William Salmon, William Sherwin, Frederick Hendrick van Hove,
William Vaughan, Margaret White, John Crump

Polygraphice

William Salmon, William Sherwin, Frederick Hendrick van Hove, William Vaughan, Margaret White, John Crump

Polygraphice

ISBN/EAN: 9783337346058

Printed in Europe, USA, Canada, Australia, Japan

Cover: Foto ©Thomas Meinert / pixelio.de

More available books at **www.hansebooks.com**

GVILIELMVS SALMON MEDICINÆ PROFESSOR ÆTATIS SVÆ 27 ANN: 1671

You see his form and years, but if you would
View his just Soule, (which can't here behold)
Into his work, following tract's looke
The lively picture of his minde & booke

Polygraphice
or
The Arts of
Drawing
Limning
Painting
&c

Zeuxis.

Apelles.

London
Printed for I: Crumpe
at the 3 bibles In St
Pauls church Yard
1675

W. Sherwin f:

POLYGRAPHICE

OR

The Arts of Drawing, Engraving,
Etching, Limning, Painting, Washing, Varnishing, Gilding, Colouring, Dying, Beautifying and Perfuming.

IN FOUR BOOKS.

Exemplified, in the *Drawing of Men, Women, Landskips, Countreys,* and Figures of various forms; The way of *Engraving, Etching* and *Limning,* with all their Requisites and Ornaments; The *Depicting of the most eminent Pieces of Antiquities*; The *Paintings of the Antients*; *Washing* of Maps, Globes or Pictures; The *Dying* of Cloth, Silk, Horns, Bones, Wood, Glass, Stones and Metals; The *Varnishing, Colouring* and *Gilding* thereof, according to any purpose or intent: The *Painting, Colouring* and *Beautifying* of the Face, Skin and Hair; The *whole Doctrine of Perfumes* (never published till now,) together with the *Original, Advancement* and *Perfection* of the Art of Painting.

To which is added

A Discourse of *Perspective* and *Chiromancy.*

The Fifth Edition, with many large Additions: Adorned with Sculptures: The like never yet extant.

By *WILLIAM SALMON* ᴏᴍᴀᴛʜᴇᴍ.

Professor of Physick.

Non quot, sed quales.

London, Printed by . . . . , for . . . . . , at the Sign of the Three Bibles in St. Paul's Church-Yard.

To the Right Honourable

HENRY

Lord HOWARD, Earl

OF

NORWICH,

EARL Marſhal of ENGLAND.

My LORD,

THE Art of Painting was a thing
which of old *Princes* admired,
Kings did affect, *Emperours* and
Noble men of almoſt all Ages did
love and make uſe of. Not to mention *Juba, Rex Mauritaniæ*, *Perſeus* King
of *Macedonia* , King *Demetrius* , *Cyrus*
King of *Perſia* , *Alexander* the Great ,
Cæſar, and others: How was *Tiberius*
the Emperour taken with the Archigal-
lus

lus of *Parrhasius*, and the Statue which
Lysippus made ? How highly did *Mna-*
son the Tyrant of the *Eleatenses* prize
the Pictures of the *Thebean* Battel done
by *Aristides* ? How did King *Nicomedes*,
who proffered an unknown sum of mo-
ney to the *Gnidians*, for the *Venus* which
Praxiteles made, admire it ? Besides many others, too tedious here to be reci-
ted, and sufficiently enough known to
your Lordship, of which to make any
repetition, might be accounted presumption, especally to your *Honour*,
whose Skill in Art is large, and whose
Knowledge of Universal Learning is not
small, chiefly in that of *History* It is
Honour, as *Cicero* saith, which gives Being, Life and Nourishment to Arts, and
where can that be found more than in
your noble Self ? Presuming therefore of
your Lordships Affection, and that un-
parallel'd Vertue, and Heroick Spirit,
which not only lodges in your Honours
Breast, but is also Hereditary to your
Noble

Noble Family, I have made bold to fhelter this Work under your Lordfhips *Patronage* : expecting either to fee it live in your *Honours* Eftimation , or perifh in your diflike. Now if thefe *Lucubrations* of mine obtain but fo much as your *Honours* leaft Approbation, I fhall think my felf happy; and hope, that with your *Name* and *Memory* this Work may be confecrated to eternity. May your *Lordfhip* daily increafe in *Honour* and *Glory*, be replenifhed with all *earthly Bleffings*, and for ever enjoy the full fruition of all *Happinefs* both in this *World*, and that which is *to come*, is the Prayer of,

MY LORD,

Your Honours moft Humble and

Affectionate Servant,

A 3   *William Salmon.*

THE
PREFACE
TO THE
READER.

THE Subject of the ensuing Work is the Art of Painting : a name not only too singular, but also too short or narrow, to express what is here intended thereby : For we do not only express that Art, (as it is generally received) but also Drawing, Engraving, Etching, Limning, Washing, Colouring and Dying : all which being considered in their proper extent, infinitely exceed that curtail'd name of Painting : which that we might joyn all in one proper and comprehensive word, we made choice of that Greek Compound POLYGRAPHICE.

To perswade any one to the Study or Practice of this Art, would be a great folly ; since ignorance (which is alwayes blind) can never be able to judge aright : For to him that already understands it, the labour would be useless and unprofitable ; to him which is already delighted therein, it would be needless and superfluous ; and to the averse and ignorant, it would be the putting a Jewel into a Swines snout : the exquisite knowledge of which, is impossible ever to be attained or understood, by such prejudicate and cloudy Souls, although it is sufficiently known to many already ; and its usefulness as apparent as it is excellent : To enumerate

The Preface to the Reader.

merate the one, or reherſe the other, is but to perſwade the world, that it is day-light, when the Sun is upon the Meridian ; or at leaſt to inculcate, an ignorance of thoſe things, which have been manifeſtly known even a long time ſince.

The Method of this work is wholly new, wherein we have united and made one, ſuch various ſubjects as have been the uncertain, obſcure and tedious diſcourſe of a great number of various and large Volumes. What ſhall we ſay? Things far aſunder, we have laid together : things uncertain, are here limited and reduced : things obſcure, we have made plain : things tedious, we have made ſhort : things erroneous, we have rectified and corrected : things hard, we have made facil and eaſie : things various, we have collected : things (in appearance) heterogene, we have made homogene : And in a word, the whole Art we have reduced to certain heads ; brought under a certain method , limited to practical rules ; and made it perſpicuous, even to a very mean underſtanding.

In the Compoſure of this Work (beſides our own Obſervations) we have made uſe of the beſt Authors now extant, that we could poſſibly procure, or get into our hands ; wherein our labour was not ſmall ; what in Reading, Comparing, Tranſcribing, Chooſing, Correcting, Diſpoſing and Reviſing every thing, in reſpect of Matter, Form and Order. The which had we any Preſident to have followed , any Path to have traced, any Example to have imitated, any Help to have conſulted, or any Subject entire : Or otherwiſe, had the Number of our Authors been ſmall , their Maxims truths, their Rules certain , their Meanings not obſcure, or their Precepts been reduced to Method and Order : We might not only, with much more eaſe, pleaſure and certainty; leſs labour, trouble and pains ; greater perſpicuity, plainneſs

A 4

and

The Preface to the Reader.

and singularity; better order, method and language; but also in shorter time *have brought to perfection,* what we here present you withal.

In this third Edition we have not only inserted several Copper Cuts, with more than two hundred several additions of singular use, through the three first Books; but there is also a whole fourth Book, containing above fourscore Chapters of such necessary matter, that the work without them may really be accounted defective. There is not only several necessary things added (which were omitted in the three first Books;) as also the various depicturings of the Antients, according to the custom of every Nation, drawn from the best, most experienced and faithfullest Authors now extant, (whether English, Italian or Latin) but also the various ways of Painting, Beautifying and Adorning the Face and Skin, so artificially, as it shall be imperceptible to the scrutiny of the most curious and piercing eye: to which we have added (as a necessary Appendice) the whole Doctrine of Perfumes, never written on (to our knowledge) in this order before; together with the Original, Advancement and Perfection of these Arts.

Lastly, the Reader is desired to take notice, that in this following Work, there are many excellent secrets, not vulgarly known, which fell into our hands from several special friends, (whose exquisite knowledge in these kinds of Mysteries truly declares them to be absolute Masters thereof) which for the publick good are freely communicated to the world.

From the East end of
Pauls, near the Free-
School, London.

William Salmon.

POLYGRAPHICES

LIBER PRIMUS.

OF

DRAWING.

CHAP. I.

Of Polygraphice in General.

I. **P**Olygraphice is an Art, so much imitating Nature, as that by proportional lines with answerable Colours, it teacheth to represent to the life (and that *in plano*) the forms of all corporeal things, with their respective passions.

II. It is called, in general, in Greek χρωματική, in Latin *Pictura*, and in English the *Art of Painting*.

III. It is sevenfold (to wit) in *Drawing, Engraving, Etching, Limning, Painting, Washing* and *Colouring*.

IV. *Drawing* is, that whereby we represent the shape and form of any corporeal substance in rude lines only.

V. It

V, It confifts in proportion and paffion, as it hath relation to motion and fituation, in refpect of Light and Vifion.

VI. *Sanderfon* faith, This admirable Art is the Imitation of the furface of Nature in Colour and Proportion. 1. By Mathematical demonftration. 2. By Chorographical defcription, 3. By fhapes of living creatures, 4. And by the forms of Vegetables; in all which it prefers Likenefs to the life, confervs it after death, and this altogether by the Senfe of Seeing.

VII. The *proportion* fhews the true length, breadth or bignefs of any part (in known meafures) in refpect of the whole, and how they bear one to another: The *paffion* reprefents the vifual Quality, in refpect of love or hatred, forrow or joy, magnanimity or cowardife, majefty or humility; of all which things we fhall fpeak in order.

CHAP. II.

Of the Infruments of Drawing.

I. THe *Infruments* of Drawing are fevenfold, *viz.* Charcoals, feathers of a Ducks wing, black and red Lead Pencils, Pens made of Ravens quills, Rulers, Compaffes and Paftills.

II. *Charcoals* are to be chofen of Sallow-wood fplit into the form of Pencils, and fharpned to a point, being chiefly known by their pith in the middle.

Their ufe is to draw lightly the draught over at firft, that if any thing be drawn amifs, it may be wiped out and amended.

III. The *Feathers* ought to be of a Ducks wing,
(though

(though others may ferve well enough) with which
you may wipe out any ftroke of the Charcoal where
it is drawn amifs, left variety of Lines breed con-
fufion.

IV. *Black and red Lead Pencils,* are to go over your
Draught the fecond time more exactly, becaufe this
will not wipe out with your hand, when you come to
draw it over with the Pen.

V. *Pens* made of Ravens quills (but others may
ferve) are to finifh the work : but herein you muft be
very careful and exact, for what is now done amifs,
there is no altering of.

VI. The *Rulers,* which are of ufe to draw ftraight or
perpendicular lines, triangles, fquares or polygons, the
which you are to ufe in the beginning, till practice and
experience may render them needlefs.

VII. *Compaffes* made of fine Brafs with Steel points,
to take in and out, that you may ufe black or red Lead
at pleafure.

*Their ufe is firft to meafure (by help of a curious fcale
of equal parts upon the edge of your Ruler) your proportions, and whether your work is exact which is done with
the Charcoal. Secondly, To draw Circles, Ovals and Arches withal.*

VIII. *Paftils* are made of feveral Colours to draw
withal, upon coloured Paper or Parchment. Thus,

*Take Plaifter of Paris or Alabafter calcined, of the colour
of which you intend to make your Paftils with, ana q. f.
grind them firft afunder, then together, and with a little
water make them into pafte, then with your hands roul
them into long pieces like black-lead Pencils, then dry them
moderately in the Air : being dryed, when you ufe them,
fcrape them to a point like an ordinary Pencil.*

And thus may you make Paftils of what colour
you pleafe, fitting them for the *Faces of Men or Wo-*
men

men, *Land-skips*, *Clouds*, *Sun-beams*, *Buildings* *and* Shadows.

IX. To the former add good Copies, Patterns and Examples of good Pictures, and other Draughts, without which, it is almost impoſſible, that the young Artiſt ſhould ever attain to any perfection in this Art.

Thoſe that deſire to be furniſhed with any excellent Patterns, Copies or Prints, may have of all ſorts, whether of Humane ſhape, Perſpective deſign, Landskip, Fowls, Beaſts, Inſects, Plants, Countreys, or any other artificial Figures, exquiſitely drawn, at very reaſonable rates, where this Book is to be ſold.

CHAP. III.

Of the Precepts of Drawing in general.

I. BE ſure to have all the neceſſaries aforeſaid in readineſs, but it will be good to practiſe as much as may be without the help of your Rule and Compaſſes ; it is your eye and fancy muſt judge without artificial meaſurings.

II. *Then firſt begin with plain Geometrical Figures,* as Lines, Angles, Triangles, Quadrangles ; Polygons, Arches, Circles, Ovals, Cones, Cylinders and the like. For theſe are the foundations of all other proportions.

III. The *Circle* helps in all orbicular forms, as in the Sun, Moon, &c. the *Oval* in giving a juſt proportion to the Face and Mouth ; the mouth of a Pot or Well, the foot of a Glaſs, &c. the *Square* confines the Picture

you

you are to copy, &c. the *Triangle* in the half-face; the *Polygon* in Ground-plats, Fortifications, and the like; *Angles* and *Arches* in Perspective; the *Cone* in Spires, tops of Towers and Steeples: the *Cylinder* in Columns, Pillars, Pilasters, and their Ornaments.

IV. Having made your hand fit and ready in general Proportions, then learn to give every object its due shade according to its convexity or concavity, and to elevate or depress the same, as the object appears either nearer or farther off the light, the which is indeed the life of the work.

V. *The second Practice of Drawing*, consists in forming *Fruits*, as Apples, Pears, Cherries, Peaches, Grapes, Strawberries, Peascods, &c. with their *Leaves:* the imitation of *Flowers*, as Roses, Tulips, Carnations, &c. *Herbs*, as Rosemary, Tyme, Hysop, &c. *Trees*, as the Oak, Fir, Ash, Wallnut, &c.

VI. *The third Practice of Drawing imitates*, 1. *Beasts*, as the Lamb, Elephant, Lion, Bear, Leopard, Dog, Cat, Buck, Unicorn, Horse, &c.   2. *Fowls*, as the Eagle, Swan, Parrot, Partridge, Dove, Raven, &c. 3. *Fishes*, as the Whale, Herring, Pike, Carp, Thornback, Lobster, Crab, &c. *of which, variety of Prints may be bought at reasonable rates.*

VII. *The fourth Praxis imitates* the Body of Man with all its Lineaments, the Head, Nose, Eyes, Ears, Cheeks, Hands, Arms, and Shadows all exactly proportional both to the whole, and one to another, as well to situation as magnitude.

VIII. *The fifth Praxis is in* Drapery, imitating Cloathing, and artificially setting off the outward Coverings, Habit and Ornaments of the Body, as Cloth, Stuff, Silk and Linen, their natural and proper folds; which although it may seem something hard to do, yet by much exercise and imitation of the
choicest

choiceſt Prints, will become facil and eaſie.

IX. In drawing of all the aforegoing forms, or what ever elſe, you muſt be perfect, firſt in the exact proportions: ſecondly in the general or outward limes, before you fall to ſhadowing or trimming your work within.

X. In mixed and uncertain forms, where Circle and Square will do no good (but only the *Idea* thereof in your own fancy) as in Lions, Horſes, and the like ; you muſt work by reaſon in your own judgement, and ſo obtain the true proportion by daily practice. *Thus* ;

Having the ſhape of the thing in your mind, firſt draw it rudely with your coal, then more exactly with your lead or pencil ; then peruſe it well, and conſider where you have erred, and mend it, according to that Idea, *which you carry in your mind ; this done, view it again, correcting by degrees the other parts, even to the leaſt* Iota, *ſo far as your judgement will inform you ; and this you may do with twenty, thirty, forty or more papers of ſeveral things at once: having done what you can, confer it with ſome excellent pattern or print of like kind, uſing no rule or compaſs at all, but your own reaſon, in mending every fault, giving every thing its due place, and juſt proportion ; by this means you may rectifie all your errors, and ſtep an incredible way on to perfection.*

XI. Having then good Patterns and Copies to draw by, the young Artiſt muſt learn to reduce them to other proportions either greater or ſmaller, and this by often and many tryals (as we ſhall hereafter more particularly teach) this requires great judgement, for in a cut, you ſhall find neither circumſcribing ſtrokes, nor difference between light and light, or ſhadow and ſhadow ; therefore ſerious obſervations are required in the ſite of thoſe things, whether coming forwards or going backwards.

XII. The

XII. The drawing after Plaifter-work , done by skilful Mafters, as the Gladiator and children of *Francifco*, the Rape of the *Sabine* Women, the Wraftler, the *Venus* of *Greece*, *Hercules*, *Hermes*, anatomical Diffecti-ons, and other pieces of antiquity, are main and ne-ceffary Introductions to attain a perfection in drawing after the life.

XIII. This done, let the young Artift now begin to exercife in drawing after the life ; (for that is the compleateft, beft, and moft perfect Copy, which Na-ture has fet for obfervation) wherein the liberty of imitation is prefented in the largeft latitude : and this muft be attained by much Practice and dili-gent Exercife , adjoining the Inftructions of a good Mafter.

XIV. In this Practice of Drawing, let there be a perfection attained, before ever there be the leaft thoughts of Colours or Painting: for that afterwards all things belonging to Painting, will in a fhort time be eafily and perfectly underftood.

CHAP. IV.

Of particular Obfervations in the Art of Drawing.

I. IN drawing after a Print or Picture, put it in fuch a light, as that the glofs of the Colours hinder not your fight, fo as that the light and your eye may equally obliquely fall upon your piece; which place at fuch a diftance, that at opening of
your

your eyes, you may view it all at once, the greater your Picture is, the further off you muſt place it to draw aſter: the which you muſt always be ſure to put right before you, a little reclining.

II. Then obſerve the middle of your Picture to be copied, which touch upon your paper with the point of your coal: then obſerve the moſt perſpicuous and uppermoſt figures (if more than one,) which touch gently in their proper places, thus running over the whole draught, you will ſee the Skeleton, as it were, of the work.

But if you go on without theſe conſiderations, whereunto your Draught will tend or run; then having ended your work, you will be forced to draw the ſame many times over and over again, and, it may be, every time to as little purpoſe; by the tedioufneſs of which, your ingenuity will be dulled.

III. Be ſecure of a right and true draught, though you do it ſlowly; what you think may be done in two or three hours, it will be better to beſtow two or three days upon: by this means (though you act leiſurely, yet you will act prudently, and) you will both ſooner and better than can be imagined, attain the perfection of what you deſire.

IV. Theſe out-ſchetches being made, view them diligently, whether they anſwer your pattern apparently; for the Geſtures of the life ought to ſhew themſelves eminently in the firſt and rudeſt draughts thereof; without which, be ſure your work will be faulty.

V. Having viewed theſe ſchetches, begin to correct and amend them (where you find them amiſs) and *gradatim* by adding or diminiſhing a little here and there, as you ſee it differ from your pattern, you will bring it nearer and nearer to the life.

This

This with a Charcoal you may easily do, because you may wipe away what is amiss.

VI. In drawing after Plaister and embossed works, choose a good North light, which let descend from above, not dilating or scattering it self too much, by which you may the more pleasantly shade your work.

If the Room has a South light, put oiled Paper before the window, or if you draw by Candle-light, have a Lamp shaded with oiled paper ; for a Candle will grow lower and lower, which causes the shades to change, all which you avoid in a Lamp.

VII. Then set your self down about three times as far from the Pattern as the Pattern is high ; so as your eyes in a direct line may view the same : then with a plumb line observe what parts of your Pattern appear to you, by the extending streight thereof, and how one under another they come in sight, and accordingly make your fundamental schetches, as we have just before taught.

VIII. In drawing the Muscles of a human body you must first have either the life or very good patterns made either of Plaister, or drawn in Pictures, enough of which are to be found in Anatomical Books ; but chiefly the Book of *Jacob Vander Gracht,* compleated with many varieties and curiosities ; from whence the alterations and changes, rising and falling, extension and contraction, and other operations of the Muscles, Arteries and particular members are in imitation of the life excellently depicted.

IX. In drawing after a naked body, all the Muscles are not so plainly to be expressed as in Anatomical Figures ; but that side whose parts are must apparent and significant in the performing of any action, most more or less appear according to the force of that action.

B   X. In

X. In young perfons the Mufcles muft not manifeftly appear fo hard, as in elder and full grown perfons : the fame obferve in fat men, and flefhy, and fuch as are very delicate and beautiful. And in Women you muft fcarce exprefs any at all, becaufe that in the life they either appear not at all, or very little, unlefs it be particularly in fome forceable action : and then you muft reprefent them but very faintly, left you fpoil the fingular Beauty of the body. The like obferve in little Children.

X I. In drawing of thefe Mufcles the motion of the whole body is alfo to be confidered : in the rifing or falling of the Arms, the Mufcles of the Breaft more or lefs appear : the Hips the like according as they bend outward or inward ; and the fame chiefly in the Shoulders, Sides and Neck, according to the feveral actions of the body : all which alterations are firft to be obferved in the life.

C H A P. V.

Of the Imitation of the Life.

I. **I**N order hereunto it will be neceffary (having fixed a convenient time and place) to choofe a good Mafter, with whom you may fpend two days in a week at leaft ; or elfe a fociety of about half a fcore or a dozen young men, who are experienced to draw after the life, by the advice and example of whom, and your own diligent obfervations and care , you may come not only to mend one anothers faults, but alfo one anothers judgements.

I I. Then choofe a well-fhap'd man , one of large
fhoulders,

shoulders, of a fair breast, strongly muscled, full thighs, long leggs, and of a proportionable height , not too tall nor too short, not too thick nor too slender, but a person every ways of an admirable shape.

I I I. Let this Exemplar be made to stand in a good posture , representing some noble action of the life , letting the head turn it self to the right side if the left be shadowed ; and contrariwise, making the parts of the apparent shoulder somewhat higher than that which is obscured ; and the head if it looks upwards, leaning no farther backwards than that the eyes may be seen ; and in the turning of it, let it move no farther than that the chin may only approach the shoulder ; making also the hip on that side the shoulder is lowest, a little to stick out ; and that arm foremost , where the leg is behind, and contrariwise.

I V. The same you must observe in all fourfooted Beasts ; and this generally to make the limbs crosswise to cohere together ; and in the turning of it forward, backward, upward, downward, sideways, ever to counterballance it by the opposition of other parts, the right knowledge of which is a great step to the Imitation of the life.

V. This done, let him, whose turn it is to begin, first schetch on the paper his own Idea's (being fixed in a convenient place and light, as in the former Chapter) wherein you must endeavour to make every part to agree with the whole, first in form, secondly in proportion , thirdly in action : after this begin again , running over your Draught, bring it to a conclusion , as we shall hereafter teach you.

V I. Observing always, that after you have schetcht your whole Figure, that you choose a part) which you most desire to finish) to perfect the same , in regard that with the rest stands in a good posture ; the rea-

son

fon is, becaufe time will not always eafily permit to
finifh or compleat a whole Figure, unlefs it be with
expert Artifts: it being much better to perfect a part
than to leave the whole imperfect; which as each Pra-
ctitioner arrives and draws nearer to perfection , he
may with fo much the more boldnefs, fecurity and
certitude attempt the compleating of the whole.

V I I. You are alfo to confider after what manner
you would have your Figure to be feen, whether upon
even ground, or from aloft; for accordingly you muft
make the pofition of your Exemplar.

VI I I. Let the young Artift alfo at his conveniency,
fometimes view the Country, and practife upon the
drawing of Landskips, as much reprefenting Nature
(1. in their diftance, 2. in their mutual pofition, 3. in
vifible afpect) as poffible may be : by this means he
will come to have a general and compleat underftanding in the univerfal meafures of all things.

C H A P. VI.

Of the Imitation of Draughts.

I. THe Learner muft, by many and often tryals ,
get a habit of Imitation; which if it be to be
done with the Pen, beware of fcratching and making
thin and lean ftroaks, but rather broad, which you
fhall draw from above, downwards; but according
to the fhades, fome of the hatches muft be fharp , fome
broad, fome unequal, and fome equal.

I I. Hold your pen or pencil fomewhat long, (and
not fo upright as when you write,) feeming as though
you laid it ftraight forward : and if they be paftils ,
                                                    accuftom

accuſtom your ſelf to turn them in your hand, by this means you will prevent their becoming ſo ſoon blunt, and they wearing to a point may ſerve without ſcraping the making of a whole Draught.

III. In ſhadowing of your Draught, you muſt firſt begin to do it faintly and ſmoothly, and ſtraight againſt the edges of the light, ſo that it may look as if it had been daſht with a bruſh-pencil ; and then here and there overſhadow it again in the darkeſt ſhades farther out, and adorn it with hatchings; and where any thing more is required, put the ſame in nimbly and clearly by gentle touches, the which will add a great grace unto your work.

IV. Doeſling (which is a certain beſmeering of the work) is to be done with Crions of red or black Chalk, touching the Draught eaſily all over ſmoothly and evenly with the points thereof, and not with Cotton or the like put up into Quills, as ſome uſe : though that may be done in ſome caſes, as where one work is to be brought into another.

V. If Copies be taken (chiefly upon coloured paper) to make it curious and neat, let the edges of the heightening be ſmoothed a little (not with cotton, but) with the like coloured paper rouled up to a ſharp point at one end, and by this means you will take away the ſharpneſs and hardneſs of your edges, and make them look ſweet and pleaſant.

VI. In performance of theſe things a certain kind of waſhing is ſometimes neceſſary, performed with Pencils dipt in ſome coloured liquor, and ſo laid upon coloured paper; and this is to be done either through the whole work, or in a part thereof, to wit, in ſome principal flat ſhades; which may be afterwards looſly wrought over with a Pen or black Chalk, the which will look very pleaſantly.

B 3

VII.

V I I. This Wafhing muft be firft done very weak and faint, yet fmooth (without fmoothing of it at the edges, except by a new ftroak of your pencil moiften-ed with your tongue ; for much fmoothing will fpoil your work) this firft wafhing being dry, go over again with your work, yet only thofe parts where there ought to be a darker fhade ; and afterwards again give fome deeper and harder touches without fmooth-ing, the which will very much fet your work off.

V I I I. Faint fhadows, and things obfcure, muft be prefented as faintly as may be, chiefly upon colour-ed paper, where the heightning helps you ; but be-ware you go not too often over your fhades, left you fpoil them, by making them too hard and ill-favoured.

I X. In drawing, whether it be after a Draught or the Life; firft obferve the thing in general, in refpect of the circumferent ftroaks ; for them are they, which bound and contain all the parts of the whole, and without which the particular parts can never be perfectly diftinguifhed, nor reprefent themfelves in their being : This done, then confider in like manner the parts, and fuppofing the parts each to be a whole; you may come to reprefent the parts of parts, and by the fame means to exprefs the whole of any Draught whatfoever.

C H A P.

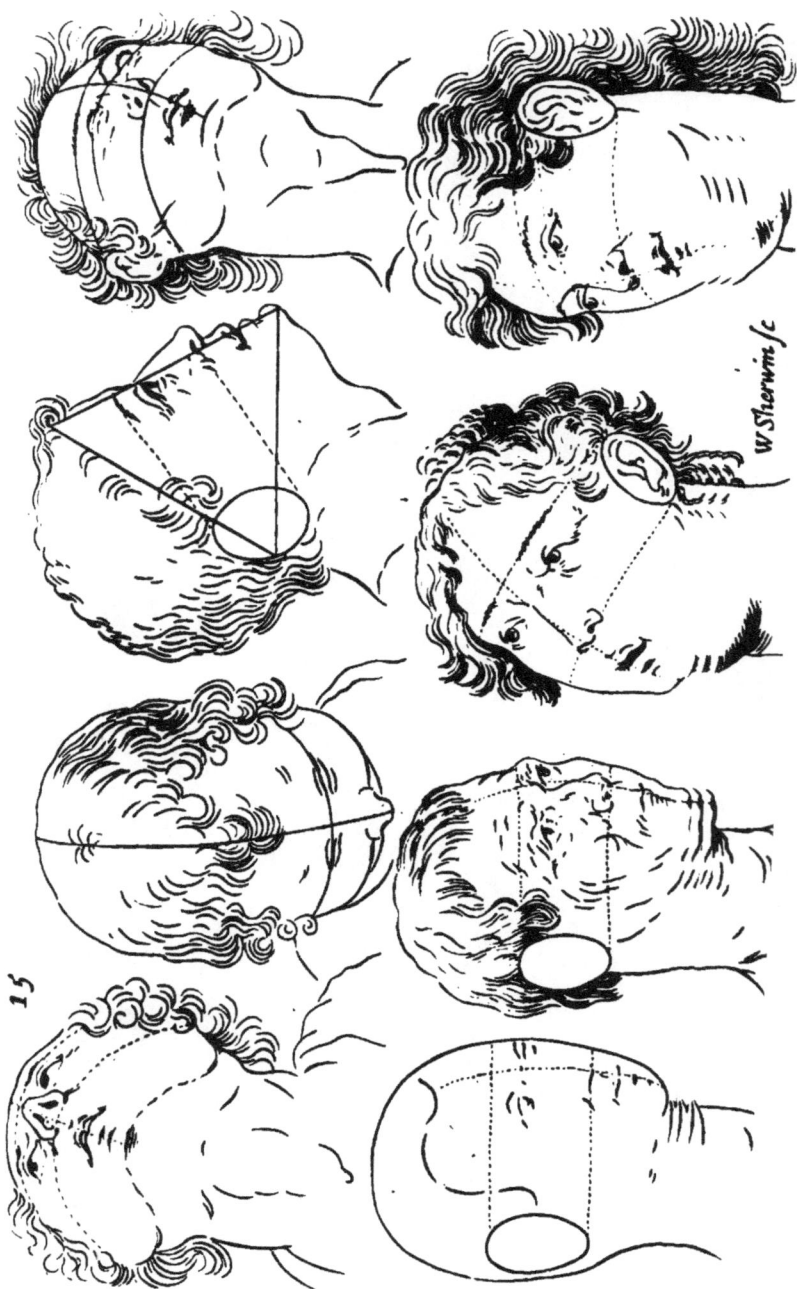

15

W.Sherwin sc

15

Sheram fe

CHAP. VII.

Of Drawing the Face of a Man.

I. IN drawing of the Face you are firſt to obſerve its motion whether upwards, downwards, forwards, or ſideways ; whether it be long or round, fat or lean, great or little.

For if it be fat, the cheeks will ſeem to ſwell : if lean, the jaw-bones will ſtick out, and the cheeks fall in ; but if neither too fat nor too lean , it will be for the moſt part round.

I I. Touch lightly the feature s where the eyes , mouth , noſe and chin ſhould ſtand , (having firſt drawn the circle or oval of the Face) then make a ſtroak down from that place of the forehead which is even with the chin, coming down where you ſhould place the middle or tip of the noſe, and middle of the mouth, which ſtroak muſt be made ſtraight down in a full right Face, but arched or oval in an oblique Face, leaning that way towards which the Face doth turn : then croſs the ſtroak about the mid- dle of the eyes, either with a ſtraight line in a right Face, or with a Curved either upwards or downwards according to the preſent action or poſture of the Face : then make another anſwerable to that, where the end of the noſe ſhould come ; and another for the mouth that it be not made crooked.

I I I. This Croſs is difficult to be underſtood *in pla- no* ; but upon a Face made upon a ſolid body, in form or ſhape of an Egg , the ſeveral variations of the ſaid croſs are moſt excellently demonſtrated : and from

B 4 hence

hence may the learner underſtand all the alterations of a Face, and thereby draw it all manner of ways, as ſideways, upwards, downwards, forwards, backwards, &c. and that only by the motion of the ſaid oval ſolid, accordingly as in the following Figures you may eaſily perceive.

I V. Then if the face look upwards towards Heaven, or downwards towards the Earth, let the Eyes, Noſe, Mouth and Brows looks accordingly with it ; and now proceed to the placing of the Features.

V. In a juſt proportioned Face, the diſtances, 1. between the top of the forehead and the eye-brows ; 2. betwen the eye-brows and the bottom of the noſe, 3. between the bottom of the noſe and the bottom of the chin are equal.

V I. In drawing the utmoſt Circumference of a Face, take in the Head and all with it, leſt you be deceived in drawing the true bigneſs.

V II. Then conſider all thoſe chief touches which give life to a face, adding grace thereto, and ſomething diſcovering the diſpoſition of the mind.

So the mouth extended and the corners a little turning up, ſhews a ſmiling countenance : the eye-brow bending, and the forehead and top of the noſe between the eyebrows wrinkled, ſhews one frowning : the upper eye-lid coming ſomething over the ball of the eye, ſhews one ſober and ſtayed : with many other touches which give life and ſpirit to a face, which in good prints, by little and little, and diligent obſervation you will at laſt find out.

V III. The diſtances between the eyes, is the length of one eye in a full face, but in a three-quarter or half-face, it is leſſened proportionably : and exactly underneath the corners of the eyes place the noſtrils.

I X. Having

5

W Sherwin Sc.

17

W Sherwin sc

I X. Having given touches where the eyes, nofe, mouth and chin fhould be placed, begin to draw them more exactly, and fo proceed till the Face be finifhed ; and then make the hair , beard , fhadows, and other things about it.

X. Be fure to make the fhadows rightly, and be fure not to make them too dark, where they fhould be faint ; for that can never be made light again, and fo the whole Face is marr'd.

The fhadows are fainter and lighter in a fair Face than in a fwarthy.

X I. When you have finifhed the Face , give here and there fome hard touches with your pen where the fhadows are darkeft ; then come the ears and hair , wherein having drawn the out-line, draw the principal curls, or mafter ftroaks in the hair, which will be a guide to you in the leffer curls, whofe dependance are on them : alway make the curls to bend exactly according to the pattern, that they may lie loofe, or carelefly, and not as if they were ftiff and forced ; the curls being rightly drawn, in the laft place ftrike in the loofe hairs which hang fcatteringly out of the Circles.

X I I. In forming the Ear, defcribe an oval as it were, and proceeding lightly, joyn ftroak to ftroak, in fuch manner as you fee in the Figures ; fo that the ear may be entirely formed, without digreffing from the bounds of Nature or Art.

X I I I. Laftly having practifed a little by rule , and brought your hand in ; in drawing of any thing, firft ftrike the out-ftroaks, principal veins and mufcles lightly , and afterwards fhadow them, ever following exquifite patterns and prints, which will both encreafe your judgement, and bring command to your hand.

C H A P.

I. **I**N drawing the Hands, draw not all the joints, veins or other things to appear plainly, but only lightly and faintly, and ftrike out the bignefs of the hand and the manner of its turning with faint touches, and not with hard ftroaks ; then that being done right, part the fingers according to the pattern with like faint ftroaks ; then mark that place where any of the fingers do ftand out from the others, with a faint refemblance : this done, proceed to draw it more perfectly, making the bending of the joynts, the wrifts and other principal things more exactly ; and laftly, go over with it again, drawing every fmall bending or fwelling of the fingers, nails, knuckles and veins, fo many as do appear.

I I. Learn by good prints the juft proportions of the hands, with their equal diftances, obferving this rule, that according as it turns one way or another, to fhorten proportionally as they appear to the eye.

For fo much as it turns away from our eye, fo much it lofes in proportion, yea fometimes a whole finger, two or three or more is loft to our fight, which you muft accordingly anfwer in your draught.

I I I. In drawing of the feet, the fame rules which we even now enumerated, at the firft and fecond Section of this Chapter, are to be underftood here.

C H A P

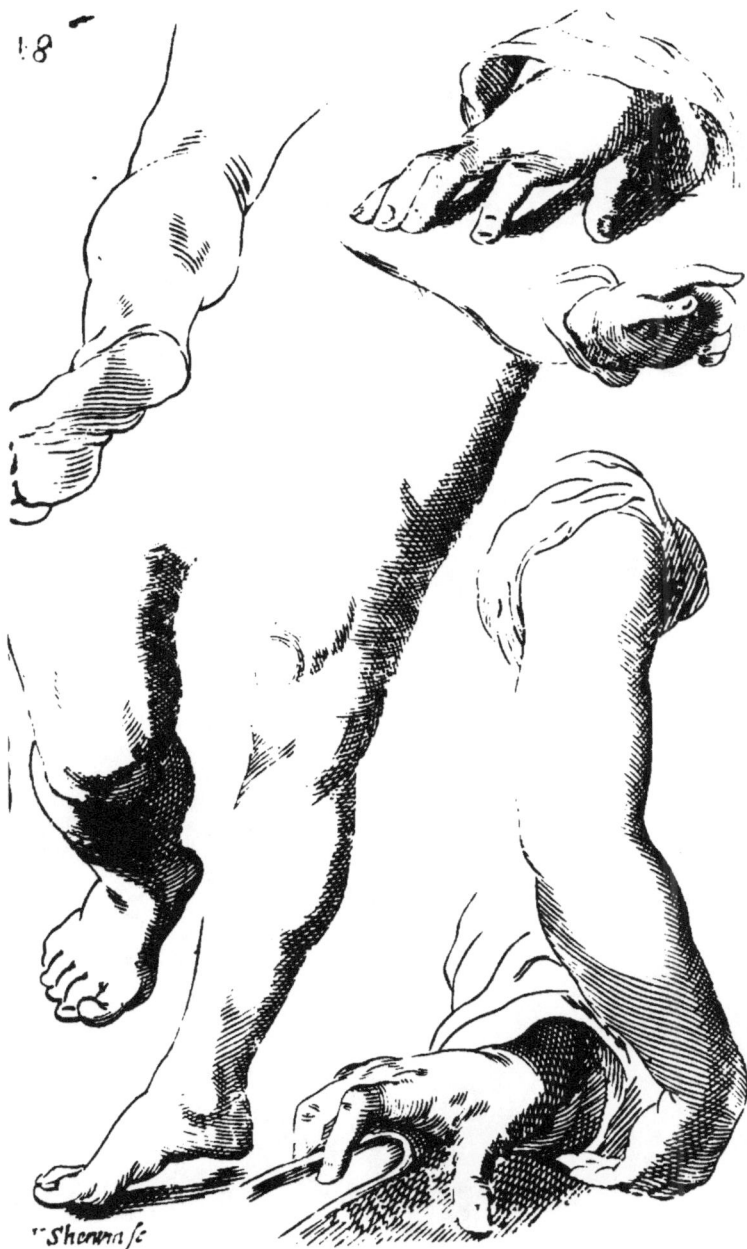

18

"Sherwin sc

19

W Sherwin fe

C H A P. IX.

Of Drawing the whole Body.

I. **F**Irſt begin with the head, and be ſure to give it
its juſt proportion, anſwerable to what you intend the whole body ſhall be; then draw the ſhoulders in their exact breadth; after them, the trunk of
the body beginning at the arm-pits, and ſo drawing
down to the hips on both ſides, obſerving withal the
exact breadth of the waſte: laſtly, draw the legs,
arms and hands, exactly to your pattern.

I I. But firſt draw with a coal, and that very
lightly and faintly, drawing nothing perfect (that
you may the eaſier mend it if it be amiſs) and then afterwards finiſh one thing after another as curiouſly as
you can.

I I I. Let the parallel ſinews, muſcles, veins and
joynts, be placed oppoſite one to another in a ſtraight
line (as ſhoulder to ſhoulder, hip to hip, knee to
knee, &c.) for which purpoſe draw ſtraight croſs
lines to guide you therein; obſerving that which way
ſoever the body turns or bows, theſe lines may anſwer
accordingly.

I V. Let all perpendicular joints, and parts alſo,
be placed in a right line one under another (as they
are in your pattern) for which end, draw a ſtraight
line (if the body be ſtraight) from the throat thorow the middle of the breaſt and privities, to the
feet, to which line draw all thoſe particular points
parallels, that the body may not appear crooked or
awry.

V. In

V. In bowings and bendings of the extuberance of the outward part be the compreſſion of the inward part things of an equal proportion, that as may be equal (as the arm to the arm, le ſo every part may be proportionable to (as the Hand not too big for the arm, for the body, nor the body for the le with this difference, that (as the one pear fully to the eye, or the other m either in part or in whole, or be ſeen ſi made ſo much leſs than the other, by l turns away from the ſight.

VI. As you obſerve a juſt proportio1 alſo in length, that as every oppoſite qual length, ſo that each part may n one for another, but according to the nitude : And in this caſe that if the bo any ways hid, thoſe parts may ſhorte: to what is out of ſight.

VII. Laſtly, Obſerve the juſt diſtan from another, for by that means you exaɛt in your draught; and in ſhort t imitate your pattern or nature.

;

21

W Sherwin fc

C H A P. X.

Of Drawing a naked Body.

I. **I**N drawing after the life, as there are variety of faces, fo no certain Rules can be delivered for the fame ; yet the following precautions may be ufeful.

II. Draw out the head in an oval, one fourth part for the hair , one fourth part for the forehead and brows , one fourth for the nofe, and the laft for the mouth and chin.

III. Having drawn out the head, meafure out eight times the length of the head (the head making one of the eight parts) and draw a ftraight line from the top of the head to the fole of the foot.

IV. One heads length from the chin is for the breaft ; the next eighth part reacheth to the navel , the fourth part to the privities, the fifth part to the middle of the thigh, the fixth part to the lower part of the knee, the feventh to the fmall of the leg, and the eighth part to the heel.

V. The mufcles you muft obferve to draw exactly as they are in the life : the breadth of the fhoulders, is about two meafures of the head : the breadth of the hips, two meafures of the face : the arms ftretched out, are juft the length of the whole figure, the breafts alfo accounted ; but without the breafts they are but fix.

VI. The arms hanging ftraight down reach within a fpan of the knee : the length of the hand is the juft length of the face. See the two figuers following.

VII. Ob-

VII. Obferve firft to draw the head exactly, and next, the fhoulders in their juft breadth: then draw the trunk of the Body, and the reft as at the firft Section of the ninth Chapter.

VIII. Be fure to place the joynts, finews, and mufcles in their natural places, and alfo proportionately; in refpect of Magnitude, Similitude, and Parts: left it feem crooked and deformed.

IX. See that every parallel joynt bend moderately, fo as to anfwer in nature its oppofite.

CHAP. XI.

Of Shadowing a Naked Body.

I. THe Shadows of the Neck, in a child or young woman, are very fine, rare and hard to be feen: In a man, the finews and veins are expreffed by fhadowing of the reft of the neck, and leaving them white: the fhoulder is fhadowed underneath: the brawn of the arm muft appear full and white, fhadowed on one fide.

II. The veins of the back of the hand and the knuckles are made with two or three hair ftroaks with a fine touch of the pen.

III. The paps of a man are fhewed by two or three ftroaks given underneath, in a woman with an orbicular fhade, fomewhat deep; the ribs retain no fhadow except you reprefent one lean or ftarved.

IV. The belly is made eminent by fhadowing underneath the breaft bone and the flank: The brawn of the thigh is fhadowed by drawing fmall hair ftroaks from

from the hip to the knee, and croſſed again over-thwartly.

V. The knee is to be finely ſhadowed underneath the joint ; the ſhin-bone appears by ſhadowing one half of the leg with a ſingle ſhadow.

VI. The ankle-bone appears by ſhadowing a little underneath (as in the knees) and the ſinews there-of muſt ſeem to take beginning from the midſt of the foot; and to wax bigger as they grow nearer to the toes.

VII. Laſtly, the ſhadows of the foot muſt take place according as reaſon and occaſion requires, for which (as alſo in all the former precepts) the having of good prints will be no ſmall advantage unto you.

CHAP. XII.

The way and manner of Shadowing.

I. IF it be a ſurface only, it is beſt ſhadowed by draw-ing lines either ſtraight or oblique, (according as the ſuperficies is) through the better half thereof.

II. If it be in a body, it is a double ſhadow, and is uſed when a ſuperficies begins to forſake your ſight, as in Columns and Pillars, where it is double dark-ned, and repreſenteth to the eye, as it were the back-ſide, leaving that unſhadowed to the light.

III. The treble ſhadow is made by croſſing over a-gain the double ſhadow, and is uſed for the inward parts of things, as in clefts of the earth, wells, caves, the inſides of pots, cups and diſhes.

IV. In ſhadowing, let the ſhadow always fall one way, that is, on the ſame ſide of the body ; leaving the other to the light.

So

So in drawing a man, if I begin to ſhadow his right cheek, I muſt ſhadow the right part of his neck, arm, ſide, thigh, leg, &c.

V. But if the light ſide of the body be darkned by the oppoſition of ſome other body ſtanding between the light and it, it muſt receive a contrary ſhadow according as the light is obfuſcated.

So if three pillars ſtand together, that in the midſt muſt receive a ſhadow on both ſides.

V I. All circular bodies muſt have a circular ſhadow (by the firſt Section of this Chapter) according to their form or appearance, and the orbicular ſhadow of the object which caſteth it.

V I I. Let your ſhadow grow fainter and fainter, according to the greatneſs of the diſtance from the opacous Body ſhadowing.

And the reaſon is, becauſe all ſhadows are pyramidal, in which caſe, ſpace of place prevails with the light againſt the ſhadow.

V I I I. Where contrary ſhadows concur, let the meaneſt and moſt ſolid body be firſt ſerved ; and in double and treble ſhadows, let the firſt lines be very dry for fear of blotting, before you croſs them.

I X. All perfect lights receive no ſhadow at all ; but being manifeſt, are only to be made apparent by that body which receives them ; whoſe ſhadow muſt be according to the efflux of light : but the colour of the light ought to agree with the medium which receives it, whether it be Air, Cryſtal, Water, Amber, Glaſs, Tranſparent-wine, or the like.

C H A P.

CHAP. XIII.

Of Expreſſing Paſſions in the Countenance.

I. **L**Ove is expreſſed by a clear, fair and pleaſant Countenance, without clouds, wrinkles, or unpleaſant bendings : giving the forehead an ample height and breadth with majeſtick grace ; a full eye with a fine ſhadow at the bottom of the eye-lid, and a little at the corner : a proportionable noſe ; noſtrils not too wide : a clear cheek made by ſtadowing of it on one ſide : and a ſmiling mouth made by a thin upper lip, and ſhadowing the mouth-line at the corners.

II. *Fear* is expreſſed by making the eyes look hollow, heavy and downward, thin faln cheeks, cloſe mouth, and ſtaring careleſs hair about the ears.

III. *Envy* is beſt decyphered by the only hanging of the cheeks, and a pale countenance ; and ſometimes by grinning of the teeth.

IV. Let every Paſſion be repreſented according to the outward appearance thereof, as it is in thoſe perſons in whom it reigns ; obſerving the rules at the ſixth Section of the ſeventh Chapter.

C   CHAP.

C H A P. XIV.

Of Humane Proportion.

I. THE length of an upright body is equal to eight times the length of the face or head: The arm hanging ſtraight down, reacheth within a ſpan of the Knee: The length of the hand muſt be the length of the face: The arms extended muſt be the juſt length of the body.

I I. Thoſe parts of the body near to the Eye muſt be made greater and longer than thoſe farther off, (becauſe the eye judgeth ſo of them) and according to the diſtance from the eye, ſo muſt you vary from that which is otherwiſe the real true proportion of thoſe parts.

I I I. In foreſhortening you muſt take things as they appear to the eye, and not to draw the full proportion of each part, but to ſhorten all, according to the rate or reaſon which is obfuſcated.

So if you would draw a ſhip foreright, there can appear but only her forepart (for the reſt being hid cannot be expreſt:) the like of an horſe looking full in my face, or a man lying along; I muſt here of neceſſity foreſhorten, to expreſs the Viſual property: And in this caſe your eye and reaſon muſt be your chief guide to give the true reaſon and meaſure of theſe appearances, whether in Drawing, Limning or Painting.

I V. The uſe of this foreſhortening is to expreſs all manner of actions in man or beaſt; to repreſent many

things

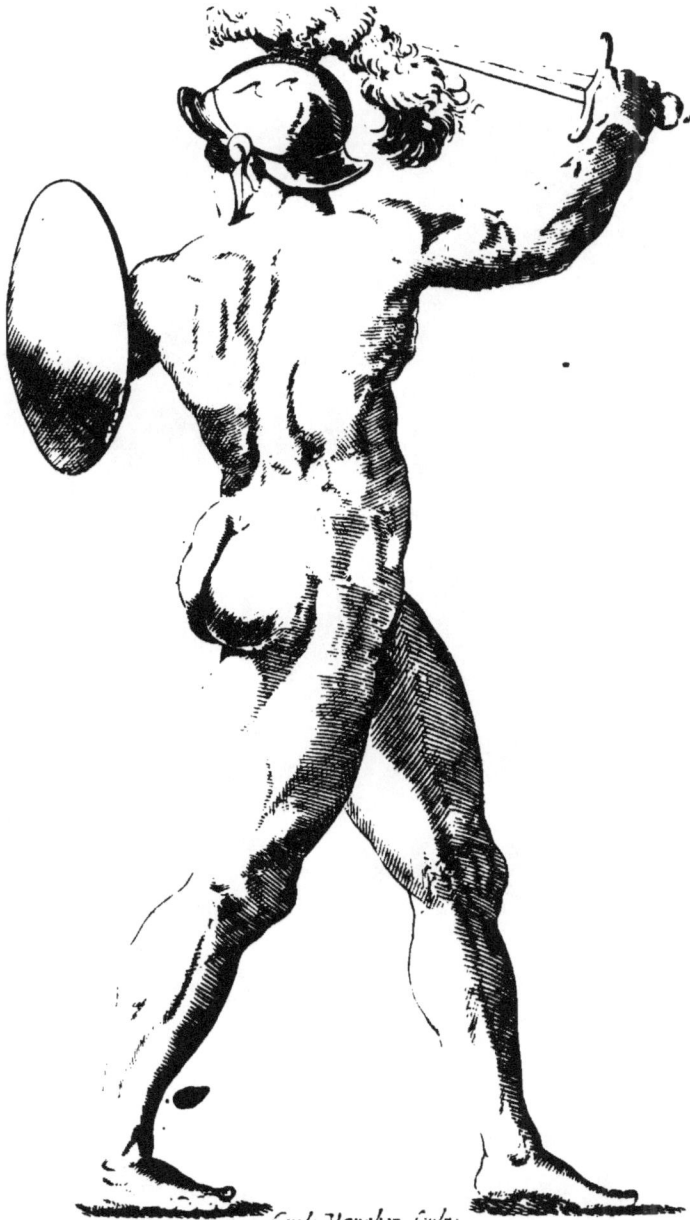

Cæl. Vaughan sculp.

things in a little room; to shew at one view to the eye and mind, the whole body of a Temple, with all its arches and pillars whether the infide or outfide, as also the fundry fides of Cities, Caftles and Forts, and fuch like.

Laftly, That in every cafe you make Nature the pattern of all draughts, fo that nothing be expreft, but what doth agree and accord with nature; and that nothing be either forced beyond nature, not yet any thing to come fhort of nature.

As if in drawing the picture of a man, be fure you draw not fuch a pofture as is impofible for him to imitate with his natural body.

C H A P. XV.

Of Drapery.

I. **D**Raw the out-lines of the Garment lightly, and herein be careful, for the whole grace of the picture lies there; then draw the greateft folds firft, and ftroak thofe into lefer; and be fure they crofs one another.

II. Sute your garments to the body and make them bend with the body, according as it ftands in or out, ftraight or crooked, or turns one way or another : the clofer the garment fits to the body, the narrower and fmaller muft the folds be.

III. All your folds muft confift of two lines and no more, which you may turn with the garment at pleafure; fhadowing the innermoft deeper, the outer-

moft

moſt more light ; and if the folds be never ſo curiouſly contrived, ſpare not to ſhadow them (if they
fall inward from the light) with a double or treble
ſhadow, as the occaſion requires.

I V. The greater folds muſt be continued through
the whole garment, the leſſer you may break off and
ſhorten as you pleaſe.

V. The ſhades of ſilk and fine linnen are very
thick and ſmall, which require little folds and a light
and rare ſhadow, commonly but double at moſt ; and
ſo alſo fine Drapery requires more and ſharper folds
than courſe.

V I. That part of a garment which ſits cloſe to the
body muſt not be folded at all, but only ſweetly
ſhaded, to repreſent the part of the body which lies
under it.

V I I. Obſerve the motion of the wind and air, for
driving looſe apparel all one way, drawing that part
of the garment firſt which lies higheſt and cloſeſt upon
the body, before you draw the looſer part that flies
off from the body, *left by drawing the looſe part of the*
garment firſt you ſhould be out, and ſo place the body
crooked or awry.

C H A P. XVI.

Of mixed and uncertain Forms.

I. FOr the drawing the form of any beaſt, begin
with your lead or coal at the forehead, drawing downward the noſe, mouth, upper and nether
chop, ending your line at the throat ; then viewing it
again where you begun, from the forehead, over the
head,

W Sherwin *fc*

head, ears, and neck, continuing till you have given the full compafs of the buttock , then mark out the legs and feet : Viewing it again touch out the breaft with the eminency thereof; Laftly, finifh the tail , paws, tongue, teeth , beard, and feveral fhadows.

II. In drawing beafts you muft be well acquainted with their fhape and action, without which you fhall never perform any thing excellent in that kind : and here if you draw it in an Emblem or the like , you ought to fhew the Landskip of the Country natural to that beaft.

III. In birds begin alfo the draught at the head, (and beware of making it too big) then bring from under the throat the breaft line down to the legs, there ftay and begin at the pinion to make the wing, which being joyned to the back line will be prefently finifhed : the eye, legs and train muft be at laft, letting always (in birds as in beafts) the fartheft leg be fhorteft ; their feathers (as the hair in beafts) muft take their beginning at the head very fmall, and fall in one way backwards in five ranks, greater and greater to the conclufion.

IV. Infects, as flies, bees, wafps, grafhoppers, worms , and fuch like, are eafie to be drawn and not hard to be laid in Colours; in doing thefe , it will at firft be abfolutely neceffary to have the living pattern before your eyes.

V. To draw a flower, begin from the bofs tufft or wart in the middle ; as in a Rofe or Marigold , with the yellow tufft, which being made , draw lines equally divided, from thence to the greateft compafs or extent of your flower : you may draw them either fully open or in the bud, and laden with dew , wet and worms, and then you may draw rudely with the coal or lead the leaves afterwards, giving them their veins or jaggednefs.

VI. To take the natural and lively fhape of the leaf of any herb or tree.

Firft, take the leaf that you would have, and gently bruife the ribs and veins on the back-fide of it : afterwards wet the fide with linfeed oyl, and then prefs it hard upon a piece of clean white paper, and fo you fhall have the perfect figure of the faid leaf, with every vein thereof fo exactly expreft, as being lively coloured it will feem to be truly natural.

C H A P. XVII.

Of Landskip.

I. **L**Andskip is that which expreffeth in lines the perfect vifion of the earth, and all things thereupon, placed above the horizon, as towns, villages, caftles, promontories, mountains, rocks, valleys, ruines, rivers, woods, forefts, chafes, trees, houfes and all other buildings, both beautiful and ruinous.

II. Firft, Always exprefs a fair horizon, fhewing the heavens cloudy or clear, more or lefs according to the occafion; and if you exprefs the Sun, let it be either as rifing or fetting, and as it were behind or over fome hill or mountain.

The Moon and Stars are feldom or never depicted, unlefs it be in reprefentation of twilight ; becaufe all things are fuppofed to be feen by day.

III. Secondly, If you exprefs the Sun, make his light to reflect upon all the trees, hills, mountains, rocks, or buildings ; fhading the contrary fide, after wich
manner

manner alſo ſhadow clouds, miſts , and the like :
making the ſhadows to fall all one way.

I V. Thirdly, be very careful to augment or leſſen
every thing proportionably to their diſtance from the
eye, making them either bigger or leſſer.

V. In expreſſing things at large diſtances, as ten ,
twenty or thirty miles off; where the object is hard
to be diſcerned, as whether it be Temple, Caſtle ,
Houſe or the like; ſhew no particular ſigns thereof,
or any eminent diſtinction; but rather as weakly ,
faintly , and confuſedly as the eye judgeth of it.

V I. If Landskips be laid in Colours, the farther
you go , the more you muſt lighten it with a thin
and airy blew , to make it ſeem as if it were aſar off,
beginning at firſt with a dark green , ſo driving
it by degrees into a blew , according to the diſtance.

V I I. Make your Landskip to ſhoot (as it were)
away, one part lower than another , making the
neareſt hill or place higheſt , and thoſe that are
farther off, to ſhoot away under that , that the
Landskip may appear to be taken from the top of
an hill.

V I I I. Let every thing have its proper motion, as
in trees when they are ſhaken with the wind, making
the ſmaller boughs yielding ; the ſtiffer leſs bending :
in clouds that they follow the winds : *in rivers* , the
general current, and flaſhing of the waters againſt
the boat ſides : *in the Sea* , the waves and other proper agitations ; and laſtly, *let every thing* which mov-
eth, whether eſſentially or accidentally, have its proper repreſentation.

I X. Let your work imitate the ſeaſon you intend it
for.

As if you intend it for a winter piece, repreſent fel-
ling

ling of wood ; sliding upon the Ice *; fowling by night ; hunting of* Bears *or* Foxes *in the snow ; making the trees every where naked or laden with the hoar frost ; the earth bare without greenness , flowers or cattel ; the air thick ; water frozen, with* Carrs *passing over it and boyes upon it,* &c.

X. Lastly , let every site have its proper *parerga,* adjuncts, or additional graces, as the Farm-house , Wind-mill , Water-mill , Woods, Flocks of sheep, Herds of cattel, Pilgrims, ruines of Temples, Castles and Monuments ; with a thousand such other only proper to particular subjects.

C H A P. XVIII.

Of Diapering and Antique.

I. **D**Iapering, is a tracing or running over your work again when you have, as it were, quite done, with damask branches, and such like.

It is used to counterfeit cloth of gold , silver, damask , velvet, chamlet and the like , with what branch and in what fashion you please : it is derived from the Greek *word* διαπερώ, *transeo, to pass over, and only signifies a light passing over the same again.*

I I. If you Diaper upon folds, let your work be broken off accordingly , and taken as it were by the half.

For reason sheweth that the fold covereth something which cannot be seen by reason of it, which if it was drawn out at length would appear plain.

I I I. Let the whole work be *homogene* ; that is ,
let

let the fame work be continued throughout the whole garment, fetting the faireft branch in the moft eminent and perfpicuous place, caufing it to run upwards, for elfe your work would be ridiculous.

I V. You may either fhadow the ground and leave your work white ; or fhadow your work and leave the ground white ; and as you fhall pleafe in this kind , your filling may be with fmall pricks, which will fhew very fair.

V. Antique (*ab antes*) are butterefles whereon the building is ftayed, as alfo the outwardmoft ranges, ufed in fore-fronts of houfes, in all manner of Compartments, curious Architecture, Armours, Jewels, and Columns.

V I. The form of it is (only for delights fake) a general or irregular compofition of men, beafts, birds, fifhes and flowers and fuch like, without either rule or reafon.

V II. Laftly, obferve the continuation of one and the fame work, through the whole piece, without the leaft change or alteration.

As if it be naked boys, playing, laying, fitting, or riding upon Goats, Eagles, Dolphins and the like ; ftrings of pearl, Satyrs, Tritons, Apes, Dogs, Oxen, bearing or drawing Fruits, Branches, or any wild fanfie after your own invention, with a thoufand fuch other idle toys ; be fure you obferve the continuation.

C H A P.

C H A P. XIX.

To take the perfect draught of any Picture:

I. TAke a sheet of fine *Venice* Paper, wet it all over with linseed oyl on one side thereof, which then wipe off as clean as you can; let the Paper dry, and lay it on any painted or printed Picture, then with a black-lead pen you may draw it over with ease : put this oyled paper upon a sheet of clean white paper, and with a little pointed stick or feather out of a swallow's wing, draw over the stroaks which you drew upon the oyled paper; so shall you have the exact form upon the white paper, which may be set out with colours at pleasure-

II. *Or thus*, The picture being drawn as before in the oyled paper, put it upon a sheet of white paper, and prick over the drawing with a pen : then take some small coal, powder it fine, and wrap it in a piece of some fine linnen, and bind it up therein loosely, and clap it lightly all over the pricked line by little and little, and afterwards draw it over again once or twice, with pen or pencil.

III. *Or thus*, Rub a sheet of white paper all over on one side with black-lead, or else with vermilion mixed with fresh butter; lay the coloured side upon a sheet of white paper, then lay the picture you would copy out upon the other side of the coloured paper, and with a small pointed stick or swallows quill, go over all the stroaks of your picture, and it will be exact on the white paper.

IV. *Or thus*, Lay a piece of Lanthorn horn upon the picture,

picture, then draw the ſtroaks of your picture with a hard nibbed pen upon the horn ; and when it is dry, breath upon the horn twice or thrice,and preſs it hard upon white paper a little moiſtned.

V. *Or thus,* Take an oyled ſheet (as at the firſt Section of this Chapter) rub one ſide of it with lamb-black or lake ; lay it upon a ſheet of fair paper with the coloured ſide downwards , and upon it lay the picture you would coppy out , and trace it over with a ſwallows feather.

V I. *Or thus,* Take fine lake mixed with linſeed oyl , and draw with it , inſtead of Ink, all the out-ſtroaks of any picture,and other material parts ; then wet the contrary ſide of the picture and preſs it hard upon a ſheet of paper, and it will leave behind it all that which you drew over.

V I I. *Or thus,* Grind Printers black fine, and temper it with water, and with a pen dipt in it, draw over the out-lines and maſter ſtroaks : wet then ſome white paper with a ſpunge or the like, and preſs it hard thereupon ; and you ſhall have the ſtroaks you drew upon the white paper.

V I I I. *Or thus,* Lay the print (the back-ſide of it) upon a clear glaſs, or oyled paper, then lay a clean paper upon the print ; hold it up againſt the light , ſo will you ſee all the ſtroaks which you may draw out, and ſhadow alſo if you pleaſe.

C H A P.

CHAP. XX.

To extend or contract a Picture keeping the proportion.

I. **E**Ncompafs your picture with one great fquare, which divide into as many little ones as you pleafe: this done, according as you would have your picture either greater or lefs, make another fquare greater or lefs, which divide into as many equal fquares which be drawn with a black-lead plummet.

I I. Take your black-lead pen, and draw the picture by little and little, paffing from fquare unto fquare (by the example of the pattern) until you have gone all over with it: obferving that in what part of the fquare the picture lies, you draw the like part in the fquare anfwerable thereto, till you have finifhed the whole.

I I I. Then draw it over with a pen, in which fecond drawing of it you may eafily mend any fault, and fhadow it at pleafure.

I V. *Laftly*, When it is throughly dry, rub it over with the crum of white-bread, and it will take off all the black-lead ftroaks, fo will your draught remain fair upon the paper.

CHAP.

CHAP. XXI.

Of Perspective in general.

OΠTIKH' in Greek, *Perspectiva* in Latin, the *Art of seeing* in English ; is that by which we behold, contemplate, and draw the likeness of all magnitudes, just in form and manner as they appear to the Eye.

II. The matter to be seen or speculated is a magnitude : the manner of speculation is by radiations of Light, either direct, reflected or broken.

III. A magnitude is that which hath form ; and it is either lineal, superficial, or solid ; that is, either a complication of points, a complication of lines, or a complication of superficies.

VI. A line is a complication of points ; that is (according to *Euclid*) a length only without either breadth or thickness.

V. A superficies is a complication of lines ; that is, a length having breadth without thickness.

For as the continuation of points makes a line : so the couching of lines makes a superficies : which is only the laying of points cross-wise.

VI. A solid is a complication of superficies ; that is, a length and breadth, having depth or thickness.

And indeed it is nothing but the continuation of points upon a superficies either perpendicularly or bending.

VII. The Contemplation of the Object represents the matter to the mind, in the same manner as its outward appearance doth to the Eye. |

And from hence comes Judgment whereby the Artist is
enabled

enabled to defcribe the fame in lines; and delineate it , according to its apparent or vifual proportions.

VIII. To draw or defcribe the Appearance in lines is the active part of this Art, whereby the *Idea* conceived in the mind (by fight and contemplation) is brought to light.

IX. A radiation is a beam of light, conveighing the likenefs of the thing, to the Eyes, or fight; and the Knowledge thereof to the mind or underftanding.

And this radiation is twofold, either external from the external light, or intellectual from its being and power.

X. *Direct radiations* are thofe which confider the direct or ftreight beams, which pafs between the eye and the object.

And this is the firft kind of perfpective; and is many times (alone) called the Opticks.

XI. *Reflected radiations* are thofe which confider the reflection of beams, and their fhape upon any polifh'd body, as on a Globe, Cone, Cylinder, Pyramid, or any regular folid.

And this is the fecond kind of Perfpective; which is called the Art Catoptrica.

XII. *Broken radiations* are thofe which confider the breaking of beams , as they are to be feen through a glafs or a Cryftal cut into feveral plains or fuperficies.

And this is the third and laft kind of Perfpective, which is called the Art Dioptrica.

CHAP. XXII.

Of the Active part of Perspective.

I. THe active part of perspective is either *Ichno-graphical, Orthographical,* or *Scenographical.*

I I. *Ichnographia,* is the description of the plain base or bottom of any body or building.

I I I. And it is twofold, to wit, either *Geometrical* or *Scenographical.*

I V. *Ichnographia Geometrical,* is that which gives the fight of the bottom or base of any body or building.

So a Circle is the base of a Column ; and a square is the base of a Pedestal , and the like ; but this Geometrical Ichnography *is not seen in Section, or through a Glass, unless it lies parallel to the base ; and so it makes no Section with it.*

V. *Ichnographia Scenographical* is the Appearance of the same base in Section, or through a Glass , erected upright on the same plain, on which the base stands.

And by this the said base is extended in length but contracted in breadth, for so it appeareth to the eye.

V I. *Orthographia,* is the vision of the foreright side of any plain ; to wit, of that plain or superficies which lies equidistant to a right line , passing through the outward or convex centers of both eyes, continued to a due length.

And therefore Perspective Orthographia, *is the delineation of the apparent right plain.*

Scenographia is the description of a plain or other
figure

figure, that declines from the apparent or foreright plain ; that is of that plain which makes Angles with the said foreright plain.

The Scenographick *vision of any form, body, or building is, of that side which declines from, or constitutes an Angle, with the right line, passing from the convex centers of both Eyes aforesaid : this Artists call the* return of the foreright side. *Now the difference between the* Ortho-graphick *and* Scenographick *vision is this ; the* Ortho-graphick *shews the side of a body or building as it is beheld when the plain of the Glass is placed equidistant to that side : but the* Scenographick *shews the side of a body or edifice as it appears through a glass raised obliquely to the said side, or making an angle therewith.*

CHAP. XXIII.

Of the Subject to be seen.

1. THe *Base* of any thing is the plain, flat, or floor upon which any solid body, or object is placed, or raised.

I I. The *Altitude* or *height* is the perpendicular space of place, between the base and eye, or height of the visual point above the base.

III. The *Visual point*, is a point in the Horizontal line, wherein all the beams of the eyes unite.

Exempli gratia. *If you look on a long straight river, the sides of which run parallel, yet by reason of the distance both sides of the river (although it be very broad) will seem to incline, touch, and unite with each other in on common point or center : and so if you look on a long ſtraight brick-wall , the ſeveral lays of brick, and courſes of mortar , will (at a great diſtance) ſeem to incline each to other in one common point or center ; this point reflected on a glaſs raiſed upright on the baſe, is called the viſual point.*

I V. The *Horizontal line* is a line proceeding from the center of the eye to the viſual point , parallel to the Horizon of the Earth.

And this is, in men of ordinary height or ſtature, commonly about five foot from the ground or baſe.

V. The *Diſtance* is the ſpace on the baſe between the Glaſs and point in the baſe which lies directly under the eyes.

. V I. The *Section* is a plain of tranſparent or perlucid matter (as of Glaſs) raiſed upright upon the plain of the baſe ſtanding before you , parallel to a ſtraight line, paſſing through the convex centers of both Eyes.

Without the knowledge of this Section *or Glaſs it is utterly impoſſible to underſtand* perſpective, *or know what it means : Or be able to give a reaſon for the difference between the* Orthographick *and* Scenographick *figure.*

V I I. If the Glaſs is placed near the viſual point, and far from the object, the figure which is ſeen will be very ſmall : and the reaſon is, becauſe all rays comprehending the Orthographical and Scenographical figures (though more remote from the object) fall into the viſual point, as their common center.

V I I I. If the viſual point be more elevated (though at the ſame diſtance) the Scenographick figure or form will appear of a much larger magnitude : becauſe the viſual radiations being higher , the various perpendiculars raiſed on the Section or Glaſs, cut them in wider diſtances , becauſe more remote from the Glaſs.

IX. If the Glass incline to the visual point, the Scenographick vision will be long-wise between the visual point and the object.

And the reason is, because the plain of the Glass heaps in more of the visual Radiations.

X. If the Glass recline from the visual point, the Scenographick figure will appear rounder, and begin to resemble the Orthographick.

XI. But if the Glass is fixed equidistant to the base, or plain the object stands upon; the Scenographick and Orthographick resemblance will be one and the same.

And the reason is, because the form of the figure is lost, or not visible in the Section.

XII. The *Visual Raies*, are those lines which proceed from the visual point, through the Glass, to any point higher or lower than the plain of the Horizor.

XIII. *Diagonals*, or lines of distance, are such as are drawn from the point of distance to any other point, higher or lower than the Horizon.

XIV. The *Object*, is that form, figure, body or edifice intended to be expressed in *Perspective* proportions.

CHAP.

CHAP. XXIV.

The General Practice of Perspective.

I. LEt every line which in the Object or Geometrical figure is ftraight, perpendicular, or parallel to its bafe, be fo alfo in its Scenographick delineation.

II. Let the lines which in the object return at right Angles from the fore-right fide, be drawn Scenographically from the Vifual point.

III. Let all ftraight lines, which in the object return from the fore-right-fide, run in a Scenographick figure into the Horizontal line.

IV. Let the object you intend to delineate ftanding on your right hand, be placed alfo on the right hand of the vifual point : and that on the left hand, on the left hand on the fame point: and that which is juft before, in the middle of it.

V. Let thofe lines which are (in the object) Equidiftant to the returning line, be drawn in the Scenographick figure, from that point found in the Horizon.

VI. In fetting off the altitude of Columns, Pedeftals and the like, meafure the height from the bafeline upward in the front or fore-right-fide ; and a vifual ray drawn, that point in the front fhall limit the altitude of the Column or pillar, all the way behind the fore-right-fide or Orthographick appearance, even to the vifual point.

This rule you muft obferve in all figures, as well where there is a front or fore-right-fide, as where there is none.

VII. In

VII. In delineating Ovals, Circles, Arches, Croffes, Spirals and Crofs-arches, or any other figure, in the roof of any room; firft draw Ichnographically, and fo with perpendiculars, from the moft Eminent points thereof, carry it up unto the Ceiling, from which feveral points carry on the figure.

VIII. The center in any Scenographick regular figure is found by drawing crofs-lines from oppofite angles : for the point where the Diagonals crofs is the Center.

IX. A ground plain of fquares is alike, both above and below the Horizontal line; only the more it is diftant above or beneath the Horizon, the fquares will be fo much the larger or wider.

X. In drawing a perfpective figure, where many lines come together, you may for the directing of your eye, draw the Diagonals in red; the vifual lines in black; the Perpendiculars in green, or other different colour from that which you intend the figure fhall be of.

XI. Having confidered the height, diftance and pofition of the figure, and drawn it accordingly, with fide or angle againft the bafe; raife perpendiculars from the feveral angles or defigned points in the figure, to the bafe, and transfer the length of each perpendicular, from the place where it touches the bafe, to the bafe on the fide oppofite to the point of diftance; fo will the Diametrals drawn to the perpendiculars in the bafe, by interfection with the Diagonals drawn to the feveral transferred diftances, give the angles of the figure : and fo lines drawn from point to point will circumfcribe the Scenographick figure.

XII. If in Landskip there be any ftanding waters, as Rivers, Ponds, and the like; place the Horizontal

rizontal line level with the farthest fight or appearance of it.

XIII. If there be any houses or the like in the picture, consider their position, that you may find from what point in the Horizontal line to draw the fronts and sides thereof.

XIV. In describing things at a great distance, observe the proportion (both in magnitude and distance) in draught, which appears from the object to the eye.

XV. In colouring and shadowing of every thing, you must do the same in your picture which you observe with your eye, especially in objects lying near; but according as the distance grows greater and greater, so the colours must be fainter and fainter, till at last they lose themselves in a darkish sky colour.

XVI. The *Catoptricks* are best seen in a common looking-glass or other polish'd matter, where if the glass be exactly flat, the object is exactly like its original : but if the glass be not flat, the resemblance alters from the original, and that more or less, according as the glass differs from an exact plain.

XVII. In drawing *Catoptrick* figures, the surface of the glass is to be considered, upon which you mean to have the reflection; for which you must make a particular *Ichnographical* draught or projection ; which on the glass must appear to be a plain full of squares , on which projection transfer what shall be drawn , on a plain divided into the same number of like squares : where though the draught may appear very confused, yet the reflection thereof on the glass will be very regular, proportional and really composed.

XVIII. The *Dioptrick* or broken beam may be seen in a tub, through a Cryftal, or Glass, which hath its

D 3   surface furface cut into many others, whereby the raies of the object are broken.

For to the flat of the Cryftal or water, the raies run ftreight; but then they break and make an Angle, the which alfo by the refracted beams is made and continued on the other fide of the fame flat.

XIX. When thefe faces on a Cryftal are returned towards a plain placed directly before it, they feparate themfelves at a good diftance on the plain; becaufe they are all directed to various far diftant places of the fame.

XX. But for the affigning to each of them a place on the fame plain, no Geometrick rule is yet invented.

C H A P. XXV.

A Rational Demonftration of Chiromantical Signatures; Added by way of Appendix to Chap. VIII. *of this Book.*

I. THe foundation of Chiromancy depends upon the true appropriation of the feveral mounts, fingers, or places in the hand, to their proper Stars or Planets.

II. The Ancients have affigned the root of the middle finger to *Saturn*; of the fore-finger to *Jupiter*: the hollow of the hand to *Mars*: the root of the ring-finger to *Sol*: of the thumb to *Venus*: of the little finger to *Mercury*: and laftly, the brawn of the hand near the wrift to *Luna*.

III. That line which comes round the ball of the
thumb

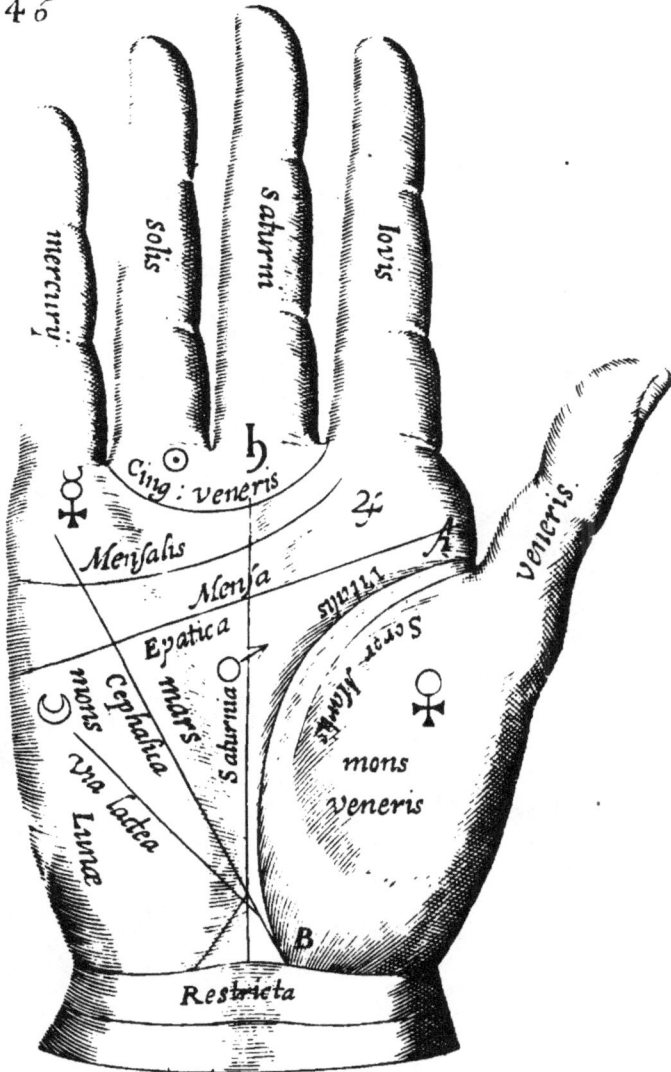

mercurij

solis

saturni

Iovis

Cing : veneris

☉ ♄

♃

Mensalis

Mensa

Epatica

Saturnia ☉

mars

Cephalica

mons

Via lactea

Lunae

Saturnia

Triesis

S Scror Mara

Veneris

♀

mons
veneris

A

B

Restricta

Iobi 37. 7.
Qui in manu omnium hominum signa posu:
it vt cognoscerent cyua eius singuli.

F. H. Vm. Houe fec:

thumb towards the root or mount of *Jupiter* is called *Linea Jovialis* or the life-line : that from the wrist to the root or mount of *Saturn*, *Linea Saturnialis* : but if it points to the root or mount of *Sol* , *Linea Solaris*, if to *Mercury*, *Linea Mercurialis* : that which goes from *Linea Jovialis* to the mount of *Luna*, *Linea Lunaris*, or the natural line : the other great line above it is called *Linea Stellata* , or the line of fortune, because it limits the mounts of the Planets , and is impressed with various vertues in those places according to the nature of the Planet whose mount it runs under or sets a boundary unto : Lastly, the space between the natural line and the line of fortune is called *Mensa*, the Table.

IV. All other lines shall either proceed out of the sides of the former, or else from some proper mount.

V. Every line great or small , long or short, hath a certain beginning or root, from which it rises ; and a certain end or point to which it tends.

VI. The distance between both ends, is the way of its passage ; in which way, it either crosses some other line, or else is crossed : if it do neither, its signification is continual, and ought so much the more to be taken notice of.

VII. Every mount hath a proper signification , which it receives from the significations of its proper Planet, being abstractly considered : the same understand of all the principal lines aforesaid.

VIII. *Saturn* is the Author of Age , Inheritances, Melancholy , Malice, Sorrow, Misery , Calamities, Enemies, Imprisonments, Sickness, Diseases, Perplexities, Cares, Poverty, Crosses, Death, and whatsoever evil can befall humane life: he signifies Fathers, Old Men, Labourers, Dyers, Smiths, and Jesuits.

IX. *Jupiter* is the Author of Health, Strength ,

Mo-

Moderation, Sobriety, Mercy, Riches, Substance, Goodness, Liberty, Religion, Honesty, Justice, Modesty, and all other things which may make a man happy : he signifies Churches, Church-men, Lawyers, Scholars, Cloathiers, and the like.

X. *Mars* is the Author of Strife, Contention, Pride, Presumption, Tyranny, Thefts, Murders, Victory, Conquest, Infortunacy, Boldness, and Dangers : he signifies Physicians, Chirurgions, Apothecaries, the Camp, all Military men and Preferments, Edge-tools, Butchers, Carpenters, Gunners, Bailiffs, and the like.

X I. *Sol* is the Author of Honour, Glory, Renown, Preferment, Life, Generosity, Magnanimity, Soveraignty, Dominion, Power, Treasures, Gold, Silver, and whatsoever may make the life of man splendid ; he signifies Kings, Princes, Rulers, and all men in power, Minters, Goldsmiths, long Life and Wisdom.

X I I. *Venus* is the Author of Joy, Pleasure, Mirth, Solace, Lust, Uncleanness, and Idleness : she signifies Woman-kind, Sisters, Ladies, Whores, Curiosities, Lapidaries, Silkmen, Taylors, Mercers, Upholsters, Pictures, Picture-drawers, the Pox, and Diseases proceeding from uncleanness.

X I I I. *Mercury* is the Author of Craft, Subtilty, Policy, Deceit, Perjury, Study, Hearing, and Merchandizing: he signifies Merchants, Clerks, Scholars, Secretaries, Ambassadors, Pages, Messengers, Poets, Orators, Stationers, Cheaters, Thieves, Petty-lawyers, Philosophers, Mathematicians, Astrologers.

X I V. *Luna* is the Author of popular Fame both Good and Evil, Joy and Sorrow, Mutability and Inconstancy, Affection and Disaffection, Moisture and every effect which may be said to be common : she signifies Waters, Ships, Seamen of all sorts, Queens, Ladies, a Governess, the Common people in general,

Neigh-

Neighbors, Mothers, Kindred, Fishmongers, Vintners, Tapsters, Midwives, Nurses and Travellers.

This being known, understand,

X V. *First,* That the lines take their signification from the mount of that Planet from whence they rise.

X V I. *Secondly,* That the place from whence any line rises shews the ground, cause, or original of the things signified by that line : the line or mount to which it points, shews the issue, to what the thing tends, and what may be the end of the matter signified.

X V I I. *Thirdly,* That whether the line signifies good or evil, if it be cut or crossed by any other line, that line so cutting it, will at a certain time not only abate the good, but also take away the evil, if it so signified.

X V I I I. *Fourthly ,* That the nature and quality of that line thus destroying the signification of the former, is known by considering from what place it rises, and to what place it tends.

X I X. *Fifthly,* That a double judgement arises from every line, by accounting its rise, first from the one , end ; secondly from the other.

X X. *Sixthly,* That little lines rising out of the sides of any other line, both augment the things signified by that line ; and also signifie new matter arising by things signified by the line from whence they rise; and the place to which they point, shew to what they tend.

X X I. *Seventhly,* That the mounts or lines adorned with stars, or small lines, not crossed, or pointing to evil places, shew great good and happiness to the person, by things signified by the same mount or line : and on the contrary, vitiated with crosses, spots , or knots shew much evil and perplexity.

X X I I. *Lastly,* The beginning of the lines , shew in the beginning or forepart of Life; the middle, in the middle part of Life ; and the ends of them, the latter

part,

part, or end of Life ; so that if any evil or good be signified by any line, you must hint the time according to the aforesaid reason.

'Tis true, here we ought to enquire into the denominated times when the things signified should come to pass ; but because that matter is something long and abstruse (being more fit to be handled in a particular tract, wherein all its curiosities may be examined) this our present work being a subject of another nature, and these things not essential to our purpose, but only added by way of appendix, we shall at this time forbear. Notwithstanding, although we have not here delineated every thing in particular, yet we have laid (as it were) the ground and foundation of the Art, out of which, as out of a fountain, the industrious Student may at his own leisure and pleasure, rear a stately fabrick.

The End of the first Book.

POLYGRAPHICES
LIBER SECUNDUS.

Of ENGRAVING, ETCHING, and LIMNING.

Shewing the Inftruments belonging to the Work ; the Matter of the Work, the way and manner of performing the fame ; together with all other Requifites and Ornaments.

CHAP. I.

Of Graving *and the Inftruments thereof.*

I. GRaving is an Art which teacheth how to transfer any defign upon Copper, Brafs, or Wood, by help of fharp pointed and cutting Inftruments.

II. The chief Inftruments are four, 1. Gravers, 2. An Oyl ftone, 3. A Cufhion, 4. A Burnifher.

III. Gravers are of three forts, round pointed, fquare pointed and Lozenge pointed. *The round is beft to fcratch withal : the fquare Graver is to make the largeft ftroaks :*

*ſtroaks : the Lozenge is to make ſtroaks more fine and deli-
cate ; but a Graver of a middle ſize betwixt the ſquare
and Lozenge pointed, will make the ſtroaks or hatches ſhew
with more life and vigour, according as you manage it in
working.*

IV. The Oyl-ſtone is to whet the Gravers upon,
which muſt be very ſmooth, not too ſoft, nor too hard,
and without pin-holes.

The uſe is thus : *Put a few drops of Oil Olive upon
the ſtone, and laying that ſide of it, which you intend ſhall
cut the Copper, flat upon the ſtone, whet it very flat and
eaven ; and therefore be ſure to carry your hand ſtedfaſt
with an equal ſtrength, placing the forefinger firmly, upon
the oppoſite ſide of the Graver. Then turn the next ſide of
your Graver, and whet that in like manner, that you may
have a very ſharp edge for an inch or more. Laſtly, turning uppermoſt that edge which you have ſo whetted, and
ſetting the end of the Graver obliquely upon the ſtone
whet it very very flat and ſloping in form of a Lozenge (with
an exaƐt and eaven hand) making to the edge thereof a
ſharp point. It is impoſſible that the work ſhould be with
the neatneſs and curioſity deſired, if the Graver be not,
not only very good, but alſo exaƐtly and carefully whetted.*

V. The Cuſhion is a leather bag filled with fine
ſand, to lay the plate upon, on which you may turn it
every way at eaſe.

*You muſt turn your plate with your left hand, accord-
ing as the ſtroaks which you grave do turn, which muſt be attained with diligent care and practice.*

VI. The burniſhing Iron is of uſe to rub out ſcratch-
es and ſpecks or other things which may fault your
work in the plate ; as alſo if any ſtroaks be graved
too deep or groſs to make them appear leſs and
fainter by rubbing them therewith.

VII. To

VII. To make your Gravers.

Provide some cross-bow steel, and cause it to be beaten out into small rods, and softned, then with a good file you may shape them at pleasure : when you have done, heat them red hot, and straight dip it into Soap, and by so doing it will be very hard : where note that in dipping them into the Soap, if you turn your hand never so little awry, the Graver will be crooked. *If your Graver be too hard, take a red-hot Charcoal and lay the end of your Graver upon it till it begins to wax yellowish, and then dip it into tallow (some say water) and it will be tougher.*

VIII. Have by you a piece of Box or hard wood, that after you have sharpned your Graver, by striking the point of it into the said Box or hard wood, you may take off all the roughness about the points, which was caused by whetting it upon the oyl-stone.

IX. Lastly, take a file and touch the edge of the Graver therewith ; if the file cut it, it is too soft, and will do no good : but if it will not touch it, it is fit for your work.

If it should break on the point, it is a sign it is tempered too hard ; which oftentimes after a little use by whetting will come into a good condition.

CHAP. II.

Of Polishing the Copper Plate.

1. **T**Ake a plate of Brass or Copper of what bigness you please, and of a reasonable thickness, taking heed that it be free from fire-flaws.

II. Beat it as smooth as you can with a hammer, and then rub it as smooth as you can, with a pumice-stone

void

void of Gravel (left it fcratch it, and fo caufe as much labour to get them out) and a little water.

III. Then drop a few drops of oyl Olive upon the plate, and burnifh it with your bernifhing Iron; and then rub it with Charcoal made of Beech wood quenched in Urine.

IV. Laftly, with a roul made of a piece of a black Felt, Caftor, or Beaver, dipt in oyl Olive, rub it well for an hour, fo fhall your plate be exactly polifhed.

C H A P. III.

Of holding the Graver.

I. **I**T will be neceffary to cut off that part of the knob of the handle of the Graver which is upon the fame line with the edge of the Graver; thereby making that lower fide next to the plate flat, that it may be no hindrance in graving.

For working upon a large plate, that part of the handle (if not cut away) will fo reft upon the Copper, that it will hinder the fmooth and even carriage of your hand in making your ftroaks, and will caufe your Graver to run into your Copper deeper than it fhould do. This done,

II. Place the knob at the end of the handle of the graver in the hollow of your hand, and having extended your fore-finger towards the point of the Graver, laying it a top, or oppofite to the edge which fhould cut the plate; place your thumb on the one fide of the Graver, and your other fingers on the other fide, fo as that you may guide the Graver flat and parallel with the plate.

III. Be wary that your fingers interpofe not between the

the plate and the Graver, for they will hinder you in carrying your Graver level with the plate, and cause your lines to be more deep, grofs and rugged, than otherwise they would be.

CHAP. IV.

Of the way and manner of Engraving.

I. HAving a Cufhion filled with fand about nine inches long and fix broad, and three or four thick, and a plate well polifhed; lay the plate upon the Cufhion, which place upon a firm Table.

II. Holding the Graver (as aforefaid) according to Art, in making ftraight ftroaks be fure to hold your plate firm upon the Cufhion, moving your hand, leaning lightly where the ftroak fhould be fine; and harder where you would have the ftroak broader.

III. But in making circular or crooked ftroaks, hold your hand and Graver ftedfaft, your arm and elbow refting upon the Table, and move the plate againft the Graver; for otherwife it is impoffible to make thofe crooked or winding ftroaks with that neatnefs and command that you ought to do.

IV. Learn to carry your hand with fuch a flight, that you may end your ftroak as finely as you begin it; and if you have occafion to make one part deeper or blacker than another, do it by degrees; and that you may do it the more exactly, obferve that your ftroaks be not too clofe, nor too wide.

For your more exact obfervation, practife by fuch prints which are more loofly fhadowed, left by imitating the more dark, you fhould not know where to begin or end.	V. After

V. After you have graved part of your work, it will be needful to scrape it with the sharp edge of a burnisher or other graver, carrying it along even with the plate, to take off the roughness of the stroaks; but in doing it beware of making scratches.

VI. And that you may the better see that which is Engraven, with the piece of Felt or Castor (at the fourth Section of the second Chapter) dipt in oyl rub the places graven.

VII. Lastly, whatsoever appears to be amiss, you may rub out with the burnisher, and very exactly polish it with your piece of Felt or Castor and oyl; which done, to cleanse the plate you may boil it a little in Wine-vinegar, and rub it gently with a brush of small grass-wire or Hogs bristles.

CHAP. V.

Of the Imitation of Copies or Prints.

I. **H**Aving a piece of Bees wax tyed up in a fine holland rag, heat the plate over the fire, till it may be hot enough to melt the wax; then rub the plate with the wax tyed up in the rag, till you see it covered all over with wax, (which let be very thin:) if it be not even, heat it again by the fire, and wipe it over gently with a feather.

II. If you would copy a printed picture, to have it print off the same way; then clap the print which you would imitate with the printed side next to the plate; and having placed it very exactly, rub the backside of the print with a burnisher, or any thing that is hard, smooth and round, which will cause it

to

to ſtick to the wax upon the plate : then take off
the print (beginning at one corner) gently and with
care , left you tear it (which may be cauſed alſo by
putting too much wax upon the plate) and it will
leave upon the wax the perfect proportion in every
part.

Where note , if it be an old picture, before you place it
upon the wax, it will be good to track it over in every limb
with a black-lead pencil.

I I I. But if you would have it print the contrary
way, take the duſt of black-lead, and rub the backſide
of the print all over therewith , which backſide put
upon the waxed plate ; and with your needle or drawing point, draw all the out-lines of the deſign or print ,
all which you will find upon the wax. This done,

I V. Take a long Graver either Lozenge or round
(which is better) very ſharp,and with the point thereof ſcratch over every particular limb in the out-ſtroak;
which done, it will not be difficult to mark out all the
ſhadows as you Engrave, having the proportion before you.

V. Laſtly, for Copies of Letters, go over every
letter with black lead, or write them with ungum'd
Ink, and clap the paper over the waxed plate as before.

C H A P. VI.

Of Engraving in Wood.

I. THe figures that are to be carved or graven in
Wood muſt firſt be drawn, traced, or paſted
upon the wood ; and afterwards all the other ſtanding
of the wood (except the figure) muſt be cut away
E   with

with little narrow pointed knives made for that purpofe.

This graving in wood is far more tedious and difficult than that in Brafs or Copper ; becaufe you muft cut twice or thrice to take out one ftroak ; and having cut it, to be careful in picking it out, left you fhould break any part of the work, which would deface it.

II. For the kind of the wood let it be hard and tough: the beft for this purpofe is Beech and Box: let it be plained inch thick ; which you may have cut into pieces according to the bignefs of the figure you grave.

III. To draw the figures upon the wood.

Grind White lead very fine, and temper it with fair water ; dip a cloth therein, and rub over one fide of the wood and let it dry throughly : This keepeth the Ink (if you draw therewith) that it run not about, nor fink: and if you draw with Paftils, it makes the ftroaks appear more plain and bright.

IV. Having whited the wood as before (if it is a figure you would copy,) black or red the blankfide of the print or copy, and with a little ftick or fwallow's quill, trace or draw over the ftroaks of the figure.

V. But if you pafte the figure upon the wood, you muft not then white it over (for then the figure will pill off) but only fee the wood be well plained : then wipe over the printed fide of the figure with Gum-Tragacanth diffolved in fair water, and clap it fmooth upon the wood, which let dry throughly : then wet it a little all over, and fret off the paper gently, till you can fee perfectly every ftroak of the figure : dry it again, and fall to cutting or carving it.

C H A P.

CHAP. VII.

Of Etching, *and the Materials thereof.*

I. **E***Tching* is an artificial Engraving of Brafs **or** Copper-plates with *Aqua-fortis.*

II. The Inftruments of Etching (befides the plate) are thefe nine. 1. *Hard Varnifh.* 2. *Soft Varnifh.* 3. *Prepared Oyl.* 4. *Aqua-fortis.* 5. *Needles.* 6. *Oyl-ftone.* 7. *Brufh-Pencil.* 8. *Burnifher.* 9. *The Frame and Trough.*

III. *To polifh the plate.*

Although in Chap. 2. of this Book, we have fufficiently taught how to polifh the plate, yet neverthelefs we think it convenient to fubjoyn thefe following words. Firft, the plate being well planifhed or forged, choofe the fmootheft fide to polifh ; then fix it upon a board a little declining, and rub it firmly and evenly all over with a piece of Grindftone, throwing water often on it, fo long till there be no dints, flaws, or marks of the hammer : wafh it clean, and with a piece of good Pumice-ftone, rub it fo long till there be no rough ftroaks or marks of the Grindftone : wafh it clean again, and rub it with a fine Hoan and water till the marks of the Pumice-ftone are rubbed out : wafh it again, and with a piece of Charcoal without knots (being heat red hot and quenched in water , the outfide being pared off) rub the plate with water till all the fmall ftroaks of the Hoan be vanifhed ; laftly, if yet there remain any fmall ftroaks or fcratches, rub them out with the end of the burnifhing Iron, fo fhall the plate be fitted for work.

I V. *To make the hard Varnish for Etching.*

Take Greek or Burgundy-pitch, Colophonium or Rozin, of each five ounces, Nut-Oyl four ounces; melt the Pitch or Rozin in an earthen pot upon a gentle fire; then put in the Oyl, and let them boil for the space of half an hour: cool it a little upon a softer fire till it appear like a Glewy fyrrup: cool it a little more, strain it, and being almost cold, put it into a glased-pot for use. Being thus made it will keep at least twenty years.

V. *To make the soft Varnish for Etching.*

Take Virgin-wax three ounces, Mastich in drops two ounces, Asphaltum one ounce : grind the Mastich and Asphaltum severally very fine : then in an earthen pot melt the wax and strew in the Mastich and Asphaltum , stirring all upon the fire till they be well dissolved and mixed, which will be in about half a quarter of an hour; then cooling it a little , pour it into a bason of fair water (all except the dregs) and with your hands wet (before it is cold) form it into rouls.

V I. *To make the prepared Oyl.*

Take Oyl Olive, make it hot in an earthen pot, and put into it a sufficient quantity of tried Sheeps fuet (so much as being dropped upon a cold thing, the oyl may be a little hardened and firm) boil them together for an hour , till they be of a reddish colour, left they should separate when you use them. This mixture is to make the fat more liquid, and not cool so fast, for the fat alone would be no sooner on the pencil, but it would grow cold ; and be sure to put in more oyl in Winter than in Summer.

V I I. *To make the Aqua-fortis.*

Take distilled White-wine Vinegar three pints; Sal-Armoniack, Bay-salt of each six ounces; Verdegriese
four

four ounces. Put all together into a large well glazed
earthen pot (that they may not boil over) cover the
pot clofe, and put it on a quick fire, and let it fpeedi-
ly boil two or three great walms and no more; when
it is ready to boil uncover the pot, and ftir it fometimes with a ftick, taking heed that it boil not over:
having boiled, take it from the fire, and let it cool being clofe covered, and when it is cold, put it into a
Glafs bottle with a Glafs ftopple: If it be too ftrong
in Etching weaken it with a glafs or two of the fame
Vinegar you made it of.   There is another fort of *A-
qua-fortis*, which is called Common, which is exhibit-
ed in *Synopfis Medicinæ*, *lib.* 3. *cap.* 7. *fect.* 4. *pag.* 656.
But becaufe that Book may not be in every mans hand,
we will here infert it ; it is thus : Take dried Vitriol
two pound, Salt-peter, one pound, mix them and diftil by a Retort, in open fire by degrees.

VIII. *To make the Etching Needles.*

Choofe Needles of feveral fizes fuch as will break
without bending, and of a fine grain ; then take good
round fticks of firm wood (not apt to fplit) about fix
inches long, and as thick as a large Goofe-quill, at
the ends of which fix your Needles fo that they may
ftand out of the fticks about a quarter of an inch or
fomething more. ·

IX. *To whet the points of the Needles with the Oyl-
ftone.*

If you would have them whetted round, you muft
whet their points fhort upon the Oyl-ftone (not as
fowing Needles are) turning them round whilft you
whet them, as Turners do. If you whet them floping, firft make them blunt upon the Oyl-ftone , then
holding them firm and fteady, whet them floping
upon one fide only , till they come to a fhort and
roundifh oval.

E 3   X. The

X. The brush pencil is to cleanse the work, wipe off dust, and to strike the colours even over the ground or varnish, when laid upon the plate.

X I. The burnisher is a well hardened piece of steel somewhat roundish at the end. Its uses are what we have spoken at the sixth Section of the first Chapter, and the third Section of the second Chapter.

X I I. *To make the Frame and Trough.*

The Frame is an entire board, about whose top and sides is fastned a ledge two inches broad, to keep the *Aqua-fortis* from running off from the sides when you pour it on : the lower end of this board must be placed in the Trough, leaning sloping against a wall or some other thing, wherein you must fix several pegs of wood to rest the plate upon. The Trough is made of a firm piece of Elm or Oke set upon four legs, whose hollow is four inches wide ; and so long as may best fit your use : the hollow must be something deeper in the middle, that the water running thither way fall through a hole (there made for that purpose) into an earthen pan well Leaded. *The inside of this board and trough must be covered over with a thick oyl colour, to hinder the* Aqua-fortis *from eating or rotting the board.*

C H A P.

CHAP. VIII.

The way and manner of using the hard Varnish.

I. **H**Aving well heat the polished plate over a Chafing dish of coals, take some of the first varnish with a little stick, and put a drop of it on the top of your finger, with which lightly touch the plate at equal distances, laying on the varnish equally, and heating the plate again as it grows cold, keeping it carefully from dust or filth; then with the ball of your thumb tap it upon the plate; still wiping your hand over all, to make it more smooth and equal.

And here beware that neither the varnish be too thick upon the plate, nor your hand sweaty.

II. Then take a great lighted candle burning clear, with a short snuff, (placing the corner of the plate against a wall) hold the varnished side downward over the candle, as close as you can, so it touch not the varnish, guiding the flame all over, till it is all perfectly black, which you must keep from dust or filth till it is dry.

III. Over a fire of Charcoals hang the varnished plate to dry with the varnish upwards, which will smoak; when the smoak abates, take away the plate, and with a pointed stick scratch near the side thereof, and if the varnish easily comes off, hang it over the fire again a little, so long till the varnish will not too easily come off; then take it from the fire and let it cool.

If

If the varnish should be too hard, cast cold water on the back-side of the plate to cool it, that the heat may not make it too hard and brittle. This done,

I V. Place it upon a low desk, or some such like thing, and cover that part which you do not work on, with a sheet of fine white paper, and over that a sheet of brown paper, on which may rest your hand, to keep it from the varnish.

V. If you use a ruler, lay some part of it upon the paper, that it may not rub off the varnish ; and have an especial care, that no dust or filth get in between the paper and the varnish, for that will hurt it.

C H A P. IX.

The way and manner of Etching.

I. IN making lines or hatches, some bigger, some lesser, straight or crooked, you must use several sorts of Needles, bigger or lesser as the work requires.

I I. The great lines are made by leaning hard on the Needle ; its point being short and thick, (but a round point will not cut the varnish clear:) or by making divers lines, or hatches, one very close to another, and then by passing over them again with a thicker Needle; or by making them with an indifferent large needle, and letting the *Aqua-fortis* lie the longer thereon.

The best Needles for this work are such as are whet sloping with an oval, because their sides will cut that which the round ones will not.

I I I. If your lines or hatches ought to be of an equal thickness from end to end, lean on the needle with an
                                                                equal

equal force; leaning lightly where you would have the lines or ftroaks fine or fmall; and more heavy where you would have the lines appear deep or large; thereby the needle may have fome Impreffion in the Copper.

I V. If your lines or hatches be too fmall, pafs over them again with a fhort round point, of fuch a bignefs as you would have the line of, leaning ftrongly where you would have the line deep.

V. The manner of holding the needle with oval points (which are moft proper to make large and deep ftroaks) is much like that of a pen, only the flat fide whetted is ufually held towards the thumb : but they may be ufed with the face of the oval turned toward the middle finger.

V I. If you would end with a fine ftroak, you ought to do that with a very fine needle.

V I I. In ufing the oval points, hold them as upright and ftraight in your hand as you can, ftriking your ftroaks firmly and freely, for that will add much to their beauty and clearnefs.

V I I I. In Landskips, in places fartheft from the fight, as alfo neareft the light, ufe a very flender point, leaning fo lightly with your hand as to make a fmall faint ftroak.

I X. In working be careful to brufh off all the duft which you work off with the needles.

C H A P.

C H A P. X.

Of uſing the Aqua-fortis.

I. IF there be any ſtroaks which you would not have the *Aqua-fortis* eat into ; or any places where the varniſh is rubbed off, melt ſome prepared Oyl , and with a pencil, cover thoſe places pretty thick.

I I. Then take a bruſh, pencil, or rag, and dip it in the prepared oyl, and rub the back-ſide of the plate all over, that the *Aqua-fortis* may not hurt it, if by chance any ſhould fall thereon.

I I I. Before you put the *Aqua-fortis* to the plate, gently warm or dry the plate by a fire to dry up the humidity, which it might contract by reaſon of the Air ; and to prevent the breaking up the varniſh upon the firſt pouring the *Aqua-fortis* thereon.

I V. Place the plate by the 12th. Section of the 7th. Chapter of this Book, and with the *Aqua-fortis* in an earthen pot pour upon the plate, beginning at the top, ſo moving your hand that it may run all over the plate, which do for eight or ten times: then turn it cornerwiſe, and pour the *Aqua-fortis* on it that way ten or twelve times ; and then turn it again corner-wiſe the other way, pouring on the *Aqua-fortis* eight or ten times as before ; doing thus ſeveral times for the ſpace of half a quarter of an hour or more, accor-ding to the ſtrength of the water, and nature of the Copper.

For there muſt be leſs time allowed to hard and brittle Copper for pouring on the Aqua-fortis *, but more to the ſoft.*

V. But

V. But you muſt have ſpecial regard to caſt on the *Aqua-fortis* as occaſion ſhall require, and work is ; caſting it on at ſeveral times, and on ſeveral places ; where you would have it very deep, often ; where leſs deep, fewer times : where light, leſs yet ; where lighter, leſſer yet : and where ſo light as it can ſcarcely be ſeen, once or twice : waſh it with water, and cover it where you would have it lighter.

V I. Having thus covered your plates as occaſion requires ; for the ſecond time, place the plate on the frame as aforeſaid, and pour on it your *Aqua-fortis* for a full half hour.

V I I. Then waſh it with water and dry it, covering the places which require lightneſs or faintneſs (that they may be proportionable to the deſign) then pour on the *Aqua-fortis* for the laſt time more or leſs according to the nature of your work, and the deepneſs that it requires.

V I I I. You may rub off the varniſh or ground, as occaſion fin your work requires with a Charcoal, to ſee whether the water hath eaten deep enough ; by which you may judge of the ſpace of time, that you are after to imploy in pouring on the *Aqua-fortis,* in the works you will have to do, which if the ſhadows require much depth, or ought to be very black, the water ought to be poured on (at the leaſt time) for an hour or better ; yet know *no certain rule of time can be limited for this.*

C H A P.

CHAP. XI.

Of Finiſhing the Work.

I. **A**LL the former operations being done, waſh the plate with fair water ; and put it wet upon the fire, till the mixture be well melted, and then wipe it very clean on both ſides with a linnen cloth, till you have cleanſed it of all the mixture.

1 I. Take Charcoal of Willow, take off the rind of it , and putting fair water on the plate, rub it with the Charcoal, as if you were to poliſh it, and it will take off the varniſh.

Where note, that the Coal muſt be free from all knots and roughneſs, and that no ſand or filth fall upon the plate.

I I I. Take ordinary *Aqua-fortis,* to which add two third parts of water, and with ſome linnen rags dipped therein rub the plate all over, ſo will you take away its diſcolouring, and recover its former beauty.

I V. Then take dry linnen rags and wipe the plate ſo as to take off all the aforeſaid water, and then holding it a little to the fire, put upon it a little Oyl Olive, and with a piece of an old Beaver rolled up rub the plate well all over, and laſtly, wipe it well with a dry cloath.

V. Then if any places need touching with the Graver, as ſometimes it happens, eſpecially where it is to be very deep or black, perfect them with care ; which done, the plate is ready for the Rolling-Preſs.

CHAP.

CHAP. XII.

The way of using the soft Varnish.

I. THE plate being prepared by cleansing it with a Charcoal and clean water, wash it well and dry it, then with fine white Chalk scraped and a fine rag, rub it well over, not touching it with your fingers.

II. Lay down your plate over a Chafing-dish of small-coal, yet so as the fire may have air; then take the ground or soft varnish (it being tied up in a fine rag) and rub it up and down the Copper, so as it may sufficiently cover it, (not too thin nor too thick:) then take a feather and smooth it as well as possibly you can all one way, and then cross it, till it lie very well.

But you must take heed that the plate be not too hot, for if it lie till the ground smoak, the moisture will be dried up, and that will spoil the work, and make the ground break or fly up.

III. Then grind some White-lead with Gum-water, so that it may be of a convenient thickness to spread on the Copper; and with a large pencil, or small brush, strike the plate cross over, twice or thrice till it is smooth; and then with a larger brush (made of Squirrels tails) gently smooth the white, and then let it lie till it is dry.

IV. Or you may black the varnish with a Candle, as we taught at the Second Section of the Eighth Chapter, and then warm it over the fire, till the varnish begin to melt.

CHAP.

CHAP. XIII.

The way of Etching upon the soft Varnish.

I. THE way of Etching is the same with that in the hard varnish ; only you must be careful not to hurt your varnish, which you may do by placing on the sides of your plate two little boards, and laying cross over them another thin one, so as that it may not touch the plate, on which you must rest your hand whilst you work.

II. Then place the plate on a Desk (if you so please) for by that means the superfluous matter will fall away of it self.

III. But if you have any design to transfer upon the plate from any Copy or Print, scrape on the backside thereof some red Chalk all over ; then go over that, by scraping some soft Charcoal, till it mingle with the Chalk ; and with a large stiff pencil rub it all over till it be fine and even, and so lay down the design upon the plate : with a blunt Needle draw over the out stroaks : *and as you work, you need not scratch hard into the Copper, only so as you may see the Needle go through the Varnish to the Copper.*

IV. Always be sure when you leave the work, to wrap the plate up in Paper, to keep it from hurt, and corrupting in the air, which may dry the varnish : and in Winter time wrap the plate up in a piece of wollen, as well as paper, for if the frost get to it, it will cause the varnish to rise from the Copper in the eating.

An inconveniency also will accrew, by letting the Varnish lie too long upon the Plate before the work is finished ;
for

for three or four months will confume the moifture and fo fpoil all.

V. The marking of the defign upon the foft var-nifh, is beft done with Black-lead or Chalk, if the ground is white; but with red Chalk, if the ground is black.

VI. Having Graved what you intend upon the var-nifh, take fome fair water, a little warm, and caft it upon the Plate; and then with a foft clean Spunge, rub upon the White-lead to moiften it all over; and then wafh the plate to take away the whiting, and dry it.

VII. Or laftly, with *Aqua-foris* mixed with fair water, wafh it all over, and by this means you may take away the whiting, which then wafh with com-mon water and dry it; and thus have you the plate prepared for the *Aqua-fortis.*

CHAP. XIV.

Of ufing the Aqua-fortis, and finifhing the Work.

I. PUt foft wax (red or green) round the brims of the plate, and let it be raifed above the var-nifh about half a Barley Corns length; fo that placing the plate level, the water being poured upon the plate may by this means be retained. This done,

II. Take common *Aqua-fortis* fix ounces, common water two ounces; mix them, and pour it gently up-on the plate, fo that it may cover it fully all over; fo will the ftronger hatchings be full of bubbles, while
the

the fainter will appear clear for a while, not making any fudden opperations to the view.

III. When you perceive the water to operate a fmall time, pour it off into a glazed earthen difh, and throw fair water upon the plate, to wafh away the *Aqua-fortis,* then dry the plate : and where you would have the Cut to be faint, tender or fweet, cover it with the prepared Oyl, and then cover the plate again with *Aqua-fortis* as before, leaving it on for eight or ten minutes, or longer : then put off the *Aqua-fortis* as before wafhing and drying the plate, and covering with the prepared Oyl other places which you would not have fo deep as the reft : Laftly, put on the *Aqua-fortis* again, for the fpace of half an hour (more or lefs) and then pour it off, wafhing the plate with fair water as before.

As you would have your lines or ftroaks to be deeper and deeper, fo cover the fweeter or fainter parts by degrees with the prepared Oyl, that the Aqua-fortis *may lie the longer on the deep ftroaks.* Then,

IV. Take off the border of wax, and heat the plate, fo that the Oyl and varnifh may throughly melt; which wipe away well with a linnen cloth : then rub the plate over with Oyl Olive and a piece of an old Beaver roll'd up, which done, touch it with the Graver where need is.

V. But if any thing be (at laft) forgotten; then rub the plate aforefaid with crums of bread, fo well that no filth or oyl remain upon the plate.

VI. Then heat the plate upon a Charcoal fire, and fpread the foft varnifh with a feather upon it (as before) fo that the hatchings may be filled with varnifh; black it and then touch it over again, or add what you intend.

VII. Let

VII. Let your hatchings be made by means of the Needles, according as the manner of the work fhall require, being careful before you put on the *Aqua-fortis*, to cover the firft graving on the plate with the prepared Oyl, (leſt the varniſh ſhould not have covered all over:) then cauſe the *Aqua-fortis* to eat into the work ; and laſtly cleanſe the plate as before.

CHAP. XV.   -

Of Limning, and the Materials thereof.

I. Limning is an Art whereby in water Colours, we ſtrive to reſemble Nature in every thing to the life.

II. The Inſtruments and Materials thereof are chiefly theſe. 1. *Gum.* 2. *Colours.* 3. *Liquid Gold and Silver.* 4. *The Grind-ſtone and Muller.* 5. *Pencils.* 6. *Tables to Limn in.* 7. *Little glaſs or China-diſhes.*

III. The *Gums* are chiefly theſe four, Gum-Arabick, Gum-Lake, Gum-Hedera, Gum-Armoniack.

IV. The principal *Colours* are theſe ſeven, *White*, *Black*, *Red*, *Green*, *Yellow*, *Blew*, *Brown* : out of which are made mixt or compound Colours.

V. The *Liquid Gold and Silver* is either natural or artificial.

The natural is that which is produced of the Metals themſelves: the artificial is that which is formed of other colours.

VI. The *Grinding-ſtone*, *Muller*, *Pencils*, *Tables*, *and Shells*, *or little China-diſhes* are only the neceſſary inſtruments and attendants, which belong to the practice of Limning.

F   CHAP.

CHAP. XVI.

Of the Gums and their Use.

I. THe chief of all is Gum-Arabick, that which is white, clear and brittle; the Gum-water of it is made thus:

Take Gum-Arabick, bruise it and tie it up in a fine clean linnen cloath, and put it into a convenient quantity of pure spring-water, in a glass or earthen vessel; letting the Gum remain there till it is dissolved; which done, if the water is not stiff enough, put more Gum into the cloath; but if too stiff, add more water: of which Gum-water have two sorts by you, the one strong, the other weak; of which you may make a third at pleasure.

But if you be where Gum-Arabick is not to be got, you may instead of that use the preparation of Sheeps-leather or parchment following.

Take of the shreds of white Sheep-skins (which are to be had plentifully at Glovers) or else of parchments, one pound; Conduit or runing water two quarts, boil it to a thin gelly, then strain it whilst hot through a fine strainer, and so use it.

II. Gum-lake, it is made of whites of Eggs beaten and strained a pint, Honey, Gum-Hedera, of each two Drachms, strong wort four spoonfuls, mix them, and strain them with a piece of spunge till they run like a clear oyl, which keep in a clean vessel till it grows hard.

This Gum will dissolve in water like Gum-Arabick, of which Gum-water is made in like manner; it is a good ordinary varnish for Pictures.

III. Gum-Hedera, or Gum of Ivy; it is gotten out
of

of Ivy, by cutting with an Axe a great branch thereof, climbing upon an Oak-tree, and bruising the ends of it with the head of the Axe ; at a Months end, or thereabouts, you may take from it a very clear, and pure fine Gum, like oyl,

It is good to put into Gold-fize and other Colours, for thefe three reafons : 1. It abates the ill fent of the fize : 2. It will prevent bubbles in Gold-fize and other Colours : 3. Laftly, it takes away the fat and clamminefs of Colours : befides which it is of ufe in making Pomanders.

. . I V. Gum-Armoniacum, It is a Forrein Gum, and ought to be brought ftrained. Grind it very fine with juice of Garlick and a little Gum-Arabick-water, fo that it may not be too thick, but that you may write with it what you will.

When you ufe it, draw what you will with it, and let it dry, and when you gild upon it, cut your Gold or Silver to the fafhion which you drew with the fize or gum, then breath upon the fize, and lay the Gold upon it gently taken up, which prefs down hard with a piece of wool ; and then let it well dry; being dryed, with a fine linnen cloath ftrike off the loofe Gold ; fo will what was drawn be fairly gilded if it was as fine as a hair : it is called Gold-Armoniack.

CHAP. XVII.

Of the feven Colours in General.

I. THE chief *Whites* are thefe, Spodium, Ceruse, White-lead, *Spanifh*-white, Egg-fhels burnt. This Colour is called in *Greek* λευκὸς of λεύσσω, *video,* to fee, becaufe λευκοτὴς ἐςι διακειτικὸν ὄψεως ; whitenefs (as *Ariftotle* faid) is the object of fight, in Latin *Albus,* from whence the *Alps* had their name, by reafon of their continual whitenefs with Snow. The *Spanifh-white* is thus made. Take fine Chalk three ounces, Alom one ounce, grind them together with fair water till it be like pap ; roul it up into balls, which dry leifurely : then put them into the fire till they are red-hot ; take them out, and let them cool : *it is the beft white of all, to garnifh with, being ground. with weak Gum-water.*

I I. The chief *Blacks* are thefe, Harts-horn burnt, Ivory burnt, Cherry-ftones burnt, Lamp-black, Charcoal.

Black, in Latin Niger *is fo called from the Greek word* νεκρὸς, *which fignifies dead, becaufe putrified and dead things are generally of that colour.* Lamp-black *is the fmoak of a Link, Torch, or Lamp gathered together.*

I I I. The chief *Reds* are thefe, Vermilion, Red-lead, Indian-lake , Red-oker. It is called in Latin *Ruber* παρὰ τὴν ῥοὴν *à corticibus vel granis mali punici* ; from the Rinds or Seeds of Pomegranates, as *Scaliger* faith.

I V. The chief *Greens* are thefe, Green Bice, Verdegriefe, Verditure, Sapgreen. This colour is called in Latin *Viridis* from *Vires* : in Greek χλωρὸν ἀ χλοὴ, Grafs or Green Herb, which is of this Colour.

V. The chief *Yellows* are thefe, Orpiment, Mafticot, Saffron, Pink-yellow, Oker-deluce. This colour is called in Latin *Flavus, Luteus,* in Greek ξανθὸς, which is *Homer*'s Epithete for *Menelaus,* where he calls him ξανθὸς ΜενελάΘ.

V I. The chief *Blews* are Ultramarine , Indico , Smalt, Blew Bice. This colour is called in Latin *Caruleus,* in Greek ΚυάνεΘ ἀ ΚύανΘ, *the name of a ftone which yields* Ultramarine.

V I I. The

V I I. The chief *Browns* are Umber, Spanish-brown, Colens Earth.   It is called in Latin *Fuscus*, quasi φῶς σκιέται, from darkning the Light, in Greek φαιός.

C H A P.   XVIII.

Of Colours in Particular.

I. **C**Eruſe, Grind it with glair of Eggs, and it will make a moſt perfect white.

II. *White-lead*, Grind it with a weak water of Gum-lake, and let it ſtand three or four days, after which if you mix with it Roſet and Vermilion, it makes a fair Carnation.

III. *Spaniſh-white*, It is the beſt white of all, to garniſh with, ground with weak Gum-water.

IV. *Lamp-black*, ground with Gum-water, it makes a good black.

V. *Vermilion*, Grind it with the glair of an Egg, and in the grinding put a little clarified honey, to make its colour bright and perfect.

VI. *Sinaper-lake*, it makes a deep and beautiful red, or rather purple, almoſt like unto a Red-roſe. Grind it with Gum-lake and Turnſole-water : if you will have it light, add a little Ceruſe, and it will make it a bright Crimſon ; if to Diaper, add only Turnſole water.

VII. *Red-lead*, Grind it with ſome Safforn, and ſtiff Gum-lake ; for the Safforn makes it orient, and of a Marigold colour.

VIII. *Turnſole*, Lay it in a Saucer of Vinegar, and ſet it over a Chafing-diſh of coals ; let it boil, then take it off, and wring it into a ſhell, adding a little

Gum-

Gum-Arabick, let it ſtand till it is diſſolved : It is good to ſhadow Carnation, and all Yellows.

I X. *Roſet*, Grind it with Brazil-water, and it will make a deep purple : put Ceruſe to it, and it will be lighter ; grind it with Litmoſe, and it will make a fair Violet.

X. *Spaniſh-brown*, Grind it with Brazil-water : mingle it with Ceruſe and it makes a horſe-fleſh Colour.

X I. *Bole-Armoniack*, It is a faint colour ; its chief uſe is, in making ſize for burniſh'd gold.

X I I. *Green bice.* Order it as you do Blew bice; when it is moiſt, and not through dry, you may Diaper upon it with the water of deep green.

X I I I. *Verdegrieſe*, Grind it with juyce of Rue, and a little weak Gum-water, and you will have a moſt pure green: if you will Diaper with it, grind it with Lye of Rue (or elſe the decoction thereof) and there will be a hoary green : Diaper upon Verdegrieſe-green with Sap-green : alſo Verdegrieſe ground with white Tartar, and then tempered with gum-water, gives a moſt perfect green.

X I V. *Virditure*, grind it with a weak Gum-Arabick water : it is the fainteſt green that is, but is good to lay upon black, in any kind of Drapery.

X V. *Sap green*; lay it in ſharp Vinegar all night ; put it into a little Alom to raiſe its colour, and you will have a good green to Diaper upon other greens.

X V I. *Orpiment*, *Arſenicum* or *Auripigmentum*, grind it with a ſtiff water of Gum-lake, becauſe it is the beſt colour of it ſelf, it will lie upon no green, for all greens, White and Red-lead, and Ceruſe ſtain it: wherefore you muſt deepen your colours ſo that the Orpiment may be higheſt, and ſo it may agree with all Colours.

X V I I. *Maſti-*

XVII. *Masticot*, grind it with a small quantity of Saffron in gum-water, and never make it lighter than it is : it will endure to lie upon all colours and metals.

XVIII. *Saffron*, Steep it in glair : it may be ground with Vermilion.

XIX. *Pink-yellow*, if you would have it sad colouredt grind it with Saffron; if light, with Cerufe : mix i with weak gum-water, and so use it.

XX. *Oker de Luce*, grind it with pure Brazil water : it makes a passing hair colour ; and is a natural shadow for gold.

XXI. *Umber*, It is a more sad colour. Grind it with gum-water, or gum-lake ; and lighten it (if you please) with a little Cerufe and a blade of Saffron.

XXII. *Ultramarine*, If you would have it deep, grind it with Litmose-water; but if light, with fine Cerufe, and a weak Gum-Arabick water.

XXIII. *Indico*, grind it with water of Gum-Arabick, as Ultramarine.

XXIV. *Blew bice*, grind it with clean water, as small as you can, then put it into a shell, and wash it thus : put as much water to it as will fill up the vessel or shell, and stir it well, let it stand an hour , and the filth and dirty water cast away ; then put in more clean water, do thus four or five times ; and at last put in Gum-Arabick water somewhat weak, that the Bice may fall to the bottom; pour off the gum-water, and put more to it , wash it again , dry it, and mix it with weak gum-water (if you would have it rise of the same colour) but with a stiff water of Gum-lake, if you would have a most perfect blew ; if a light blew, grind it with a little Cerufe ; but if a most deep blew, add water of Litmose.

XXV. *Smals*,

XXV. *Smalt*, grind it with a little fine Rofet, and it will make a deep Violet: and by putting in a quantity of Cerufe, it will make a light Violet.

XXVI. *Litmofe-blew*, grind it with Cerufe: with too much Litmofe it makes a deep blew; with too much Cerufe, a light blew: grind it with the weak water of Gum Arabick.

Take fine Litmofe, cut it in pieces, lay it in weak water of Gum-lake for twenty four hours, and you fhall have a water of a moft perfect Azure; with which water you may Diaper and Damask upon all other blews, to make them fhew more fair and beautiful.

XXVII. *Orchal*, grind it with unflak'd Lime and Urine, it makes a pure Violet: by putting to more or lefs Lime, you may make the Violet light or deep as you pleafe.

CHAP. XIX.

Of mixt and compound Colours.

I. **M**Urry, It is a wonderful beautiful colour, compofed of purple and white: it is made thus. *Take Sinaper-lake two ounces; White-lead one ounce, grind them together.* See the 24. Section.

II. *A glafs gray*, mingle Cerufe with a little Azure.

III. *A bay colour*, mingle Vermilion with a little Spanifh brown and black.

IV. *A deep purple*, It is made of Indico, Spanifh-brown and white.

It is called in Latin Purpureus, *in Greek* πορφυρ⊙ *from* πορφυες, *a kind of fhell-fifh that yields a liquour of that colour.*

V. *An*

V. *An Aſh-colour, or Gray*, It is made by mixing White and Lamp-black; or white with Sinaper ; Indico and black make an Aſh-colour.

It is called in Latin Cæſius, *and* color Cinereus; *in Greek* Γλαυκὸς *and* τεφρώδης.

VI. *Light Green*, It is made of Pink and Smalt ; with white to make it lighter if need require.

VII. *Saffron colour*, It is made of Saffron alone by infuſion.

VIII. *Flame colour*, It is made of Vermilion and Orpiment, mixed deep or light at pleaſure : or thus, Take Red-lead and mix it with Maſticot , which heighten with white.

IX. *A Violet colour*, Indico, White and Sinaper-lake make a good Violet. So alſo Ceruſe and Litmoſe, of each equal parts.

X. *Lead colour* , It is made of White mixed with Indico.

XI. *Scarlet colour* , It is made of Red-lead, Lake, Vermilion : yet Vermilion in this caſe is not very uſeful.

XII. *To make Vermilion.*

Take Brimſtone in powder one ounce, mix it with Quickſilver a pound, put it into a Crucible well luted, and upon a Charcoal-fire heat it till it is red-hot ; then take it off and let it cool.

XIII. *To make a bright Crimſon.*

Mix tincture of Brazil with a little Ceruſe ground with fair water.

XIV. *To make a ſad Crimſon.*

Mix the aforeſaid light Crimſon with a little Indico ground with fair water.

XV. *To make a pure Lake.*

Take Urine twenty pound, boil it in a Kettle and ſcum it with an Iron ſcummer till it comes to ſixteen pound ;

pound ; to which add Gum-lake one pound, Alom five ounces ; boil all till it is well coloured , which you may try by dipping therein a piece of linnen cloth ; then add fweet Alom in powder a fufficient quantity, ftrain it and let it ftand ; ftrain it again through a dry cloth till the liquor be clear : that which remains in the cloth or bag is the pure Lake.

XVI. *To make a Crimfon Lake.*

Its ufually made of the flocks fhorn off from Crimfon cloth by a Lye made of Salt-peter, which extracts the colour ; which precipitate, edulcorate, and dry in the Sun or a Stove.

XVII. *A pure Green.*

Take white Tartar and Verdegriefe, temper them with ftrong White-wine Vinegar, in which a little Gum-Arabick hath been diffolved.

XVIII. *A pure Violet.*

Take a little Indico and tincture of Brazil, grind them with a little Cerufe.

XIX. *A pure Purple colour.*

Take fine brimftone an ounce and an half , Quickfilver, Sal- Armoniack, Jupiter, of each one ounce ; beat the Brimftone and Salt into powder, and make an Amalgamy with the Quickfilver and Tin, mix all together, which put into a great glafs goard ; make under it an ordinary fire, and keep it in a conftant heat for the fpace of fix hours.

XX. *To make a Yellow colour.* . .

Take the Yellow chives in white Lillies, fteep them in gum-water, and it will make a perfect Yellow ; the fame from Saffron and Tartar tempred with gumwater.

XXI. *To make a Red colour.*

Take the roots of the leffer Buglofs, and beat them, and ftrain out the juyce, and mix it with Alom-water.

XXII. *To*

XXII. *To make excellent good Greens.*

The Liver of a Lamprey makes an excellent and durable grafs green : and yellow laid upon blew will change into green : fo likewife the juyce of a blew Flower-de-luce, mixed with gum-water , will be a perfect and durable green or blew, according as it it ufed.

XXIII. *To make a Purple colour.*

Take the juyce of Bilberries and mix it with Alom and Galls, and fo paint with It.

XXIV. *To make a good Murry.*

Temper Roffet with a little Rofe-water, in which a little gum hath been diffolved, and it will be good, but not exceeding that at the firft Section of this Chapter.

XXV. *To make Azure or Blew.*

Mix the Azure with glew-water, and not with gum-water.

XXVI. *To make a Yellow Green, or Purple.*

Buckthorn-berries gathered green and fteeped in Alom-water yield a good yellow : but being through ripe and black (by the eighteenth Section of the twenty feventh Chapter of the third Book) they yield a good green : and laftly, being gathered when they are ready to drop off, which is about the middle or end of *November* , their juyce mixt with Alom water yields a good Purple colour.

C H A P.

C H A P. XX.

Of Colours for Drapery.

I. **F**Or *Yellow Garments.* Take Maſticot deepened with brown-Oker and Red-Lead.

II. *For Scarlet.* Take Virmilion deepened with Sinaper-lake , and heightened with touches of Maſticot.

III. *For Crimſon.* Lay on Lake very thin and deepen with the ſame.

IV. *For Purple.* Grind Lake and Smalt together : or take Blew-bice, and mix it with Red and White-Lead.

V. *For an Orient Violet.* Grind Litmoſe , Blew-Smalt, and Ceruſe ; but in mixture let the blew have the upper hand.

VI. *For Blew.* Take Azure deepned with Indy-Blew or Lake heightened with white.

VII. *For black Velvet.* Lay the garment firſt over with Ivory black , then heighten it with Cherryſtone black, and a little white.

VIII. *For black Sattin.* Take Cherryſtone black ; then white deepened with Cherryſtone black; and then laſtly, Ivory black.

IX. *For a pure Green.* Take Verdegrieſe, bruiſe it, and ſteep it in Muſcadine for twelve hours, then ſtrain it into a ſhell, to which add a little Sap-green : (but put no gum thereto.)

X. *For a Carnation.* Grind Ceruſe , well waſhed, with Red-lead ; or Ceruſe and Vermilion.

XI. *For Cloth of Gold.* Take brown Oker, and liquid

quid Gold water, and heighten upon the fame with fmall ftroaks of Gold.

XII. *For white Sattin.* Take firft fine Ceruſe, which deepen with Cherryſtone-black, then heighten again with Ceruſe, and fine touches where the light falleth.

XIII. *For a Ruſſet Sattin.* Take Indy-blew and Lake, firft thin and then deepned with Indy again.

XIV. *For a hair Colour.* It is made out of Maſticot, Umber, Yellow Oker, Ceruſe, Oker-de-luce, and Sea-coal.

XV. *For a Popenjay Green.* Take a perfect green mingled with Maſticot.

XVI. *For Changeable Silk.* Take water of Maſticot and Red-lead; which deepen with Sap-green.

XVII. *For a light Blew.* Take Blew bice, heightened with Ceruſe or Spodium.

XVIII. *For to ſhadow Ruſſet.* Take Cherryſtone-black and white; lay a light Ruſſet, then ſhadow it with white.

XIX. *For a Skie Colour.* Take Blew-bice and Venice Ceruſe: but if you would have it dark, take ſome blew and white.

XX. *For a Straw Colour.* Take Maſticot, then white heightened with Maſticot, and deepned with Pink. Or thus. Take Red-lead deepned with Lake.

XXI. *For Yellowiſh.* Thin Pink deepned with Pink and green.: Orpiment burned makes a Marigold colour.

XXII. *For a Peach Colour.* Take Brazil water, Log water and Ceruſe.

XXIII. *For a light Purple.* Mingle Ceruſe with Logwood water: or take Turnſole mingled with a little Lake, Smalt and Bice.

XXIV. *For*

XXIV. *For a Walnut colour.* Red-lead thinly. laid, and shadowed with Spanish brown.

XXV. *For a Fire colour.* Take Masticot, and deepen it with Masticot for the flame.

XXVI. *For a Tree.* Take Umber and white, wrought with Umber, deepned with black.

XXVII. *For the Leaves.* Take Sap-green and green Bice, heighten it with Verditure and white.

XXVIII. *For Water.* Blew and white , deepned with blew, and heightned with white.

XXIX. *For Banks.* Thin Umber, deepned with Umber and black.

XXX. *For Feathers.* Take Lake frizled with Red-lead.

CHAP. XXI.

Of Liquid Gold and Silver.

I. **L**	*Iquid Gold and Silver.*
Take five or six leaves of Gold or Silver , which grind (with a stiff Gum-lake water , and a good quantity of Salt) as small as you can ; then put it into a vial or glazed vessel ; add so much fair water as may dissolve the stiff gum-water ; then let it stand four hours, that the Gold may settle : decant the water, and put in more, till the Gold is clean washed : to the Gold put more fair water, a little Sal-Armoniack and common Salt, digesting it close for four days : then put all into a piece of thin Glovers leather (whose grain is peeled off) and hang it up , so will the Sal-Armoniack fret away , and the Gold remain behind, which keep.

Or

Or thus. *Grind fine leaf Gold with strong or thick gum-water very fine; and as you grind add more thick gum-water being very fine, wash it in a great shell, as you do Rice : then temper it with a little quantity of Mercury sublimate, and a little dissolved gum to bind it in the shell; shake it, and spread the Gold about the sides thereof, that it may be all of one colour and fineness, which use with fair water, as you do other colours. The same observe in liquid Silver; with this observation, That if your Silver, by length of time, or humidity of the air become rusty; then cover the place with juyce of Garlick before you lay on the Silver, which will preserve it.*

When you use it, temper it with glair of Eggs, and so use it with pen or pencil. Glair of Eggs is thus made. Take the whites and beat them with a spoon, till that rise all in a foam; then let them stand all night, and by morning they will be turned into clear water, which is good glair.

II. *Argentum Musicum.*

Take one ounce of Tin, melt it, and put thereto of Tartar and Quicksilver of each one ounce, stir them well together untill they be cold, then beat it in a mortar and grind it on a stone; mix it with gum water, write therewith, and afterwards polish it.

III. *Burnished Gold or Silver.*

Take Gum lake and dissolve it into a stiff water; then grind a blade or two of Saffron therewith, and you shall have a fair Gold: when you have set it, being throughly dry, burnish it with a dogs tooth. Or thus having writ with your pen or pencil what you please, cut the leaf Gold or Silver into pieces, according to the draught, which take up with a feather and lay it upon the drawing, which press down with a piece of wool; and being dry, burnish it.

IV. *Gold*

IV. *Gold Armoniack.*

This is nothing but that which we have taught at the fourth Section of the sixteenth Chapter of this Book.

V. *Size for burnished Gold.*

Take Bole-Armoniack three drachms, fine Chalk one drachm; grind them as small as you can together with fair water, three or four times, letting it dry after every time: then take glair and strain it as short as water, with which grind the Bole and Chalk, adding a little Gum-Hedera, and a few blades of Saffron: grind all as small as possible, and put them into an Ox horn (I judge a glass vessel better) and set it to rot in horse dung for six weeks; then take it up, and let it have air, and keep it for use.

Its use is for gilding parchments, book-covers, and leather, thus lay this size first upon the parchment, then with a feather lay the Gold or Silver upon it, which when dry burnish it.

VI. *To Diaper on Gold or Silver.*

You must Diaper on Gold with Lake and Yellow Oker: but upon Silver with Ceruse.

VII. *Aurum Musicum.*

Take fine Crystal, Orpiment, of each one ounce, beat each severally into a fine powder, then grind them together well with glair.

You may write with it, with pen or pencil, and your letter or draught will be of a good Gold colour.

C H A P.

CHAP. XXII.

Of Preparing the Colours.

I. COlours, according to their natures have each a particular way of preparation : to wit, by grinding, washing or steeping.

II. The chief *Colours to be ground* are these ; White-lead, Ceruse, Sinaper-lake, Oker pink, Indico, Umber, Colens Earth, Spanish-brown, Ivory-black, Cherryftone-black.

III. The chief *Colours to be wash'd* are Red-lead, Mafticot, Green Bice, Cedar Green, Ultramarine, Blew Bice, Smalt, Verditure.

IV. The chief *Colours to be fteep'd*, are Sap-green, Saffron, Turnfole, Stone-blew, Venice Berries.

V. *To grind Colours.*

Take the colour you would grind, and fcrape off from it all the filth, then lay it upon the ftone, and with the muller bruife it a little ; then put thereto a little fpring water, and grind all together very well, till the colour is very fine ; which done pour it out into certain hollows or furrows cut in Chalkftone, and there let it lie till it is dry, which referve in papers or glaffes.

VI. *To wash colours.*

Put the colour into a glazed veffel, and put thereto fair water plentifully, wafh it well, and decant (after a while) the water; do this fix or feven times; at laft put the water (being juft troubled) into another glazed veffel, leaving the dregs at bottom: then into

G   this

this second veffel put more fair water, wafhing it as before, till the water (being fettled) be clear, and the colour remain fine at bottom : we have taught another way at the twenty fourth Section of the eighteenth Chapter of this Book.

V I I. *To fteep Colours.*

Take a quantity thereof, and put it into a fhell, and fill the fhell with fair water, to which add fome fine powder of Alom, to raife the colour ; let it thus fteep a day and night, and you will have a good colour.

Where note , Saffron fteeped in Vinegar gives a good colour ; and the Venice Berries in fair water and a little Alom, or a drop or two of oyl of Vitriol makes a fair yellow.

V I I I. *To temper the Colours.*

Take a little of any colour, and put it into a clean fhell, and add thereto a few drops of gum-water , and with your fingers work it about the fhell, then let it dry ; when dry, touch it with your fingers , if any colour comes off, you muft add ftronger gum-water : but being dry, if the colour glifter or fhine, it is a fign there is too much gum in it, which you may remedy by putting in fair water.

I X. *To help the defects.*

Some colours, as Lake, Umber, and others which are hard, will crack when they are dry ; in this cafe, in tempering them add a little white Sugar-candy in very fine powder, which mix with the colour and fair water in the fhell, till the Sugar-candy is diffolved.

X. Thefe colours, Umber, Spanifh-brown, Colen earth, Cherryftone, and Ivory-black, are to be burnt before they be ground or wafh'd.

X I. *To burn or calcine Colours.*

This

This is done in a crucible, covering the mouth thereof with clay, and fetting it in a hot fire, till you are fure it is red-hot through: which done, being cold, wafh or grind it as aforefaid.

XII. *To prepare fhadows for Colours.*

White is fhaded with Black, and contrariwife: Yellow with Umber and the Okers: Vermilion with Lake: Blew-bice with Indie: Black-coal with Rofet, *&c.*

CHAP. XXIII.

Of the Manual Inftruments.

I. THE manual Inftruments are four (by the fecond Section of the fifteenth Chapter of this Book) to wit, The *Grinding-ftone* and *Muller*, *Pencils*, *Tables* to Limn on, and fhells or little glaffes or China-difhes.

II. The *Grinding-ftone* may be of Porphyry, Serpentine or Marble, but rather a Pebble, for that is the beft of all others: *Muller* only of Pebble, which keep very clean.

Thefe may be eafily got of Marblers or Stone-cutters in London.

III. Choofe your pencils thus: by their faftnefs in the quills, and their fharp points after you have drawn or wetted them in your mouth two or three times; fo that although larger, yet their points will come to as fmall as a hair, which then are good; but if they fpread or have any extravagant hairs they are naught.

IV. *To wafh your pencils.*

G 2   After

After ufing them, rub the ends of them well with Soap, then lay them a while in warm water to fteep, then take them out and wafh them well in other fair water.

V. *To prepare the Table.*

It muft be made of pure fine pafte-board, fuch as Cards are made of (of what thicknefs you pleafe) very finely flick'd and glazed. Take a piece of this pafte-board of the bignefs you intend the Picture, and a piece of the fineft and whiteft parchment you can, get (virgin parchment) which cut of equal bignefs with the pafte-board; with thin, white, new made ftarch, pafte the parchment to the pafte-board, with the outfide of the skin outwardmoft : lay on the ftarch very thin and even; then the grinding ftone being clean, lay the card thereon with the parchment fide downwards, and as hard as you can, rub the other fide of the pafte-board with a Boars-tooth fet in a ftick; then let it be thorow dry, and it will be fit to work or Limn any curious thing upon.

V I. The fhells holding or containing your colours, ought to be Horfe-mufcle fhells, which may be got in *July* about Rivers fides; but the next to thefe are fmall Mufcle-fhells, or in ftead thereof little China or glafs veffels.

C H A P. XXIV.

Of Preparations for Limning.

I. **H**Ave two fmall glafs or China-difhes, in either of which muft be pure clean water, the one to wafh the pencils in being foul; the other to temper

per the colours with , when there is occasion.

II. Besides the pencils you Limn with ; a large, clean and dry pencil , to cleanse the work from any kind of dust, that may fall upon it, which are called Fitch-pencils.

III. A sharp Pen-knife to take off hairs that may come from your pencil, either among the colours or upon the work ; or to take out spots that may fall upon the Card or Table.

IV. A paper with a hole cut therein, to lay over the card , to keep it from dust and filth, to rest your hand upon, and to keep the soil and sweat of your hand from sullying the parchment, as also to try your pencils on before you use them.

Let the small glasses, waters, pencils and pen-knife lie all on the right hand.

V. Have ready a quantity of light Carnation or flesh colour temper'd up in a shell by it self with a weak gum-water ; if it be a fair complexion , mix White and Red-lead together ; if a brown or swarthy , add to the former, Masticot, or English Oker, or both : but be sure the flesh colour be always lighter than the complexion you would Limn ; for by working on it you may bring it to its true colour.

VI. In a large Horse-muscle shell place your several shadows (for the flesh colour) in little places one distinct from another.

VII. In all shadowings have ready some white , and lay a good quantity of it by it self besides what the shadows are first mixed with : for Red for the cheeks and lips, temper ·Lake and Red-lead together : for blew shadows (as under the eyes and in veins) Indico or Ultramarine and white : for gray faint shadows , white , English Oker , sometimes

Masticot : for deep shadows , white, English Oker,
Umber : for dark shadows, Lake and Pink , which
make a good fleshy shadow.

VIII. To make choice of the light.

Let it be fair and large and free from shadows of Trees
or Houses, but all clear Skye-light , and let it be direct
from above , and not transverse ; let it be Northerly and
not Southerly ; and let the room be close and clean , and
free from the Sun-beams.

IX. Of the manner of sitting.

Let your desk on which you work be so situate, that sit-
ting before it, your left arm may be towards the light ,
that the light may strike sidling upon your work : Let the
party that is to be Limned, be in what posture themselves
will design, but not above two yards off you at most, and
level with you ; wherein observe their motion , if never so
small, for the least motion, if not recalled, may in short
time bring on you many errors : Lastly, the face being
finished, let the party stand (not sit) at a farther distance
(four or five yards off) to draw the posture of his clothes.

CHAP. XXV.

Of the Practice of Limning in Miniature, or
Drawing of a Face in Colours.

I. TO begin the Work.

Have all things in a readiness (as before)
then on the Card lay the prepared colour (answerable
to the complexion presented) even and thin, free from
hairs and spots, over the place where the Picture is to
be : the ground thus laid, begin the work, the party
being

being set, which must be done at three sittings : at the first sitting the face is only dead coloured, which takes up about two hours time : at the second sitting, go over the work more curiously , adding its particular graces or deformities, sweetly couching the colours, which will take up about five hours time : at the third sitting, finish the face, in which you must perfect all that is imperfect and rough, putting the deep shadows in the face, as in the eyes, eye-brows, and ears, which are the last of the work, and not to be done till the hair curtain, or backside of the Picture, and the drapery be wholly finished.

II. *The operation or work at first sitting.*

The ground for the complexion being laid, draw the out-lines of the face, which do with Lake and white mingled ; draw faintly, that if you miss in proportion or colour you may alter it : this done, add to the former colour Red-lead, for the cheeks and lips; let it be but faint (for you cannot lighten a deep colour) and make the shadows in their due places, as in the cheek, lips, tip of the chin and ears, the eyes and roots of the hair : shadow not with a flat pencil, but by small touches (as in hatching) and so go over the face. In this dead covering rather than to be curious, strive as near as may be to imitate nature. The red shadows being put in their due places; shadow with a faint blew, about the corners and balls of the eyes ; and with a grayish blew under the eyes and about the temples, heightening the shadows as the light falls, as also the harder shadows in the dark side of the face, under the eye-brows, chin and neck. Bring all the work to an equality, but add perfection to no particular part at this time ; but imitate the life in likeness, roundness, boldness, posture, colour, and the like. Lastly, touch at the hair with a sutable colour in such

G 4　　　　　　　curls,

curls, folds and form, as may either agree with the life, or grace the Picture : fill the empty places with colour, and deepen it more ftrongly, than in the deepeft fhadowed before.

III. *The operation or work at fecond fitting.*

As before rudely, fo now you muft fweeten thofe varieties which Nature affords, with the fame colours and in the fame places driving them one into another, yet fo as that no lump or fpot of colour, or rough edge may appear in the whole work ; and this muft be done with a pencil fharper than that which was ufed before. This done, go to the backfide of the Picture which may be Landskip, or a curtain of blew or red Sattin : if of blew, temper as much Bice as will cover a card, and let it be well mixed with gum ; with a pencil draw the out-lines of the curtain; as alfo of the whole Picture ; then with a large pencil lay thinly or airily over the whole ground, on which you mean to lay the blew ; and then with a large pencil, lay over the fame a fubftantial body of colour ; in doing of which be nimble, keeping the colour moift, letting no part thereof be dry till the whole be covered. If the curtain be Crimfon, trace it out with Lake ; lay the ground with a thin colour ; and lay the light with a thin and waterifh colour, where they fall ; and while the ground is yet wet, with a ftrong dark colour tempered fomething thick, lay the ftrong and hard fhadows clofe by the other lights. Then lay the linnen with faint white, and the drapery flat of the colour you intend it. In the face, fee what fhadows are too light or too deep, for the curtain behind, and drapery, and reduce each to their due perfection ; draw the lines of the eye-lids, and fhadow the entrance into the ear, deepnefs of the eye-brows, and eminent marks in the face, with a very fharp pencil : laftly, go over the

hair,

hair, colouring it as it appears in the life, cafting over the ground fome loofe hairs, which will make the Picture ftand as it were at a diftance from the curtain : *fhadow the linnen with white, black, and a little yellow and blew ; and deepen your black, with Ivory-black mixed with a little Lake and Indico.*

I V.   *The operation or work at third fitting.*

This third work is wholly fpent in giving ftrong touches where you fee caufe ; in rounding, fmooth- ing and colouring the face, which you may better fee to do, now the curtain and drapery is limned, than before. And now obferve whatfoever may conduce to the perfection of your work, as gefture, fcars or moles, cafts of the eyes, windings of the mouth, and the like.

C H A P.   XXVI.

Of Limning Drapery.

I.   A Full and fubftantial ground being laid all over where you intend the drapery ; as if blew , with Bice fmoothly laid, deepen it with Lake and Indico ; lightening it with a fine faint white, in the extreme light places, the which underftand of other colours.

I I.   If the body you draw be in *Armour*, lay liquid Silver all over for a ground, well dried and burnifhed ; fhadow it with Silver , Indico and Umber, according as the life directs you.

III.   For *Gold Armour* lay liquid Gold as you did the Silver, and fhadow upon it with Lake, Englifh Oker, and a little Gold.

I V. For

I V. For *Pearls,* your ground muſt be Indico and white; the ſhadows black and pink.

V. For *Diamonds,* lay a ground of liquid Silver, and deepen it with Cherry-ſtone-black and Ivory-black.

V I. For *Rubies,* lay a Silver ground, which burniſh to the bigneſs of a Ruby : then with pure Turpentine temper'd with Indian Lake, from a ſmall wire heated in a Candle, drop upon the burniſhed place, faſhioning it as you pleaſe with your Inſtruments, which let lie a day or two to dry.

V I I. For *Emeraulds,* or any green ſtone, temper Turpentine with Verdigrieſe, and a little Turmerick root, firſt ſcraped, with Vinegar, drying it, grind it to fine powder and mix it.

V I I I. For *Saphyres,* mix or temper Ultramarine with pure Turpentine, which lay upon a ground of liquid Silver poliſht.

To make liquid Gold or Silver : ſee the firſt Section of the twenty firſt Chapter of this Book.

C H A P. XXVII.

Of Limning Landskip.

ALL *the variable expreſſions of Landskip are innumerable, they being as many as there are men and fancies; the general rules follow.*

I. Alway begin with the Sky, Sun-beams or lighteſt parts firſt; next the yellowiſh beams (which make of Maſticot and white) next the blewneſs of the Sky, (which make of Smalt only.)

II. At

II. At firſt colouring, leave no part of the ground uncovered, but lay the colours ſmooth all over.

III. Work the Sky downwards, towards the Horizon fainter and fainter, as it draws nearer and nearer the earth : the tops of mountains far remote, work ſo faint that they may appear as loſt in the air.

IV. Let places low, and near the ground be of the colour of the earth, of a dark yellowiſh, or brown green ; the next lighter green ; and ſo ſucceſſively as they loſe in diſtance, let them abate in colour.

V. Make nothing which you ſee at a diſtance perfect, by expreſſing any particular ſign which it hath, but expreſs it in colours, as weakly and faintly as the eye judgeth of it.

VI. Always place light againſt darkneſs and darkneſs againſt light, by which means you may extend the proſpect as a very far off.

VII. Let all ſhadows loſe their force as they remove from the eye ; always letting the ſtrongeſt ſhadow be neareſt hand.

VIII. Laſtly, Take Iſinglaſs in ſmall pieces half an ounce, fair Conduit-water two quarts, boil it till the glaſs is diſſolved, which ſave for uſe : with which mix ſpirit or oil of Cloves, Roſes, Cinnamon or Ambergrieſe, and lay it on and about the Picture where it is not coloured (left it ſhould change the colours : but upon the colours uſe it without the perfumes) ſo it will varniſh your Pictures, and give them a gloſs, retaining the glory of their colours, and take from them any ill ſcent which they might otherwiſe retain.

CHAP.

CHAP. XXVIII.

Of Light and Shadow.

L Ights and shades set in their proper places in such a just and equal proportion, as Nature doth give, or the life require give a true Idea of the thing we would represent; so that 'tis not any colour whatsoever, nor any single stroak or stroaks which is the cause thereof, but that excellent Symmetry of Light and Shadow, which gives the true resemblance of the light.

II. In shadowing, be careful you spoil not your work by too grofs a darkness, whether it be hard or soft.

III. This Observation of light and dark is that which causeth all things contained in your work to come forward or fall backward, and makes every thing from the first to the last to stand in their just places, whereby the distance between thing and thing seems to go from you or come to you as if it were the work of Nature it self.

IV. Suppose it were a plaister Figure, take good notice what appears forwards and what backwards, or how things succeed one another; then confider the cause which makes them in appearance either to incline or recline, and confider the degrees of light and darkness, and whether they fall forward or backward, accordingly in your draught give first gentle touches, and after that heighten by degrees according as the example and your own ingenuity shall direct.

V. Those parts are to be heighten'd in your work
which

which appear higheſt in your Pattern : The greateſt life which we can give on white paper is the paper it ſelf, all leſſer lights muſt be faintly ſhadowed in proportion to their reſpective degrees. But on coloured paper white Crions and Tobacco-pipe-clay are uſed for the firſt and ſecond heightenings, putting each in their proper places, as more or leſs light is required, which is a ſingular obſervation in this manner of drawing. Then you muſt take heed you heighten not too many places, nor heighten any thing more than what is needful, nor too near the dark or ſhadows, or any out-line, (except where you intend ſome reflection,) leſt your work ſhew hard and rough. In heightening, or ſuch figures as require great light, put the greateſt light in the middle, and the leſſer towards the edges for the better perſpicuity of your work. Laſtly, leave ſufficient faint places on the ground of your paper between your lights and ſhades, that they may appear pleaſantly with a ſingular plainneſs and ſmoothneſs.

VI. In reflection, uſe it in delineating, glittering, or ſhining bodies, as Glaſs, Pearl, Silver, &c. let the cauſe of the reflection, be it more or leſs, be ſeen in the thing it ſelf.

VII. In plain drawing, lay all your ſhades ſmooth, whether it be in hatching or ſmutching, keeping every thing within its own bounds, and this is done by not making your ſhades at firſt too hard, or putting one ſhadow upon another too dark.

VIII. Obſerve that the greater parts of light and ſhadows, and the ſmall parts intermixt in the ſame, may always ſo correſpond as thereby to make more apparent the greater.

IX. In Pictures, let the higheſt light of the whole, (if any darkneſs ſtand in the middle of it) appear

more

more dark than indeed it is: and in working always compare light with light and dark with dark, by which you will find the power of each, and the general use thereof in all operations.

X. We think it necessary to shew another way of making all sorts of Crions or Pastills than what we taught in the beginning of this Book, Thus: Take Tobacco-pipe-clay and with a little water temper the same what colour you please, making several according to the several heights you intend, which mix with the said Tobacco-pipe-clay so much as the clay will bear, work all well together, make it into Pastills, and let them dry for use.

C H A P. XXIX.

Of Colours more Particularly.

I. O*Ker* is a good colour, and much in use for shadows, in Pictures of the life, both for hair and drapery: In Landskips it is used for Rocks and high ways.

II. *Pink,* the fairest, with blew, makes the fastest greens for Landskip and Drapery.

Sap-green and green-bice are good in their kind; but the first is so transparent and thin, the other of so course and gross body, that in many things they will be useless, especially where a beautiful green (made of Pink and Bice mixed with Indico) is required.

III. *Umber*, is a greasie foul colour; but being calcined and ground, it works sharp and neat.

IV. *Spanish-brown*, is exceeding course and full of gravel; being prepared, it is used for a mixture made

made of Red-lead mixt with a little Umber, which makes the same colour.

V. *Colens earth* or *Terra Lemnia,* it is used to close up the last and deepest touches in the shadows of Pictures of the life, and in Landskips ; use it when new ground.

VI. *Cherry-stone-black,* is very good for Drapery and black apparel : mixt with Indico, it is excellent for Sattin ; it appears more beautiful or shining if mixed with a little white : if deepned with Ivoryblack, in hard reflections, and strong deep touches, it is wonderful fair.

VII. *Ivory black,* it serves for a deep black, but is not easie to work without it be well tempered with Sugar-candy, to prevent peeling.

VIII. *Red-lead,* well wash'd, is a glorious colour, for those pieces which require an exquisite redness.

IX. *Indian-lake,* is the deareft and moſt beautiful of all reds ; it is to be ground as white-lead, and mixt with a little white Sugar-candy and fair water, till the colour and Sugar-candy be throughly diſſolved, which being dry will lie very faſt, without danger of cracking or peeling.

CHAP. XXX.

Obſervations of making ſome Original Colours.

I. *To make white-lead.*

Put into an earthen pot ſeveral plates of fine Lead, cover them with White-wine Vinegar, covering

vering the top of the pot close with clay, bury it in a Cellar for seven or eight weeks, and you will have good white lead upon the plates, which wipe off.

II. *To make Verdigriese.*

This is made by hanging plates of Copper over the fumes of *Aqua-fortis* or spirit of Nitre : or by dipping them in the same or in Vinegar.

III. *To make an Emerald Colour.*

Take Verdigriese in fine powder, which temper with varnish, and lay it upon a ground of liquid Silver burnisht, and you have a fair Emerald.

IV. *To make a Ruby Colour.*

Mix the same with Florence Lake, and you shall have a very fair Ruby colour.

V. *To make a Saphyre Colour.*

The same, *viz.* Verdigriese mixt with Ultramarine, makes a glorious Saphyre.

VI. *To make a Crimson Velvet.*

Take Turnsoil and mix it with Indico-lake (well ground with gum and Sugar-candy) lay it full, and when it is wet, wipe away the colour with a dry pencil, where you would have the heightening of the Crimson Velvet appear, and the stronger reflections will be well expressed.

VII. *To make a Silver Black.*

Take fine Silver filings or plates, which dissolve in spirit of Nitre or *Aqua-fortis*, and evaporate to driness, or precipitate with *Oleo Sulphuris* or Salt-water, and you shall have a snow-white precipitate, which mixt with water makes the best black in the world, to dy all manner of Hair, Horns, Bones, Wood, Metals, *&c.*

VIII. *To make a Murry or Amethyst.*

It is made of Indian Lake ground with Gum-Arabick water only.

IX. *To*

IX. *To make a Red or Ruby for Limning.*

It is made of Indian-lake (which breaks off a Scarlet colour) ground with Gum-water and Sugar-candy.

X. *To make Azure blew, or Saphyre.*

It is made of Ultramarine of *Venice* (which is best) the best blew Smalt, or blew bice ground with gum-water only : you may make good shadowing blews of Indico, Flory and Litmose, all which need no washing, nor Litmose no grinding , but only infused in a Lixivium of Soap-ashes.

XI. *To make a green or Emerald.*

It is made of Cedar green : in place whereof, take tripal to draw with : Pink is good also for Landskips, mixed with Bice-ashes ; as also with Masticot and Cerufe.

XII. *To make a Yellow or Topaz.*

It is made of Masticot which is the best, of which there are divers forts , *viz* deeper and paler : Yellow-Oker also for want of better may do. Shadow Masticot with Yellow-Oker; deepen it with Oker-de-Luce.

XIII. *To make Ultramarine.*

Take the deepest coloured *Lapis Lazuli* (having few veins of Gold upon it) heat it red-hot in a Crucible close covered, then quench it in Urine, Vinegar or water in a Leaded earthen pot, dry it well, then with a pair of pinsers nip off the hard, gray, and whitest part from it , and grind the remainder with honied water as fine as may be, then dry it for use. The honied water is made of water a quart, boiled with honey two spoonfuls.

H

CHAP.

C H A P. XXXI.

The sum of the Observations of Limning to the life in general.

I. LE T the Table be prepared very exactly by the fifth rule of the twenty third Chapter of the second Book.

II. Let the ground be of flesh colour, tempering it according to the complexion to be painted.

III. If it be a fair complexion, mix a good quantity of Red and White Lead together somewhat thick.

IV. If swarthy or brown, mix with the former a little fine Masticot or English Oker, or both, always observing that your ground be fairer than the complexion painted.

For fairness may be shadowed or darkened at pleasure; but if it be sad or dark, you can never heighten it, for in Limning the picture is always wrought down to its exact colour.

V. Lay the ground upon the Card or Tablet, with a larger pencil than ordinary, free from spots, scratches of the pencil, or dust, and as even as possible may be; and let the colour be rather thin and waterish than too thick, doing it very quick and nimbly with two or three dishes of the pencil.

VI. This done, prepare your shadows in order, by the seventh rule of the four and twentieth Chapter of the second Book.

VII. Then draw the out-lines of the face with Lake and white mingled together very fine; so that if you
should

should mistake in your first draught, you may with a strong stroak draw it true, the other line by reason of its faintness being no hinderance.

These lines must be truly drawn, sharp and neat, with the greatest exactness imaginable.

VIII. Observe the most remarkable and deep shadows, to keep in memory when you go over them with more exactness; drawing out also (if you so please) the shape of that part of the body next adjoining to the face, *viz.* a little beneath the shoulders, with a strong and dark colour, which in case of mistake in proportion may easily be altered.

IX. The first sitting is to dead colour the face: the second sitting is the exact colouring and observation of the several shadows, graces, beauties or deformities, as they are in Nature: the third sitting is in making smooth what was before rough and rude; clothing what was naked, and giving strong and deepning touches to every respective shadow.

X. The dead colour is thus made.

Take of the aforesaid ground (at the third or fourth Section of this Chapter) and mix it with fine Red-lead, tempering it exactly to a dead colour of the cheeks and lips, having a great care, that you make it not too deep; which if light, you may do at pleasure.

XI. The face is first begun to be coloured in the reds of the cheeks and lips, and somewhat strongly in the bottom of the chin (if beardless) also over, under, and about the eyes with a faint redness.

XII. The ear is most commonly reddish, as also sometimes the roots of the hair.

XIII. The ground being wash'd over with this

reddish

reddifh or dead colour, let the fhadows be as well bold and ftrong as exact and curious.

A good Picture, if but dead coloured only, and feeming near hand very rough, uneven and unpleafant, yet being boldly and ftrongly done and fhadowed will appear very fmooth, delicate, and neat if but viewed at a diftance from the eye. Therefore curiofity and neatnefs of Colour, is not fo much to be regarded, as bold, lofty, and ftrong expreffing what is feen in the life.

XIV. The next thing to be done is the ufe of the faint blews, about the corners and balls of the eyes and temples, which you muft work out exceeding fweetly, and faint by degrees.

XV. Always be fure to make the hard fhadows fall in the dark fide of the face, under the nofe, chin, and eye-brows, as the light falls, with fomewhat ftrong touches.

XVI. The light fhadows being done and fmoothed work the hair into fuch forms, curlings, and difpofitions as beft adorn the piece.

Firft draw it with colours, neatly and to the life; then wafh it roughly as the reft; and the next time perfect it: filling up the empty places with colour, and the partings thereof with blew.

XVII. And ever remember, when you would have your colours or fhadows deep, ftrong, and bold; that you do them by degrees, beginning faintly, and then encreafing the fame.

XVIII. Firft, ufe the former colours in the fame places again, driving and fweetning them into one another, that no part may look uneven, or with an edge, or patch of colour, but altogther equally mixt and difperfed, lying foft and fmooth, like fmoak or vapour.

XIX. Se.

XIX. Secondly, this work being done for an hour or two, lay the ground for behind the Picture of Blew, or Crimſon, like to a Sattin or Velvet Curtain.

XX. If blew, let it be done with Biſe well tempered in a ſhell : Firſt draw the out-lines with the ſame colour, with a ſmall pencil : then with a thin and waterish blew waſh over the whole ground with a larger pencil : laſtly, with thicker colour cover the ſame which you before waſh'd, ſwiftly, that it dry not before all be covered, ſo will it lie ſmooth and even.

XXI. If Crimſon, work with Indian-lake, in thoſe places where the ſtrong lights, and high reflexions fall : let the light be done with thin and waterish Lake ; the deepning and ſtrong ſhadows, cloſe by the light with thicker colour : this done, the Picture will be much changed ; the beauty of theſe grounds will much darken and dead it.

XXII. Let the apparel with ſuitable colours be done only flat with heightening or deepning ; and then go over the face again, reducing the ſhadows to ſmoothneſs and neatneſs with a ſharp and curious pencil : drawing the eyes, the lines of the eye-lids ; redneſs of the noſtrils ; ſhadow of the ears ; deepneſs of the eye-brows, and thoſe other remarkable marks of the face : *ſo ſweetning the out-lines of the face (by darkning the ground, above from the light ſide, and below on the dark ſide) that when the work is done, the ground may ſtand as it were at a diſtance from the face behind ; and the face may ſeem to ſtand off forward from the ground.*

XXIII. Then go over the hair, making it light or deep by the life : and in apparel make the ſeveral folls and ſhadows, and what elſe is to be imitated, as it is in

the life it felf; lightning the lines with the pureft
white, a little yellow and fome blew ; and deepening
with lvory black, and heightning with black mixed
with a little Lake or Indico.

XXIV. This done, and the perfon gone, your work
being yet rough, by your felf polifh it, and ftrive to
make it finooth and pleafant , filling up the empty
places, and fweetning the fhadows, which yet lie uneven and hard.

XXV. The apparel, hair, and ground being finifhed, now give ftrong touches for the rounding of the
face ; and obferve whatfoever may conduce to likenefs and refemblance, as moles, fmilings, or glancings
of the eyes, motion of the mouth, &c. for which purpofe, you may find an occafion of difcourfe, or caufe
the perfon to be in action, and to look merrily and
chearfully.

XXVI. Laftly conclude, that the eye gives the life ;
the nofe the favour; the mouth the likenefs ; and the
chin the grace.

XXVII. In fair coloured drapery, if the lightning
be done with fine fhell Gold it will add a moft wonderful luftre, and be a fingular ornament to your work ;
and if this Gold be mixt with the very ground it felf,
the apparel will appear much the fairer.

CHAP. XXXII.

Of Limning Landskip, more particularly.

I. TO make the Tablet for Landskip.

Take a piece of *Vellom,* and *share it thin upon a Frame, faftning it with paft or glew, and pafting it upon a board; and this manner of Tablets are altogether ufed in* Italy *for Landskip, and Hiftory.*

II. If you draw a Landskip from the life take your ftation from the rife of ground, or top of an hill, where you fhall have a large Horizon, marking your Tablet into three divifions downwards from the top to the bottom : then your face being directly oppofed to the midft of the finitor, keeping your body fixed, depict what is directly before your eyes, upon your Tablet on your middle divifion, then turning your head (not your body) to the right hand, depict what is there to be feen : adjoining it to the former. *In like manner doing by that which is to be feen on the left hand, your Landskip will be compleated.*

III. Make every thing exact, not only in refpect of diftance, proportion and colour; but alfo in refpect of form, as if there be *Hills, Dales, Rocks, Mountains, Catarafts, Ruines, Aquædufts, Towns, Cities, Caftles, Fortifications, or whatfoever elfe may prefent it felf to view;* making always a fair Sky, to be feen afar off; letting your light always defcend from the left hand to the right.

IV. In beginning your work, firft begin with a large Sky; and if there be any fhining or reflexion of the Sun, beware you mix no Red-lead in the Purple

H 4

of the Sky, or Clouds, but only with Lake and white: the yellow and whitish beams of Sol work with Masticot and white.

V. Then with a fresh or clean pencil finish the blewish Sky, and Clouds, with Smalt only : at the first working, dead all the work over, with colours suitable to the Air, green Meadows, Trees, and ground, laying them somewhat smooth, not very curiously, but slightly and hastily ; make a large Sky, which work down in the Horizon, faintly, but fair ; and drawing nearer to the earth, let the remote Mountains appear sweet and misty, almost indistinguishable, joyning with the Clouds, and as it were lost in the Air.

V I. The next ground colour downwards must encrease in magnitude of reason, as nearer the eyes , somewhat blewish or Sea-green : but drawing towards the first ground, let them decline into a reddish or popinjay-green : the last ground colour, must be nearest the colour of the earth, *viz.* a dark yellow, brown and green ; with which, or some colour near it, you must make your first Trees ; making them, as they come near in distance, to encrease proportionably in colour and magnitude, with great judgement : the leaves flowing and falling one with another, some apparent, others lost in shadow.

V I I. Let your Landskip lie low, and as it were under the eye (which is most graceful and natural) with a large and full Sky not rising high, and lifting it self into the top of the piece, as some have done.

V I I I. Be sure to make your shadows fall all one way, *viz.* to make light against darkness, and darkness against light ; thereby extending the prospect, and making it to shew as afar off; by losing its force and vigour, by the remoteness from the eye.

I X. In touching the Trees, Boughs and Branches,
put

put all the dark shadows first, raising the lighter leaves above the darker, by adding Masticot to the dark green, which may be made with Bice, Pink, and Indico: the uppermost of all, exprest last of all, by lightly touching the exteriour edges of some of the former leaves, with a little green, .Masticot, and white: the darkest shadows you may set off with Sapgreen and Indico.

X. Trees and their leaves, Rivers, and Mountains far distant, you must strive to express with a certain real softness and delicateness: in making Cataracts, great falls of Waters, and Rocks, you must first lay a full ground near the colour, then with a stronger in the dark places, and slight heightning in the light: remarking all disproportions, cracks, ruptures and various representations of infinitely differing matters; the manner whereof is abundantly exprest, in almost every Landskip.

CHAP. XXXIII.

Of the various Forms or Degrees of Colouring.

I. THere are four various Forms or degres of colouring, *viz.* 1. *Of Infants, or Children.* 2. *Of Virgins, or fair Women.* 3. *Naked bodies.* 4. *Old or aged bodies.*

II. *Infants or young Children* are to be painted of a soft and delicate complexion; the Skin and ears of a ruddy and pleasant colour, almost transparent; which may be done with White-lead, Lake, and a little Redlead; shadowing it thin, faint and soft; letting the

Cheeks,

cheeks, lips, chin, fingers, knees, and toes, be more ruddy than other parts; making all their linnen very fine, thin, and transparent, or perspicuous, with strong touches in the thickest folds.

III. *Virgins and fair Women* are as curiously to be express'd as the former, but their Muscles are to be more apparent, their shape more perfect; and their shadows to be of a whitish yellow, blewish, and in some places almost purple; but the most perfect and exquisite direction is the life, which ought rather to be followed than any thing delivered by rule.

IV. *Naked bodies* are to be painted strong, lively, and accurate; exactly matching the respective pairs of Muscles and Nerves, fixing each Artery in its due and proper place, giving each limb its proper motion form and situation, with its true and natural colour; all which to do well may be the study and practice of almost ones whole life.

V. *Old or aged bodies* ought to be eminent for exact and curious shadows, which may be made of Pink, Lake, and Ivory-black, which make notable shadows, in appearance like the wrinkles and furrows of the face and hand in extream old age: let the eyes be dark, the aspect melancholy, the hair white (or else the pate bald) and all the remarks of Antiquity or age be very apparent and formidable.

VI. But notwithstanding all the aforegoing rules, the posture or form of standing, and being either of the whole body, or any of its parts, ought diligently to be observed, that the life may be imitated, in which, it only lies in the breast and judgment of the Painter to set it off with such various colours, as may best befit the respective complexion and accidental shadows of each accidental

tal pofition or pofture, which are fometimes more
pale, fometimes more ruddy; fometimes more faint,
fometimes more lively.

CHAP. XXXIV.

Of the Limning of the Skie, Clouds, &c.

I. FOR a beautiful Sky, fitted for fair weather,
take Bice tempered with white, laying it in
the upper part of the Sky, (as you fee need) under
which you may lay a thin or faint purple with a fmall
foft brufh: working the undermoft purple into the
uppermoft blew; but fo as that the blew may ftand
clear and perfect: then for the Horizon or near the
fame lay a fine thin Mafticot, which work from below upwards, till it mix with the purple, after which
you may take a ftronger purple, making here and
there upon the former purple, as it were the form of
Clouds, as nature requires: upon the Mafticot you
may alfo work with Minium mixed with Cerufe, to
imitate the fiery beams which often appear in hot and
clear Summer weather.

II. To imitate glory, with a great fhining light of
a yellowifh colour or the Sun-beams, you muft take
Mafticot, or Saffron mixt with Red-lead, and heightned with fnell gold, and the like.

III. A Cloudy Sky is imitated with pale Bice,
afterwards fhading the Clouds with a mixture of feveral colours: a fair Sky requires clouds of a greater
fhade, with purple: the clouds in a rainy Sky, muft
be fhaded with Indico and Lake: in a night Sky,
with black and dark blew fmoaky, making a blaze with
purple

purple, Minium and Cerufe: the clouds in a Sun rifing or fetting muft be done with Minium, Cerufe and purple, making underneath the clouds fcattering ftroaks, with Minium and Mafticot, or Minium and Saffron; fo that the fcatterings upwards may appear faint: and below, afar off near the Landskip, fomewhat fiery.

IV. A fiery Sky, let be made with a pale blew, fmoothing it downwards, which afterwards, you muft mingle with a ftrong Red-lead, mixt with Cerufe, making long diminutive ftroaks like the Sunbeams upon the blew Sky, with which let fall fome purple ftroaks, much like the faid beames; laftly, fweeten one into another with a foft brufh pencil, wet in gum-water, not too ftrong.

V. Laftly, you may make a fair Sky, by ufing fair Bice alone, and tempering it by degrees with more and more white, fmoothing one into another, from above downwards, and fhading it as you fhall fee reafon and nature require.

CHAP. XXXV.

Of the Limning of Towns, Caftles, and Ruines.

I. THofe Towns, or Cities, which feem at fartheft diftance, muft have but little fhadowing or heightening, and fometimes none at all, thefe if they appear againft the Sky, muft be laid with Bice, and a little purple, and fhaded faintly with a good blew.

II. Thofe which lie at a farther diftance, muft be laid

laid with Bice and purple as aforefaid, and fhaded
with light blew, and heightened with white.

III. Thofe which appear at an ordinary diftance,
muft be done with Vermilion and purple, and fhaded
with a ftrong purple fhaded with white.

IV. Thofe which are near, muft be done with
Vermilion and white, and then fhaded with a ftrong
Vermilion and brown Oker, mixt with white.

CHAP. XXXVI.

Of Mountains, Hills, and the like.

I. THofe Mountains which are next in fight, muft
be laid with a fair green, and fhaded with
Sap-green; fometimes with brown Oker, and *French*
Berries, to diftinguifh them from fuch as are farther
off.

II. Such as lie farther off, muft be laid with green,
blew, and Mafticot, and be fhaded with blew, green,
and Verdegriefe.

III. Such as lie yet farther, muft be laid with fome
ftrong blew, white, and Bergh-green, and fhaded
with ftrong blew.

IV. Such as lie yet farther, muft be laid with
ftrong blew and white, and fhaded with blew only.

V. Such as lie yet farther, with Bice and white,
and fhaded with Bice.

VI. Such as lie farther off, are only laid with white,
and fhaded with a faint Bice.

VII. Fields being near, muft be done with a fingular good green, the which muft always be fainteft, according as they are farther diftant; heightening them
with

with Mafticot, or a light green, and fhading with Sap-green, but not too much : thofe which lie far, are to be laid with a *French* berry yellow, made of a blew greenifh, fhaded with Oker.

VIII. And in Fields, Hills, and Dales (whether near, or far off) there are many roads, paffages and ways, which muft be laid either fainter or ftronger according to their diftance and fituation.

CHAP. XXXVII.

Of Trees, Boughs, Cottages, and the like.

I. THofe Trees of divers colours which ftand up-on the fore-ground, muft be laid with divers colours as with Verdegriefe, mixt with other green, or with mafticot, and Bergh-green mixt, and then fha-ded with Sap-green ; which you may heighten with Mafticot, mixt with White-lead.

II. If they appear yellow, ufe Verdegriefe and Ma-fticot mixt, and fhadow with Verdegriefe.

III. If they be of a whitifh colour, let them be laid with Verdegriefe mixt with White-lead, and fhade them with Verdegriefe, mixt with Indico faint ; heighten them with Cerufe, that they may look of a faint yellow green ; or elfe with a little Indico and yellow.

IV. Thofe which ftand at a great diftance, lay with Indico, and white, and fhadow with Indico, and heighten with the fame made a little lighter.

V. If Trees be very old with mofs upon them, give them the appearance of green and yellow, which commix of Pink, and Bergh-green : if they be of a

whitifh

whitifh yellow, do them with Pink and white mixt . with a little green.

VI. Country Cottages lay with light Oker, which order acording to the newnefs or oldnefs of the building.

VII. Cottages of Timber, let be laid of the colour of Trees and Wood-work.

VIII. Thatcht Cottages if new, lay with Pink, fha-dow with brown Oker, and heighten with Mafticot mixt with white: but if old, lay them with brown Oker mixt with white, and heighten with the fame.

IX. Straw colours at a diftance are done with In-dico and white, mixt fometimes with brown Oker , and fhaded with Indico.

CHAP. XXXVIII.

Of the Colouring of Naked Figures.

I. FOR Women and Children, take the beft Flake White-lead , and a little good Lake , with which if you pleafe you may mix a little Vermilion, but take heed that your mixture be neither too red or too pale, but exactly agreeable to the life it felf; the which in this cafe is the beft director : this being dry touch the lips, cheeks , chin, fingers, and toes with thin Lake, and then heighten with white mixt with a little Lake or Vermilion.

II. But if you would cover them fomewhat brownifh, mix with your Carnation, a little brown Oker ; and fhade it with Red-Oker, and coal-black with a little Lake.

III. In old Women take White, Vermilion and brown-

Brown-Oker , and give the luſtre where it ought to be with Vermilion mixt with a little Lake : ſhade it with Red-Oker and Lake, or with Wood ſoot, or Lamp-black , and heighten with white mixt with a ſmall quantity of Vermilion.

I V. Dead Children and young Women, paint with Brown-Oker, white and ſome Vermilion , and ſhadow the ſame with the ſoot of wood.

V. Dead old Women colour with Brown-Oker mixt with a little white, which ſhade with a thin ſoot of wood firſt, then with a ſtronger.

V I. Young men paint with Ceruſe, Vermilion and Lake, making it a little browner than for young Women ; giving them luſtre with Vermilion and Lake, ſhadowing with Lamp-black and Brown-Oker ; and heightening with Ceruſe and Vermilion.

V I I. Old Men Limn with Vermilion, Brown-Oker, and white; ſhade with ſoot and Lamp-black ; heighten with Vermilion , Brown-Oker , and white, and give it a luſtre with Lake or Vermilion.

V I I I. Dead men colour with Brown-Oker, white, and a little Vermilion , as your diſcretion ſhall inform you, and ſhade with ſoot , or Lamp-black mixt with a little Ceruſe.

I X. Devils, Satyrs, and the like Limn with Brown Oker, mixt with a little white and red, which mixture let be made ſome part whiter, ſome part browner ; and ſtrongly ſhade it with ſoot, as your own ingenuity may inform you.

C H A P.

CHAP. XXXIX.

Of the Colouring of Hair.

I. THE Hair of Women and Children is coloured with fimple Brown-Oker, and heightened with Mafticot: The fame in the hair of men, only making it fadder or lighter as the life requires.

II. Hair which is black may be done with foot, or Lamp-black, but it will abide no heightning.

III. Childrens Hair is fometimes laid with brown, oker and white, and heightned with the fame; and fometimes with Alom.

IV. Sometimes alfo they are done with light-oker, and deepned with brown-oker, and heightened with Mafticot fimple.

V. Old Womens Hair with brown-oker and black, heightned with brown-oker and white.

VI. In Gray Hair take more black than white, and heighten with pure white.

CHAP. XL.

Of Walls, Chambers, and the like.

I. FOR a brick Wall take Vermilion and white, and fhadow with Red-oker.

II. If the ground of the wall is laid with black and white, fhade it with a thin black, if with Red-oker

I   and

and white, fhade it with purple : or with Lake and black, or Red-oker fimple.

III. If it be laid with black, white, and purple , fhade it with purple and black,

IV. If the wall belongs to any Chamber or Hall , having Figures or Statues ; fo order and temper your colours, with fuch diftinction, that the Figures and Wall be not drowned in each other.

V. Sandy fore-grounds do thinly with brown-oker, fad or light as the life prefents; fhadow the fame with the fame brown-oker , and Rocks with Red-oker, according as they are near to, or far from the fight.

CHAP. XLI.

Of Marble Pillars, Rocks, and the like.

I. MArble muft be done with a good and light pencil, after a carelefs manner in imitation of Nature, wherein all fuch ftains , colours , veins, and reprefentations of the faces of living things muft be carefully obferved.

II. The like is to be obferved in Rocks, of Sandy colours, and ragged forms ; which if feen at a great diftance, muft be coloured with thin Bice, and then heightened with purple and white , and fhaded with Smalt or a deep blew.

III. If they feem near, colour them with brown-oker mixt with white , which go over again with Vermilion mixt with white, after which lay here and there fome Verdegriefe mixt with fome other green.

IV. In thefe works you muft make fpots, ftains and
breakings,

breakings, with hatchings, which shade with the foot of Wood or Lamp-black mixt with a little white.

CHAP. XLII.

Of the Colouring of Metals.

I. **F**OR Gold colour, take Red-lead, Saffron, and very light Oker, with which colour all manner of Cups, Dishes and the like, which shade with foot, and heighten with shell Gold.

II. For Silver, lay a thin white, which shade with a thin blew, mixt with a little black, and heighten with shell Silver.

III. For Tin and Iron, take white and Indico, and shade it with Indico and Bice, and heighten with white or shell Silver.

IV. For Brass, take thin Pink, shade it with Indico mixt with green, or with almost all Indico, and heighten it with shell Gold.

V. For Copper, take Red-oker and white, shade it with Red-oker, and heighten with Red-oker and white, heightening also here and there, where the light falls, with shell Silver.

C H A P. XLIII.

Of the Colouring of Flowers.

I. THE Tulip, draw it firſt with black-lead upon a white ground, then ſhade it a little (as for a white Flower) with thin Indian Ink, or with green yellow Ink, or with black-lead ground with thick gum water ; then lay on your ſeveral colours reſembling Nature, which being dry, ſhade with a higher colour, and then farther ſhadow it, according to the nature of the Flower : ſo that being finiſhed it may be like flame, red, blew, lake, purple, ſpotted, or otherwiſe, in imitation of the life.

II. The Damask Roſe, lay with Lake mixt with white, ſhadow with the ſame mixt with thin Lake ; and heighten with white.

III. The green leaves are done with Verdegrieſe mixt with ſome *French* berry green, ſhade it with Verdegrieſe mixt with Sap-green ; the ſtalks lay ſome-what browner with brown-oker.

IV. Red Roſes do with fine Lake mixt with white , ſhade it with brown Lake, and heighten it with Lake mixt with white.

V. White Roſes colour with Flake Lead , ſhade it with white and black (but the chief ſhadows with a ſtronger black) and heighten with white.

VI. The little thrums (which ſome erroneouſly call ſeeds) in the middle of the Roſe, lay with Maſticot, and ſhadow with Minium, and heighten with white.

VII. The Clove-gilliflower is done almoſt like the Red-

Red-rose: the fpecking or fpotting of it is done with Lake; thofe which are lighter, with a lighter red upon a pure white; thofe like flames with Vermilion and Lake, which fhade with a ftronger Lake; and fpeck the white with Lake and Vermilion, to refemble the life.

VIII. The green ftalks, or branches and leaves lay with Bergh-green, and fhade with Sap-green.

IX. The Marigold do with yellow Orpiment and Minium, fhadow with Vermilion and Lake mixt with Minium; and heighten with white and Mafticot.

X. Corn-flowers lay with blew mixt with fome white, fhadow with Indico, and fhadow with blew and white.

CHAP. XLIV.

Of Radishes, Turneps, Melons, Cucumers, and Cabage.

I. R Adifhes are done with white, fhaded with Lake, and as it were behind fweetned with purple; and fometimes with green from the top downwards: The green leaves at top with Verdegriefe mixed with Sap-green, fhaded with Sap-green, and heightned with Mafticot.

II. Turneps are laid with white, fhaded with foot; the leaves as the Radifh leaves.

III. Yellow Melons with yellow, fhaded with brown-oker; the veins with a ftronger brown-oker, and then heightned with white.

IV. Green Melons, with Indico mixt with Verde-

griefe

griefe and Sap-green, fhaded with Sap-green and Indico ; and heightened with Mafticot.

V. Cucumers, the ends with a thin yellow, the
middle with green, fweetned the one into the other,
and fhaded with Sap-green ; but the whole fruit with
brown-oker, the fpecks lay with red and black to the
life.

V I, Cabbage white with very thin yellow, and in
fome places with very thin green (or yellowifh green)
fweetning with very thin brown-oker mixt with Sap-
green ; heighten with pure white.

V I I. Cabbage red, lay with purple, fhade with
Lakmus, and heighten with purple mixt with white.

C H A P. XLV.

How to Colour Fruits.

I. CHerries, with Vermilion and fome Brazil, fhade
with Lake, heighten with Vermilion mixt
with white.

I I. Heart Cherries in the middle with Vermilion
and Lake mixt with white, the Circumference remaining whitifh, here and there fweetning them with
Lake, and heightening with white, or mixt with a
little Lake.

I I I. A Pear with mafticot, fhaded fweetly with
brown-oker ; its blufh with Lake not too high, heighten with white.

I V. Apples with a thin Mafticot mixt with Verdegriefe, fhade them with brown-oker, and give
their blufh with a thin or deep Lake (refembling
Nature) and heighten with white : if you will have
them

them very high, mix your white with some Masticot, but this must be according to the condition of the Fruit whether ripe or unripe , red , yellow or green, &c.

V. Mulberries with a very strong Brazil, and then lay'd over with black, so that between the stalks and berries they make look a little reddish according to Nature.

V I. Strawberries with a white ground , which draw over with Vermilion and Lake very thin ; shade it with fine Lake, and heighten with Masticot mixt with Minium; and then with white only speck them with Lake, by one side of which put a smaller speck of white.

V I I. Wall-nuts with their green on, with Verdegriese mixt with Sap-green , shade with Sap-green and a little white.

V I I I. Wall-nuts without their green, with brown-oker, shaded with soot.

I X. Blew Plums with purple, shadowed with Bice, and about the stalks with a little green, well sweetned ; heighten with purple and white.

X. White Plums and Peaches with thin Masticot , shaded with brown-oker ; give them a blush with Lake, and heighten them with white.

X I. Red and Blew Grapes with purple, shaded with blew, and heightned with white.

X I I. White Grapes with thin Verdegriese (called also *Spanish* green) mixt with Masticot, shadow with thin Verdegriese ; and heighten with Masticot mixt with white.

CHAP.

CHAP. XLVI.

Of the Limning of Fowls.

I. THE Eagle with black and brown-oker, fhadow it with black, the feathers heighten with brown-oker mixt with white: the bill and claws lay with Saffron, and fhade it with foot or Lamp-black : the eyes with Vermilion heightned with Mafticot, or with Saffron fhaded or deepned with Vermilion ; let the talons be done with black.

II. The Swan with white mixt with a little black, heighten it with fine and pure white, · fo that its plumes or feathers by that heightning may look well: the legs with a black colour : the bill with Vermilion, fhaded with Lake : the eyes yellow with a black round in the middle ; from which falls a blackifh vein, defcending to the bill.

III. The Goofe with more white than black, *viz.* a light gray, heighten it with a grey white ; the legs with black : the bill like the Swan.

IV. The Duck with a light grey, the head with a dark blew, and dark green neck fweetly enterwoven, the belly with white, the legs with black mixt with a little white, *&c.* but be fure to imitate the life.

V. The Turkey with black mixt with a little white, from the back towards the belly whiter by degrees, but the belly fpeck with black, and in like manner the wings : let him be fhaded with black, the wings with Indico, fhaded with ftronger Indico , the bill with black , the eyes blew, heightned with white. He being angry the naked skin of his neck
will

will be blood red, which lay with Vermilion mixt with Lake, fhaded with Lake: but otherwife lay it of a whitifh blew colour.

VI. The Griffon with Saffron, fhadowed with brown-oker or foot.

VII. The Pheafant with grey, made of white and black, the feathers of a white grey, the whole muft be fhaded with black, and heightened with pure white; the eyes like the Falcon, the legs with Pink, and fhaded with black.

VIII. The Falcon with brown-oker, and black mixt with white, and fhadowed with black, the feathers muft be pleafantly drawn with black, and fprinkled upon its breafts; heighten it with white, let his talons be black, above the eyes lay with Saffron, and fhade with Vermilion, the bill with grey.

IX. The Stork with grey, heightned with white, and the corners of his wings (near one half) with black, his long bill and legs with Vermilion, fhaded with Lake.

X. The Owl with Cerufe, black and foot, fhadowed with foot, and heightned with yellow-Oker and white, fometimes white alone, the eyes yellow, circled with white, the legs of a brown yellow.

CHAP.

CHAP. XLVII.

Of *Limning of Beasts.*

I. SHeep with a thin white, fhaded with Indico and foot, and heightened with white.

II. Hogs with brown-oker, fhaded with foot, and heightened with Mafticot: you may as you fee occafion colour the hair here and there with ftronger brown-oker ; his eyes with Vermilion, which heighten with Mafticot, his mouth with Indico, or white and black, fhaded with black.

III. A Bear with brown-oker, red-oker, and black mixt ; fhadow with foot alone, or mixt with black, and heighten with brown-oker and white.

IV. A Wolf with brown-oker and foot, fhadow with more foot.

V. A gray Wolf with black, white, and brown-oker, fhaded with black and foot, or black only ; the mouth with black and red-oker, fhaded with black and foot heightned with red-oker and white.

VI. The Elephant (which is of a Moufe gray) with black and white mixt with foot, and fhaded with black and foot, and heightened with the fame, with a little more white ; the nofe at the end of his trunk, inwardly muft be laid with Vermilion and Cerufe, fhadowed with black, or black mixt with Lake : in the fame manner the inner part of the ears, the eyes with white tending to a grey.

VII. Mice are coloured as the Elephant : Rats a little browner.

VIII. The Unicorn with a pure white, fhaded
with

with black: the chaps red, the eye and hoofs with a thin black.

IX. The Heart with brown-oker, fhaded on the back with foot, which fweetly drive towards the belly, and fhade over again with a ftronger foot; the neck and belly with white, the mouth and ears a little reddifh, the hoof black, the horns with foot, and fhaded with foot mixt with black.

X. The Hind with the fame colours as the Hart, but thinner, and higher, not fo brown.

XI. The Coney with black and white, his belly all white, fweetned with black; and heightned with a ftronger white.

XII. The Hare with brown-oker, his belly below a little whitifh; fhade it on the back with foot, and heighten on the belly with white.

XIII. Apes, Monkeys and the like, with Pink and black, heightned with Mafticot and white; the face lay with a thin black mixt with foot, fhaded with black and Pink mixt with a little red-oker.

XIV. Cats if gray and brownifh, or tabby, with Indico, blew and white, heightened with pure white, and fhaded with Indian blew and black mixt: in other colours ufe your difcretion.

XV. The Afs with black mixt with white like grey; if the Afs be of a mingled brown, black and white mixt with brown-oker, fhaded with black in the mouth; heighten with white.

XVI. The Leopard with brown-oker and red-oker mixt with black, fhadow it with foot, the fpots with red-oker and black, the mouth with black and white: heighten him with light Oker.

XVII. Horfes, Dogs, Oxen and fuch like, if white, with white mixt with a little foot, or Oker, fhaded with a black and white, and heightened with perfect white.   XVIII. It

XVII. If of a Cheſtnut-brown, with red-oker and black, ſhaded with black and ſoot, and heightned with red-oker and white.

XIX. If an Aſh grey, with black mixt with white, ſhaded with black, and heightned with white.

XX. If black, with a thin black, ſhaded with a ſtronger black, and heightned with black and white.

XXI. A bay Horſe with Vermilion and brown-oker; or only with red-chalk, ſhaded with red-oker, and heightned with red-chalk mixt with white.

XXII. If ſpotted, by mixture of the aforeſaid colours, and diſcreetly putting every one in its proper apart-ment or place.

CHAP. XLVIII.

Of the Limning of Serpents.

I. THE Serpents on the back with Bice , and downwards towards the belly with a pale black, the back ſpeckled with black; the belly ſha-ded with red, ſprinkled alſo with black ſpecks.

II. The Adder with red-lead, Vermilion and ſaf-fron, with blew in the back, and on the belly below Maſticot and white, ſpeckled all over with black ſpots.

III. The Crocodile with a dark thin green, from the back down-wards to the belly ; below the belly with Maſticot, ſo that the yellow and green may melt, or vaniſh away into one another ; ſhadow him with Indico and ſmalt, and heighten the belly with Ma-ſticot and white: the mouth before and within rediſh,

the

the fcales black, the claws of blackifh green, the nails wholly black.

IV. The Frog with a fair green, fpeckled with black, and towards the belly with green mixt with Mafticot, fweetned with green fpeckled : the eyes with Saffron, and black round them, the back heightned with Saffron.

CHAP. XLIX.

Of Limning waters and Fifh.

I. **W**Ater at a diftance with white and Indico, fhaded with Indico mixt with Bice , and heightned with white: if near the Horizon much like the Sky.

II. Waters near lay with ftronger Indico, heighten and fhadow with the fame mixt with Bice : laftly heighten with pure white.

III. Waters nearer with ftronger Indico, fhaded and heightned as before.

IV. Waters in fields overgrown, with Pink and the like ; always imitating Nature.

V. Fifh in green Waters, with Indico mixt with *Ferench*-berry-yellow, fhaded with a thin Indian blew, and heightned with pure white.

But Fifhes ought alfo to be done according to their Nature and Colour , for fome are yellow , fome brown, fome fpeckled, fome grifled, fome black, &c. in all which to conferve in Figure the true Idea, you ought to take directions only by the life.

Horat.

Horat. Epod. 16.

Vos, quibus est virtus, muliebrem tollite luctum,
    Etrusca præter & volate littora.
Nos manet Oceanus circumvagus ; arva , beata
    Petamus arva, divites & insulas :
Reddit ubi Cererem tellus inarata quotannis,
    Et imputata floret usquè vinea.
Germinet & nunquam fallentis termes olivæ ,
    Suámque pulla ficus ornat arborem.
Illis injussæ veniunt ad mulctra capellæ ;
    Refértque tenta grex amicus ubera.
Nec Vespertinus circumgemit ursus ovile;
    Nec intumescit alta viperis humus :
Pluráque felices mirabimur : ut neque largis
    Aquosus Eurus arva radat imbribus,
Pinguia nec siccis urantur semina glebis :
    Utrumque rege temperante Cœlitum.
Non huc Argoo contendit remige pinus,
    Neque impudica Colchis intulit pedem
Non huc Sidonii torserunt cornua nautæ,
    Laboriosa nec cohors Ulyssei.
Nulla nocent pecori contagia, nullius astri
    Gregem æstuosa torret impotentia.
Jupiter illa piæ secrevit littora genti ,
    Ut inquinavit ære tempus aureum.

You nobler spirits, hence with womens tears,
Sail from Etruscan confines free from fears:
The Earth-encirc'ling Ocean us invites,
Rich Islands, Fields, Fields blest with all delights.
Where Lands untill'd are yearly fruitful seen,
And the unpruned Vine perpetual green.

                                    Still,

Of Landskip.

Still, Olives by the faithful branch are born,
And mellow Figgs their native Trees adorn.
There milchy Goats come freely to the pail,
Nor do glad flocks with dugs distended fail.
The nightly Bear roars not about the fold,
Nor hollow earth doth poisonous Vipers hold.
Add to this happiness, the humid East
Doth not with frequent showers the Fields infest.
Nor the fat seeds are parcht in barren land,
The powers above both temp'ring with command.
No Bark came hither with Argoan oar,
Nor landed wanton Colchis on this shoar:
Cadmus with filled sails turn'd not this way,
Nor painful troops that with Ulysses stray.
Here amongst cattel no Contagions are,
Nor feel flocks droughty power of any star.
When brass did on the Golden Age intrude,
Jove for the pious did this place seclude.

The End of the Second Book.

POLYGRAPHICES
LIBER TERTIUS.

Of Painting, Waſhing, Colouring, Dying, Varniſhing, and Gilding.

*Containing the Deſcription and Uſe of all the
chief Inſtruments and Materials, and the way
and manner of working.*

The Dying of Cloath, Silks, Horns, Bones,
Woods, Glaſs, Stones, and Metals : Together with the Gilding and Varniſhing
thereof, according to any purpoſe or intent.

CHAP. I.

Of Painting in General.

I. THE Art of *Painting* (which is the imitation
of Nature) conſiſts in three things, to
wit, *Deſign, Proportion,* and *Colour* : all
which are expreſt in three ſorts of Painting, *viz.*
Landskip, Hiſtory, and *Life.*

K

II. *Land-*

I I. *Landskip* or Perspective, wonderfully respects freedom and liberty, to draw even what you please. *History* respects proportion and figure : *Life,* respects colour : In each of which there is a necessary dependency of all the other.

I I I. The work of the Painter is to express the exact imitation of natural things; wherein you are to observe the excellencies and beauties of the piece, but to refuse its vices.

For a piece of Painting may in some part want Diligence, Boldness, Subtilty, Grace, Magnificence, &c. *while it is sufficiently in other parts excellent; and therefore you are not so much to imitate Ornaments, as to express the inward power and strength.*

I V. In *Imitation,* always be sure to follow the examples and patterns of the best masters; lest evil precedents beget in you an evil habit.

V. The force of *Imitation* resides in the fancy or imagination, where we conceive (what we have seen) the form or *Idea* of that, or those things which we would represent in lines and colours.

V I. This *Fancy* or *Imagination* is strengthened, by lodging therein all variety of visible rarities ; as 1. Forms made by light and darkness; such as are to be seen in Summer in the clouds, near Sun-setting (which vanish before they can be imitated :) 2. Forms made by proximity or distance of place, such as are Trees, Woods, Buildings, appearing perfect being near, or confused in their parts being far off: 3. Forms of dreams, of which (whether sleeping or waking) the fancy must be fully possest.

V I I. Where *Design* is required; you must fancy every circumstance of the matter in hand, that in an instant, with a nimble had, you may depict the same with liveliness and grace.

Slow

*Slow performance caufes a perturbation in the fancy ,
cooling of the mind, and deſtruction of that paſſion which
ſhould carry the work one : but quickneſs and diligence
brings forth things even excellent indeed : Care, Induſtry
and Exerciſe are the props, ſupporters and upholders of
Art.*

VIII. Be fure you dwell not too long upon defigning : alter not what is well, left for want of exquifite
judgment you make it worfe: and if in defigning,
you want that ability to follow the quickneſs of fancy,
fubmit to a willing negligence ; a careleſs operation
adds fometimes fuch a fingular grace, as by too much
curiofity would have been totally loft ; then by re-
viewing what is done, *make a regular connexion of all
the* Idea's *conceived in your mind.*

IX. With *Apelles* amend thofe things which others
juftly find fault with ; the reprehenfions of an Artift
are as demonftrative rules of experience ; and weigh
every ones opinion for the advancement of Art.

X. Laftly, be fure your piece be of a good *Defign,
Hiſtory* or *Life* ; that the parts be well *difpofed* , the
Characters of Perfons, *proper* ; the Form *magnificent* ,
the colour *lively*, and the fpirit *bold* : that it may appear to be the work of a nimble fancy, ready memory,
clear judgment, and large experience.

CHAP.

CHAP. II.

Of Painting in Oyl, and the Materials thereof.

I. PAinting in Oyl is nothing but the work or Art of Limning performed with colours made up or mixed with Oyl.

II. The Materials of Painting are chiefly Seven, 1. The *Easel.* 2. The *Pallet.* 3. The *Straining Frame.* 4. The *Primed cloath.* 5. *Pencils.* 6. The *Stay.* 7. *Colours.*

III. The *Easel* is a Frame made of wood (much like a Ladder) with sides flat, and full of holes, to put in two pins to set your work upon higher or lower at pleasure ; something broader at bottom than at the top : on the backside whereof is a stay, by which you may set the *Easel* more upright or sloping.

IV. The *Pallet* is a thin piece of wood, (Pear-tree or Walnut) a foot long, and about ten inches broad, almost like an Egg, at the narrowest end of which is made an hole to put in the thumb of the left hand, near to which is cut a notch, that so you may hold the *Pallet* in your hand. *Its use is to hold and temper the Colours upon.*

V. The *Streining Frame* is made of wood, to which with nails is fastned the *Primed cloath,* which is to be Painted upon.

These ought to be of several sizes according to the bigness of the cloath.

VI. The *Primed cloath* is that which is to be Painted upon : and is thus prepared.

Take

Take good Canvas and smooth it over with a slick-stone, size it over with size, and a little honey, and let it dry; then white it over once with whiting and size mixed with a little hony, so is the cloath prepared, on which you may draw the Picture with a coal; and lastly lay on the Colours.

Where note, honey keeps it from cracking, peeling or breaking out.

VII. *Pencils* are of all bigneſſes, from a pin to the bigneſs of a finger, called by ſeveral names, as *Ducks-quill fitched* and *pointed*; *Gooſe-quill fitched* and *pointed*; *Swans-quill fitched* and *pointed*; *Jewelling pencils*, and *briſtle pencils*: ſome in quills, ſome in Tin caſes, and ſome in ſticks.

VIII. The *Stay* or *Molstick*, is a Brazil ſtick (or the like) of a yard long; having at the one end thereof, a little ball of Cotten, fixed hard in a piece of Leather, of the bigneſs of a Cheſtnut; which when you are at work you muſt hold in your left hand; and laying the end which hath the Leather ball upon the cloath or Frame, you may reſt your right arm upon it, whilſt you are at work.

IX. The Colours are in number ſeven (*ut ſuprà*) to wit, White, Black, Red, Green, Yellow, Blew, and Brown.

Of which some may be tempered on the Pallet at first, some must be ground, and then tempered; and other some must be burnt, ground, and lastly tempered.

X. To make the Size for the Primed cloath at the ſixth Section of this Chapter.

Take Glew, and boil it well in fair water, till it be dissolved, and it is done.

XI. To make the Whiting for the ſixth Section of this Chapter.

Take of the aforesaid Size, mix it with whiting

K 3 *ground,*

ground, *and so white your boards or cloath (being made smooth) dry them, and white them a second or third time; lastly, scrape them smooth, and draw it over with White-lead tempered with Oyl.*

XII. To keep the Colours from skinning.

Oyl Colours (if not presently used) will have a skin grow over them, to prevent which put them into a glass, and put the glass three or four inches under water, so will they neither skin nor dry.

XIII. To cleanse the Grinding stone and Pencils.

If the Grinding stone be foul, grind Curriers shavings upon it, and then crumbs of bread, so will the filth come off: if the pencils be foul, dip the ends of them in oyl of Turpentine, and squeeze them between your fingers, and they will be very clean.

CHAP. III.

Of the Colours in General, and their significations.

I. **T**HE chief *Whites* for Painting in Oyl are, White-lead, Ceruse and Spodium.

II. The chief *Blacks* are Lamp-black, Seacoal-black, Ivory-black, Charcoal, and earth of Colen.

III. The chief *Reds* are, Vermilion, Sinaper Lake, Red-lead, Indian Red, Ornotto.

IV. The chief *Greens* are, Verdegriese, Terra-vert, Verditer.

V. The chief *Yellows* are, Pink, Masticot, English Oker, Spruce Oker, Orpiment.

VI. The chief *Blews* are, Blew Bice, Indico, Ultramarine, Smalt.

VII. The

VII. The chief *Browns* are Spanish-brown, burnt Spruce, Umber.

VIII. These Colours, Lamp-black, Verditer, Vermilion, Bice, Smalt, Masticot, Orpiment, Ultramarine, are not to be ground at all, but only tempered with oyl upon the Pallet.

IX. These Colours, Ivory, Ceruse, Oker and Umber are to be burnt, and then ground with oyl.

X. All the rest are to be ground upon the Grinding stone with Linseed oyl (except White-lead, when it is to be used for Linnen, which then is to be ground with oyl of Walnuts, for Linseed oyl will make it turn yellow.

And now since we are engaged to treat of colours, it may neither be unnecessary, nor unuseful for the young Artist to know their natural significations; which take as followeth.

XI. *Blew* signifieth truth, faith, and continued affections; *Azure,* Constancy; *Violet,* a religious mind.

XII. *Orange-tawny* signifies Pride, also integrity; *Tawny* forsaken, *Limmon,* jealousie.

XIII. *Green* signifies hopes: *Grass-green,* youth, youthfulness, and rejoycing: *Sea-green,* Inconstancy.

XIV. *Red* signifies Justice, Vertue and Defence: *Flame-Colour,* Beauty and desire: *Maidens-blush,* Envy.

XV. *Yellow* signifies Jealousie: perfect yellow, Joy, Honour, and greatness of Spirit: *Gold-colour,* Avarice.

XVI. *Flesh-colour* signifieth Lasciviousness: *Carnation,* Craft, Subtilty and Deceipt: *Purple,* Fortitude and Strength.

XVII. *Willow-colour* signifieth forsaken: *Popingjay green,* Wantonness: *Peach-colour,* Love.

XVIII. *White* signifieth Death: *Milk-white,* Innocency, Purity, Truth, Integrity: *Black,* Wisdom, Sobriety, and Mourning,

K 4

XIX. *Straw.*

XIX. *Straw-colour* fignifieth Plenty : *Ruft of Iron*, Witheredneſs: *Ermine*, Religion and Holineſs.

XX. *The White, Black, Red, and green, are colours held ſacred in the Church of* Rome: *White* is worn in the Feſtivals of Virgins, Saints, Confeſſors and Angels, to ſhow their Innocency: *Red* in the Solemnities of the Apoſtles and Martyrs of Jeſus : *Black* in Lent and other Faſting dayes: *Green* is worn between the *Epiphany* and *Septuageſima* : and between *Pentecoſt* and *Advent.*

CHAP. IV.

Of the fitting of Colours for Painting.

I. **U**PON the Pallet diſpoſe the ſeveral colours , at a convenient diſtance, that they may not intermix : firſt lay on the Vermilion, then the Lake, then the burnt Oker, then the Indian Red, Pink, Umber, Black and Smalt, each in their order, and lay the White next to your thumb, becauſe it is ofteneſt uſed, for with it all ſhadows are to be lightned ; and next the White a ſtiff ſort of Lake; thus is the Pallet furniſhed with ſingle colours for a face.

Now to temper them for ſhadowing various complexions do thus.

II. For a fair complexion.

Take White one drachm, Vermillion, Lake of each two dreachms, temper them, and lay them aſide for the deepeſt Carnation of the face : to part of the aforeſaid mixture put a little more white, for a light Carnation ; and to part of that put more white (which temper on the Pallet) for the lighteſt colour of the face.

III. The

III. The faint shadows for the fair complexion.

Take Smalt, and a little white, for the eyes ; to part of that add a little Pink, and temper by it self for faint greenish shadows in the face.

IV. The deep shadows for the same.

The Sinaper Lake, Pink, and black of each, which temper together ; if the shadows ought to be redder than what is tempered, add more Lake ; if yellower, add more Pink ; if blewer or grayer, add more black: thus shall the Pallet be fitted with colours.

V, For a brown or swarthy complexion.

The single colour being laid on the Pallet as before, and tempered ; to the white, Lake and Vermilion, put a little burnt Oker for a Tawny ; and for heightening add some Yellow Oker, so much as may just change the colours. The faint and deep shadows are the same at the third and fourth *Section of this Chapter.*

VI. For a Tawny complexion.

The colours are the same with the former, but the shadows are different ; which must be made of burnt Oker and Umber, (which will fit well :) if the shadow be not yellow enough, add a little Pink to it.

VII. For a black complexion.

The dark shadows are the same with the former : but for heightening take White, Black, Lake, and burnt Oker ; in tempering of which put in the white by degrees, till you come to the lightest of all. Where note that the single colours at first laid upon the Pallet and tempered, serve for shadows for all complexions ; and that all deepnings ought to be with black, Lake and Pink tempered together.

CHAP.

CHAP. V.

Of Colours for Velvet.

I. FOR *black Velvet.* Take Lamp-black and Verdegriefe for the firſt ground; that being dry,
take Ivory-black, and Verdegriefe, ſhadow it with
White-lead mixt with Lamp-black.

II. *For Green.* Take Lamp-black and White-lead,
and work it like a Ruſſet Velvet, and let it dry; then
draw it over with Verdegriefe tempered with a little
Pink.

III. *For Sea-green.* Take only Verdegriefe and
lay it over Ruſſet: If a *Graſs-green*, put a little Maſticot to it; ſhadow theſe greens with Ruſſet, which
lay according to the deepneſs of the green.

IV. *For Red.* Take Vermilion, and ſhadow it
with Spaniſh-brown; and where you would have it
darkeſt, ſhadow with Seacoal-black and Spaniſh-brown
with the aforeſaid colours, dry it, and then gloſs it
over with Lake.

V. *For Crimſon or Carnation.* Take Vermilion, to
which add White-lead at pleaſure.

VI. *For Blew.* Take Smalt tempered alone.

VII. *For Yellow.* Take Maſticot and yellow Oker,
and where you would have it darkeſt, ſhadow it with
Umber.

VIII. *For Tawny.* Take Spaniſh-brown, White-
lead, and Lamp-black, with a little Verdegriefe, to
ſhadow where need is: when dry, gloſs it over with
Lake and a little Red-lead.

IX. *For hair colour.* Take Umber ground alone;
and

and where it fhould be brighteft, mix fome White-lead about the folds, lighten or darken with White-lead and Umber.

X. *For Afh-colour.* Take Charcoal, black and White-lead; lighten with white-lead: *a colour like to a dark Ruffet will be an Afh colour.*

XI. *For Purple.* Take Smalt and Lake, of each alike, temper them (light or deep as you pleafe) with white-lead.

XII. *Laftly note,* that in Painting Velvet you muft at firft work it fomewhat fad, and then give it a fudden brightnefs.

·CHAP. VI.

Of Colours for Sattins.

I. FOR *Black.* Take Lamp-black ground with Oyl and tempered with white-lead; and where you would have it fhine moft, mix Lake with the white-lead.

II. *For Green.* Take Verdegriefe ground alone and mixed with white-lead; adding Pink where you would have it brighteft: to the deepeft fhadows add more Verdegriefe.

III. *For Yellow.* Take Mafticot, yellow Oker and Umber (ground each by themfelves) where it fhould be brighteft ufe Mafticot alone; where a light fhadow, ufe Oker, where darkeft ufe Umber.

IV. *For Purple.* Take Smalt alone, and where it fhould be brighteft ufe white-lead.

V. *For Red.* Take Spanifh-brown (ground alone) mix it with Vermilion, and where it fhould be bright-eft mix white-lead with the Vermilion.

V I. *For White.* Take White-lead (ground alone)
and Ivory-black, which temper light or dark.

V I I. *For blew.* Temper Smalt and White-lead ;
where it should be saddest, use Smalt ; where lightest ,
White-lead.

V I I I. *For Orange colour.* Take Red-lead and Lakes ;
where brightest, Red lead, where saddest, Lake.

I X. *For Hair colour.* Temper Umber and white-
lead ; where it should be brightest, put more White-
lead, and where the greatest shadow, use Seacoal-black
mixed with Umber.

C H A P. VII.

Of Colours for Taffaty, Cloth and Leather.

I. **T**Affaties are Painted much as Sattins, thus : Take
such colours as are fit for the purpose, and lay
them one by another upon the work, and shadow them
with others.

I I. *Cloth* is the same work with Sattin, save, you
must not give to Cloth so sudden a shining gloss.

I I I. *Cloth of Gold* is made of brown Oker and liquid Gold ; water and heighten upon the same with
small gold stroaks.

I V. *For Buff,* mix yellow Oker and White-lead ;
and where it should be dark by degrees, mix it with a
little Umber ; when you have done, size it over with
Umber and Seacoal-black.

V. *For yellow Leather,* take Masticot and yellow
Oker, shadow it with Umber.

V I. *For black Leather,* take Lamp-black , and shadow it with White-lead.

VII. *For*

VII. *For White Leather*, take White-lead, and shadow it with Ivory-black.

CHAP. VIII.

Of Colours for Garments in general.

I. FOR *Black*. Let the dead colour be Lamp-black and Verdigriefe : being dry, go over with Ivory-black and Verdigriefe; but before the fecond going over, heighten it with white.

II. *For Hair colour*. Take Umber and White for the ground; Umber and black for the deeper fhadows; Umber and Englifh Oker for the meaner fhadows; white and Englifh Oker for heightening.

III. *For Blew*. Take Indico and White: firft lay the White, then the Indico and White mixed; then deepen it with Indico, and when dry, glaze it with Ultramarine which will never fade.

Smalt will turn black, and Bice will turn green.

IV. *For Purple*. Take Smalt tempered with Lake and White-lead; then heighten with White-lead.

V. *For a fad Red*. Take Indian Red heightened with White.

VI. *For a light Red*. Take Vermilion, glaze it over with Lake, and heighten it with White.

VII. *For a Scarlet*. Take Vermilion and deepen it with Lake, or Indian Red.

VIII. *For Green*. Take Bice and Pink, heighten it with Mafticot, and deepen with Indico and Pink.

IX. *For yellow*. Take Mafticot, yellow Oker, Umber; lay Mafticot and white in the lighteft places; Oker and White in the mean places, and Umber in the darkeft, glaze it with Pink. X. *For*

X. *For Orange colour.* Lay the lighteſt parts with Red-lead and white, the mean parts with Red-lead alone; the deeper parts with Lake, and if need is, heighten it with white.

XI. *For a ſad Green.* Mix Indico with Pink: *for a light Green* mix Pink and Maſticot: *for a Graſs-green* mix Verdegriefe and Pink.

XII. Remember always to lay yellows, blews, reds and greens, upon a white ground, for that only giveth them life.

CHAP. IX.

Colours for Metals and precious Stones.

I. FOR *Iron.* Take Lamp-black and White-lead; if you would have it ruſty, take Seacoal-black, and mix it with a little white.

II. *For Silver.* Take Charcoal-black and White-lead; where you would have it darkeſt, uſe more Charcoal: work Silver ſomewhat ruſtiſh, and give it a ſudden gloſs with White-lead only.

III. *For Gold.* Take Lake, Umber, Red-lead, Maſticot; lay the ground with Red-lead, and a little dry Pink: where you would have it darkeſt, ſhadow it moſt with Umber, where lighteſt with Maſticot.

Note, in grinding Red-lead for the Gold ſize, put in a little Verdegriefe to make it dry ſooner.

IV. *For Pearls.* Temper Charcoal-black with white-lead, till it be a perfeſt ruſſet; then make the Pearl with it, and give it a ſpeck of White-lead only to make it ſhine.

Where note, that Ceruſe tempered with Oyl of white Poppy is excellent to heighten up Pearls. V. For

V. *For precious Stones.* For Rubies, *&c.* lay their counterfeit grounds with tranſparent colours ; and Lake , Verdegrieſe and Verditer give them a ſhining colour.

C H A P. X.

Of Colours for Landskip.

I. FOR *a light Green* , uſe Pink and Maſticot heightned with white : *for a ſad Green,* Indico and Pink heightned with Maſticot.

II. *For ſome Trees,* take Lake, Umber and White, *for others* Charcoal and white, *for others* Umber, black and white, with ſome green ; adding ſometimes Lake or Vermilion, with other colours.

III. *For Wood,* take Lake, Umber and white, mixing ſometimes a little green withal.

IV. *For Fire,* lay Red-lead and Vermilion tempered together where it is reddeſt : where it is blew, lay oyl, Smalt, and white-lead : where it is yellow, take Maſticot, and work it over in certain places ; where you would have it ſhine moſt, with Vermilion.

V. *For an Azure Skie,* which ſeems a far off, take Oyl, Smalt, or Bice, and temper them with Linſeed-oyl. *But grind them not : for Smalt or Bice utterly loſe their colour in grinding.*

VI. *For a Red Skie,* take Lake and white ; and for Sun-beams, or yellow clouds at Sun-riſing or ſetting, take Maſticot and white.

VII. *For a Night Skie,* or clouds in a ſtorm, take Indico deepned with black, and heightned with white.

VIII. *For Wood colours,* they are compounded either

of

of Umber and white , Charcoal and white, Seacoal and white, Umber black and white ; or with fome green added : to which you may adjoin fometimes , as in barks of Trees, a little Lake or Vermilion.

IX. *Laftly for the practical performing of the work* have recourfe to the rules delivered in *chap.* 13. *lib.* 1. and *chap.* 27. *lib.* 2.

C H A P. XI.

Of the Painting of the Face.

I. **H**Ave your neceſſary pencils in readineſs, as two pencils ducks quill fitched ; and two ducks quill pointed ; two Goofe quill fitched , and two pointed : two briftles both alike ; one Swans quill fitched, and one pointed ; one larger pencil in a Tin cafe fitched ; and a briftle of the fame Bigneſs, every one having a ſtick of a bout nine inches long put into the quill thereof, the farther end of which ſtick muſt be cut to a point.

I I. The *pencils* in a readineſs in your left hand , with the *pallet* upon your thumb, prepared with fit co-lours, and your *molftick* to reſt upon ; you muſt work according to the directions following.

I I I. The *cloth* being pinned, and ſtrained upon the Frame, take a knife, and with the edge thereof ſcrape over the cloth, left knots or the like ſhould trouble it.

I V. Then fet the *Frame* and *cloth* upon the *Eafel,* at a convenient heighth , that fitting on a ſtool (even with the party you draw) you may have the face of the Picture equal , or fomething higher than your
own :

own : fet the Eafel to the light (as in Limning we have taught) letting it come in upon your left hand, cafting the light towards the right.

V. Let the Perfon to be drawn, fit before you in the pofture he intends to be painted in, about two yards diftant from you.

VI. Then with a piece of painted chalk draw the proportion of the face upon the cloth, with the place of the eyes, nofe, mouth, ears, hair, and other poftures.

Here is no difficulty in this, if you mifs much, the colours will bring all to rights again.

VII. Then take a pencil Swans quill pointed, and begin to paint fome of the lighteft parts of the face with the lighteft colour, (as the heightning of the fore-head, nofe, cheek-bone of the lighteft fide :) the mean parts next (as the cheek-bone of the dark-fide, chin, and over the upper lip :) proceeding gradually till you come to the reddeft parts of all.

VIII. Lay faint greenifh fhadows in convenient places, and where it is neceffary to foften harfher fhadows, but take heed of putting green where red fhould be.

IX. The faint or light parts thus done, take one of the Goofe quill pointed, or Ducks quill fitched, and begin at the eyes to fhadow with Lake, going over the nofe, mouth, compafs of the ear, &c. before you lay on any colour, wiping it lightly over with a linnen rag, to prevent the overcoming of the other colours.

X. The colours both light and dark being put in, take a great fitch pencil, and fweeten the colours therewith, by going over the fhadows with a clean foft pencil, which being well handled will drive and intermix the colours one into another, that they will look as if they were all laid on at once, and not at divers times.

L   *Where*

Where note, that the bigger pencils you use, the sweeter and better your work will lie.

XI. *At the second sitting,* begin again with clean pencils, of such bigness as the work requires, and observe well the person, and see what defects you find in your work at first sitting, and amend them; then heighten or deepen the shadows as occasion requires.

XII. *Lastly,* take a Goose quill bristle, and put in the hair about the face (if there must be any) and rub in the greater hair, with the greater bristle, heightning it up with the Goose quill pencil.

C H A P. XII.

Of the cleansing of any old Painting.

I. TAke good wood ashes, and searce them, or else some Smalt or powder-blew, and with a Spunge and fair water gently wash the Picture you would cleanse (taking great care of the shadows) which done, dry it very well with a clean cloth.

II. Then varnish it over again with some good varnish, but such as may be washed off again with water if need be.

We shall hereafter shew the way of making varnish of several sorts, mean season this following may serve.

III. Take either common varnish (made with Gum sandrack dissolved in Linseed-oyl by boiling) or glair of Eggs, and with your pencil go over the Picture once, twice, or more therewith as need requires.

CHAP. XIII.

Of a Picture in general.

I. IN every Picture there are always four principal confiderations: to wit, 1. *Invention.* 2. *Proportion.* 3. *Colour.* and 4. *Life.*

I I. *Invention* muft be free, and flow from a general knowledge of Antiquities, Hiftory, Poetical Fictions, Geometrical conclufions, and Optical confiderations, according to its Situation or Afpect, either near or far off.

I I I. And this *Invention* muft exprefs proper and fit things, agreeing to the Circumftances of *Time, Place, Matter,* and *Perfon*; and having refpect to the modes of habits belonging to the Country or People whether *Antient* or *Modern.*

I V. *Proportion, Analogy,* or *Symmetry* (which you pleafe) is that wich limits each part to its proper bignefs, in refpect to the whole.

Whatfoever differs from this recedes from beauty, and may be called Deformity.

V. This *Proportion* is called by Artifts the defigning lines; which are firft drawn before the whole is painted.

Thefe proportions or lineal defigns, draughts, and fcotches, may be called Picture, which being well done, fhew not only the fhape, but alfo the intent: In lines only, we may draw the proportion of a Black-Moor, and fuch as fhall be like him: Now this skill proceeds from the very higheft principles of Art.

I V. *Colour* is that which makes the Picture refem-

ble

ble what we defire to imitate; by mixing of various colours together.

VII. In making any thing apparent, it is neceffary to exprefs its oppofite or contrary.

So light and fhadows forward, fet forth Paintings out-wards, as if you might take hold of them with your hand : blacknefs makes things feem farther off, and is ufed in things hollow, as Caves, Wells, &c. the more deep the more black.

VIII. Brightnefs exceeds light fparkling in fplendor.

It is ufed in the Glory of Angels; twinkling of Gems, Armory, Gold and Silver veffels, fires and flames.

IX. In Painting of a man, grace each limb with its proper and lively colour; the black make fincerely black; the white pure, with rednefs intermixt. But to paint purely the exquifite beauty of a woman, is never to be well done (except it be by a very ingenious Artift indeed) her rare complexion being fcarcely poffible to be imitated with colours: *There is none really knows the exact mixture for fuch a Countenance.*

X. Life or Motion is that from whence action or paffion doth refult, which in coloured Pictures is feen with a lively force of Gefture and fpirit.

To do this it is neceffary that the Artift be well acquainted with the nature, manners, and behaviour of men and women, as in anger, fadnefs, joy, earneftnefs, idlenefs, love, envy, fear, hope, defpair, &c. Every difturbance of the mind alters the Countenance into feveral poftures.

XI. The head caft down fhews humility; caft back, arrogancy or fcorn; hanging on the neck, languifhing; ftiff and fturdy, morofity of mind : the various poftures of the head fhew the paffions; the Countenance the fame; the eyes the like : and in a word, all the other parts of the body contribute fomething to the ex.

expreſſion of the ſaid paſſions of the mind, as is eaſily to be obſerved in the life.

In excellent pieces you may at a view read the mind of the Artiſt in the formality of the Story.

XII. Laſtly, Be alway ſure firſt to conceive that in your thoughts , which you would expreſs in your work ; that your endeavours being aſſiſted by an intellectual energy, or power of operation, may at length render your productions perfect.

CHAP. XIV.

Of the Choice of Copies, or Patterns.

I. HE that chuſeth a Pattern, ought to ſee 1. that it be well deſigned : 2. that it be well coloured.

II. In the well deſigning, be ſure that it be true in every part ; and that the proportion of the figure be juſt and correſpond to the life.

III. If the Picture be a fiction, ſee that it be done boldly, not only to exceed the work (but alſo the poſſibility) of nature, as in *Centaurs, Satyrs, Syrens, Flying-horſes , Sea-horſes, Tritons, Nereides,* &c.

Alexander ab Alexandria *ſaith that* Theodore Gaza *caught one of theſe* Nereides *in* Greece, *and that in* Zealand, *another was taught to ſpin* : *theſe* Tritons and Nereides *are thoſe which are called Mare-maids,* *the Male and the Female.*

IV. Natural figures ſhew property , and are required to agree with the life : forced figures expreſs novelty, and are to be beautified by exorbitancies according to the fancy of the Painter without limitation :

L 3　　　　　　　　novelty

novelty caufes admiration, and admiration curiofity, a kind of delight and fatisfaction to the mind.

Thefe things are not the products of ftupid brains, nor are they contained within the perimetre of clouded and dull Conceptions.

V. In the well colouring, know that in obfcurity or darknefs there is a kind of deepnefs; the fight being fweetly deceived *gradatim* in breaking the Colours, by infenfible change from the more high to the more dull.

In the Rain-bow this mixture is perfect; the variety of Colours are throughly difpers'd (like Atoms in the Sun-beams) among one another, to create its juft appearance.

V I. See that the fwellings of the work agree with the exactnefs of nature, and as the parts thereof require, without fharpnefs in out-lines, or flatnefs within the body of the piece; as alfo that each hollownefs exactly correfpond in due proportions.

V I I. Laftly, View precifely the paffions, as *Joy, Sorrow, Love, Hatred, Fear, Hope,* &c. and fee that they correfpond with their proper poftures; for a touch of the pencil may ftrangely alter a paffion to its juft oppofite or contrary, as from Mirth to Mourning, &c.

C H A P.

CHAP. XV.

Of the Diſpoſing of Pictures and Paintings.

I. **A**Ntique works, or *Grotesco*, may become a wall, the borders and freezes of other works; but if there be any draughts in figures of men and women to the life upon the wall, they will be beſt of black and white, or of one colour heightened: if they be naked, let them be as large as the place will afford; if of Marbles, Columns, Aquæducts, Arches, Ruines, Cataracts, let them be bold, high, and of large proportion.

II. Let the beſt pieces be placed to be ſeen with ſingle lights, for ſo the ſhadows fall natural, being always fitted to anſwer one light; and the more under or below the light the better, eſpecially in mens faces and large pieces.

III. Let the *Porch* or entrance into the houſe, be ſet out with *Ruſtick* figures, and things rural.

IV. Let the *Hall* be adorned with Shepherds, Peaſants, Milk-maids, Neat-heards, Flocks of Sheep and the like, in their reſpective places and proper attendants; as alſo Fowls, Fiſh, and the like.

V. Let the *Stair-caſe* be ſet off with ſome admirable monument or building, either new or ruinous, to be ſeen and obſerved at a view paſſing up: and let the *Ceiling* over the top-ſtair be put with figures foreſhortened looking downwards out of Clouds, with Garlands and Cornucopia's.

VI. Let *Landſkips*, Hunting, Fiſhing, Fowling, Hiſtories and Antiquities be put in the Great *Chamber*.

VII. In

VII. In the *Dining-room* let be placed the Pictures of the King and Queen; or their Coat of Arms ; forbearing to put any other Pictures of the life, as not being worthy to be their Companions ; unlefs at the lower end, two or three of the chief Nobility, as attendants of their Royal Perfons : for want hereof you may put in place, fome few of the neareft blood.

VIII. In the *inward or with-drawing Chambers,* put other draughts of the life, of Perfons of Honour, intimate or fpecial friends, and acquaintance, or of Artifts only.

IX. In *Banqueting-rooms*, put cheerful and merry Paintings, as of *Bacchus*, *Centaures*, *Satyrs*, *Syrens*, and the like, but forbearing all obfcene Pictures.

X. Hiftories, grave Stories, and the beft works become *Galleries*; where any one may walk, and exercife their fenfes, in viewing, examining, delighting, judging and cenfuring.

XI. In *Summer-houfes* and *Stone-walks*, put Caftles, Churches or fome fair building: In *Tarraces*, put Bofcage, and wild works. Upon *Chimney-pieces*, put only Landskips, for they chiefly adorn.

XII. And in the *Bed-chamber*, put your own, your Wives and Childrens Pictures; as only becoming the moft private Room, and your Modefty : left (if your Wife be a beauty) fome wanton and libidinous gueft fhould gaze too long on them, and commend the work for her fake.

XIII. In hanging of your pictures; if they hang high above reach, let them bend fomewhat forward at the top ; becaufe otherwife it is obferved that the vifual beams of the Eye, extending to the top of the Picture, appear further off, than thofe at the foot.

CHAP.

C H A P. XVI.

Of Frefcoe, or Painting of Walls.

I. IN Painting upon Walls, to make it endure the weather, you muſt grind your colours with Lime water, Milk, or Whey, mixt in ſize colour in pots.

II. The paſte or plaiſter muſt be made of well waſh'd Lime, mixt with fine powder of old rubbiſh ſtones : the Lime muſt be ſo often waſh'd, till all its ſalt is abſtracted ; and all your work muſt be done in clear and dry weather.

III. To make the work endure, ſtrike into the wall ſtumps of headed nails, about five or ſix inches aſunder, and by this means you may preſerve the plaiſter from peeling.

IV. Then with this paſte, plaiſter the wall, a pretty thickneſs, letting it dry : being dry, plaiſter it over again about the thickneſs of half a Barley corn , very fine and ſmooth, then your colours being ready prepared work this laſt plaiſtering over, whileſt it is wet, ſo will your Painting unite and joyn faſt to the plaiſter, and dry together as a perfect compoſt.

V. In Painting be nimble and free, let your work be bold and ſtrong, but be ſure to be exact, for there can be no alteration after the firſt painting ; and therefore heighten your paint enough at firſt, you may deepen at pleaſure.

VI. All earthy colours are beſt, as the Okers, Spaniſh-white, Spaniſh-brown, Terræ-vert, and the like, mineral colours are naught.

VII. Laſtly, let your pencils and bruſhes be long and ſoft, otherwiſe your work will not be ſmooth ; let
your

your colours be full, and flow freely from the pencil or brush; and let your design be perfect at first, for in this, there is no after alteration to be made.

C H A P. XVII.

Of Colours for Painting Glass.

I. *YEllow.* Take a very thin piece of pure fine Silver, and dip it into melted Brimstone; take it out with a pair of plyers, and light it in the fire, holding it till it leaves burning; then beat it to powder in a brasen mortar; then grind it with Gum-Arabick water, and a little yellow Oker.

II. *Yellow.* Take fine Silver one Drachm, Antimony in powder two Drachms, put them in a hot fire, in a Crucible for half an hour, and then cast it into a Brass mortar, and beat it into powder, to which add yellow Oker six Drchams, old earth of rusty Iron seven Drachms, grind all well together.

This is fairer than the former.

III. *White.* This is the colour of the glass it self: you may diaper upon it with other glass or Crystal ground to powder.

IV. *Black.* Take Jet and Scales of Iron, and with a wet feather take up the Scales that fly from the Iron, after the Smith hath taken his heat, grind them with Gum-water.

V. *Black.* Take Iron scales, Copper scales, of each one Drachm, heat them red hot in a clean fire shovel; then take Jet half a Drachm, first grind them small and temper them with Gum-water.

VI. *Red.*

VI. *Red.* Take *Sanguis Draconis* in powder, put to it rectified ſpirit of Wine ; cover it cloſe a little while, and it will grow tender ; wring it out into a pot, that the droſs may remain in the cloth ; the clear preſerve for uſe. This is a fair red.

VII. *Carnation.* Take Tin-Glaſs one ounce, Jet three ounces, Red.oker five ounces, gum two drachms, grind them together. It is a fair Carnation.

VIII. *Carnation.* Take Jet four drachms, Tin-glaſs or Litharge of Silver two drachms ; gum and ſcales of Iron of each one drachm, red chalk one ounce, grind them.

IX. *Green.* Take Verdegrieſe and grind it well with Turpentine, and put it into a pot ; warming it at the fire when you uſe it.

X. *Blew.* Provide the cleareſt leads you can get of that colour, beat them to powder in a brazen mortar ; take Goldſmiths Amel of the ſame colour, clear and tranſparent, grind each by it ſelf, take two parts of Lead, and one of Amel, grind them together as you did the Silver. *The ſame underſtand of Red and Green.*

CHAP. XVIII.

Of the way of Painting upon Glaſs.

I. **T**Here are two manner of ways of painting upon glaſs ; the one is for oyl colour, the other for ſuch colours as are afterwards to be annealed or burnt on.

II. To lay oyl colours upon glaſs, you muſt firſt grind them with gum-water once, and afterwards temper it with Spaniſh Turpentine, lay it on and let it dry by the fire, and it is finiſhed.   III. To

III. To anneal or burn your glafs, to make the colours abide, you muſt make a four ſquare brick Furnace, eighteen inches broad and deep ; lay five or ſix croſs Iron bars on the top of it, and raiſe the Furnace eighteen inches above the bars : then laying a plate of Iron over the bars, ſift (through a ſieve) a lay of ſlack'd Lime over the plate, upon which lay a row of glafs, upon that a bed of Lime, and upon that Lime, another row of glafs ; thus continue *ſtratum ſuper ſtratum,* till the Furnace is full.

IV. Lay alſo with every bed of glafs a piece of glafs, which you may wipe over with any colour (theſe are called watches) and when you think your glafs is burnt enough, with a pair of plyers take out the firſt and loweſt watch, and lay it on a board, and being cold, try if you can ſcrape off the colour, if it hold faſt on, take out that row ; always letting it abide the fire, till the colour will not ſcrape off.

CHAP. XIX.

Of waſhing, and the Materials thereof.

I. BY waſhing here we intend nothing elſe ; but either to ſet out Maps or Printed Pictures in proper Colours, or elſe to varniſh them.

II. The Inſtruments and materials of waſhing are chiefly ſix : to wit, 1. *Alom-water.* 2. *Size.* 3. *Liquid Gold.* 4. *Pencils.* 5. *Colours.* 6. *Varniſh.*

III. *To make Alom-water.* Take Alom eight ounces, fair water a quart, boil them till the Alom is diſſolved.

IV. *To make Size.* Take glew, which ſteep all night
in

in water, then melt it over the fire, to see that it be neither too strong nor too weak : then let a little of it cool ; if it be too stiff when it is cold, put more water to it, if too weak more glew, using it luke-warm.

V. *Liquid Gold,* It is exactly made by the first Section of the 21 Chapter of the second Book.

V I. *Pencils* are to be of all sorts both fitch'd and pointed, as also a large pencil brush to paste Maps upon Cloth ; another to wet the paper with Alom water ; a third to starch the face of the picture withal before it be coloured : and a fourth to varnish withal.

V I I. The colours are the same with those which we mentioned in *Chap.* 17. *lib.* 2. to which add, 1. *Of Black,* Printers black, *Frankford* black. 2. *Of Red,* Vermilion, Rosset. 3. *Of Blew*, Verditure, Litmos Flory. 4. *Of Yellow,* Cambogia, Yellow-berries, Orpiment. 5. Brazil, Logwood (ground) and Turnsole, Cochenele, Madder.

C H A P. XX.

Of Colours simple for Washing.

I. **P**Rinters black, Vermilion, Rosset, Verditure and Orpiment are to be ground, as we have taught at the fifth Section of the 22 Chapter of the second Book.

I I. *Brazil.* To some ground Brazil put small Beer and Vinegar, of each a sufficient quantity, let it boil gently a good while, then put therein Alom in powder to heighten the colour, and some Gum-Arabick to bind it ; boil it till it taste strong on the tongue, and make a good red.

I I I. *Logwood.* Ground Logwood boiled as Brazil,

makes

makes a very fair tranfparent Purple Colour.

I V. *Cochenele.* Steeped as Brazil was boiled, makes a fair tranfparent purple : as thus, take Cochenele and put it into the ftrongeft Sope-lees to fteep, and it will be a fair purple, which you may lighten or deepen at pleafure.

V. *Madder.* Take Madder four drachms, ground Brazil one ounce, Rain-water a quart ; boil away a third part ; then add Alom half an ounce, boil it to a pint ; then Gum-Arabick one ounce, which boil till it is diffolved, cool it ftirring it often, and ftrain it for ufe. It is a good Scarlet die for Leather.

V I. *Verdegriefe.* Take Verdegriefe ground finely one ounce, put to it a good quantity of common varnifh, and fo much oyl of Turpentine, as will make it thin enough to work withal ; it is a good green. And Verdegriefe, Alom, of each one drachm, Logwood three drachms, boiled in Vinegar, make a good Murry.

V II. *Gambogia.* Diffolve it in fair fpring water, and it will make a beautiful and tranfparent yellow : if you would have it ftronger, diffolve fome Alom therein: it is good for Silk, Linnen, white Leather, Parchment, Vellom, Paper, Quills, &c.

V III. *To make Verdegriefe and Ceruse, according to* Glauber.

Thefe colours are made with Vinegar in earthen pots fet into hot horfe dung : but if you diffolve your Venus or Saturn with fpirit of Nitre, and precipitate your Venus with a lye made of Salt of Tartar, and your Saturn with Salt water, edulcorating and drying them ; the Venus will yield an excellent Verdegriefe, which will not corrode other colours as the common Verdegriefe doth ; and the Saturn yields a Ceruse whiter and purer than the ordinary much better for Painting or Chirurgery.

IX. *Yel-*

IX. *Yellow Fuftick-berry.* Boil it in water or fteep them in Alom water, it makes a good yellow for the fame purpofe.

X. *Turnfole.* Put it into fharp Vinegar over a gentle fire till the Vinegar boil, and is coloured; then take out the Turnfole and fqueeze it into the Vinegar, in which diffolve a little Gum-Arabick ; it fhadows very well on a Carnation or yellow.

XI. *Litmos.* Cut it into fmall pieces, and fteep it a day or two in weak Gum-Lake water, and you will have a pure blew water to wafh with.

XII. *Flory Blew.* Grind it with glair of Eggs, if then you add a little Roffet it makes a light Violet blew; mixed with White and Red-lead, it makes a Crane-feather colour.

XIII. *Saffron.* Steeped in Vinegar and mixed with gum-water is a good yellow.

CHAP. XXI.

Of Compounded Colours for Wafhing.

I. ORange Colour. Red-lead and Yellow berries make a good Orange colour: or thus, take Arnotto half an ounce , Pot-afhes one Drachm, water one pound, boil it half away, then ftrain it, and ufe it hot.

It is good for White Leather, Paper, Vellom, Quills, Parchment, &c.

II. *Green.* Take diftilled vinegar, filings of Copper, digeft till the vinegar is blew, which let ftand in the Sun or a flow fire till it is thick enough, and it will be a good green.

Or

Or thus, *Take Cedar-green (which is best of all) or instead thereof green Bice, steep it in Vinegar, and strain it; then grind it well with fair water , and put to it a little honey, and dry it well; when you use it, mix it with gum-water.*

III. *To make fine Indico.*

Take the blossoms of Wode three ounces, Amylum one ounce, grind them with Urine and strong Vinegar, of which make a Cake, then dry it in the Sun and so keep it for use.

IV. *A Blew to wash upon paper.*

Take of the best Azure an ounce, Kermes two ounces, mix them, which temper with clear gum-water, and it will be a glorious colour.

V. *To make a Venice Blew.*

Take quick Lime, make it into past with strong Vinegar, half an hour after put thereto more Vinegar to soften it; then add Indico in fine powder one ounce, mix them and digest it in horse-dung for thirty or forty days.

VI. *Another excellent Blew.*

Mix fine white Chalk with juyce of Elder-berries full ripe, to which put a little Alom-water.

VII. *To make blew Smalt.*

Take fluxible sand, Sal-Nitre and Cobalt , mix them together.

VIII. *A lively Yellow.*

Dissolve Orpiment in gum-water, to which put a little ground Vermilion ; grind them together and you shall have a very lively colour.

IX. *A light Green.* Take juyce of Rew, Verdegriese, and Saffron, grind them well together and use them with gum-water.

Or thus, *Take Sap-green, Flower-deluce, or Tawny green , which steep in water: Verditure and Ceruse mixt*
with

with a little Copper green , make a good light colour.

X. *Blew* Ultramarine, blew Bice, Smalt, and Verditure, ground singly with gum-water, or together, make a good blew.

XI. *Brown.* Ceruse, Red-lead, English Oker, and Pink, make a good brown.

XII. *Spanish-brown.* To colour any horse, dog, or the like, you must not calcine it; (yet not calcined it is a dirty colour:) but to shadow Vermilion, or lay upon any dark ground, behind a picture, to shade berries in the darkest places, or to colour wooden posts, wainscot, bodies of Trees and the like, it is very good (being burnt.)

XIII. *Flesh Colour.* Mix white, Indian Lake, and Red-lead (according as you would have it light or deep,) and to distinguish a mans flesh from a womans, mingle with it a little Oker.

XIV. *Colours of Stones.* Verdegriese with Varnish makes an Emerald : with *Florence* Lake a Ruby: with Ultramarine a Saphire.

XV. *A never fading Green.*

Take juice of flowers of Flower-de-luce, put it into Gum-water and dry it in the Sun.

CHAP. XXII.

Of mixing Colours and Shadowing.

I. IN mixing be careful not to make the colour too sad, nor take the pencils out of one colour and put them into another.

II. In mixing colours, stir them well about the water severally till they are well mixed; then put them together, making the colour sadder or lighter at pleasure.   M   III. *Green*

III. *Green* is shadowed with Indico and yellow-berries.

IV. *Blew* is shadowed with Indico, Litmose and Flory; or any of them being steeped in Lees of Sope-ashes, and used with gum-water.

V. *Garments* are shadowed with their own proper colours: or you may mingle the colour with white (for the light) and shadow it with the same colour unmingled: or you may take the thinnest of the co-lour for the light, aud shadow with the thickest or bottom of the same.

VI. *Sap-green* is only used to shadow other greens with, and not to be laid for a ground in any Garment.

VII. *Lake* ought not to be shaded with any colour, for it is a dark red; but for variety you may shadow it with Bice, or blew Verditure, which will make it like changeable Taffata.

VIII. The shadow for *Yellow-berries* is Umber; but for beauties sake with Red-lead, and the darkest touches with Spanish-brown; and for variety with Copper green, blew Bice or Verditure.

IX. *White* sets off *blews* and *blacks* very well: *Red* sets off well with *yellow*: *Yellows* with *reds*, sad *blews*, *browns*, *greens*, and *purples*.

X. *Blews* set off well with *yellows*, *reds*, *whites*, *browns*, and *blacks*: and *Green* sets off well with *purples*, and *reds*.

C H A P.

C H A P. XXIII.

Of Colours for Landskips.

I. GReen mixed with white, Pink, Bice, Masticot, Smalt, Indico, or Cerufe ; or blew Verditure mixt with a few yellow-berries makes a good green for Landskips.

II. For the *faddeft hills* ufe Umber burnt; for the *lighteft places*, put yellow to the burnt Umber : for *other hills* lay Copper green thickened on the fire, or in the Sun : for the next *hills farther off* mix yellow-berries with Copper green: let the fourth part be done with green Verditure ; and the *furtheft and fainteft places* with blew Bice, or blew Verditure mingled with white, and fhadowed with blew Verditure, in the fhadows indifferent thick.

III. Let the *high-ways* be done with red and white Lead, and for variety Yellow-oker ; fhadow it with burnt Umber, which you may ufe for fandy Rocks and Hills.

IV. *Rocks* may be done with feveral colours ; in fome places black and white, in other places red and white, and in others blew and white, and the like, as you fee convenient.

V. *The water* muft be black Verditure and white, fhadowed with green and blew Verditure, when the *banks* caft a green fhadow upon the water ; and the water is dark fhadowed, then fhade it with Indico, green thickned, and blew Verditure.

VI. Colour *buildings* with as much variety of pleafant colours ; as may be imaginable, yet let reafon be your rule in mixing your colours : you may fometimes

M 2 . ufe

ufe white and black for the *wall, conduits* or other things: for *Brick-houfes* and the like, Red-lead and white : if *many houfes* ftand together, fet them off with variety of colours, as Umber and white; Lake and white; Red-lead and white, and the like.

VII. Laftly, *for the Skie,* ufe Mafticot or yellow-berries, and white for the *loweft and lighteft places*; red Roffet and white for the *next degree*; blew Bice and white for *the other*; blew Bice, or blew Verditure for *the higheft.*

Thefe degrees and colours muft be fo wrought together, that the edge of each colour may not receive any fharpnefs; that is, fo as that you cannot perceive where you began to lay them, being fo drowned one in another.

C H A P. XXIʲV.
Of the Practice of Wafhing.

I. With the *Alom-water* wet over the pictures to be coloured, for that keeps the colours from finking into the paper, and will add a luftre unto them, make them fhew fairer, and keep them from fading.

II. Then let the paper dry of it felf (being wafhed with *Alom-water*) before you lay on the colours ; or before you wet it again, for fome paper will need wetting four or five times.

III. The wafhing of the paper with the *Alom-water* muft be done with a large pencil brufh, fuch as we have advifed to at the fixth Section of the nineteenth Chapter of this Book.

IV. But if you intend to varnifh your pictures after you have coloured them; inftead of wafhing them with *Alom-water*, firft fize them with new fize made of good white ftarch, with a very fine brufh; and this
you

you muſt be ſure to do all over, for elſe the varniſh will ſink through.

V. Having thus prepared your work go to laying on your colours according to the former directions, ſuiting them, as near as may be, to the life of every thing.

V I. The Picture being painted, you may with ſize (as at the fourth Section of the nineteenth Chapter of this Book) paſte your Maps or pictures upon cloth, thus : wet the ſheet of cloth therein, wring it out, and ſtrain it upon a Frame, or nail it upon a wall or board, and ſo paſte your Maps or pictures thereon.

V I-I. Laſtly, if the Picture be to be varniſhed, having thus fixed it into its proper Frame, then varniſh it with a proper varniſh (by the following rules) and the work will be fully finiſhed.

C H A P. XXV.

Of the making of Varniſhes.

I. **V**Arniſh for painting in Oyl.

Take Maſtich two ounces, oyl of Turpentine one ounce ; put the Maſtich in powder into the oyl , and melt it over the fire, letting it boil little or nothing (leſt it be clammy;) when it is enough, you may know by putting in a hens feather, for then it will burn it.

I I. *Varniſh for painted Pictures.*

Take white Rozine one pound, Plum-tree gum (or Gum-Arabick) Venice Turpentine, Linſeed-oyl, of each two ounces; firſt melt the Rozin and ſtrain it very hot ; ſteep the Gum in oyl Olive (oyl ben is better) till it is diſſolved, and ſtrain it, to which put the Trupentine and Rozin, and over a ſlow fire mingle them till

they

they are well diſſolved. When you uſe it, uſe it hot.

III. *Another for the ſame.*

Take Olibanum and gum-Sandrack in powder, which mingle with Venice Turpentine, melting and incorporating them ſtill over a gentle fire, then ſtrain it hot.

When you uſe it let it be hot, and your Varniſh will ſhine well; it dries immediately.

IV. *Another for the ſame.*

Take oyl of Linſeed, which diſtill in a glaſs Retort, one ounce, fair Amber diſſolved three ounces, mix them over a ſlow Fire, and it is done.

V. *A very good Varniſh for Gold, Silver, Braſs, Iron, Stone, Wood, Vellom, or Paper.*

Take Benjamin (made into fine powder between two papers) put it into a vial, and cover it with Spirit of Wine four fingers above it, and let it ſtand three or four days; then ſtrain it, and it will be bright and ſhining, drying immediately, and retaining its brightneſs many years.

If you Varniſh Gold, or any thing gilded, before the ſtraining you ſhould put in a few blades of Saffron for colour ſake: but if Silver or any thing white, you ought to uſe the white part of the Benjamin only.

VI. *A Varniſh particularly for Gold, Silver, Tin, or Copper.*

Take Linſeed oyl ſix ounces, Maſtick, Aloes Epatick of each one ounce; put the gums in powder into the oyl, into a glazed earthen pot, which cover with another, luting them together, in the bottom of which I be a hole, whereinto put a ſmall ſtick with a broad end to ſtir withal; cover them all over with clay, (except the hole,) ſet it over the fire, and ſtir it as often as the oyl begins to boyl a little while, then ſtrain it for uſe. And when you would uſe it, then brush it over with

VII. *A*

VII. *A Varnish for Wood and Leather.*

Take Tincture of Saffron or Turmerick in Spirit of Wine a pint, prepared Gum-lake a sufficient quantity, dissolve the gum in the Tincture, and it is done.

This is a Varnish of great use to lay over Gold, and Silver or any thing which is exposed to the Air.

VIII. *To make the common Varnish.*

Take spirit of Wine a quart, Rozin one ounce, Gum-lake a sufficient quantity, dissolve the gums in a gentle heat (being close covered) and let them settle: then gently decant off the clear, which keep in a close Glass-bottle for use.

The thick which remains, you may strain through a cloth, and keep for other purposes.

IX. *To make a red Varnish.*

Take spirit of Wine a quart, Gum-lake four ounces, *Sanguis Draconis* in fine powder eight ounces, Cochenele one ounce, digest a week over a gentle heat, then strain it for use.

X. *To make a yellow Varnish.*

Take spirit of Wine a pint, in which infuse (three or four days) Saffron half an ounce, then strain it, and add Aloes Succotrina one ounce, *Sanguis Draconis* two ounces, which digest a week over a gentle heat close covered, then strain it for use.

XI. *An Universal Varnish, the best of all others.*

Take good Gum-Sandrack (but Gum-Anime is better) dissolve it in the highest rectified spirit of Wine (an ounce and half more or less to a pint) and it is done.

Where note, 1. That unless the Spirits be highly rectified the Varnish cannot be good. 2. That some put into it Linseed oyl (which is naught; oyl of ben is better) and mix them together. 3. Some mix boiled Turpentine with it; others Chymical oyls of deep colours (as of Cloves, Mace, Nutmegs,

*megs, Caraways, Cinnamon) according to the intent. 4.
That it ought to be kept in a glafs bottle clofe ſtopped, leſt
it curdle, and the Gums ſeparate.*

XII. *The Indian Varniſh for Cabinets, Coaches, and
ſuch like.*

Take the higheſt rectified ſpirit of Wine a quart,
ſeed Lake or ſhell Lake five ounces, put them into a
glaſs body; and diſſolve the Lake in Balneo (but beware leſt the water in the Balneum boil, for that will
turn the Varniſh white) this done ſtrain the matter
through a Flannel bag, and keep it in a glaſs bottle
cloſe ſtopt for uſe.

Where note, 1. *That if the ſpirit is good, it will (if you
put Gun-powder into it) burn all away and fire the
Gun-powder.* 2. *That this Varniſh done over leaf Silver,
turns the Silver of a Gold colour.* 3. *That this is that
Varniſh which Coach-makers and others uſe for that purpoſe.*
4. *That it preſerves the Silver which it is laid upon from the
injuries of the Air.* 5. *That being laid upon any colour it
makes it look infinitely the more beautiful.* 6. *That if it lies
rough you may poliſh it with the impalpable powder of Emery
and water.*

CHAP. XXVI.

Of the manner of Varniſhing.

I. THE intent of Varniſhing is either to preſerve
the gloſs of paintings or pictures, or elſe to
repreſent and imitate the forms of ſhining and perlucid bodies.

II. To Varniſh paintings and pictures, 'tis no more
but with a pencil dipt in the varniſh to go over the
ſame,

fame, then letting it dry; and fo going over it fo often as in reafon you fhall fee convenient.

III. If you are to imitate anything, as Marble,
Tortoife-fhell, Amber, *Lapis Lazuli* or the like; you
muft firft make the imitation of them, upon that which
you would varnifh, with their proper colours, as in
Limning or Painting with oyl; which muft be throughly dry: then by the fecond Section go over all with
the varnifh, fo often till you fee it thick enough;
letting it dry every time leifurely. *For example fake.*

IV. *To imitate Marble.*

Take of the Univerfal varnifh at the eleventh
Section of the five and twentieth Chapter, with
which mingle Lamp-black (or other black) and
White-lead finely beaten, and with a brufh pencil,
Marble the thing you would varnifh according to your
fancy; laftly, being dry ftrike it again two or three
times over with clear varnifh alone, and it will be
perfect.

V. *To imitate Tortoife-fhell.*

Firft lay a white ground, then with convenient
colours (as Vermilion with Auripigment) duly mixt
with common varnifh, ftreak and fhadow the white
ground with any wild fancy (as nearly imitating Tortoife-fhell as you can) which being dry, ftrike it here
and there with the red varnifh (mixed with a little
Sinaper or Indian Lake) then up and down the work
as nature requires touch it with varnifh mixed with
any good black; then ftroke it over with Univerfal *varnifh* four or five times, letting it dry every times; laftly,
let it dry well a week, and with Pumice ftone (in fine
powder) and a wet cloth polifh it by rubbing; then go
over it again three or four times with the Univerfal
varnifh, and (if need require) polifh it again with
fine putty as before; after which you may once again
ftrike

ftrike it over with the faid Varnifh, and it will be done.

VI. *To imitate Tortoife-fhell upon Silver or Gold.*

A white ground being laid, and fmeared over with Vermilion or the like; lay over the fame leaves of Silver or Gold (as we have taught in other places) either with Gum-Ammoniacum, Lake, common *Varnifh* or glair; this done, and being dry-ed, fhadow it according to reafon; ftriking it over here and there with yellow *Varnifh*, and with the yellow *Varnifh* mixed with a little red *Varnifh*; (all things being done in imitation of the fhell) ftrike it feveral times over with the Univerfal *Varnifh*, and polifh it (in all refpects) as before.

VII. *To imitate* Lapis Lazuli.

Upon a ground of White-lead, Spodium or the like in common Varnifh (being firft dry) lay Ultramarine or fome other pure blew well mixed with the Univerfal Varnifh, fo as that the ground may not appear: then with wild, irregular ftreaks (in refemblance of Nature) with liquid or fhell Gold, run ftraglingly all over the blew, adding very fmall fpecks upon the blew part, of fuch various colours, as are ufually to be feen upon the ftone.

CHAP.

CHAP. XXVII.

Experimental Observations of Vegetable Co-
lours in General.

I. **A** Strong infusion of Galls filtred, mixed with
a strong and clear solution of Vitriol, makes a
mixture as black as *Ink* : which with a little strong
Oyl of Vitriol is made *transparent* again : after
which the *black* colour is regained again, by the affusion of a little quantity of a strong solution of Salt of
Tartar.

The first black (although pale in writing, yet) being
dry, appears to be good Ink.

I I. Decoction of dried red Roses, in fair water,
mixed with a little filtrated solution of blew Vitriol
made a black colour : this mixed with a little *Aqua-*
fortis turn'd it from a black, to a deep red ; which by
affusion of a little spirit of Urine, may be reduced
straight to a thick and black colour.

I I I. *Yellow wax* is whitened by dissolving it over the
fire in spirit of Wine, letting it boil a little, and then
exhaling the spirit of Wine ; or else whilst it is hot,
separating it by filtration.

I V. Fair water mixed with a blood red Tincture
of *Benjamin* drawn with spirit of Wine, immediately
makes it of a milk white colour.

V. *Blackness* may be taken away with oyl of Vitriol ;
so black pieces of Silk or Hair I have turn'd to a kind
of yellow.

V I. A handful of *Lignum Nephriticum* rasped, infused in four pound of spring water, yields between the
light

light and the eye and almoſt golden colour (unleſs the infuſion be too ſtrong) but with the eye between the light and it (in a clear vial) a lovely blew as indeed it is : this with ſpirit of Vinegar may be made to varniſh (ſtill keeping its golden colour) and after with oyle of Tartar *per deliquium* may be reſtored again.

VII. Cloth died with blew and Woad, is by the yellow decoction of *Luteola* died into a green.

VIII. Syrup of Violets mixed with a high ſolution of Gold in *Aqua regia*, produces a reddiſh mixture ; and with a high ſolution of filings of Copper in ſpirit of Urine, a lovely fair green.

IX. Syrup of Violets mixt with a little juyce of Lemons, ſpirit of Salt, Vinegar, or the like acid Salt, will be immediately red; but mixt with oyl of Tartar, or a ſolution of pot-aſhes, it will in a moment be perfect green : the like in juice of blew-bottles.

X. A good quantity of oyl of Tartar, put into a ſtrong ſolution of Verdegrieſe, gives a dightful blew, which may be variouſly changed by adding ſpirit of Urine, or Hartſhorn.

XI. Although red Roſes hung over the fume of Sulphur, loſe all their redneſs, and become white : yet oyl of Sulphur (which is nothing but the fumes condenſed) doth wonderfully heighten the tincture of the ſame.

XII. *Cochenele* will have its colour far more heightned by ſpirit of Urine, than by rectified ſpirit of Wine : and one grain of Cochenele in a good quantity of ſpirit of Urine, being put into one hundred twenty ſix ounces of water, tinged it (although but faintly :) which amounts to above one hundred twenty five thouſand times its own weight.

XIII. Twenty grains of *Cochenele* being mixed with an ounce of *Saccharum Saturni,* makes a moſt
glori-

glorious purple colour: and so accordingly as the quantity is either diminished or encreased, so the purple colour shall be either lighter or deeper.

XIV. A few grains of *Cochenele* being mixed with the *Lixivium* of Quick-lime in a due proportion, makes a fading purple colour, of the greatest glory imaginable in the world.

XV. The juice of privet berries with spirit of Salt, is turned into a lovely red: but with a strong solution of pot-ashes into a delightful green.

XVI. Upon things red by nature, as Syrup of Clove-gilliflowers, juice of Buckthorn berries, infusion of Red Roses, Brazil, *&c.* Spirit of Salt makes no considerable change, but rather a lighter red: but other salts turn them into a greenish; especially juice of buckthorn berries.

XVII. Juice of *Jasmin* and snow drops, by a strong *alcalizate* solution, was (although of no colour) turned into a deep greenish yellow.

XVIII. *Buckthorn berries* being gathered green and dried are called *Sap-berries,* which being infused in Alom-water gives a fair yellow *(which is used by Book-binders for the edges of their Books, and to colour Leather also:)* being gathered when they are black, they are called *Sap-green,* and make a green colour being put into a Brass or Copper vessel for three or four days; or a little heated upon the fire, and mixed with Alom in powder, and pressed forth; so put into bladders hanging it up till it is dry: and being gathered about the end of *November,* (when they are ready to drop) they yield a purplish colour.

XIX. Tincture of *Cochenele,* diluted never so much with fair water, will never yield a yellow colour: a single drop of a deep solution in spirit of Urine, diluted in an ounce off fair water, makes a fair Pink, or Carnation. XX. Oyl

XX. Oyl or fpirit of Turpentine, digefted with pure white Sugar of lead, yields in a fhort time a high red tincture, which Chymifts call *Balfamum Saturni*.

XXI. Spirit of Salt dropt into a ftrong infufion of *Cochenele* or juice of black cherries, makes immediately a fair red : but dropt into the infufion of Brazil, a kind of yellow : fo the filtrated tincture of *Balauftins* mixed with good fpirit of Urine, or the like , turns of a darkifh green ; but with fpirit of Salt, a high rednefs, like rich Claret wine ; which glorious colour may in a moment be deftroyed, and turned into a dirty green, by fpirit of Urine.

XXII. A high infufion of *Lignum Nephriticum*, mixed with fpirit of Urine gives fo deep a blew, as to make the liquor *opacous* : which after a day or two vanifhes, and leaves the liquor of a *bright amber colour*.

Where note that inftead of Spirit of Urine you may ufe oyl of Tartar, or a ftrong folution of pot afhes.

XXIII. Infufion of Logwood in fair water (mixt with fpirit of *Sal Armoniack*) ftraight turns into a deep, rich, lovely purple ; two or three drops to a fpoonful is enough , left the colour be fo deep, as to be opacous.

XXIV. Spirit of *Sal Armoniack* will turn fyrup of Violets to a lovely green.

XXV. Infufion of *Litmofe* in fair water gives in a clear glafs a purple colour : but by addition of fpirit of Salt, it will be wholly changed into a *glorious yellow*.

XXVI. The Infufions and juices of feveral plants, will be much altered by a folution of Lead in fpirit of Vinegar : it will turn infufion of red rofe leaves into a fad green.

XXVII. So Tincture of red rofes in fair water, would be turned into a thick green, with the folution of *Minium* in fpirit of Vinegar ; and then with the addition

of

of oyl of Vitriol the refolved Lead would percipitate white, leaving the liquor of a clear, high red colour again.

XXVIII. We have not yet found, that to exhibit ftrong variety of colours, there need be imployed any more than thefe five, White, Black, Red, Blew, Yellow: *for thefe being varioufly compounded and decompounded exhibit a variety and number of colours; fuch as thofe who are ftrangers to painting can hardly imagine.*

XXIX. So *Black* and *White* varioufly mixed, make a vaft company of light and deep *Grays*: *Blew* and *Yellow,* many *Greens*: *Red* and *Yellow, Orange-tawnies*: *Red* and *White, Carnations*: *Red* and *Blew, Purples,* &c. producing many colours for which we want names.

XXX. Acid falts deftroy a blew colour: Sulphureous, Urinous or fixed reftore it.

XXXI. Acid and *Alcalizate* falts with many bodies that abound with *Sulphureous* or oyly parts will produce a red, as is manifeft in the Tincture of Sulphur, made with *Lixiviums* of Calcined Tartar or pot-afhes.

XXXII. *Laftly it may be worth tryal (fince it hath fucceeded in fome experiments) fo to take away the colour of a Liquor, as that it may be colourlefs*: which in what we have tryed, was thus: firft by putting into the Tincture, Liquor, or Juice, a quantity of the folution of pot-afhes or oyl of Tartar *per deliquium;* and then affufing a good or ftrong folution of Alom, which in our obfervations precipitated the tinging matter, or gathered it into one body (like as it were curds) and fo left the Liquor *tranfparent and clear as Cryftal.*

CHAP.

CHAP. XXVIII.

General Experimental observations of Mineral Colours.

I. *SUblimate* diſſolved in fair water, and mixed with a little ſpirit of Urine, makes a milk white mixture in a moment: which by addition of *Aquafortis*, immediately again becomes *tranſparent*.

II. If *Sublimate* two ounces, and *Tin-glaſs* one ounce be ſublimed together, you will have a ſublimate not inferiour to the beſt *Orient Pearls* in the world.

III. *Silver* diſſolved in *Aqua-fortis* and evaporated to dryneſs, and fair water poured two or three times thereon, and evaporated, till the *calx* is dry, leaves it of a Snow whiteneſs : which rubbed upon the ſkin, (wetted with ſpittle, water or the like) produces a deep blackneſs, not to be obliterated in ſome days.

With this, Ivory, Hair, and Horns may be dyed in fair water of a laſting black.

IV. *Coral* diſſolved by oyl of Vitriol, Sulphur, or ſpirit of vinegar, and precipitated by oyl of Tartar, yields a Snow whiteneſs. The ſame of Crude Lead and Quickſilver diſſolved in *Aqua-fortis*: So butter of *Antimony* rectified by bare affuſion in much fair water, will (though Unctuous) be precipitated into that Snow white powder which (being waſhed from its corroſive ſalts) is called *Mercurius Vitæ* : the like of which may be made without the addition of any *Mercury* at all.

V. *Mercury Sublimate* and *precipitate* yields (with the ſpirit of Urine, Hartſhorn, or the like) *a white precipitate* : but with the ſolution of Pot-aſhes, or other

Lixiviate

Lixiviate Salts an *Orange Tawny*. And if on a filtrated solution of Vitriol, you put the solution of a *fixed salt,* there will subside a copious substance far from whiteness, which Chymists call the Sulphur of Vitriol.

VI. If Copper two ounces be mixed with Tin one ounce, the reddishness will vanish : and if Arsenick (calcined with Nitre) in a just proportion be mixed with melted Copper, it will be blanched both within and without.

VII Fine powders of blew Bice, and yellow Orpiment slightly mixed, give a good green : and a high yellow solution of good Gold in *Aqua regia,* mixed with a due quantity of a deep blew solution of crude Copper in strong Spirit of Urine, produces a *transparent green*: And so blew and yellow *Amel* fused together in the flame of a Lamp, being strongly blowed on without ceasing, produces at length a green colour.

VIII. An urinous salt, largely put into the dissolution of blew Vitriol in fair water, turn'd the liquor and corpuscles (which resided) into a yellowish colour like yellow Oker.

IX. Verdegriese ground with Salt *Armoniack* and the like (digested for a while in a dunghil) makes a glorious blew.

X. The true glass of *Antimony* extracted with acid spirits (with or without Wine) yields a red tincture.

XI. Balsom of Sulphur (of a deep red in the glass) shaked about, or dropt on paper gives a yellow stain.

XII. If Brimstone and *Sal-Armoniack* in powder, of each five ounces, be mixed with quick-lime in powder six ounces, and distilled in a Retort in sand by degrees; you will have a volatil spirit of Sulphur of excellent redness, though none of the ingredients be so.

So also oyl of Anniseeds mixed with oyl of Vitriol, gives

N   *in*

in a trice a blood red Colour, which soon decays.

XIII. Fine Silver diffolved in *Aquafortis,* and precipitated with fpirit of Salt ; upon the firft decanting the liquor, the remaining matter will be purely white; but lying uncovered, what is fubject to the ambient Air will lofe its whitenefs.

XIV. *Sublimate* diffolved in a quantity of water and filtred, till it is as clear as Cryftal, mixed (in a Venice glafs) with good oyl of Tartar *per deliquium* filtred , (three of four drops to a fpoonful) yields an opacous liquor or a deep Orange colour ; after which if four or five drops of oyl of Vitriol be dropt in, and the glafs ftraightway be ftrongly fhaked, the whole liquor will (to admiration) be colourlefs without *fediment.* And if the filtred folution of *fublimed Sal-Armoniack* and *Sublimate* of each alike be mixt with the folution of an *Alcali,* it will be white.

XV. Spirit of *Sal-Armoniack* makes the folution of Verdigriefe an excellent *Azure* ; but it makes the folution of *Sublimate* yield a white precipitate.

XVI. So the folution of filings of Copper in fpirit of Urine (made by fermentation) gives a lovely *Azure* colour : which with oyl of Vitriol (a few drops to a fpoonful) is deprived in a trice of the fame, and makes it like fair water. And fo a folution of Verdigriefe in fair water, mixed with ftrong fpirit of Salt , or dephlegmed *Aqua-fortis,* makes the greenefs almoft totally to difappear.

XVII. Quick-filver mixed with three or four times its weight of good oyl of Vitriol,and the oyl drawn off in fand, through a glafs Retort , leaves a Snow white *precipitate* ; which by affufion of fair water, becomes one of the lovelieft light yellows in the world, and a durable colour.

XVIII. Tin calcined *per fe* by fire,affords a very white
calx

calx called *Putty*: Lead, a red powder called *Minium*: Copper a dark or greyish powder: Iron a dirty yellowish colour, called *Crocus Martis*: and Mercury a red powder.

XIX. Gold diffolved in *Aqua Regia* Ennobles the *Menftruum* with its own colour : Silver Coyn diffolved in *Aqua-fortis* yields a tincture like that of Copper ; but fine Silver a kind of faint blewifhnefs : Copper diffolved in fpirit of Sugar (drawn off in a glafs Retort) or in oyl or fpirit of Turpentine, affords a green tincture ; but in *Aqua-fortis* a blew.

XX. *Vermilion* is made of *Mercury* and *Brimftone* fublimed together in a due proportion.

XXI. Glafs may have given to it a lovely golden colour with Quick-Silver ; but it is now coloured yellow generally with *calx* of Silver : yet fhell-Silver , (fuch as is ufed with pen or pencil) mixed with a convenient proportion of powdered glafs, in three or four hours fufion, gave a lovely Sapphirine blew.

XXII. Glafs is tinged green (by the Glafs-men) with the *Calx of Venus*: which *Calx* mixed with an hundred times its weight of fair glafs, gave in fufion a blew coloured mafs.

XXIII. *Putty* (which is Tin calcined) as it is white of it felf, fo it turns the purer fort of glafs metal into a white mafs, which when opacous enough, ferves for white *Amel*.

XXIV. This white *Amel* is as it were the Bafis of all thofe fine Concretes, that Gold-fmiths , and feveral Artificers ufe, in the curious Art of *Enameling* ; for this white and fufible fubftance, will receive into it felf, without fpoiling them, the colours of divers other Mineral fubftances, which like it will endure the fire.

N 2   XXV. Glafs

X X V. Glafs is alfo tinged blew with the dark mineral called *Zaffora* ; and with *Manganefs* or *Magneffia* in a certain proportion, which will tinge glafs of a red colour ; and alfo of a Purplifh or Murry ; and with a greater quantity, into that deep colour which paffes for black.

X X V I. Yellow Orpiment fublimed with Sea-Salt, yields a white and Cryftalline Arfenick ; Arfenick coloured with pure Nitre being duly added to Copper in the fufion, gives it a whitenefs both within and without.

X X V I I. So *Lapis Calaminaris* turns Copper into Brafs.

X X V I I I. And *Zink* duly mixed with Copper when 'tis in fufion, gives it the noblest golden colour that was ever feen in the best gold.

X X I X. Copper diffolved in *Aqua-fortis* will imbue feveral bodies of the colour of the folution.

X X X. Laftly, Gold diffolved in *Aqua regia* will (though not commonly known) dye *Horns*, *Ivories* and other *Bones* of a durable purple colour : And the Cryftals of Silver made with *Aqua-fortis*, (though they appear white) will prefemtly dye the *Skin*, *Nails*, *Hair*, *Horn*, and *Bones*, with a *Black* not to be wafhed off.

C H A P.

CHAP. XXIX.

Of Metals.

I. **To harden *Quick-silver.***

Cast your Lead separated from its dross into a vessel, and when it begins to cool, thrust in the point of a stick, which take out again and cast in the Argent Vive, and it will congeal : then beat it in a mortar, and do so often; when it is hard, melt it often and put it into fair water, doing it so long till it is hard enough, and may be hammered.

I I. *To tinge Quick-silver of the colour of Gold.*

Break it into small pieces (being hardned) which put into a Crucible, with the powder of *Cadmia, stratum super stratum,* mixed with Pomegranate peels, Turmerick (beaten fine) and Raisons, cover the Crucible and lute it well, dry it well; and then set it on a fire for six or seven hours, that it may be red-hot; then blow it with bellows till it run, which then let cool whilst covered with coals, and it will have the colour of gold.

III. *To fix Quick-silver being hardned.*

This is done with fine powder of Crystal glass, laid with the Metal *stratum super stratum* in a Crucible covered and luted; heating it all over red-hot, and then melting of it.

IV. *To make Quick-silver malleable.*

First harden it by the first Section, then break the Metal into small pieces, and boil it a quarter of an hour in sharp vinegar : then add a little *Sal-Armoniack,* and digest all together for ten or twelve days; then boil all together in a luted Crucible, till it is red-hot, and by

degrees

degrees crack : laſtly, hang the Mercury in a pot with Brimſtone at bottom to cover it ; lute it and ſet it into the fire, that it may grow hot by degrees, and receive the fume of the Sulphur ; do thus for a month once a day, and the Mercury will run and be hammered.

V. *Another way of tinging Mercury.*

Take purified Mercury one ounce, Sulphur two ounces, *Aqua-fortis* three ounces, let them all ſtand till the water grow clear ; diſtil this with its ſediment, and at bottom of the Limbeck you ſhall find the Mercury hard, and of an exact colour.

VI. *To colour and ſoften Gold.*

Diſſolve Verdegrieſe in vinegar, and ſtrain it through a felt, then congeal, and when it begins to wax thick, put to it ſome Sal-Armoniack, and let it harden a good while, then melt gold with it, and it will heighten the colour and make it ſoft.

VII. *To make Gold and Silver ſofter.*

Take Mercury Sublimate, Sal-Armoniack, of each alike, powder them, melt the gold, and put to it a little of this powder, and it will be ſoft.

VIII. *Another way to do the ſame.*

Take Vitriol, Verdet, Sal-Armoniack, burnt Braſs, of each half an ounce, mix them with *Aqua-fortis*, let it ſo repoſe in the heat two days, then let it harden, do thus three times with *Aqua-fortis*, and let it dry, make it into powder, to one dram put one ounce of gold three times and it will be ſofter.

IX. *Another way to do the ſame in Silver.*

Take Salt-peter, Tartar, Salt, Verdet, boil all together, till the water is comſumed, then put to it Urine, and let it ſo conſume, and you ſhall have an oyl, which put into melted Silver will do the ſame.

Or thus, *Take as many wedges as you have melted, put them*

them one night into a crucible in a furnace, but so as they melt not, and they will be soft and fair.

Or thus, *Take honey, oyl, of each alike, in which quench the Gold or Silver three or four times, and it will be softer.*

Or thus, *Take Maftich, Frankincenfe, Myrrh, Borax, Vernix, of each alike all in powder.*

Or thus, *Quench the Gold or Silver in water of Sal-Armoniack, and it will be foft.*

X. *To tinge Silver of a Gold colour.*

Take fine Gold, fine Silver, good Brafs, and Brafs or Copper calcin'd with Sulphur-vive, of each alike, melt them down together, and it fhall appear to be gold of eighteen carets fine.

XI. *Another way to tinge Silver.*

Take Quick-filver purged three ounces, leaf-gold one ounce, mix them and put them into a glafs Retort well luted, put it on the fire till it grow hot; then take it off, and add to it Quick-filver purged two ounces, *Sal-Armoniack* one ounce, *Sal Ellebrot* half an ounce, *Borax* two drachms; then feal up the glafs hermetically, and put it into a continual fire for three dayes; then take it out, let it cool, open the Retort, take out the matter, and powder it very fine: of which powder mix one ounce with filver fine ounces, and it will tinge it into a good gold colour.

Note, Sal Ellebrot is thus made. Take pure common Salt, Sal Gem, Sal Alcali in powder, of each one ounce, juice of mints four ounces, spring water four pound, mingle them, and evaporate. And Quick-filver is purged by wafhing it in fharp Vinegar three or four times and ftraining it; or by fubliming it which is bettter.

XII. *To bring Silver into a Calx.*

This is done by amalgamating of it with Quick-filver, and then fubliming of it; or by diffolving it in

Aqua-fortis, and precipitating it with the folution of Salt in fair water, and then wafhing it with warm water often to free it from the falts: or elfe by mingling the filings with fublimed Mercury, and in a Retort caufing the Mercury to afcend, which will leave at bottom the Calx of Silver, fit for Jewels, *&c.*

XIII. *To blanch Silver.*

Take *Sal-Armoniack, Roch-Alom, Alom Plumofum, Sal gem, Argol, Roman-Vitriol, of each alike*; powder and mix them, and diffolve them in fair water, in which boil the Silver fo long, till you fee it wonderful white.

XIV. *To colour Silver of a Gold-colour*

Take Salt-peter two pound, Roch-Alom five pound, mingle, and diftil them, keeping the water for ufe. When you ufe it, melt the Silver, and quench it in the faid water.

XV. *To tinge Brafs of a Gold colour.*

Diffolve burnt Brafs in *Aqua-fortis* (made of Vitriol, Salt-peter, Alom, Verdegriefe, and Vermilion) and then reduce it again, and it will be much of a gold colour.

XVI. *To make Brafs through white.*

Heat Brafs red-hot, and quench it in water diftilled from Sal-Armoniack, and Egg-fhells ground together, and it well be very white.

XVII. *To make Brafs white otherwife.*

Take Egg-fhells and calcine them in a Crucible, and temper them with the whites of Eggs, let it ftand fo three weeks; heat the Brafs red-hot, and put this upon it.

XVIII. *To make Brafs.*

Take Copper three pounds, *Lapis Calaminaris* one pound in powder, melt them together the fpace of an hour, then put it out.

XIX. *The way to colour Brafs white.*

Diffolve

Diſſolve a peny weight of Silver in *Aqua-fortis*, putting it to the fire in a veſſel, till the Silver turn to water; to which add as much powder of white Tartar as may drink up all the water, make it into balls, with which rub any Braſs, and it will be white as Silver.

X X. *To tinge Copper of a Gold colour.*

Take Copper, *Lapis Calaminaris*, of each four drachms, Tutty two drachms; heat the Copper red-hot twice, quenching it in piſs: doing the like by the *Lapis* and Tutty: take of the diſſolved Copper half an ounce, adding to it Honey one ounce, boil them till the Honey look black and is, dry that it may be powdered, which then beat with the *Lapis* and Tutty: boil them again, till the Copper is melted, and it is done.

X X I. *Another way to make Copper of a Gold colour.*

Take the Gall of a Goat, Arſnick, of each a ſufficient quantity, and diſtil them; then the Copper being bright being waſhed in this water, will turn into the colour of Gold.

X X I I. *Another way to do the ſame.*

Melt Copper, to which put a little *Zink* in filings, and the Copper will have a glorious golden colour.

X X I I I. *To make Copper of a white colour.*

Take Sublimate, Sal-Armoniack, of each alike; boil them in Vinegar, in which quench the Copper being made red-hot; and it will be like Silver.

X X I V. *Another way to whiten Copper.*

Heat it red-hot divers times, and quench it in oyl of Tartar *per deliquium*, and it will be white.

X X V. *Another way to whiten Copper.*

Take Arſnick three ounces, Mercury Sulimate two ounces, Azure one ounce, mix them with good and pure greaſe like an ointment, with which anoint any Copper veſſel, then put that veſſel into another, and
    ſet

set it into a digestive heat for two months, after which cleanse it with a brush and water, and it is done.

XXVI. *Another way to whiten Copper.*

Take Arsnick calcined with Salt-peter, and Mercury Sublimate, which cast upon melted Copper, and it will be white like Silver.

XXVII. *To soften Copper.*

Melt burnt Brass with *Borax* in a Crucible, quench it in Linseed-oyl, and then beat it gently on an Anvil; boil it again and quench it in oyl as before, doing thus five or six times, till it is soft enough; and this will neatly unite with Gold, of which you may put in more by half than you can of other Brass.

XXVIII. *To tinge Iron with a Gold colour.*

Lay in a Crucible plates of Iron and Brimstone, *stratum super stratum,* cover and lute it well, and calcine in a furnace, then take them out and they will be brittle: put them into a pot with a large mouth, and put in sharp distilled vinegar, digesting till they wax red over a gentle heat: then decant the vinegar, and add new, thus doing till all the Iron be dissolved; evaporate the moisture in a glass Retort or *Vesica,* and cast the remaining powder on Silver, or other white Metal, and it will look like Gold.

XXIX. *To make Iron or Silver of a Brass colour.*

Take Flowers of Brass, Vitriol, *Sal-Armoniack,* of each alike in fine powder; boil it half an hour in strong vinegar, take it from the fire, and put in Iron or Silver, covering the vessel till it be cold, and the Metal will be like to Brass, and fit to be gilded: or rub polished Iron with *Aqua-fortis* in which filings of Brass is dissolved.

XXX. *To tinge Iron into a Brass colour.*

Melt the Iron in a Crucible casting upon it Sulphur *vive,* then cast it into small rods, and beat it into pieces

(for

(for it is very brittle) then in *Aqua-fortis* diffolve it, and evaporate the *menftruum*, reducing the powder by a ftrong fire into a body again, and it will be good Brafs.

XXXI. *To whiten Iron.*

Firft purge it, by heating it red hot and quenching it in a water made of Ley and Vinegar, boil'd with Salt and Alum, doing this fo often till it is fomewhat whitened.   The fragments of the Iron beat in a mortar till the Salt is quite changed, and no blacknefs is left in the Liquor of it, and till the Iron is cleanfed from its drofs: then *Amalgamate* Lead and Quick-filver together, and reduce them into a powder : lay the prepared plates of Iron and this powder *ftratum fuper ftratum* in a Crucible, cover it, and lute it all over very ftrongly, that the leaft fume may not come forth, and put it into the fire for a day; at length encreafe the fire, fo as it may melt the Iron (which will quickly be) and repeat this work till it is white enough : It is whitened alfo by melting with Lead, the Marchafit or fire-ftone and Arfnick. If you mix a little Silver (with which it willingly unites) with it, it gives a wonderful whitenefs, fcarcely ever to be changed any more , by any art whatfoever.

XXXII. *To keep Iron from Rufting.*

Rub it over with vinegar mixt with Cerufe; or with the marrow of a Hart : if it be rufty, oyl of Tartar *per deliquium* will prefently take it away and cleanfe it.

XXXIII. *To cleanfe Brafs.*

Take *Aqua-fortis* and water of each alike, fhake them together, and with a woollen rag dipt therein rub it over : then prefently rub it with an oyly cloth; laftly, with a dry woollen cloth dipt in powder of *Lapis Calaminaris*, it will be clear and bright as when new.

XXXIV. *To foften Iron.*

Take

Take Alom, Sal-Armoniack, Tartar, of each alike, put them into good Vinegar, and set them on the fire, heat the Iron, and quench it therein : or quench it four or five times in oyl, in which melted Lead hath been put six or seven times.

XXXV. *To make Iron of a Gold colour.*

Take Alom of Melancy in powder, Sea-water; mix them : then heat the Iron red-hot, and quench it in the same.

XXXVI. *To make Iron of a Silver colour.*

Take powder of Sal-Armoniack, unslak'd-lime, mix and put them into cold water, then heat the Iron red-hot, quench it therein, and it will be as white as Silver.

XXXVII. *To soften steel to grave upon.*

This is done with a *Lixivium* of Oak-ashes and un-slak'd-Lime, by casting the Steel into it, and letting it remain there fourteen days. Or thus, take the Gall of an Ox, man's Urine, Verjuice, and juice of Nettles of each alike, mix them ; then quench Steel red-hot therein four or five times together, and it will become very soft.

XXXVIII. *To harden Iron or Steel.*

Quench it six or seven times in Hogs blood mixed with Goose-grease, at each time drying it at the fire before you dip it again, and it will become very hard and not brittle.

XXXIX. *To solder on Iron.*

Set the joynts of Iron as close as you can, lay them in a glowing fire, and take of Venice-glass in powder, and the Iron being red-hot, cast the powder thereon, and it will solder of it self.

XL. *To counterfeit Silver.*

Take Crystal Arsnick eight ounces, Tartar six oun-ces, Salt-peter two ounces, Glass one ounce and an half,

Sub-

Sublimate half an ounce : make them feverally into fine powder and mix them : then take three pound of Copper in thin plates which put into a Crucible (with the former powder *ftratum fuper ftratum*) to calcine, covering it and luting it ftrongly, let it ftand in the Furnace for about eight or ten hours : then take it out, and (being cold) break the pot, and take out all the matter, and melt it with a violent fire, cafting it into fome mold. Then take purged Brafs two pound, of the former metal one pound; melt them together, cafting in, now and then, fome of the aforefaid powder, after which add half as much of fine Silver melting them together, and you have that which is defired : laftly, to make it as white as Silver, boil it in Tartar.

XLI. *Another way to counterfeit Silver.*

Take purified Tin eight ounces, Quick-filver half an ounce, and when it begins to rife in the firft heat, take powder of Cantharides, and caft into it, with a lock of hair, that it may burn in it; being melted put into it the powder aforefaid, then take it fuddenly from the fire, and let it cool.

XLII. *To purge the Brafs.*

It is cleanfed or purged, by cafting into it when it is melted, broken Glafs, Tartar, Sal-Armoniack and Salt-peter, each of them by turns, by little and little.

XLIII. *To tinge Lead of a Gold colour.*

Take purged Lead one pound, Sal-Armoniack, in powder, one ounce, Salt-peter half an ounce, Sal-Elebrot two drachms; put all into a Crucible for two days, and it will be throughly tinged.

XLIV. *To purge Lead.*

Melt it at the fire, then quench it in the fharpeft Vinegar; melt it again and quench it in the juice of Celandine: melt it again and quench it in Salt-water:
then

then in vinegar mixed with *Sal-Armoniack* : and laſtly melt it, and put it into aſhes, and it will be well
cleanſed.

XLV. *To make Lead of a Golden colour.*

Put Quick-ſilver one ounce into a Crucible , ſet it
over the fire till it is hot, then add to it of the beſt
leaf-gold one ounce , and take it from the fire , and
mingle it with purified Lead melted one pound ;
mingle all well together with an Iron rod, to which
put of the filtrated ſolution of Vitriol in fair water
one ounce ; then let it cool, and it will be of a gold colour. Diſſolve the Vitriol in its equal weight of water.

XLVI. *To take away the ringing and ſoftneſs of Tin.*

Melt the Tin, and caſt in ſome Quick-ſilver, remove it from the fire, and put it into a glaſs Retort,
with a large round belly, and a very long neck , heat
it red-hot in the fire , till the Mercury ſublimes and
the Tin remains at bottom ; do thus three or four
times. The ſame may be done by calcining of it three
or four times, by which means it will ſooner be red-hot
than melt.

XLVII. *To take away the ſoftneſs and creaking noiſe
of Tin.*

This is done by granulating of it often, and then
reducing it again, and quenching it often in vinegar
and a Lixivium of Salt of Tartar. The creaking noiſe
is taken away by melting it ſeven or eight ſeveral times
and quenching it in Boys Urine, or elſe oyl of Walnuts.

XLVIII. *To take away the deaf ſound of Tin.*

This is done by diſſolving it in *Aqua-fortis* over a
gentle fire, till the water fly away : doing thus ſo long
till it is all turned to a *calx* ; which mixed with *calx*
of Silver, and reduced, performs the work.

XLIX. *To make that Tin crack not.*

Take

Take Salt, Hony, of each alike, and mix them : melt your Tin and put it twelve or more times into it, then ſtrain out the Tin, and it will purge and leave cracking ; put it into a Crucible, which lute, and cal-cine it four and twenty hours, and it will be like *calx* of Gold.

L. *To take away the brittleneſs of any Metal.*

Firſt calcine it and put it under dung, then do thus; when it is red-hot at the fire, or melted, quench it of-ten in *Aqua vita* often diſtilled ; or uſe about them Roſin or Turpentine, or the oyl of it, or wax, ſuet, Euphorbium, Myrrh, artificial Borax: for if a metal be not malleable, unctuous bodies will oftentimes make them ſofter, if all theſe, or ſome of theſe be made up with ſome moiſture into little cakes : and when the metal yields to the fire, by blowing with the bellows, we caſt in ſome of them and make them thick like mud, or clear, then ſet the Metal to the fire, that it may be red-hot in burning coals, take it forth and quench it in them, and ſo let it remain half an hour to drink in.   Or anoint the Metal with Dogs greaſe, and melt it with it, for that will take away much of the brittleneſs of it, and make it ſo that it may be hamme-red and wrought.

LI. *To colour Metal like Gold.*

Take Sal-Armoniack, White Vitriol, Stone-ſalt, Verdegrieſe,of each alike, in fine powder ; lay it upon the Metal, then put it into the fire for an hour, take it out and quench it in Urine, and the Metal will have the colour of Gold.

LII.   *To make a kind of Counterfeited Siver of Tin.*

This is done by mingling Silver with Tin melted with Quick-ſilver, continuing it long in the fire, then being brittle, it is made tough, by keeping it in a gen-tle

tle fire or under hot embers (in a Crucible) for about twenty four hours.

LIII. *To solder upon Silver, Brass or Iron.*

Take Silver five peny weight, Brass four peny weight, melt them together for soft Solder, which runs soonest.

Take Silver five peny weight, Copper three peny weight, melt them together for hard Solder.

Beat the Solder thin and lay it over the place to be Soldred, which must be first fitted, and bound together with Wire as occasion requires : then take Borax in powder, and temper it like pap, and lay it upon the Solder, letting it dry, then cover it with quick coals and blow, and it will run immediately ; then take it presently out of the fire, and it is done.

Note, 1. *If a thing is to be Soldred in two places, (which cannot be well done at one time) you must first Solder with the hard Solder, and then with the soft ; for if it be first done with the soft, it will unsolder again before the other be Soldred.* 2. *That if you would not have your Solder run about the piece to be Soldred, rub those places over with Chalk.*

LIV. *To make the Silver Tree of the Philosophers.*

Take *Aqua-fortis* four ounces, fine Silver one ounce, which dissolve in it : then take *Aqua-foris* two ounces, in which dissolve Quick-Silver : mix these two Liquors together in a clear glass, with a pint of pure water ; stop the glass close, and after a day, you shall see a Tree to grow by little and little, which is wonderful and pleasant to behold.

LV. *To make the Golden Tree of the Philosophers.*

Take oyl of Sand or Flints, oyl of Tartar *per deliquium*, of each alike, mix them well together, then dissolve Sol in *Aqua Regis*, and evaporate the *menstruum*, dry the Calx by the fire, but make it not too hot (for then it will lose its growing quality)

lity) break it into little bits (not into powder)
which bits put into the aforesaid liquor, a fingers
breadth one from another in a very clear glass, keep
the liquor from the Air, and let the Calx stand still,
and the bits of Calx will presently begin to grow : first
swell ; then put forth one or two stems ; then divers
branches and twigs, so exactly, as you cannot but wonder to see.

*Where note , that this growing is not imaginary but
real.*

LVI. *To make the Steel Tree of the Philosophers.*

Dissolve Steel in rectified spirit or oyl of Salt, so
shall you have a green and sweet solution, smelling
like Brimstone ; filter it, and abstract all the moisture
with a gentle heat, and there will distil over a liquor,
as sweet as rain water (for Steel by reason of its dry-
ness detains the Corrosiveness of the spirit of Salt,
which remaineth in the bottom, like a blood-red mass,
and it is as hot on the tongue as fire :) dissolve this
blood-red mass in oyl of Flints or Sand, and you shall
see it grow up in two or three hours like a Tree with
stem and branches.

*If you prove this Tree at the test, it will yield good Gold,
which it draweth from the oyl of Sand or Flints ; the said
oyl being full of a pure golden Sulphur.*

LVII. *To make oyl of Flints or Sand.*

Take of most pure Salt of Tartar in fine powder
twenty ounces, small Sand, Flints, Pebbles, or Cry-
stals in fine powder five ounces, mix them ; put as
much of this as will fill an Egg-shell into a Crucible,
set it in a Furnace, and make it red-hot, and presently there will come over a thick and white spirit, take
out the Crucible whilest it is hot, and that which is in
it, like transparent glass, keep from the Air ; after
beat it to powder, and lay it in a moist place, and it will

O   dissolve

diſſolve into a thick, fat oyl, which is the oyl of Flints, Sand, Pebbles or Cryſtals. *This oyl precipitateth Metals, and makes the Calx there more heavy than oyl of Tartar doth; it is of a golden nature, and extracts colours from all Minerals; it is fixed in all fires, maketh fine Cryſtals, and Borax, and maturateth imperfect Metals into Gold.*

LVIII. *To melt Metals quickly.*

Take a Crucible, and make in it a lay or courſe of the powder of any Metal, then lay upon it a lay of Sulphur, Salt-peter and Saw-duſt, of each alike mixed together, put a coal of fire to it, and the Metal will immediately be in a maſs.

LIX. Laſtly, He that ſhall obſerve the work and reaſon of the Silver, Golden and Steel Trees, may in like manner produce the like out of the Calx of other Metals.

CHAP. XXX.

Of the Inſtruments and Materials of Caſting.

I. **H**E that would learn to caſt muſt be provided of all the chief Tools thereto belonging; which are 1. *A Trough.* 2. *Sand.* 3. *A Flask.* 4. *Skrew.* 5. *Tripoli.* 6. *The Medal or Form.* 7. *A Furnace.* 8. *Crucibles.* 9. *A Pipe.* 10. *Tongs.* 11. *Two Oak Plates.* 12. *Pledgets of wool.* 13. *Oyl and Turpentine.* 14. *A Hares Foot.* 15. *Bruſhes.*

II. The *Trough* is a four-ſquare thing about half a foot deep, or ſomething more; and its uſe is to hold the Sand.

III. Of

III. Of *Sand* there is various forts, the chief are High-gate Sand, and Tripoli ; the which to make fit for the work you muft order thus :

If it is High-gate Sand, you muft finely fift it ; if Tripoli, you muft firft beat it fine, then fift it through a fine Sieve : to either of thefe fine Sands you muft put of pure fine Bole (an ounce to nine ounces) well beaten, diffolved in water, and laftly reduced into fine powder ; which powders you muft moderately moiften with this Magifterial water, viz. *filtrated Brine made of decrepitated common Salt : or the fame, mixed with glair of Eggs.*

IV. The *Flask* is a pair of Oval Irons, containing only fides to hold the Sand, which muft be prefled hard thereinto : and a paffage or mouth for the Metal to run in at.

V. The *Skrew* is an Iron Prefs, between which the Flask is put and preft , after that it is filled with Sand, and hath received the form or impreffion to be caft.

VI. *Tripoli* is that of which the fecond fort of Sand is made, which here ought to be calcined and beaten into impalpable powder, to ftrew over the fandy moulds ; firft that the fides of the Flask may not cleave together when they are full ; fecondly that the thing caft may have the perfect form and impreffion, without the leaft fcratch or blemifh imaginable.

VII. The *Medal* or Form, is that which is to be impreffed upon the Sand, whofe likenefs we would imitate.

VIII. The *Furnace* is that which contains the fire, where the Crucible is put, for the Metal to melt in, which is generally melted with Charcoal.

IX. The *Crucibles* are calcining or melting pots, (commonly three-fquare) made fo as they may endure

dure

dure the fire all over, in which the Metal is to be melted.

X. The *Pipe* is a hollow Reed, or piece of Tin, to blow coals and filth out of the Crucible.

XI. The *Tongs* are a crooked Inſtrument to take coals out of the Crucible with, as alſo to ſtir and repair the fire; and to take the pot out of the Furnace when you go to Caſt.

XII. The *two Oak plates* are to be ſmooth, and to be put between the Flask and the ſides of the Skrew, on each ſide.

XIII. *Pledgets of wool* are to be put between the Oak plates and the Sand, to fill up empty ſpaces if there be any.

XIV. The *Oyl and Turpentine* is to wet ſome paper or cotton threads, which muſt be ſet on fire, to ſmoak the Impreſſion or Mould (being dry) that the Metal may run the better.

XV. The *Hares-foot* is to wipe the hollow places in the Mould, if they ſhould be too much filled with ſmoak.

XVI. The *Bruſhes* ought to be two, to wit, one with thick bar Wire ſtrings, another with Hogs-briſtles, wherewith the work (both before and after caſting) ought to be rubbed and cleanſed.

CHAP.

CHAP. XXXI.

The way and manner of Casting.

I. WAsh the Medal in Vinegar, in which put some Salt and Straw-ashes; and rub it well with the aforesaid hair-brush, then wash it with water, and dry it well.

II. Place the female part of the Flask upon one of the Oak plates; so that the middle part, *viz.* that which is joyned to the other, may lie downwards.

III. Then put the cleansed Medal in the Flask upon the Oak plate, in a right line to the mouth of the Flask: and if there be two, let them be placed so, that there may be a place left in the middle for the melted Metal to run in at.

IV. Then take of the aforesaid earth or sand prepared, (that is, so much moistened with the Magisterial water, that being crushed between the hands or fingers, it will not stick but like dry flour, and will stand with the print of the hand closed together) and press it on well in the Flask upon the Medal with the fleshy part of your fingers or hand ; then with a rule strike off all the superfluous sand that sticks about the Flask.

V. This done, the pledgets of wool, or a woollen cloth, must be laid upon it, and then the other Oak plate, and then turned up with both hands, the plates being both held close.

VI. Then taking off the upper plate ; put upon it the male part of the Flask, which fill with sand in like manner (the Medal being now between) pressing it

O 3   down

down as before, and then with a ruler ftriking away the fuperfluous fand.

VII. Upon which lay a woollen cloth, and gently lift off the top, or upper part of the Flask, fo that the medal may be taken forth.

VIII. All things being thus done with a knife (or fome fuch like) cut the paffage for the Metal, which let be a little dry'd: then,

IX. Either ftrew over the fide of the impreffion (now taken off) with a calcined Tripoli ground impalpable; applying it upon the female Flask again; turn the female Flask uppermoft, which take off, and ftrew it in like manner, with the calcined Tripoli, and putting them together again, prefs them fo hard, as that the fine Tripoli may receive the moft perfect impreffion of the Medal, which then take out, by feparating the fides of the Flask, and gently fhaking that part which holds it, till it falls out.

X. Or with Cotton wet in Oyl and Turpentine and fet on fire let the impreffion be fmoaked; and if any fuperfluous fume be taken, wipe it off with a Haresfoot.

XI. Then joyn the fides of the Flask together, putting them with the woollen cloaths between the Oaken plates, which put into the Prefs, and skrew them a little.

XII. Then the Metal being melted, put it into the mould being hot, which if it be Silver, or blanched Brafs, or Copper, it will run well enough.

XIII. But if it runs not well, you may caft in about the hundredth part of Mercury fublimate, and an eighth part of Antimony; for fo it will not only run well, but alfo be a harder Metal.

XIV. Laftly, the Medal being cooled, take it neatly out and keep it.

Where

Where note, 1. *That so long as the Impression or Mould is not spoiled, you may still cast more Medals therein; but when it decays, you must perfectly renew the whole work as at first.* 2. *That you may blanch them with a pure whiteness by the ninth Section of the nine and twentieth Chapter of this Book: or thus, if they be of whitened Brass, Take Sal-Armoniack one ounce and an half, Salt-peter two ounces and an half, Leaf-silver twenty four grains; mix them and evaporate them in a luted Crucible, having a hole in the cover, till all the moisture is gone; being cold beat all into fine powder; of which take one ounce, Salt, Alom, Tartar, of each one handful, fair water a sufficient quantity; mix and boil all in a glazed vessel, in which put the Medals boiling them till they are purely white: then rub them with the Tartar in the bottom very well, wash them in fair water and dry them.* 3. *That if the Medals be of Gold, or of a golden colour, you may heighten it with Verdegriese and Urine.*

CHAP. XXXII.

Of Glass and Precious Stones.

I. *To melt Crystal.*

Beat Crystal to bits, and put them into an Iron spoon, cover it and lute it well, and heat it in the fire till it is red-hot, which quench in oyl of Tartar: this do so often, till they will easily beat to powder in a mortar, which will then easily melt.

This is of use to counterfeit Jewels with.

II. *To make a Cement for broken Glasses.*

Glair of Eggs mixed with Quick-lime will joyn broken pieces of glass together, and all earthen-pots, so

O 4   as

as that they fhall never be broken in the fame place a-
gain.

Or thus, Take old liquid Varnifh, and joyn the pieces
therewith ; bind them together, and dry them well
in the Sun or in an Oven, and they will never unglew
again : but put no hot liquor into them then.

Or thus, Take White-lead, Red-lead, Quick-lime,
Gum-fandrack, of each one ounce, mix all with glair
of eight Eggs.

Or thus, Take White-lead, bole, liquid varnifh as
much as fufficeth.

Or thus, Take White-lead, Lime, glair of Eggs as
much as fufficeth.

Or thus, Take fine powder of glafs, Quick-lime,
liquid varnifh, of each a fufficient quantity.

Or thus, Take Quick-lime powdered, liquid varnifh, glair of Eggs, of each alike : grind them upon a
ftone : this is a ftrong glew even for ftones.

Or thus, Take calcined flints and Egg-fhells of each
alike, and with whites of Eggs and Gum-tragacanth,
or diffolution of Gum-fandrack make glew, this in few
days will be as hard as ftone.

Or thus, Take calcined flints two pound, Quick-
lime four pound, Linfeed-oyl fo much as may temper
the mixture, this is wonderful ftrong; but with liquid
varnifh it would be ftronger.

Or thus, Take Fifh glew, and beat it thin, then
foak it in water till it is like pafte, make rouls thereof which draw out thin : when you ufe it, diffolve it
in fair water over the fire, letting it feeth a while and
fcumming of it, and whileft it is hot ufe it. This not
only cements glafs, but Tortoife-fhell and all other
things.

III. *To make Glafs green.*

Green glafs is made of Fern afhes, becaufe it hath
much

much of an Alkaly Salt.   Cryſtal or Venice-Glaſs is tinged green with Ore of Copper ; or with the Calx of Copper five or ſix grains to an ounce.

IV.   *To counterfeit a Diamond.*

Take a ſaphyre of a faint colour, put it into the mid-dle of a Crucible in Quick-lime, and put it into a gen-tle fire, and heat it by degrees till it is red-hot, keep it ſo for ſix or ſeven hours ; let it ſtand in the Crucible till it is cold, (left taking it out hot it ſhould break) ſo will it loſe all its colour, and be perfectly like a Dia-mond, ſo that no file will touch it : if the colour is not all vaniſhed at the firſt heating, you muſt heat it again till it is perfect.

V.   *To prepare the Salts for counterfeit Gems.*

The Salts uſed in making counterfeit Gems, are chiefly two, the firſt is made of the Herb Kali ; the ſe-cond of Tartar ; their preparations are according to the uſual way (but in Glaſs veſſels.)

VI.   *To prepare the matter of which Gems are made.*

The matter is either Cryſtal or Flint that is clear and white : put them into a Crucible in a reverbera-tory heat (the Crucible being covered) then take them out and caſt them into cold water, ſo will they crack and eaſily reduce to powder : of which powder take an equal quantity with Salt of Tartar (or *Sal Alkali*) to which mixture add what colour you pleaſe, which muſt be either Metalline or Mineral : put them into a very ſtrong Crucible (filling it about half full) cover it cloſe, and melt all in a ſtrong fire till it becomes like glaſs.

Where note, in melting you muſt put an Iron rod into it, and take up ſome of it, and if it is free from bubbles, grains, or ſpecks, it is fuſed enough : if not, you muſt fuſe it till it is free.

VII.   *To make a counterfeit Diamond of Cryſtal.*

Put

Put Cryſtal in a Crucible and ſet it in a Glaſs Furnace all night, and then bring it to fine powder, mix it with equal parts of *Sal Tartari*, digeſt all night in a vehement heat, but yet not to melt, then take them out, and put them into another veſſel which will ſtoutly endure the fire;let them ſtand melted two days and take out the maſs.

VIII. *To make a Chalcedon.*

Mingle with the powder of Cryſtal, a little calcined Silver, and let it ſtand in fuſion twenty four hours.

IX. *To make counterfeit Pearls.*

Mix Calx of Luna and Egg-ſhells with Leaf ſilver ground with our beſt varniſh, of which make paſte,and having bored them with a Hogs briſtle, dry them in the Sun, or an Oven.

X. *To counterfeit a Ruby.*

Take Sal-Alkaly four ounces, Cryſtal three ounces, Scales of Braſs half an ounce, Leaf-gold ſix grains, mix all, and melt them in a Reverberatory.

XI. *To counterfeit a Carbuncle.*

Mix Cryſtal with a little Red-lead, putting it into a Furnace for twenty four hours, then take it out, powder and ſearce it, to which add a little calcined Braſs ; melt all again, and add a ſmall quantity of Leaf-gold, ſtirring it well three or four hours, and in a day and night it will be done.

XII. *An Artificial Amethyſt.*

Take Cryſtal one pound, Manganeſs one drachm, mix and melt them.

Or thus, Take Sal Alkaly three ounces, powder of Cryſtal four ounces, filings of Braſs half an ounce, melt all in a ſtrong fire.

XIII. *An Artificial Jacynth.*

Put Lead into a ſtrong Crucible, and ſet it into a Furnace, let it ſtand there about ſix weeks till it is like glaſs, glafs, and it will have the natural colour of a Jacynth not eafily to be difcerned.

XIV. *An Artificial Chryfolite.*

Mix with melted Cryftal a fixth part of fcales of Iron, letting it ftand in a vehement fire for three days. *Or thus,* to the mixture of the *Topaze* add a little Copper.

XV. *An Artificial Topaze.*

To Cryftal one pound, add *Crocus Martis* two drachms, Red-lead three ounces, firft putting in the Lead, then the *Crocus.*

XVI. *Artificial Corals.*

Take the fcrapings of Goats horns, beat them together, and infufe them in a ftrong *Lixivium* made of *Sal fraxini* for five days : then take it out and mingle it with Cinnaber diffolved in water ; fet it to a gentle fire that it may grow thick; make it into what form you pleafe, dry, and polifh it. *Or thus,* Take *Minii* one ounce, Vermilion ground fine half an ounce, Quick-lime, and powder of calcined Flints, of each fix ounces, a *Lixivium* of Quick-lime and Wine, enough to make it thick : add a little Salt, then make it into what form you pleafe, and boil it in Linfeed-oyl.

XVII. *An Artificial Emerald.*

Take Brafs (three days) calcined in powder, which put again into the Furnace with oyl and a weaker fire; let it ftay there four days, adding a double quantity of fine fand or powder of Cryftal : after it is fomething hard, keep it at a more gentle fire for twelve hours, and it will be a lovely, pleafant and glorious green. *Or thus,* Take fine Cryftal two ounces and an half, Sal Alkaly two ounces, *flos æris* infufed in Vinegar and ftrain'd one ounce, *Sal Tartari* one ounce and a half; mix and lute them into a crucible, and put all into a Glafs-makers furnace for twenty four hours, and it

will

will be glorious indeed. *Or thus*, Take Cryſtal ten ounces, *Crocus Martis*, and Braſs twice calcined, of each one pound, mix and melt them, ſtirring them well with an Iron rod.

XVIII. *An Artificial Saphire.*

To melt Cryſtal put a little *Zaphora* (two drachms to a pound of Cryſtal) then ſtir it continually from top to bottom with an Iron hook, till it is well mixed, keep it in the Furnace three days and it is done : yet when it is well coloured, unleſs it be preſently remo-ved from the fire, it will loſe its tincture again.

XIX. *Artificial Amber.*

Boil Turpentine in an earthen pot, with a little cotton (ſome add a little oyl) ſtirring it till it is asthick as paſte, then put it into what you will, and ſet it in the Sun eight days, and it will be clear and hard, of which you may make beads, hafts for knives, and the like.

XX. *Another way to counterfeit Amber.*

Take ſixteen yolks of Eggs, beat them well with a ſpoon; Gum-Arabick two ounces, Cherry-tree Gum an ounce, make the Gums into Powder, and mix them well with the yolks of Eggs; let the Gums melt well, and put them into a pot well leaded, then ſet them ſix days in the Sun, and they will be hard, and ſhine like glaſs; and when you rub them, they will take up a Wheat-ſtraw, as other Amber doth.

XXI. *To make yellow Amber ſoft.*

Put yellow Amber into hot melted wax well ſcum'd and it will be ſoft, ſo that you may make things thereof in what form and faſhion you pleaſe.

XXII. *Another Artificial Amber.*

Take whites of Eggs well beaten, put them into a veſſel with ſtrong white-wine Vinegar, ſtop it cloſe, let it ſtand fourteen days, then dry it in the ſhade, and it will be like to Amber.

XXIII. *Ano-*

XXXIII. *Another Artificial Amber.*

Break whites of Eggs with a ſpunge, take off the froth, to the reſt put Saffron, put all into a glaſs cloſe ſtopped, or into a Copper or brazen veſſel, let it boil in a kettle of water, till it be hard ; then take it out and ſhape it to your liking, lay it in the Sun and anoint it often with Linſeed-oyl mixed with a little Saffron; or elſe being taken out of the Kettle, boil it in Linſeed-oyl.

XXIV. *To make white Enamel.*

Take Calx of Lead two ounces, Calx of Tin four ounces, make it into a body with Cryſtal twelve oun-ces, roll it into round balls, and ſet it on a gentle fire for a night, ſtirring it about with an Iron rod, till it is melted, and it is done.

XXV. *The general preparations and proportions of Mine-ral colours.*

Plates of Copper muſt be made red-hot, and then quenched in cold water ; of which five or ſix grains mixed with Cryſtal and *Sal Tartari* of each half an ounce, and melted, will colour a Sea-green. *Iron* muſt be made into a Crocus in a reverberatory fire ; of which eight or ten grains will tinge the ſaid ounce of mix-ture in a Yellow or Hyacinth colour. *Silver* is to be diſſolved in *Aqua-fortis,* and precipitated with oyl of Flints, then dulcifyed with water and dry'd ; of this five or ſix grains to an ounce, gives a mixed colour. *Gold* muſt be diſſolved in *Aqua Regis,* and precipitated with liquor of Flints, then ſwectned and dry'd ; of which five or ſix grains to one ounce gives a glorious Saphirine colour. *Gold* melted with *Regulus Martis nitroſus* five or ſix grains to one ounce, gives an in-comparable Rubine colour. *Magneſia* in powder on-ly ten or twelve grains to one ounce, makes an Ame-thyſt colour. *Granata* in powder only ten or fifteen

grains

grains to one ounce, will tinge the mafs into a glorious Smaragdine colour, not unlike to the natural.

XXVI. *Laftly,* Common Copper makes a *Sea-green*: Copper of Iron a *Grafs-green* : Granats, a *Smaragdine* : Iron, *Yellow* or *Hyacinth*: Silver, *White, Yellow, Green,* and *Granat*: Gold, *a fair Skie colour*: Wifmut, *a common Blue*: Magnefia, *an Amethyft colour*: Copper and Silver, *an Amethyft colour*: Copper and Iron, *a pale green*: Wifmut and Magnefia, *a purple colour*: Silver and Magnefia, *an Opal, and the like.*

XXVII. *To make Azure.*

Take Sal-Armoniack three ounces, Verdegriefe fix ounces, make them into powder, and put them into a glafs with water of Tartar, fo that it may be fomewhat thick, ftop the glafs and digeft in fand in Horfe-dung for eight or ten days, and it will be good Azure.

XXVIII. *Another way to make good beyond Sea Azure.*

Beat common Azure with Vinegar , and anoint therewith thin plates of Silver, and put the fame over a veffel full of Urine, which fet over hot afhes and coals, moving and ftirring it till it looks like good Azure.

CHAP.

CHAP. XXXIII.

The ways and manner of Gilding.

I. *TO lay Gold on any thing.*
Take Red-lead ground fine, temper it with Linseed-oyl : write with it and lay Leaf-gold on it, let it dry, and polish it.

II. *To lay Gold on Glass.*
Take Chalk and Red-lead, of each alike, grind them together, and temper them with Linseed-oyl : lay it on, and when it is almost dry, lay Leaf-gold on it ; let it dry, then polish it.

III. *To gild Iron with a water.*
Take spring water three pound, Roch-Alom three ounces, Roman Vitriol, Orpiment, one ounce, Verde-griese twenty four grains, Sal-gem three ounces, boil all together, and when it begins to boil, put in Tartar and Bay-salt, of each half an ounce; continue the boiling a good while, then take it from the fire, strike the Iron over therewith, dry it against the fire, and burnish it.

IV. *To lay Gold on Iron, or other Metals.*
Take liquid Varnish one pound, oyl of Linseed and Turpentine, of each one ounce ; mix them well together : strike this over any Metal, and afterwards lay on the Gold or Silver, and when it is dry polish it.

IV. *To Gild Silver, or Brass with Gold water.*
Take Quick-silver two ounces, put it on the fire in a Crucible, and when it begins to smoak, put into it an Angel of fine Gold ; then take it off immediately, for the Gold will be presently dissolved : then if it be

too

too thin, ſtrain a part of the Quick-ſilver from it, through a piece of Fuſtian : this done, rub the Gold and Quick-ſilver upon Braſs or Silver, and it will cleave unto it, then put the ſaid Braſs or Silver upon quick coals till it begin to ſmoak, then take it from the fire, and ſcratch it with a hair bruſh ; this do ſo long till all the Mercury is rubbed as clean off as may be, and the Gold appear of a faint yellow : which colour heighten with Sal-Armoniack, Bole and Verdegrieſe ground together and tempered with water.

Where note, that before you gild your Metal, you muſt boil it with Tartar in Beer or water, then ſcratch it with a wire bruſh.

VI. *Another water to gild Iron, Steel, Knives, Swords and Armour with.*

Take Fire-ſtone in powder, put it into ſtrong red Wine-vinegar for twenty four hours, boil it in a glazed pot, adding more Vinegar as it evaporates, or boils away : into this water dip your Iron, Steel, &c. and it will be black ; dry it, then poliſh it, and you will have a gold colour underneath.

VII. *Another water to gild Iron with.*

Take Salt-peter, Roch-alom burnt, of each half an ounce, Sal-Armoniack an ounce, all being in fine powder, boil with ſtrong Vinegar in a Copper veſſel ; with which wet the Iron, &c. then lay on Leaf-gold.

VIII. *Another water to gild Iron with.*

Take Roch-Alom, and grind it with boys Urine, till it is well diſſolved, with which anoint the Iron, heat it red-hot in a fire of wood coals, and it will be like Gold.

IX. *To gild Books.*

Take Bole-Armoniack four peny weight, Sugar-candy one peny weight, mix and grind them with glair of Eggs, then on a bound Book, (while in the preſs, after it hath been ſmeared with glair of Eggs,
and

and is dryed) smear the said composition, let it dry,
then rub it well and polish it: then with fair water
wet the edges of the Book, and suddenly lay on the
gold, pressing it down with Cotton gently, this done,
let it dry, and then polish it exactly with a tooth.

X. *Another way of gilding Iron.*

Take water three pound, Alom two ounces, Sal-gem
three ounces, Roman Vitriol, Orpiment of each one
ounce, *flos Æris* twenty four grains ; boil all with
Tartar and Salt as at the third Section.

XI. *To make Iron of the colour of Gold.*

Take Linseed-oyl three ounces, Tartar two ounces,
yolks of Eggs boiled hard and beaten two ounces,
Aloes half an ounce, Saffron five grains, Turmerick two
grains: boil all in an Earthen vessel, and with the oyl
anoint Iron, and it will look like Gold. *If there be not
Linseed-oyl enough, you may put in more.*

XII. *A Golden liquor to colour Iron, Wood, Glass, or
Bones with.*

Take a new laid Egg, through a hole at one end take
out the white, and fill up the Egg with Quick-silver two
parts, Sal-armoniack finely powdered one part ; mix
them all together with a Wire or little stick: stop the
hole with melted wax, over which put an half Egg-
shell : digest in horse-dung for a month, and it will be
a fine golden coloured Liquor.

XIII. *To gild Silk and Linnen.*

Take Glew made of Parchment, lay it on the Linnen, or Silk, *&c.* gently, that it may not sink: then
take Ceruse, Bole and Verdegriese, of each alike, mix
and grind them upon a stone : then in a glazed vessel
mix it with varnish , which let simper over a small fire,
then keep it for use.

XIV. *Another of a pure Gold colour.*

Take juyce of fresh Saffron, or (for want of it)
P

Saffron

Saffron ground, the beſt clear Orpiment of each alike : grind them with Goats gall or gall of a Pike (which is better) digeſt twenty eight days in horſe-dung, and it is done.

XV. *To gild on wood or ſtone.*

Take Bole-Armoniack, Oyl Ben, of each a ſufficient quantity ; beat and grind them together : with this ſmear the wood or ſtone, and when it is almoſt dry, lay on the Leaf gold, let it dry, then poliſh it.

XVI. *To gild with Leaf-gold.*

Take leaves of gold , and grind them with a few drops of honey, to which add a little gum-water, and it will be excellent to write or paint with.

XVII. *To gild Iron or Steel.*

Take Tartar one ounce , Vermilion three ounces, Bole-Armoniack , *Aqua-vitæ* of each two ounces , grind them together with Linſeed-oyl, and put thereto *Lapis Calaminaris* the quantity of a haſle-nut ; and grind therewith in the end a few drops of varniſh ; take it off the ſtone, ſtrain it through a liunen cloth (for it muſt be as thick as honey) then ſtrike it over Iron or Steel, and let it dry ; then lay on your Silver or Gold, and burniſh it.

XVIII. *To colour Tin or Copper of a gold colour.*

Take Linſeed-oyl, ſet it on the fire, ſcum it, then put in Amber. Aloes Hepatick, of each alike, ſtir them well together till it wax thick ; then take it off, cover it cloſe, and ſet it in the earth three days : when you uſe it, ſtrike the Metal all over with it, with a pencil, let it dry, and it will be of a golden colour.

XIX. *To gild any Metal.*

Take ſtrong *Aqua-fortis,* in which diſſolve fine Silver, to which put ſo much Tartar in fine powder, as will make it into paſte, with which rub any Metal, and it will look like fine Silver.

XX. *To*

XX. *To gild so as it shall not out with any water.*
Take Oker calcined , Pumice-stone of each alike,
Tartar a little, beat them with Linseed oyl, and five
or six drops of varnish, strain all through a linnen
cloth, with which you may gild.

CHAP. XXXIV.

Of Paper, Parchment, and Leather:

I. **T**O *make Paper waved like Marble.*
Take divers oyled colours, put them severally in drops upon water, and stir the water lightly :
then wet the Paper (being of some thickness) with it,
and it will be waved like Marble; dry it in the Sun.

II. *To write golden Letters on Paper or Parchment.*
This may be done by the ninth, tenth and twelfth
Sections of the three and thirtieth Chapter of this
Book : or write with Vermilion ground with Gum-
Armoniack, ground with glair of Eggs, and it will be
like gold.

III. *To take out blots, or make black Letters vanish in
Paper or Parchment.*
This may be done with Alom-water ; or with
Aqua-fortis mixed with common-water.

IV. *To make Silver Letters in Paper or Parchment.*
Take Tin one ounce, Quick-silver two ounces, mix
and melt them, and grind them with Gum-water.

V. *To write with green Ink.*
Take Verdegriese, Litharge, Quick-silver , of each
a sufficient quantity , grind and mingle them with
Urine, and it will be a glorious green like an Emerald
to write or paint with;

Or

Or thus, Grind juyce of Rue and Verdegriefe with a little Saffron together; and when you would write with it mix it with Gum-water : *Or thus,* Diffolve Verdegriefe in Vinegar, ftrain it, then grind it with common water, and a little honey, dry it; then grind it again with gum-water, and it is done.

VI. *To write on Paper or Parchment with blew Ink.*

Grind blew with honey, then temper it with glair of Eggs or Gum-water made of Ifinglafs.

VII. *To dye Skins Blew.*

Take berries of Elder or Dwarf-elder, firft boil them, then fmear and wafh the Skins therewith, and wring them forth : then boil the berries as before, in the diffolution of Alom-water, and wet the Skins in the fame water once or twice, dry them and they will be very Blew.

VIII. *To dye Skins into a reddifh Colour.*

Firft wafh the Skin in water and wring it well : then wet it with the folution of Tartar and Bay-falt in fair water, and wring it again : to the former diffolution, add afhes of Crab-fhells, and rub the Skin very well therewith, then wafh with common water and wring them out : then wafh them with tincture of Madder, in the folution of Tartar, Alom and the aforefaid afhes; and after (if not red enough) with the tincture of Brazil.

IX. *Another way to dye them Red.*

Wafh the Skins, and lay them in galls for two hours; wring them out, and dip them into a colour made with *Liguftrum,* Alom and Verdegriefe in water: Laftly, twice dye them with Brazil boiled with Lye.

X. *Another way to dye them Blew.*

Take the beft Indico and fteep it in Urine a day, then boil it with Alom, and it will be good. *Or,* temper the Indico with red Wine, and wafh the Skins there-with

XI. *To*

XI. *To dye Skins Purple.*

Take Roch-alom, diſſolve it in warm water, wet the Skins therewith drying them again ; then take raſped Brazil, boil it in water well, then let it cool ; do thus thrice : this done, rub the dye over the Skins with your hand, which being dry poliſh.

XII. *To dye Skins of a ſad Green.*

Take the filings of Iron and Sal-armoniack of each, ſteep them in Urine till they be ſoft, with which beſmear the Skin, being ſtretched out, drying it in the ſhade : the colour will penetrate and be green on both ſides.

XIII. *To dye Skins of a pure Skie Colour.*

For each Skin take Indico an ounce, put it into boiling water, let it ſtand one night, then warm it a little, and with a bruſh-pencil beſmear the Skin twice over.

XIV. *To dye Skins of a pure Yellow.*

Take fine Aloes one ounce, Linſeed-oyl two pound, diſſolve or melt them, then ſtrain it ; beſmearing the Skins therewith, being dry, varniſh them over.

XV. *To dye Skins Green.*

Take Sap-green, Alom-water, of each a ſufficient quantity, mix and boil them a little : if you would have the colour darker, add a little Indico.

XVI. *To dye Skins Yellow.*

Infuſe Wold in Vinegar , in which boil a little Alom : *Or thus,* having dyed them green by the fifteenth Section, dip them in decoction of Privet-berries and Saffron and Alom-water.

XVII. *To dye them of an Orange Colour.*

Boil Fuſtick-berries in Alom-water : but for a deep Orange, uſe Turmerick-root.

XVIII. *A Liquor to gild Skins, Metals, or Glaſs.*

Take Linſeed-oyl three pound, boil it in a glazed veſſel till it burns a feather being put into it, then put

to

to it Pitch, Rozin, dry varnish, or Gum-Sandrach, of each eight ounces, Aloes Hepatica four ounces; put all in powder into the oyl, and stir them with a stick, the fire being a little encreased: if the liquor is too clear or bright, you may add an ounce or two more of Aloes Socratine, and diminish the varnish, so the liquor will be darker and more like Gold. Being boiled, take it, and strain it, and keep it in a Glass for use: which use with a pencil.

CHAP. XXXV.

Of *Wood, Horns and Bones.*

I. *To dye Elder, Box, Mulberry-tree, Pear-tree, Nut-tree of the colour of Ebony.*

Steep the wood in Alom-water three or four dayes, then boil it in common oyl, with a little Roman-Vitriol and Sulphur.

Where note, the longer you boil the wood, the blacker it will be, but too long makes them brittle.

II. *To dye Bones green.*

Boil the Bones in Alom-water, then take them out, dry them and scrape them, then boil them in Lime-water with a little Verdegriese.

III. *To dye Wood like Ebony, according to Glauber.*

Distil an *Aqua-fortis* of Salt-peter and Vitriol.

IV. *To make Horns black.*

Vitriol dissolved in Vinegar and Spirit of Wine will make Horns black: so the Snow-white Calx of Silver in fair water.

V. *To makes Bones white.*

They

They are ſtrangely made white by boiling with water and Lime ; continually ſcumming of it.

VI. *To dye Bones green.*

Take white Wine-vinegar a quart, filings of Copper,
Verdegrieſe, of each three ounces, Rue bruiſed one
handful , mix them, and put the Bones therein for
fifteen days.

VII. *To dye Wood, Horns, or Bones red.*

Firſt boil them in Alom-water, then put them into
tincture of Brazil in Alom-water for two or three
weeks : or into tincture of Brazil in Milk.

VIII. *To dye them Blew.*

Having firſt boiled them in Alom-water, then put
them into the diſſolution of Indico in Urine.

IX. *To dye them green like Emeralds.*

Take *Aqua-fortis,* and put as much filings of Copper
into it, as it will diſſolve ; then put the Wood, Horns,
or Bones therein for a night.

X. *To dye Briſtles and Feathers.*

Boil them in Alom-water, and after, while they are
warm, put them into tincture of Saffron, if you would
have them yellow : or juyce of Elder-berries, if blew :
or in tincture of Verdegrieſe, if green.

XI. *To dye an Azure colour.*

Take Roch-alom, filings of Braſs, of each two ounces,
Fiſh-glew half an ounce, Vinegar, or fair water a pint,
boil it to the conſumption of the half.

XII. *To ſoften Ivory and Bones.*

Lay them twelve hours in *Aqua-fortis,* then three days
in the juyce of Beets, and they will be tender, and you
may make of them what you will: *To harden them again,*
lay them in ſtrong white Wine-vinegar.

XIII. *To make Horns ſoft.*

Take Urine a month old, Quick-lime one pound,
calcined Tartar half a pound, Tartar crude, Salt, of

each four ounces, mix and boil all together, then ſtrain it twice or thrice, in which put the Horns for eight dayes, and they will be ſoft.

XIV. *Another way to make them ſoft.*

Take aſhes of which glaſs is made, Quick-lime of each a pound, water a ſufficient quantity, boil them till one third part is conſumed, then put a feather into it, if the feather peel it is ſodden enough, if not, boil it longer, then clarifie it, and put it out, into which put filings of Horn for two dayes; anoint your hand with oyl, and work the Horns as it were paſte, then make it into what faſhion you pleaſe.

XV. *Another way to ſoften Horns.*

Take juyce of Marubium, Alexanders, Yarrow, Celandine and Radiſh roots, with ſtrong Vinegar, mix them, into which put Horns, and digeſt ſeven dayes in horſe-dung, then work them as before.

XVI. *To caſt Horns in a mould like as Lead.*

Make a Lixivium of calcined Tartar and Quick-lime, into which put filings or ſcrapings of Horn, boil them well together, and they will be as it were pap, tinge it of the colour you would have it, and then you may caſt it in a mould, and make thereof what faſhioned things you pleaſe.

XVII. *To make Ivory white.*

If Ivory be yellow, ſpotted or coloured, lay it in Quick-lime, pour a little water over it, letting it lye twenty four hours, and it will be fair and white.

C H A P.

CHAP. XXXVI.

Of Dying Yarn, Linnen Cloth, and the like.

I. **T**O dye a *sad Brown*.

First infuse the matter to be dyed in a strong tincture of Hermodacts: then in a bag put Saffron and ashes, *stratum super stratum*, upon which put water two parts mixed with Vinegar one part; strain the water and Vinegar through hot, fifteen or sixteen times, in this Lixiviate tincture of Saffron put what you would dye, letting it lye a night, then take it out, and hang it up to dry without wringing, which do in like manner the second and third times.

II. *To dye a blew Colour.*

Take *Ebulus* berries ripe and well dryed, steep them in Vinegar twelve hours, then with your hands rub them, and strain them through a linnen cloth, putting thereto some bruised Verditer and Alom.

Note, if the blew is to be clear, put more Verditer to it.

III. *Another excellent blew Dye.*

Take Copper scales one once, Vinegar three ounces, Salt one drachm; put all into a Copper vessel; and when you would dye, put the said matter into the tincture of Brazil.

IV. *Another excellent blew Dye.*

Take calcined Tartar three pugils, unslak'd Lime one pugil, make a Lixivium, and filtrate it; to twelve or fifteen quarts of the same water put Flanders blew one pound, and mix them well: set it to the fire, till you can scarcely endure your hand in it: then first boil
what

what you would dye in Alom-water, then dry it: afterwards dip it in hot Lye twice or thrice; then put it into the Dye.

V. *A good red Dye.*

Take Brazil in powder, fine Vermilion, of each half an ounce, boil them in Rain-water, with Alom one drachm, boil it till it is half consumed.

VI. *Another excellent good red Dye.*

Take of the *Lixivium* of unflak'd Lime one pint, Brazil in powder one ounce, boil to the half; then put to it Alom half an ounce, keep it warm, but not to boil: then dip what you would dye, firſt in a *Lixivium* of Red-wine Tartar, let it dry; then put it into the Dye.

VII. *Another very good Red.*

Take Roſſet with Gum-Arabick, boil them a quarter of an hour, ſtrain it: then firſt boil what you would dye, in Alom-water two hours; after put it into the Dye.

VIII. *To make fair Ruſſet Dye.*

Take two quarts of water, Brazil one ounce, boil it to a quart; put to it a ſufficient quantity of Grany and two drachms of Gum-Arabick.

IX. *A good Purple Colour.*

Take Myrtle-berries two pound, Alom, calcined Braſs, of each one ounce, water two quarts, mix them in a Braſs Kettle, and boil half an hour, then ſtrain it.

X. *A Yellow Colour.*

Take berries of purging Thorn, gathered about *Lammas-day*, bruiſe them, adding a little Alom in powder; then keep all in a Braſs veſſel.

XI. *Another good Yellow.*

Put Alom in powder to the Tincture of Saffron in Vinegar.

XII. *A*

XII. *A very good green Colour.*

Take Sap-green, bruife it, put water to it, then add a little Alom, mix and infufe for two or three days.

XIII. *To take out Spots.*

Wafh the fpots with oyl of Tartar *per Deliquium,* two or three times and they will vanifh, then wafh with water. Spirit of Wine to wafh with is excellent in this cafe. If they be Ink fpots, juyce of Limmons or Spirit of Salt is incomparable, wafhing often and dry-ing it: fo alfo Caftle-fope and Vinegar.

CHAP. XXXVII.

Of the Dying of Stuffs, Cloaths and Silks.

I. **T**O *make a fubftantial blew Dye.*

Take Woad one pound, and mix it with four pound of boiling water: infufe it twenty four hours; then dye with it all white colours.

II. *To make a firm black Dye.*

Firft Wad it with the former Blew: then take of Galls one pound, water fixty pound; Vitriol three pounds: firft boil the Galls and water with the Stuff or Cloath, two hours; then put in the Coperas at a cooler heat for one hour: then take out the Cloath or Stuff and cool it, and put it in for another hour, boiling it: Laftly, take it out again, cool it, and put it in once more.

III. *To make an excellent Yellow Dye.*

Take liquor or decoction of wheat-bran (being very clear) fixty pound: in which diffolve three pound of Alom: then boil the Stuff or Cloath in it.

for

for two hours : after which take Wold two pounds, and boil it till you fee the colour good.

IV. *To make a very good green Dye.*

Firſt dye the Cloth or Stuff yellow by the third Section, then put it into the blew Dye, in the firſt Section of this Chapter.

V. *To make a pure clear red Dye.*

Take liquor or infuſion of Wheat bran (being ſtrained and made very clear) ſixty pounds, Alom two pounds, Tartar one pound ; mix and diſſolve them, with which boil the Stuff or Cloth for two hours : take it then out, and boil it in freſh Wheatbran liquor, ſixty pounds : to which put Madder three pounds ; perfect the colour at a moderate heat, without boiling.

VI. *To make a very pleaſant purple Dye.*

Firſt dye it blew, by the firſt rule of this Chapter ; then boil it in the former red at the fifth rule hereof : laſtly, finiſh it with a decoction of Brazil.

VII. *To dye Crimſon in Grain.*

Firſt boil it in the red at the fifth rule of this Chapter ; then finiſh it in a ſtrong tincture of Cochenele made in the Wheat-bran liquor aforeſaid: Where note, that the veſſels in which the Stuff and Liquors are boiled muſt be lined with Tin, eiſe the colour will be defective. The ſame obſerve in Dying of Silks (in each colour) with this Caution, that you give them a much milder heat, and a longer time.

VIII. The Bow-dyers know, that diſſolved Tin (that is the ſolution of *Jupiter*) being put into a Kettle to the Alom and Tartar makes the Cloth attract the colour into it, ſo that none of the Cochenele is left ; but is all drawn out of the water into the Cloth.

The Spirit of Nitre being uſed with Alom and Tartar, in the firſt boiling makes a firm ground, ſo that they ſhall not spot nor lose their colour by the Sun, Fire, Air, Vinegar, Wine, Urine or Salt-water.

To enumerate all the great variety of Dyes, or Colours; or offer at an essay to reduce them to a certain method, as it is a labour needless, so it is as altogether impossible, there being infinite colours to be produced, for which (as yet) we have no certain, known or real name : And out of what we have already enumerated in this Chapter, the ingenious (if they please) shall find (by little Practice and Experience) such great variety to be apparent , that should we express the number though but in a very low or mean degree, we could not but be exposed in censure to an Hyperbole even of the highest : Every of the aforegoing colours, will alone or singly, produce a great number of others, the first more deep or high; the latter, all of them paler than each other : And according to the variety of colours the matter is of, before it is put into the Dye, such new variety also shall you have again when it comes out; not according to what the colour naturally gives, but another clean contrary to what you (although an Artist) may expect. For if strange colours be dipt into Dyes not natural to them, they produce a forced colour of a new texture, such as cannot possibly be preconceived by the mind of man, although long and continued experience might much help in that case. And if such variety may be produced by any one of those single colours; what number in reason might be the ultimate of any two or three or more of them being complicate or compounded? Now if such great numbers or varieties may be produced,   1. By any one single colour,   2. By being complicate; how should we (without a certain and determinate limitation by denomination or name) ever order such confused, unknown,

                                                          various,

various, and undeterminate species of things, in any pleasant, intelligible method? Since therefore that the matter (as yet) appears not only hard, but also impossible, we shall commend what we have done to the Ingenuity of the Industrious; and desire that Candor or Favour from the Experienced, with love to correct our Errors; which act or kindness will not only be a future obligation to the *Author*, but also enforce Posterity to acknowledge the same.

The End of the Third Book.

POLY-

POLYGRAPHICES

LIBER QUARTUS.

Containing the Original , Advancement and
Perfection of the Art of Painting : Par-
ticularly Exemplified in the various
Paintings of the Ancients.

To which is added the Art of Beautifying of the
Face and Skin, according to the choiceſt wayes
yet known: the whole Art of Perfuming never
Publiſhed till now : A brief contemplation of
Chiromantical Idea's : together with many
other things of excellent Uſe,

CHAP. I,

Of the Original of theſe Arts.

I. **T**HE *Original of the Art of Painting was*
taken from the Forms of things which do
appear ; expreſſing the ſame (as Iſidorus
Peluſiota *ſaith) with proper colours, imitating the Life,*
either

either hollow or swelling, dark or light, hard or soft, rough or smooth, new or old.

Of such things (amongst Vegetables) Flowers yield the greatest variety : of Animals, Man : of things Inanimate, Landskips, &c. For this matter of imitation was presented in the chief things only; for who should learn to imitate all things in Nature? the greater being attained, the lesser will follow of themselves; if any shall attempt so great a burthen, two inconveniencies, saith *Quintilian,* will necessarily follow, to wit, *Alwayes to say too much, and yet never to say all.*

II. *And this imitation of things seen with the Eye, was much helped by the Idea's of things conceived in the mind, from the continual motion of the imagination.*

Wherefore as *Quintilian* saith (*lib. 10. cap. 3.* of his Institutions of Oratory) " We shall do well to "accustome our minds to such a stedfast constancy of "conceiving, as to overcome all other impediments "by the earnestness of our intention: for if we do "altogether bend this intention upon things concei-"ved, our mind need never take notice of any thing "which the Eye sees, or the Ear hears. And there-fore those which would profit much, must take care and pains to furnish their minds with all sorts of useful Images and Idea's. " This treasury of the mind "(saith *Cassiodorus cap. 12. de Anima*) is not over-"loaden in haste: if it be once furnished, the Artist "shall find upon any sudden occasion, all things ne-"cessary, ready at hand; whereas those which are "unprovided shall be to seek. It is like to the Ana-letical Furniture in *Algebra,* without the knowledge of which, no notable thing can be performed. Now although the imagination may be easily moved, yet this same excellency is not attained in an instant : And without the ability of expressing of the conceived

Images,

Images, all the exercise of the fancy is worth nothing.

III. *These Forms and Idea's were not singly considered, but complicately.*

For whereas nature scarcely ever represents any one thing perfect in beauty (in all its parts) left it should be said, that she had nothing more to distribute to others: So Artists of old chose out many Patterns, which were absolutely perfect in some of their parts, that by designing each part after that Pattern, which was perfect therein, they might at last present something perfect in the whole. And so when *Zeuxis* intended an exquisite Pattern of a beautiful woman, he sought not for this perfection in one particular body ; but chose five of the most well-favoured Virgins, that he might find in them that perfect beauty, which (as *Lucian* faith) must of necessity be but one. And *Maximus Tyrius* faith, you shall not find in haft a body so accurately exact, as to compare it with the beauty of a Statue. And *Proclus* faith, if you take a man brought forth by nature, and another made by Art of Carving, that by nature shall not seem the statelier, because Art doth many things more exactly : To which *Ovid* assents, when that he faith that *Pygmalion* did Carve the Snow-white Image of Ivory, with such a happy dexterity, that it was altogether impossible that such a woman should be born.

IV. *From this manner of imitation did arise the skill of designing ; from whence sprang the Arts of Painting, Limning, Washing, Casting, and all others of that kind.*

These Arts in their infancy, were so mean, that the first Artist was forced (as *Ælianus* faith *lib.* 10. *cap.* 10. *of his History*) in Painting to write this is an Ox, this a Horse, this a Dog : But as *Tully* faith (*in libro*

Q   *de*

de claris oratoribus) there is nothing both invented
and finished at a time. And *Arnobius in libro secundo
adversus Gentes* saith, " The Arts are not together
" with our minds, brought forth out of the heavenly
" places; but are all found out here on earth, and
" in process of time, softned, forged, and beautified,
" by a continual meditation: Our poor and needy
" life, perceiving some casual things to fall out prof-
" perously, whilest it doth imitate, attempt, try, slip,
" reform, and change, hath out of the same assiduous
" reprehension made up some small pieces of Arts,
" the which it hath afterwards by study brought to
" some perfection.

V. *The persons who were the first inventers of these Arts
are scarcely known (because daily new inventions were added) but those famous Persons who either strove to bring
them to perfection, or add to what was already invented,
or otherwise were famous in any one particular thing, History
has in part informed us of.*

The famous *Pausias* was the first that attempted to
bring the Art of Painting to perfection. *Apelles* was
the first that undertook the expressing of invisible
things, as Thunder, Lightning, and the like; the
which consideration of these almost impossibilities
made *Theophylactus Simocatus* (in *Epist.* 37.) say, that
Painters undertake to express such things, as nature
is not able to do: And the same *Apelles* had a certain
invention and grace, proper to himself alone, to
which never any other Artificer ever attained. And
although *Zeuxis, Apelles, Aglaophon,* did none of them
seem to lack any thing of, yet they differed very much,
and had each of them some peculiar excellency, of
which neither of the other two could boast. Here is but
one Art of Casting, in which *Myron, Polycletus, Lysippus,* have been excellent, yet did One very much differ
from

from another: *Zeuxis* did surpass all other Artizans in Painting womens bodies : *Lysippus* is most excellent in fine and subtle workmanship: *Polycletus* made excellent Statues upon one Leg : *Samius* did excel in conceiving of Visions and Phantasies: *Dionysius* in Painting of men only : *Polygnotus* most rarely expressed the affections and passions of men : *Antimochus* made noble women : *Nicias* excellent in Painting of women, but most excellent in four footed creatures, chiefly Dogs : *Calamis* made Chariots, with two or four horses; the horses were so excellent and exact, that there was no place left for Emulation : *Euphranor*, the first and most excellent in expressing the dignity, and marks of Heroical Persons ; *Arestodemus* Painted Wrestlers : *Serapion* was most excellent in Scenes: *Pyreicus* (inferiour in the Art of Painting to none) painted nothing but Coblers and Barbers : *Ludio* the first and most excellent in Painting Landskips : *Apollodorus, Asclepiodorus, Androbulus, Alevas,* were the only Painters of Philosophers, *&c.*

VI. *Another reason of the Invention hereof, was from the moving of the passions.*

For as *Simonides* saith, (comparing Painting with Poesy) Picture is a silent Poesy, and Poesy is a speaking Picture : Upon the occasion of these words, *Plutarch* saith, *The things represented by Painters, as if they were as yet doing, are propounded by Orators, as done already: Painters express in colours and lines, what Poets do in words; the one doth that with the Pencil, which the other doth with the Pen.* When *Latinus Pacatus* had made a full description of the miserable end of the wicked *Maximus,* he calls upon all the Painters to assist him : Bring hither, bring hither you pious Poets (saith he) the whole care and study of your tedious nights : Ye Artificers also, despise the vulgar

Ar-

Argument of Ancient Fables; thefe, thefe things deferve better to be drawn by your cunning hands: let
the Market-places and Temples be filled with fuch
Spectacles; work them out in Ivory; let them live
in colours; let them ftand in Brafs; let them exceed
the price of precious Stones. It doth concern the fecurity of all Ages, that fuch things might be feen to
have been done, if by chance, any one filled with
wicked defires, might drink in innocency by his Eyes,
when he fhall fee the (horrid and deplorable) Monuments of thefe our times. And *Gregory Nyſſen,* upon
the Sacrificing of *Iſaac* faith, *I often ſaw in a Picture
the Image of this Fact, upon which I could not look without tears ; ſo lively did Art put the Hiſtory before my
Eyes.*

' VII. *The* Egyptians *were the firſt inventers of Painting : The* Greeks *brought it (out of its rudeneſs) to proportion : The* Romans *adorned it with colours: The* Germans
*(following them) made their works more durable by painting
in Oyl : of whom the* Engliſh, Dutch, Italian, *and* French,
are become imitators.

It is reported that the *Grecians* were the firſt painters, and that their colours were (in the infancy thereof) only white and black : but it appears more with
reaſon and truth, that the invention thereof ſhould be
aſcribed to the *Egyptians,* who (before the invention of Letters) ſignified their conceptions by *Hierogly-
phicks* of Figures, Cyphers, Characters, and Pictures
of divers things, as *Birds, Beaſts, Inſects, Fiſhes, Trees,
Plants,* and the like, which by Tradition they tranſ-
fer'd to their Children ; ſo they made the *Falcon* to
ſignifie Diligence, Strength, and Swiftneſs : the *Bee*
a King ; its *Honey,* Mildneſs; its *Sting,* Juſtice : a *Serpent* (tail in mouth) the revolution of the Year : the
Eagle, Law ; the *Earth,* a labouring Beaſt ; a *Hare,*
Hearing,

Hearing, *&c.* Now our bare learning to imitate is not enough; it is requisite that since we are not first in invention, we should study rather to outgo than to follow. *If it were unlawful (saith* Quintilian *) to add any thing to things invented, or to find out better things, our continual labour would be good for nothing ; for it is certain that* Phydias *and* Apelles, *have brought many things to light, which their Predecessors knew nothing of.* *Apelles* did all things with compleatness, *Zeuxis*, with an inestimable grace : *Protogenes* with an indefatigable diligence : *Timanthes* with a great deal of subtilty and curiosity : *Nicophanes* with a stately magnificence. Now to attain to these kind of Excellencies, it is necessary to have recourse to variety of great Masters, that something out of the one, and something out of the other, may be as so many ornaments to adorn our works; and as so many steps to lead us on to the door of perfection.

VIII. *About the time of* Philip *King of* Macedon, *this Art began to flourish: growing into great estimation in the days of* Alexander *and his Successors: from thence through all the series of time even to this day, it hath received by degrees, such wonderful advancements that it may be now said, it is arrived at perfection.*

For without doubt there is a perfection of Art to be attained, and it is as possible that I, or thou, or he, may as well attain it, as any body else, if we resolve to strive, and take pains, without fainting, or fear of despair. And since the Art of Painting is (as *Socrates* saith) the resemblance of visible things, the Artist ought to beware that he abuses not the liberty of his imagination, in the shapes of monstrous and prodigious Images of things not known in nature; but as a true lover of Art, prefer a plain and honest work (agreeing with nature) before any phantastical and conceited device whatsoever.

Q 3   IX. *Last-*

IX. *Laftly, that from* Time, Form, Magnitude, Number, Proportion, Colour, Motion, Reft, Scituation, Similitude, Diftance, Imagination, and Light, *in a fingle and complicate confideration, this Art hath its effence or being, and at laft had by the help of induftrious and unwearied minds, its Original production, and manifeftation.*

Light is that only thing, without which all thofe other things from which this Art fprings, would be ufelefs ; without which the Art it felf cannot be. " It " is (as *Sanderfon* faith) the heavens off-fpring, the " eldeft daughter of God, *fiat lux*, the firft days Crea-"tion : it twinkles in a Star, blazes in a Comet ; "dawns in a Jewel, diffembles in a Glow-worm ; "contracts it felf in a Spark, rages in a Flame, is "pale in a Candle, and dyes in a Coal. By it the "fight hath being, and the imagination life, which "comprehends the univerfality of all things without "fpace of place : the whole Heavens in their vaft and "full extent, enter at once through the apple of the "Eye, without any ftraitnefs of paffage : the fight "is a fenfe, which comprehends that, which no other "fenfe is capable of ; it judgeth and diftinguifheth "between two contraries in an inftant, it confiders "the excellency and beauty of every object : the "fpangled Canopy of Heaven by night, the wander-"ing Clouds by day, the wonderful Form of the "Rain-bow, the glorious matutine appearance of "*Phœbus* ; the meridional exaltation, the golden rays "which furround him, the mutability of his fhadows, "his vefpertine fetting : the lofty tops of Mountains, "unacceffible and ridgy Rocks, profound Valleys, "large Plains, which feem to meet Heaven, green "Trees, and pleafant Groves, delightful Hills, fweet "and flowery Meadows, pleafant Streams, fpringing
Foun-

" Fountains, flowing Rivers, stately Cities, famous
" Towers, large Bridges, magnificent Buildings, fruit-
" ful Orchards and Gardens, shapes of living Crea-
" tures, from the Elephant to the Ant, from the Eagle
" to the Wren, and from the Whale to the Shrimp,
" the wonderful forms of Insects, the marching of
" Armies, the besieging and storming of Garisons,
" the insolencies of rude People, and flight of the
" Distressed, the desolation and depopulation of King-
" doms and Countries, the sailing of Ships, terrible Sea-
" fights, great beauty of Colours, together with thou-
" sands of other things, all which it digests, and Mar-
" shals in ample Order, that when occasion may be, it
" may exert its store, for the benefit, advantage, ad-
" vancement, and perfection of Art.

CHAP. II.

Of the farther progress of these Arts.

I. **A**S *God Almighty (who is the Author of all wisdom)
was the first institutor hereof, so also was he the pro-
mulgator, by whom these Arts have made progression in the
world.*

Certainly, saith *Philostratus*, Picture is an invention
of the Gods, as well for the painted faces of the Meadows adorned with Flowers, according to the several
Seasons of the year; as for those things, which appear in the Sky. What wonderful Eloquence is this!
that in so few words, this Philosopher should clear so
great a point. But what saith *Gregorius Nyssenus*?
Man, saith he, is an earthen Statue: and *Suidas in
Oratione prima de Beatitudinibus*; speaking of *Adam*,
saith,

ſaith, This was the firſt Statue, the Image named by God, after which all the Art of Carving uſed by men receiveth directions : *Lot's* Wife was another, turned into a durable Pillar of Salt, of whom *Prudentius* (in *Harmartigenia*) ſaith, ſhe waxed ſtiff, being changed into a more brittle ſubſtance, ſhe ſtandeth Metamorphoſed into Stone, apt to be melted, keeping her old poſture in that Salt-ſtone Image ; her comlineſs, her ornaments, her forehead, her eyes, her hair, her face alſo (looking backward) with her chin gently turned, do retain the unchangeable Monuments of her Antient offence : and though ſhe melteth away continually in Salt ſweat ; yet doth the compleatneſs of her ſhape ſuffer no loſs by that fluidity ; whole droves of beaſts cannot impair that ſavoury ſtone ſo much, but ſtill there is liquor enough to lick, by which perpetual loſs, the waſted skin is ever renewed. To theſe let us add the pattern of the *Tabernacle* ſhewed unto *Moſes* upon Mount *Sinai* : The *Brazen Serpent* made by the expreſs command of God : The *Pattern of the Temple* (which *David* gave unto *Solomon*) after the form which God made with his own hand : *Ezekiel's* portrait of *Jeruſalem* with its formal *Siege* upon a Tile by expreſs command from God alſo : The *Brazen Statue* of our Lord *Jeſus Chriſt* erected by the woman healed of the bloody Iſſue, as is mentioned by *Photius,* and *Aſterius* Biſhop of *Amaſa,* and other Eccleſiaſtick Writers : The *Picture* alſo of our Lord made without hands, as it is related by *Damaſcenus Cedrenus* and others : The *Picture* of *Chriſt* in a Napkin or Towel, ſent by our Lord himſelf, unto *Augarus* King of *Edeſſa* ; together with many more too tedious here to relate.

II. *By vertue of this divine hand it was that many Artiſts of old attained to a certain kind of perfection in theſe Arts.*

We will only refer the proof of this to the examples in the 31 of *Exodus* of *Bezaleel* and *Aholiab*; of whom God himself witnesseth, that he called them by name to make the *Tabernacle*; and filled them with his spirit, not only to devise curious works *in Gold, in Silver, in Brass, and in Silk*; but also gave them skill to teach others the same.

III. *Nature also hath not been idle, but hath acted a Master-piece herein.*

To pass by the glory of Flowers, the excellent comliness of beasts (as in the spots of *Leopards*, tails of *Peacocks*, and the like) I will only remark the same of a Gem, which *Pyrrhus* (who made War with the *Romans*) had, of which *Pliny* in *lib.* 34. *cap.* 1. of his natural History, reports, that it being an *Agath* had the *nine Muses* and *Apollo* holding of a Lute depicted therein; the spots not by Art, but by nature, being so spread over the stone, that each Muse had her peculiar mark. See *Gafferel cap.* 5.

IV. *The care of Parents in the Education of their Children, was another reason of the progress hereof.*

The *Grecians*, saith *Aristotle in cap.* 3. *lib.* 8. of his Politicks, did teach their children the Art of Painting: and *Plutarch* saith, that *Paulus Æmilius* had Sculptors and Painters amongst the Masters of his children as well as Philosophers and Rhetoricians? and *Pliny* saith, that by the Authority of *Pamphilus*, this Art hath been ranked among the liberal Sciences, and that only Free-born children should learn it. And *Galen* enumerating several Arts as *Physick, Rhethorick, Musick, Geometry, Arithmetick, Logick, Grammer, and knowledge of Law*; add unto these, saith he, *Carving and Painting*. And as the *Grecians* were the first, that taught their children these Arts, so also they provided betimes for them choice Masters.

V. *These*

V. *Theſe Maſters by their carefulneſs and vigilancy, not deceiving thoſe that put their truſt in them, became main Pillars of theſe Arts, and propagated them to Poſterity; which by the addition of conſiderable gifts and rewards had an honourable eſteem in the world.*

Their care was manifeſt in laying down ſolid Principles of Art; of which *Quintilian in cap.* 2. *lib.* 12. of his Inſtitutions of Oratory ſaith, though vertue may borrow ſome forward fits of nature, yet ſhe niuſt attain to perfection by doctrine. Their vigilancy was ſeen in watching, to apprehend their Scholars capacities, that they might ſuit themſelves accordingly; as in *Tully*'s inſtance of *Iſocrates*, a ſingular good teacher, who was wont to apply the ſpur to *Ephorus*, but the bridle to *Theopompus*; And their reward was eminent, as *Pliny* noteth in *Pamphilus* his School, out of which *Apelles* and many other excellent Painters came, who taught no body under a Talent (which is about 175 pound ſterling) thereby the better to maintain the Authority of Art.

VI. *Their practice exactly agreed with their precepts.*

As with *Seneca*, that labour is not loſt, whoſe experiments agree with precepts; ſo with *Quintilian*, thoſe examples may ſtand for teſtimonies : And it was the practice of Painters of old, as *Galen* witneſſeth concerning *Polycletus*, who hath not only ſet down in Writing the accurate precepts of Art; but alſo that he made a Statue according to the rules of Art contained in thoſe precepts.

VII. *Theſe precepts which they taught their Scholars, they delivered in writing, that they might ever accompany them whereſoever they went.*

Apelles gave the precepts of this Art to his diſciple *Perſeus* in writing, as *Polycletus* did to his; beſides innumerable others now in being too tedious here to
recite.

recite. The like did these following, *Adæus*, *My-lenæus*, *Alcetas*, *Alexis* the Poet, *Anasimenes*, *Antigonus*, *Aristodemus*, *Carius*, *Artimon*, *Callixenus*, *Christodorus*, *Democritus*, *Ephesus*, *Duris*, *Eupherion*, *Euphranor*, *Isthmius*, *Hegesander Delphicus*, *Hippias Eleus*, *Hypsicrates*, *Iamblicus*, *Juba* Rex Mauritaniæ, *Malchus Bizantius*, *Melanthius*, *Menæchmus*, *Menetor*, *Pamphilus*, *Polemon*, *Porphyrius*, *Praxiteles*, *Protogenes*, *Theophanes*, *Xenocrates*, and many others, the chief of whole works are now lost.

VIII. *As Arts came new into estimation, so at length Laws were established for their preservation; and punishments for their prevarication.*

The beginning of these Laws was first at *Argos*, *Ephesus*, *Thebes* and *Athens*, as also in *Egypt*, where a workman (saith *Diodorus Siculus*) is fearfully punished, if he undertake any charge in the Commonwealth, or meddle with any Trade but his own : the which Law, saith *Herodotus*, the *Lacedæmonians* did also approve of.   By means of which Laws it was, that the Artists of those Nations attained to such a perfection of Art, as we shall hereafter relate.

IX. *The fervent desire and love of emulation to excel others; the commendable simplicity of Art; together with the content and satisfaction of doing something well, gave a large progress towards the advance of Art.*

It was nobly said of *Scipio Africanus*, that every magnanimous spirit compares himself, not only with them that are now alive; but also with the famous men of all ages; whereby it appears that great wits are always by the sting of emulation, driven forwards to great matters ; but he that by too much love of his own works, compares himself with no body, must needs attribute much to his own conceits.   Dost thou desire the glory of swiftness? saith *Martial* (*in Epigr.* 36. *lib.*

36. *lib.* 12. ſtrive to out-go the *Tyger,* and the light *Oſtrich*; it is no glory at all to out-run *Aſſes.* This *emulation* is the force of great wits, whereby our imitation is provoked ſometimes by envy, and ſometimes by admiration, whereby it falls out, that the thing we earneſtly ſeek after, is ſoon brought to ſome height of perfection; which perfection conſiſts in exact imitation, according to the ſimplicity of Art, and not in gaudy appearances, which adorns the ſhadows much more than ever nature adorned the ſubſtance. This imitation of the life gave the *Artizan* fame; which fame quickened his aſpiring thoughts, adding more fuel to the flames, till ſuch time, as he brought forth a moſt abſolute work, whereby he conceived a joy, content and ſatisfaction, as durable as the work it ſelf, upon which he now conceived himſelf a happy man, and through a juſt affiance of his vertues knows himſelf to be lifted up above the reach of envy, where he ſtands ſecure of his fame, enjoying in this life (as if he were now conſecrated unto Eternity) the veneration that is like to follow him after his death; thus an honeſt *emulation* and *confidence,* bringing forth works of general applauſe, procureth unto its author an everlaſting Glory. Now what a comfortable thing is this, to have a fore-feeling of what we hope to attain to?

X. *Another reaſon of the augmentation of theſe Arts, was the manifold uſes thereof among men, either for good or evil purpoſes.*

As in natural Sciences, where words come ſhort, a little Picture giveth us the knowledge of Beaſts, Birds, Fiſhes, and other forms, as well inanimate as animate : In the *Tacticks,* how ſhould a General know how to ſet his men in array, unleſs he try the caſe by deſign or delineation? ſo in *Architecture* to pourtray Platforms
after

after any fashion, and to work out the Patterns of high and mighty buildings in a little wax, keeping in so small an example the exact proportion of the greater Structure: In *Geometry* the exactness of Lines, Angles, Surfaces and Solids: In *Botonalogia*, the exact shapes of Herbs, Plants and Trees: In *Zoologia*, the shapes of all living creatures: In *Anthropologia*, the exact description of all the parts of mans body inward and outward: In *Chymia*, the forms of all Chymical vessels and operations: In *the lives of illustrious men and Princes*, to express their forms and shapes to the life, that age might not prevail against them, deserving thereby (as *Varro* saith) the envy of the Gods themselves: In *Geography*, to describe in small Maps Kingdoms, Countreys, and Cities, yea, the whole World: In *Policy,* as *Michal* in saving her husband *David*, *Ptolomæus* in the Image of *Alexander*, which he willingly let *Perdiccas* catch from him, supposing it to have been the body it self, thereby avoiding much blood-shed: *Cyrus* his wooden *Persians* in the Siege of *Sardis* , by which the Towns-men being frighted, yielded the City: *Epaminondas* at *Thebes* by the Image of *Pallas* did wonders: *Amasis* King of *Egypt*, his golden Image made of the Bason, in which his feet used to be washed, which the *Egyptians* religiously worshipped, whereby he brought them to affect him being now a King, who was of an ignoble and base Parentage ; the *wooden Elephants* of *Perseus* King of *Macedonia*, with which he wonted his herses, that they might not be frighted in time of Battel. The Ornaments of Temples, Market-places and Galleries, places both publick and private. *Julius Cæsar*'s Image in wax, hideous to look to, for twenty three gaping wounds he received, did mightily stir up the *Romans* to revenge his death. Worthy men which had deserved well of the world, had

their

their memories conferved with their Images; by which all thofe that afpire to goodnefs, and to follow their fteps, are likewife filled with hope. The *Athenians* have erected unto *Æfop* a moft goodly Statue, faith *Phædrus,* and have fet a contemptible flave upon an everlafting bafe, *that all might underftand, how the way of honour lieth open to every one, and that glory likewife doth not fo much follow the condition of our birth, as the vertues of our life.* *Berofus* excelled in *Aftrology,* wherefore the *Athenians* for his divine Prognofticatons, erected him a Statue with a golden Tongue, fet up in their publick Schools, as *Pliny* faith, *lib.* 7. *cap.* 37. Publick Libraries were furnifhed alfo with Golden, Silver, and Brafs Images of fuch, whofe immortal fouls did fpeak in thofe places. The provocations of vices have alfo augmented the Art; it hath been pleafing to engrave *wanton lufts* upon their cups; and to drink in *Ribauldry* and *Abominations,* as *Pliny* faith in the Proem of his 33. Book.

XI. *The ufe therefore of thefe Arts extending it felf fo univerfally to all intents both in war and peace, it came to pafs that Artificers were honoured by all forts of men, which themfelves perceiving, did ftill endeavour to encreafe this erjoyed favour by a daily advance of their skill.*

By Kings they were honoured; for *Demetrius,* whileft at the Siege of *Rhodes,* came to *Protogenes,* leaving the hope of his Victory to behold an Artificer. *Alexander* the Great came alfo to *Apelles* his Shop, often accompanied with many Princes. It was his will that none but *Polycletus* alone, fhould caft his Statue in *Brafs,* that none but *Apelles* alone fhould paint him in *Colours,* that none but *Pyrgoteles* alone fhould *Engrave* him. The eftimation of the Artifts were alfo underftood from the efteem and high rates their works were

prized

prized at ; a picture of *Bularchus* a Painter, was valued
at its weight in Gold by *Candaules* King of *Lydia*:
Aristides was so singular in his Art, that it is reported
of King *Attalus* that he gave an hundred Talents
(which is about seventeen thousand and five hundred
pounds sterling) for one of his Pictures. As much
had *Polycletus* for one of his. *Apelles* had for painting the Picture of *Alexander* the Great, three thousand and five hundred pounds given him in golden
Coin. *Cæsar* payed to *Timomachus* eighty Talents,
(about fourteen thousand pounds sterling) for the
Pictures of *Ajax* and *Medea.* Many more examples
we might produce, but these may suffice ; at length
no price was thought equal to their worth : so *Nicias*
rather than he would sell his Picture called *Necyia* to
King *Attalus*, who proffered him sixty Talents, (worth
near eleven thousand pound sterling) bestowed it as a
Present upon his Country.

XII. *Art meeting with such Successes, created a boldness
in Artificers, to attempt even the greatest matters.*

The great *Colosses* of the Antients may serve here
for an example ; *Zeuxis* above all the rest, hath been
admired for his boldness : *Euphranor* also excelled
Parrhasius in this kind, in that the *Thesius* of the one
so infinitely excelled the *Thesius* of the other. So great
an excellency of Spirit arose in the old Artificers, as
not to be daunted by the authority of those, who were
like to censure their works : it was a great mark they
aimed at, to avoid a prosperous shame or fear. And
this they accomplished by taking care, not only to give
them content, who must of necessity be contented
with the work ; but also that they might seem admirable unto them which may judge freely without
controul. So they heeded to do well in the opinion
of accurate and judicious spectators, rather than to
do

do that which liked themfelves. And therefore what-foever is dedicated unto pofterity, and to remain as an example for others, had need be well done, neat, po-lifhed, and made according to the true rule and law of Art, forafmuch as it is likely to come into the hands of skilful Artificers, judicious cenfurers, and fuch as make a narrow fcrutiny into every defect. But as it is impoffible to attain to an excellency, or height of any thing without a beginning, fo do the firft things in going on of the work feem to be the leaft; the height of Arts, as of Trees, delighteth us very much, fo do not the roots; yet can there be no height with-out the roots. And therefore we fhall find that a fre-quent and continual exercife, as it is moft laborious, fo it is moft profitable; feeing *nature doth begin, hope of profit doth advance, and exercife doth accomplifh the thing fought after.* In fum, by doing quickly, we fhall never learn to do well; but by doing well, it is very likely we may learn to do quickly. To this fpeedy and well doing there belongeth three things, *viz.* to add, to detract, and to change. To add or detract, requireth lefs labour and judgement; but to deprefs thofe things that fwell, to raife thofe things that fink, to tye clofe thofe things which are fcattered, to digeft things that are without order, to compofe things that are different, to reftrain things that are infolent, requireth double pains: for thofe things may be condemned, which once did pleafe, to make way for inventions not yet thought of. Now with-out doubt, the beft way for emendation is to lay by the defign for a time, till it feem unto us as new, or anothers invention; left our own, like new births, pleafe us too much.

XIII. Laftly, *That which gave the greateft and as it were, the laft ftep towards the augmentation of Art, was that*

*that free liberty which Artizans gave every one, to cen-
ſure, to find fault with their works, and to mark their
defects.*

It was the opinion of *Seneca*, that many would
have attained unto wiſdom, if they had not conceived themſelves to be wiſe already. When *Phidias*
made *Jupiter* for the *Eleans*, and ſhewed it, he ſtood
behind the door liſtning what was commended, and
what diſcommended in his work : one found fault
with the groſsneſs of his noſe, another with the length
of his face, a third had ſomething elſe to ſay : now
when all the ſpectators were gone, he retired himſelf
again to mend the work, according to what was liked
of the greater part; for he did not think the advice
of ſuch a multitude to be a ſmall matter, judging that
ſo many ſaw many things better than he alone, though
he could not but remember himſelf to be *Phidias.* But
yet Artificers did not from hence admit their judgements generally in every thing , but they followed
their directions only *in ſuch things as did belong to
their Profeſſion.* As when *Apelles* made a work, he ex-
poſed it in a place where all that paſſed by might ſee
it; hiding himſelf in the mean time behind the Picture, to hear what faults were marked in his works,
preferring the common people before his own judgement. And he is reported to have mended his work,
ſipon the *cenſure of a Shoo-maker*, who blaming him
for having made fewer latchets in the inſide of one of
the Pantoffles, than of the other : the Shoo-maker
finding the work the next day mended according to
his advice, grew proud, and began to find fault with
the Leg alſo; whereupon *Apelles* could not contain
himſelf any longer, but looking forth from behind the
Picture, *Ne ſutor ultra crepidam,* bid the Shoo-maker
not go beyond his Laſt ; from whence at laſt came

R   **that**

that Proverb. He is the beſt man that can adviſe himſelf what is fit to be done; and he is next in goodneſs, that is content to receive good advice: but he that can neither adviſe himſelf, nor will be directed by the advice of others, is of a very ill nature.

CHAP. III.

Of the Conſummation or Perfection of the Art of Painting.

I. **A**S *Invention gave way to the advancement of Art, ſo the advancement of the ſame made way for its Perfection.*

The Invention aroſe from the appearance of things natural, conceived in *Idea's*, as we have abundantly ſignified (*in the firſt Chapter of this Book*) the Advance from the bringing of thoſe *Idea's* to light through practice (*by Chap. 2.*) from whence aroſe things *very excellent for greatneſs : very good for their uſefulneſs , choice for their novelty, and ſingular for their kind.*

II. *Eaſe of Invention, Plenty of Matter, and Neatneſs of Work, were ſteps by which Art was conſummated.* For eaſe of Invention gave Encouragement, Plenty of Matter gave Formation, and Neatneſs gave Delight, all which ſo conſpired together, to put ſo much of emulation into the Artificer, to undertake, or endeavour to do thoſe things, which in their kind might never after be exceeded : this indeed was their aim of old, which although the antients of this Art could never attain unto, yet did they make ſuch way, that ſome of their followers have done thoſe things , which never any after them could ever mend, nor themſelves ſcarcely

come

come near. Eafie invention fprings out of a great and well rooted fulnefs of learning; by being converſant in all forts of ftudies, having familiarity with Antiquities; the knowledge of innumerable Hiftorical and Poetical narrations, together with a through acquaintance with all fuch motions and Idea's of the mind, as are naturally incident unto men: for the whole force of this Art doth principally confift in thefe things, nothing bearing a greater fway in the manifold varieties of *Painting.*

III. *It was the opinion of* Pamphilus *(the maſter of* Apelles *) that without the knowledge of Arithmetick, Geometry, and the Opticks, this Art could not be brought to Perfection.*

The examples of *Phidias* and *Alcamenes* is pertinently brought here: The *Athenians* intending to fet up the Image of *Minerva* upon a high Pillar, employed thofe two Workmen, purpofing to chufe the better of the two; *Alcamenes* (having no skill in *Geometry* nor the *Opticks*) made her wonderful fair to the eye of them that faw her near. *Phidias* contrariwife (being skilful in all Arts, chiefly the *Opticks*) confidering that the whole fhape would change according to the height of the place, made her lips wide open, her nofe fomewhat out of order, and all the reft accordingly, by a kind of refupination: the two Images being brought to view, *Phidias* was in great danger to have been ftoned by the multitude, until at length the Statues were fet up; where the fweet and excellent ftroaks of *Alcamenes* were drowned, and the disfigured diftorted hard-favourednefs of *Phidias* his work vanifhed (and all this by the height of the place;) by which means *Alcamenes* was laughed at, and *Phidias* much more efteemed. Of like perfection is *Amulius* his *Minerva*; the Image of *Juno* in the Temple of the

R 2   *Syrian*

Syrian goddeſs ; the head of *Diana* exalted at *Chios*, made by *Bupalus* and *Anthermus*, *Hercules* in the Temple of *Antonia*, &c. An Artificer, ſaith *Philoſtratus* in *Proœmio Iconum*, muſt underſtand the nature of a man throughly, to expreſs all his manners, guiſe, behaviour, &c. he muſt diſcern the force in the conſtitution of his cheeks, in the turning of his eyes, in the caſting of his eye-brows ; in ſhort, he muſt obſerve all things which may help the judgement ; and whoſoever is thus furniſhed will doubtleſs excell, and bring things to perfection ; he then may eaſily paint a mad man, an angry man, a penſive man, a joyful man, an earneſt man, a lover, &c. in a word, the perfection of whatſoever may poſſibly be conceived in the mind.

IV. *Continual obſervation of exquiſite pieces (whether Artificial or Natural) nimble conceptions, and tranquillity of mind, are great means to bring Art to Perfection.*

The works of the Antients could never have been ſo exquiſite in the expreſſion of Paſſions, but by theſe means. How perfectly did *Zeuxis* paint the modeſt and chaſte behaviour of *Penelope* ; *Timomachus* the raging mad fit of *Ajax* ; *Silanion* the frowardneſs of *Apollodorus* ; *Protogenes* the deep penſiveneſs of *Philiſcus* ; *Praxiteles* the rejoycings of *Phryne* ; *Parrhaſius* a boy running in Armour ; and *Ariſtides* his *Anapauomenos* dying for love of his Brother ? *Bodius* his Image of *Hercules* is of the ſame nature: *Themiſtius* ſhews us the true Image of feigned friendſhip ; *Agellius* a moſt lively Image of *Juſtice* ; *Apelles* an admirable Picture of *Slander* ; thouſands of examples more might be drawn out of antient Authors to approve theſe things , if theſe may be thought not ſufficient.

V. *This Perfection alſo lyeth in the truth of the matter, the occaſion thereof, and diſcretion to uſe it.*

The moſt antient and famous Painters did make

much

much account of *Truth,* and had rather lose the neatnefs and glory of their pieces, than to endanger the
truth of their ftory ; which indeed is the great commendation of a Picture, for as much as *Lucian* faith,
That nothing can be profitable but what proceeds
from truth. *Occafion* alfo is a great matter ; the Picture of *Bacchus* may here ferve for an excellent example, whofe paffion of love was fo clearly expreffed
therein ; cafting afide his brave apparel, Flowers,
Leaves, Grapes, *&c.* Now in reprefenting things
truly according to the occafion, *difcretion* ought to be
your guide ; for as in Tragedies, fo alfo in Pictures
all things ought not to be reprefented ; let not *Medea*
(faith *Horace in libro de Arte*) Murder her own children in the prefence of all the people ; let not the
wicked *Atreus* boil humane flefh openly ; there are
doubtlefs many things, which had better be left out,
though with fome lofs of the ftory , than with the
lofs of modefty ; wanton , unlawful and filthy lufts
(though they may gain the vain title of wit, yet)
they diminifh not only the eftimation of the workman, but alfo the excellency of the work, debarring
it of perfection. Precepts help Art much, in pro-
pounding unto us the right way ; but where they fail,
our wits muft fupply, by warily confidering what is
decent and convenient ; for this Art requireth ftudi-
ous endeavours, affiduous exercitations, great experience, deep wifdom, ready counfel, veracity of mind,
diligent obfervations, and great difcretion.

VI. *To the former add Magnificence, which gives Authority to things excellent.*

Great minded men are moft of all given to entertain ftately conceits ; therefore an *Artizan* ought to
be of a *magnanimous* nature ; if not, yet that at leaft
he ought with a determined refolution to aim at *mag-*

nificent

nificent things. So it seems that nature did difpofe *Nicophanes* to a high ftrain of invention ; *Nicophanes* (faith *Pliny, lib.* 35. *cap.* 10.) was gallant and neat, fo that he did paint *Antiquities* for *Eternity* , whereby he was commended for the magnificence of his work, and gravity of his Art. Such *Artificers* therefore as do bring any thing to perfection, muft be of an exceeding great fpirit , and entertain upon every occafion great thoughts , and lofty imaginations ; by this means they fhall gain an everlafting fame ; but this is impoffible (faith *Longinus*) for any who bufie the thoughts and ftudies of their life about vile and flavifh matters, to bring forth any thing which might deferve the admiration of fucceeding ages. If any *Artizan* be not naturally of fo great a fpirit, let him help himfelf by the reading of *Hiftory* and *Poefie* ; *Hiftory* cannot but infpire a *magnanimous Spirit* , when fhe reprefents to us fo many rare exploits, and the examples of fo many great noble and valiant fouls, who *throughout all ages*, in the midft of moft eminent dangers, have demonftrated their vertues and fpirits not only to thofe prefent, but *all fucceeding times*. *Poefie* alfo being of a haughty and lofty ftile, doth much enlarge the mind, and from thence many excellent things are brought : The much admired *Elean Jupiter* which *Phidias* made, himfelf confeffed to be formed after the Image of *Jupiter* defcribed in *Homer*. From the fame Poet did *Apelles* paint the Image of *Diana* among the facrificing Virgins. It is not the prefent age, but the facred memory of all pofterity, which gives unto us a weighty and durable crown of Glory.

VII. *Exact Analogy or proportion* , *not only advanced Art*, *but alfo brought it a degree nearer Perfection*.

Philoftratus calls it *Symmetrie*, fome *Analogy*, others *Harmony* ; this is the appellation of the *Greeks* ; what
the

the Latines called it fcarcely appears (as *Pliny* faith *lib.* 34. *cap.* 8.) yet words equivalent in power thereto are found, as *Congruence, equality,* and *Tully* (*libro primo de Officiis*) calls it *Agreement* and apt *compofition* ; *Vitruvius, Commodulation* ; *Agellius* calls it a *natural competence* ; *Quintilian* approves the word *Proportion* ; by which faith *Plutarch* beautiful things are perfected : it is one of thofe things which the moft High ufed in the fabrication of the world, (Wifd. 11. 20.) *He hath difpofed all things in meafure and number and weight.* The firft giver of *Symmetrie* or *Analogy* was *Parrhafius* ; *Polycletus* was a diligent obferver thereof; *Afclepiodorus,* an exact practifer thereof, whofe admirer was *Apelles,* who efteemed it to proceed out of fome perfections in an *Artificer* furpafling in Art, and which is moft apparent in naked and undifguifed bodies. *Strabo* faith, that *Phidias* exactly obferved this proportion in the Image of *Jupiter Olympicus* fitting. The fame *Phidias,* as *Lucian* reports, could exactly tell upon the firft fight of a Lions claw, how big a Lion he was to make in proportion to the fame claw. Lineal Picture is the foundation of all imitation, which if it be done after the true rules of proportion, will lively reprefent the thing delineated : this is a perfection in kind, which yet cannot be compared to the perfection of a coloured Picture.

VIII. *This point of Perfection was further advanced by the exquifitenefs of Colouring.*

The perfection of Colouring arifeth from a certain right underftanding of each colour feverally, without which it is impoffible to mix any thing rightly, as *Hermogenes* faith. The *Greeks* (as *Porphyrius*) call this mixtion of colours, *corruption,* which word *Plutarch* alfo ufed when he faid that *Apollodorus* (who firft found out the *corruption* or way of fhadowing in co-

R 4 lours)

lours)was an *Athenian*. *Lucian* calls it *confusion*, where he faith, that by the Art of Painting, Images were made by a moderate *confusion* of Colours, as White, Black, Yellow, Red, &c. by which, as *Philoftratus* faith in *Proæmio Iconum*, we know how to imitate the diverfities of looks in a mad-man, in a fad or cheerful countenance ; the colour of the eye, as brown, gray or black ; of the hair, as golden, ruddy, bright, or flaxen ; of the cloaths, as cloth, leather, or armour ; of places, as chambers, houfes, forefts, mountains, rivers, fountains, &c. this is done by the accurate mixtion, due application, and convenient fhadowing, as *Lucian* faith in *Zeuxide* ; through the obfervation of light, fhadow, obfcurity and brightnefs, as *Plutarch* will have it. For this caufe, faith *Johannes Grammaticus*, is a white or golden Picture made upon a black ground. *Light* is altogether neceffary, feeing there can be no fhade without it : light and fhadow cannot fubfift afunder, becaufe by the one, the other is apparent, for thofe things which are enlightned feem to ftick out more, and to meet the eyes of the beholder ; thofe which are fhaded to be depreffed. This fame of light and fhadow, *Nicias* the *Athenian* did moft accurately obferve ; as alfo *Zeuxis*, *Polygnotus*, and *Euphranor*, as *Philoftratus* faith in *libro fecundo de vita Apollonii, cap.9*. *Apelles* painted *Alexander*, as if he held lightning in his hand, *Philoftratus* obferved the fame. in the picture of an Ivory *Venus*, fo that one would think it an eafie matter to take hold of her ; *Paufias* arrived to fuch an excellency in this, as fcarcely any after could attain unto, as in the painted Ox, faith *Pliny*, which he made inimitable. *Obfcurity* or *Darknefs* is only the duskinefs of a deeper fhadow, as *brightnefs* is the exaltation of light : if white and black be put upon the fame fuperficies, the white will feem neareft, the black farther off: this being

being known to make a thing feem hollow, as a ditch, cave, ciftern, well, &c. it is coloured with black or brown; and fo much the blacker, fo much the deeper it feems; extream black reprefenting a bottomlefs depth; but to make it rife, as the breafts of a maid, a ftretched out hand, &c. there is laid round or on each fide fo much black or brown, as may make the parts feem to ftick out by reafon of the adjacent hollownefs; *brightnefs* is fometimes ufed for necefity, but generally for ornament, (as in the pictures of *Angels*, *Gems*, *Armour*, *Flame*, *Flowers*, *Gold, and the like*) the which is made alwayes with a mixture of light; which mixtion Painters call *Harmoge*, but is nothing elfe fave an undifcernable piece of Art, by which the *Artizan* ftealingly paffeth from one colour into another, with an infenfible diftinction; this *Harmoge* is moft perfect in the *Rainbow*, which containing evident variety of Colours, yet leaves them fo indiftinguifhable, as that we can neither fee where they begin, nor yet where they end, as *Boethius* obferves in *libri quinti de arte mufica capite quarto.* The laft and chief perfection of colouring lyeth in the out-lines, or extremities of the work, being cut off with fuch a wonderful fubtilty and fweetnefs, as to prefent unto us things we do not fee, but that we fhould believe that behind the pictures, there is fomething more to be feen, than can eafily be difcerned; thereby fetting forth, as it were, thofe things which are really concealed, this was *Barrhafius* his chief glory; but herein *Apelles* exceeded all others whatfoever, as *Petronius in Satyrico* feems to affirm.

IX. *Action and Paffion is next to be confidered, in which confifts life and motion.*

There is not any thing that can add a more lively grace to the work, than the extream likenefs of motion, proceeding from the inward Action or Paffion

of

of the mind. It is therefore a great point of Art, which leads unto *Perfection*, the which we are to learn by casting our eyes upon nature, and tracing her steps. Consider all the gestures of the body, as the head, by which is expressed the affections of the mind. The casting down of the head, sheweth dejection of mind, being cast back, arrogance; hanging on either side, languishing, being stiff or sturdy, churlishness: by it we grant, refuse, affirm, threaten; or passively are bashful, doubtful, sullen, envious, &c. by the motions of the Countenance appears sorrow, joy, love, hatred, courtesie, courage, dejection, &c. by the motions of the countenance, are exprest the qualities of the mind, as modesty and shamefacedness, or boldness and impudence; but of all the parts of the countenance, the eyes are most powerful, for they, whether we move or move not, shew forth our joy or sorrow; this is excellently exprest by the Prophet, in *Lam.* 3. 48. פלג־מים תרד עיני על־שבר בת־עמי *palge majim terrad gneni, gnal shcber bat gnammi,* which *Tremellius* renders, *Rivis aquarum perfluit oculus meus ,* *propter contritionem filiæ populi mei* : and again עיני נגרה ולא תרמה *gneni niggerah velo tidma,* i. e. *oculus meus defluit nec desistit.* For the same purpose it is that nature hath furnished them with tears; but their motion doth more especially express the intention, as meekness, pride, spitefulness, and the like; all which are to be imitated, according as the nature of the action shall require, as staring, closed, dull, wanton, glancing, asking or promising something. The *eye-brows* also have some actions, for they chiefly command the fore-head by contracting, dilating, raising and depressing it; wrinkled brows shew sadness and anger; displayed, cheerfulness; hanging, shame; elation, consent; depression, dissent, &c. The *Lips* shew mocking, scorning,

loath-

loathing, *&c.* The *Arm* gently caſt forth, is graceful in-familiar ſpeech ; but the arm ſpread forth towards one ſide, ſhews one ſpeaking of ſome notable matter ; without the motion of the *hands* all motion is maimed : The hands as it were *call, diſmiſs, threaten, requeſt, abhor, fear, ask, demand, promiſe, deny, doubt, confeſs, repent, number, meaſure, rejoyce, encourage, beſeech, hinder, reprove, admire, relate, commend,* &c. In admiration we hold the hand up, bent ſomewhat backward, with all the fingers cloſed : In relating we join the top of the fore-finger to the thumb-nail : In promiſing we move it ſoftly : In exhorting or commending, more quick : In penitence and anger, we lay our cloſed hand to the breaſt : We cloſe the fingers ends, and lay them to our mouth when we conſider, *&c.* It is not yet enough that the Picture or Image reſembles the proportion and colour of the life, unleſs it likewiſe reſembles it in the demeanour of the whole body ; therefore *Calliſtratus* calls this Art, the art of counterfeiting manners. *Ulyſſes* is evidently, ſaith *Philoſtratus,* diſcerned by his auſterity and vigilancy; *Menelaus* by his gentle mildneſs; *Agamemnon* by a kind of Divine Majeſty ; *Ajax Telamonius,* by his grim look ; *Locrus* by his readineſs and forwardneſs. The beſt Artiſts ever change their hands, in expreſſing of *Gods, Kings, Prieſts, Senators, Orators, Muſicians, Lawyers,* &c. *Zeuxis* painted the modeſty of *Penelope* : *Echion* made a new married but ſhamefaced woman: *Ariſtides* painted a running Chariot drawn with four horſes : *Antiphilus* made a boy blowing the fire : *Philoxenus Eretrius* depicted the Picture of Wantonneſs : *Parrhaſius* made the *Hoplitides* or Pictures of two armed men, as may be ſeen in *Pliny lib.* 35. *cap.* 9, 10, and 11. *Boethius* made a babe ſtrangling a gooſe : *Praxiteles* made a weeping woman, and a rejoycing whore; *Euphranor* drew the picture of

Paris

Paris as a Judge, a Wooer and a Soldier : See *Pliny
lib.* 34. *cap.* 8. where you may have many other examples. It is worth our pains to see in *Calliftratus* thefe
defcriptions at large, whereby we may fee it is a fingular *Perfection of Art.*

‘ X. *The laft ftep of Perfection is the right ordering and
difpofing of things.*

This order or difpofition muft be obferved as well
in a picture confifting of one figure, as in a picture of
many figures. The nature of man, faith *Xenophon
in Oeconomico,* cannot name any thing fo ufeful and
fair, as order ; a confufed piece of work cannot deferve admiration ; thofe things only affect us, wherein
every part is not only perfect in it felf, but alfo well
difpofed by a natural connexion. It is not enough
in a building to bring hair, lime, fand, wood, ftones,
and other materials , unlefs we take care that all this
confufed ftuff be orderly difpofed to the intent. *Nature*
it felf feems to be upholden by *Order,* and fo are all
things elfe which are fubjugated to the fame Law.
Now the way to attain to this true *order of difpofition,*
is *firft* to conceive the *Idea* of the hiftory in the imagination , that the prefence of the things in the mind
may fuggeft the order of difpofing each thing in its proper place, yet with that fubtilty that the whole may
reprefent one entire body. *Secondly,* That the frame of
the whole ftructure of this difpofition, may be analo-
gous to the things themfelves ; fo that we may at
once reprefent things which are already done, things
which are doing, and things which are yet to be done ;
perfecting, as *Philoftratus* faith, in every one of thefe
things, what is moft proper, as if we were bufied about
one only thing. *Thirdly,* An hiftorical Picture muft
reprefent the feries of the hiftory, which although the
Picture be filent, yet that the *connexion* might (as it
were)

were) fpeak, putting the principal figures in the principal places. *Fourthly*, The parts muſt be connected eaſily rolling on, gently flowing or following one another, hand in hand, feeming both to hold and be upheld, free from all abruption, well grounded, finely framed, and ſtrongly tyed up together; that the whole may be delightſome for its equality, grave for its ſimplicity, and graceful for its univerſal analogical compoſure. *Fifthly*, That moſt excellent pieces (if the hiſtory will ſuffer it) be ſhadowed about with rude thickets, and craggy rocks, that by the horridneſs of ſuch things, there may accrew a more *excellent grace* to the principal ; (juſt as diſcords in Muſick make ſometimes concords) from whence reſults a ſingular delight. *Sixthly*, That to theſe things be added *perſpicuity*; which, as *Lucian* ſaith, through the mutual connexion of things, will make the whole compleat and perfect. *Seventhly* and laſtly, that the *diſpoſition of the proportion* be obſerved , in the due diſtance of each figure, and the poſition of their parts, of which we have ſaid ſomething, Section ſeventh ; but in general *Pliny* (*lib.* 35. *cap.* 10.) ſaith that in this general diſpoſition of proportional diſtances , we have no rules ; our eye muſt teach us what to do ; to which *Quintilian* aſſents, where he ſaith, that theſe things admit no other Judgement, but the judgement of our eyes.

XI. Laſtly, *For the abſolute Conſummation or Perfection of the Art, excellency of Invention, Proportion, Colour, Life and Diſpoſition, muſt univerſally concur, and conſpire, to bring forth that comely gracefulneſs, which is the very life and ſoul of the work, the entire and joint Sum of all perfections.*

It is not enough, that a Picture is excellent in one or more of the aforeſaid perfections, but the conſumma-

tion is, that they all concur; for if but one be wanting, the whole work is defective. A good invention
affects the mind; true proportion draws the eyes;
lively motion moves the foul; exquifite colours be-
guile the phantafie; and an orderly difpofition, wonderfully charms all the fenfes; if all thefe unite, and
center in one piece, how great an excellence and perfection will appear? *What a comely Grace?* this *Grace*
it is, which in beautiful bodies is the life of beauty,
and without which, its greateft accomplifhments cannot pleafe the beholder. For it is not fo much the perfection of Invention, Proportion, Colours, Motion
and Difpofition apart, which affect the fenfes, but *all*
thofe perfections abfolutely *united*, which brings forth
that comely *Grace,* and *higheft Perfection*, which Art
aims at, and the Artizan ftrives after. This *Grace* proceeds not from any rules of Art, but from the excellent fpirit of the Artificer; it is eafier attained by obfervation and a good judgement, than learned by Precepts, as *Quintilian* in his Inftitutions *lib.* 11. *cap.* 1.
learnedly obferves. And this *Grace* is moft *graceful,*
when it flows with facility, out of a free Spirit, and is
not forced or ftrained out with labour and toil, which
quite fpoils and kills the life of the work : Now this
facility fprings from Learning, Study and exercitation.
Art and *Nature* muft concur to the Conftitution of this
Grace; *Art* muft be applied difcreetly to thofe things
which we *naturally* affect, and not to things which we
loath; left we mifs of *that Glory* which we feek after.

CHAP.

CHAP. IV.

How the Ancients depicted their Gods: and first of Saturn.

WE here intend to comprehend the various wayes of the *Antients* in depicting their Idols, according to the customs of those several Nations, where they were adored and worshipped, and that from the most *Ancient*, chiefest and best approved *Authors* now extant.

I. The Ancient *Romans* figured *Saturn* like an old man, with a Sythe or Hook in his hand, by some signifying *Time*, as his name *Chronos* also intimates.

II. They also figured him in the shape of a very Aged man, as one who began with the beginning of the World, holding in his hand a Child, which by piecemeals he seems greedily to devour.

By this is signified the revenge he took for being expulsed Heaven by his own Children, of which those which escaped his fury , were only four , Jupiter, Juno, Pluto, *and* Neptune, *by which is shadowed forth the four Elements,* Fire, Air, Earth, *and* Water, *which are not perishable by the all-cutting Sickle of devouring Time.*

III. *Martianus Capella* depicts him an old man , holding in his right hand a Serpent, with the end of its tail in its mouth, turning round with a very slow pace, his temples girt with a green wreath, and the hair of his head and beard milk white.

The wreath on his head shews the Spring time , his snowy hair and beard, the approach of churlish winter; the slowness of the Serpents motion, the sluggish revolution of that Planet.

IV. *Macro-*

IV. *Macrobius* deſcribes him with a Lions head, a Dogs head, and a Wolfs head.

By the Lions head is ſignified the time preſent , (which is alwayes ſtrongeſt, for that which is muſt needs be more powerful than that which is not:) by the Dogs head, the time to come, (which alwayes fawns on us, and by whoſe alluring delights we are drawn on to vain and uncertain hopes :) and by the Wolfs head, time paſt, (which greedily devoureth whatſover it finds, leaving no memory thereof behind.)

V. *Macrobius* alſo ſaith, that among the reſt of his deſcriptions, his feet are tyed together with threds of Wooll.

By which is ſhewed, that God does nothing in haſte, nor ſpeedily caſtigates the iniquities of man , but proceeds ſlowly and unwillingly, to give them time and leiſure to amend.

VI. *Euſebius* ſaith, that *Aſtarte* (the daughter of *Cœlum*, wife and ſiſter of *Saturn)* did place alſo upon his head two wings, demonſtrating by the one, the excellency and perfection of the mind ; by the other, the force of ſenſe and underſtanding.

The Platonicks underſtand by Saturn the mind, and its inward contemplation of things cœleſtial , and therefore called the time in which he lived, the golden Age, it being replete with quietneſs, concord, and true content.

CHAP.

CHAP. V.

How the Antients depicted Jupiter.

I. ORpheus describes him with golden locks, having on his temples peeping forth two golden horns, his eyes shining, his breast large and fair, having on his shoulders wings.

By the golden locks is signified the Firmament, and its glorious army of tralucent Stars: by his two Horns, the East *and* West *: by his eyes, the Sun and Moon : by his breast, the spacious ambulation of the air ; and by his wings the fury of the winds.*

II. *Porphyrius* and *Suidas* depicture the Image of *Jupiter* sitting upon a firm and immoveable seat ; the upper parts naked and uncloathed, the lower parts covered and invested ; in his left hand a Scepter ; in his right hand a great Eagle, joined with the figure of *Victoria.*

This Image was erected in Piræus, *a stately and magnificent Gate of* Athens : *by the seat is shewed the permanency of Gods power : the naked parts shew that the compassion of the Divine power is always manifest to those of an understanding Spirit : the lower parts covered, shew that while we wallow in the world, and as it were rock'd asleep with the illecebrous blandishments thereof, that the divine knowledge is hid and obscured from us : by the Scepter is signified his rule over all things : by the Eagle and* Victoria *how all things stand in vassalage and subjection to the all-commanding power.*

III. *Martianus* depictures him with a regal crown, adorned with most precious and glittering stones; over his shoulders, a thin vail (made by *Pallas* own

S   hands)

hands) all white, in which is inserted divers small pieces of glass representing the most resplendent Stars; in his right hand he holdeth two balls, the one all of Gold, the other half Gold, half Silver; in the other hand an Ivory Harp with nine strings, sitting on a foot-cloth, wrought with strange works, and Peacocks feathers; and near his side lieth a tridental gold embossed mass.

IV. *Plutarch* saith that in *Crete*, he had wholly humane shape and proportion, but without ears.

By that was signified that Superiours and Judges ought not to be carried away by prejudice nor perswasion, but stand firm, stedfast and upright to all without partiality.

V. Contrariwise the *Lacedæmonians* framed his picture with four ears.

By that they signified that God heareth and understandeth all things; and that Princes and Judges ought to hear all informations, before they deliver definitive sentence or judgment.

VI. *Pausanias* saith that in the temple of *Minerva* (among the *Argives*) the statue of *Jupiter* was made with three eyes; two of them in their right places; the other in the middle of his fore-head.

By which is signified his three Kingdoms; the one Heaven; the other Earth; the last Sea.

VII. With the *Eleans* (a people of *Greece*) the Statue of *Jove* was compacted of Gold and Ivory, empaled with a Coronet of Olive leaves; in his right hand the Image of *Victoria*; in his left a Scepter, on the top of which was mounted the portraicture of an Eagle, upon a feat of Gold, enchased with the forms of many unknown birds and fishes, upheld and supported by four Images of *Victoria*.

VIII. In *Caria* (a place of the lesser *Asia*) the
Statue

Statue of *Jupiter* was made holding in one of his hands a Pole-axe.

The reason of this was, as Plutarch *saith, from* Hercules, *who overthrowing* Hippolyta *the Amazonian Queen, took it from her, and gave it to* Omphale *his wife a Lydian.* The Platonists *understand by* Jupiter, *the soul of the world ; and that divine spirit through whose Almighty Power, every thing receives its being and preservation.*

IX. He is also painted with long curled black hair in a purple robe, trimmed with Gold, and sitting on a golden throne, with bright yellow clouds dispersed about him.

CHAP. VI.

How the Antients depicted Mars.

I. **M**Acrobius saith that the Pictures of *Mars* were adorned and beautified with the Sun-beams, in as lively a manner as could be devised ; with an Aspect fierce, terrible, and wrathful, hollow red eyes, quick in their motion, face all hairy with long curled locks on his head, depending even to his shoulders, of a coal black colour, standing with a spear in the one hand, and a whip in the other.

II. He is also sometimes depicted on horse-back and sometimes in a Chariot, drawn with horses called *Fear* and *Horror :* some say the Chariot was drawn with two men, which were called *Fury* and *Violence.*

III. *Statius* saith he wore on his head a helmet most bright and shining, so fiery as it seemed, there issued

flashes

flaſhes of lightning; a breaſt-plate of Gold, inſculp'd with fierce and ugly Monſters; his ſhield depainted all over with blood, enchaſed with deformed beaſts, with a ſpear and whip in his hands, drawn in a Chariot with two horſes, *Fury* and *Violence*, driven with two churliſh Coach-men, *Wrath* and *Deſtruction*.

IV. *Iſidorus* ſaith that the Picture of *Mars* was depainted with a naked breaſt.

By which is ſignified that men ought not to be timorous in war, but valiantly and boldly expoſe themſelves to hazards and dangers.

V. *Statius* ſaith that the houſe of *Mars* was built in an obſcure corner of *Thracia*, made of ruſty, black Iron; the *Porters* which kept the gates were *Horror* and *Madneſs*; within the houſe inhabited *Fury, Wrath, Impiety, Fear, Treaſon* and *Violence*, whoſe governeſs was *Diſcord*, ſeated in a regal throne, holding in one hand a bright ſword, and in the other a baſin full of humane blood.

VI. *Arioſto*, deſcribing the Court of *Mars*, ſaith, that in every part and corner of the ſame were heard moſt ſtrange Echoes, fearful ſhrieks, threatnings, and diſmal cryes; in the midſt of this Palace was the Image of *Vertue*, looking ſad and penſive, full of ſorrow, diſcontent and melancholy, leaning her head on her arm: hard by her was ſeated in a chair *Fury* in triumph: not far from her ſate *Death*, with a bloody ſtern countenance, offering upon an *Altar* in mens skulls, humane blood, conſecrated with coals of fire, fetch'd from many Cities and Towns, burnt and ruinated by the tyranny of War.

CHAP.

CHAP. VII.

How the Antients depicted Phœbus *or* Sol.

I. MAcrobius faith that in *Affyria* was found the Statue of *Apollo, Phœbus* or *Sol,* the father of *Æfculapius,* in the form of a young man, and beardlefs, polifhed with Gold, who ftretching out his Arms, held in his right hand a Coachmans whip; and in his left a thunderbolt with fome ears of Corn.

The Tyrant of Syracufe, Dionyfius, *with fury pulled off the beard from the figure of* Æfculapius, *faying it was very incongruous that the father fhould be beardlefs, and the fon have one fo exceeding long.*

II. *Eufebius* faith that in *Egypt* the Image of *Sol* was fet in a fhip, carried up, and fupported by a *Crocodile :* and that they (before letters were invented) framed the fhape of the Sun, by a Scepter, in the top of which was dexteroufly engraven an eye.

The Scepter fignified Government : the Eye, *the power which over-fees and beholds all things.*

III. The *Lacedæmonians* depicted *Apollo* with four ears, and as many hands.

By which was fignified the judgment and prudence of God being fwift and ready to hear, but flow to fpeak, and from thence grew that proverb among the Grecians.

IV. *Herodotus* reporteth that the *Phœnicians* had the Statue of the Sun made in black ftone, large and fpacious at bottom, but fharp and narrow at top, which they boafted to have had from Heaven.

V. *Lactantius* faith that in *Perfia, Phœbus* or *Apollo* was their chiefeft God, and was thus defcribed; he had

the

the head of a Lyon habited according to the Perſian cu-
ſtom, wearing on his head ſuch ornaments as the women
of *Perſia* uſed, holding by main force a white Cow by
the horns.

*The head of the Lion ſheweth the Suns dominion in the
ſign* Leo *; the Cow ſhews the Moon, whoſe exaltation is*
Taurus *: and his forceable holding, the Moons Eclipſe which
ſhe cannot avoid.*

VI. *Pauſanias* telleth that in *Patra* a City of *Achaia,*
a metalline Statue of *Apollo* was found in the proportion
of an Ox or Cow.

VII. *Lucianus* ſaith that the *Aſſyrians* ſhaped him
with a long beard (ſhewing his perfection ;) upon his
breaſt a ſhield ; in his right hand a ſpear, in the top of
which was *Victoria* ; in his left hand *Anthos,* or the Sun
flower : this body was covered with a veſtment upon
which was painted the head of *Meduſa,* from which
dangled downwards many ſwarms of ſnakes ; on the
one ſide of him *Eagles* flying, on the other ſide a lively
Nymph.

VIII. The *Egyptians* compoſed the ſtatue of the Sun
in the ſhape of a man, with his head half ſhaven.

*By the head half ſhaven, is ſignified that though his
beauty or ſhining may be clouded for a time, yet that he
will return and beautifie the ſame with his priſtin brightneſs ; as the growing of the hairs (which ſignifie his
beams) to their full extent and perfection again may denote.*

IX. *Martianus* thus deſcribes him ; upon his head
(ſaith he) he wears a royal and gorgeous Crown, in-
chaſed with multitudes of precious Gems ; three of
which beautifie his fore-head ; ſix his temples ; and
three other the hindermoſt part of the Crown : his
hair hanging down in treſſes, looks like refined Gold,
and his Countenance wholly like flame : his veſtment
                                                        is

is thin, subtil, and wrought with fine purple and gold; in his right hand he holds a bright shield; and in his left a flaming fire-brand: on his feet he hath two wings, beset with fiery Carbuncles.

X. *Eusebius* writeth that in *Elephantinopolis* (a City in *Egypt*)the Image of *Apollo* was framed to the due likeness of a man throughout the body, save only, that he had the head of a Ram, with young and small horns; and his aspect of a *Cerulean* and blewish green, not unlike to that of the Sea.

The head of the Ram signifies the Sun's exaltation in the sign Aries ; *and the young horns the change or New of the Moon, made by her conjunction with the Sun, in which she looks blewish.*

XI. He is also drawn with long curled golden hair, crowned with a lawrel in a purple robe a silver bow in his hand, sitting on a throne of Emeralds.

There might you see with greatest skill intexed,
The portraicture of Phœbus *lively drawn ;*
And his fair Sisters shape thereto annexed,
Whose shining parts seem'd shadow'd o're with lawn.
And though with equal art both were explai ..
And workmens care gave each of them the ..,
Yet to the view great difference remain'd,
In habit, shape, aspect, and in their h..
   For one of them must give the da   ..
   And th' other reign Commandress of ..

CHAP. VIII.

How the Antients depicted Venus.

I. **H**ER Statue is framed in the shape of a most beautiful and young woman, standing upright in a huge shell of fish, drawn by two other most ugly and strange Fishes, as *Ovid* at large noteth.

II. *Paufanias* saith she is drawn in a Coach, through the airy passages, with two white Doves (as *Apuleius* also affirmeth) which are called the birds of *Venus*.

III. *Horace* and *Virgil* affirm that the Chariot of *Venus* is drawn by two white Swans, of which *Statius* also maketh mention, who saith that those birds are most mild, innocent, and harmless, and therefore given unto *Venus*.

IV. *Praxiteles* an excellent engraver in the Island of *Gnidos*, made her Image naked, and without clothes, as also did the Grecians.

By which was signified that all luxurious and licentious people were by their inordinate lusts, like beasts deprived of sense, and left as it were naked and despoiled of reason, and understanding; and oftentimes also stripped thereby of their riches, goods and estates.

V. *Lactantius* saith that the *Lacedemonians* framed and composed the Image of *Venus* all armed like a Warriour, holding in one hand a spear, in the other a shield or target.

And this was by reason of a certain Victory which the women of that place got over their enemies, the people of Messenia, *which success they supposed to have proceeded from the power and assistance of* Venus, *as inspiring these womens hearts with courage, stoutness and resolution.*

VI. She

VI.She is also depicted with yellow hair attired with black ; a scarlet, or else dun-coloured robe.

C H A P. IX.

How the Antients depicted Mercury.

I. **T**HE Antients described him in the shape of a young man without a beard, with two small wings fixed behind his shoulders and ears, his body almost all naked, save that from his shoulders depended a thin vail, which winded and compassed about all his body ; in his right hand he held a golden purse, and in his left a *Caduceus*, or snaky staff, to wit, a slender white wand, about which two Serpents do annodate and entwine themselves, whose heads meet together just at the top, as their tails do at the lower end.

This resemblance was called Concordia *or* Signum Pacis ; *upon which it came to pass, that Embassadours, and great men in matters of State, carried always in their hand such a like staff, and were called* Caduceators.

II. *Apuleius* writeth that *Mercury* was a very youth, having very short hair on his head of an Amber colour, and curled, having for a vestment only a subtil and thin vail made of purple Silk.

III. *Martianus Capella* describes him young, yet of a strong and well composed body , with certain young hairs of a yellowish colour sprouting out of his chin.

IV. *Pausanias* saith that in a Province of *Corinth*, he was depicted like a young man carrying a ram upon his shoulders: and that a Statue (brought from *Arcadia*

cadia unto *Rome*) erected in the temple of *Jupiter Olym-picus,* had on its head a helmet of engraven steel ; and over his shoulder, a coat, who held under his arm the Image of a ram.

V. Among some of the *Egyptians* his Image was fra-med with a head like a dog's, holding in his right hand a *Caduceus* or snaky wand ; shaking with his left a green bough of a Palm.

By the head of the dog was understood subtilty and crafti-ness (no beast being so subtil as a dog ;) by the snaky wand the power of wisdom and Eloquence in producing of peace, signi-fied by the green palm.

VI. By some he was depicted in the similitude of a very aged man, his head almost bald, saving that on the sides there remained some few hairs, short and curled ; his look grim, severe and sowre ; his com-plexion of a tawny, antient hue; his upper garment, of a Lions skin ; in his right hand a huge pole-ax, in his left hand an Iron bow : at his back hanging a Qui-ver of steel-headed arrows : to the end of his tongue were fastned many small chains of Gold, at whose ends were tyed multitudes of all sorts of men, which he seemed to draw unto him ; looking always backward, to behold the innumerable troops of people following him.

By this description is signified the all powerful and at-tractive vertue of Eloquence ; which by his age is under-stood to be found only in old, wise and experienced men, as being in them more mature and perfect, than in those of younger years, of which Homer *speaks at large in his Commendation and Praise of* Nestor : *from whose mouth (saith he) plentifully rolled forth most pleasant and dul-cid streams ; whose pen distilled Crystalline drops of deli-cious sweetness ; whose works and fruits so compleatly adorned with golden sentences, assuageth the malice of time, and miti-gateth*

gateth and allayeth the spight of forgetfulness, that his per-
petuity is engraven in the brass-leaved books of eternal memo-
ry, never to be blotted out.

VII. He is also drawn with long curled yellow hair in
a coat of flame colour, with a mantle purely white, trimmed with Gold and Silver; his Beaver white, with white
feathers, his Shooes Golden, his Rod Silver.

CHAP. X.

How the Antients *depicted* Diana *or* Luna.

I. **D**Iana, *Cynthia, Lucina* or *Luna* was according
to *Propertius* depicted in the likeness of a
young beautiful virgin ; having on either side of her
forehead two small glistering horns, newly putting
forth, drawn through the air in a purple colored Coach,
by two swift paced horses, the one of a sad Colour, the
other of a white.

These two differing horses Boccace *saith, shew that she*
hath power both in the day and night.

II. *Claudianus* saith that her Chariot is drawn by two
white Bullocks, (which Image the *Egyptians* worshipped
with great zeal and reverence) having one of their flanks
bespotted with divers stars, and on their heads two such
sharp horns, as the Moon hath in her chiefest wane.

III. *Cicero* describes her statue (which he brought
out of a temple in *Cicilia*) of a wonderful height,
and large dimension, the whole body covered with a
thin vail, of a youthful aspect, holding in her right
hand a lively burning torch, and in her left an Ivory
bow, with a Quiver of Silver-headed arrows hanging
at her back.

IV. The

IV. The Poets (who call her the goddeſs of hunting and imperial governeſs of Woods and Groves)deſcribe her in the habit of a young *Nymph*, with her bow ready bent in her hand, and a Quiver of arrows hanging by her left ſide; a ſwift paced Grey-hound faſt tyed to her right ſide, with a collar about his neck; and after her following troops of *Sylvan Virgins*, which are chaſt, and are called the *Nymphs* of *Diana*.

V. Theſe Virgins and Votreſſes of the Goddeſs, we thus deſcribe.

Scarce mounted Sol *upon his glorious Car,*
When o're the lofty hills, and lowly plain,
Running apace, you might perceive afar
A Troop of Amazons to poſt amain.
    But when they nearer came unto your view,
    You might diſcern Diana *and her Crew.*
A careleſs crew of lively Nymphs, deſpiſing
The joyous pleaſures and delights of love ;
Waſting their days in rural ſports deviſing :
Which know no other, nor will other prove.
    Wing'd with deſire to overtake the chaſe,
    Away they flung with unreſiſted pace.
Their necks and purple veined arms are bare,
And from their Ivory ſhoulders to their knee,
A Silken veſtment o're their skin they wear,
Through which a piercing eye might chance to ſee.
    Cloſe to their bodies is the ſame engirted,
    Bedeck'd with pleaſing flowers there inſerted.
Each in her hand a Silver bow doth hold,
With well-ſtor'd Quivers hanging at their backs :
Whoſe arrows being ſpent they may be bold
To borrow freely of each others packs.
    Thus are theſe nimble skipping Nymphs diſplay'd,
    That do attend that Goddeſs, Queen and Maid.

VI. In

VI. In *Arcadia* faith *Paufanias* was a ftatue of *Diana*, covered over with the skin of a Hind, and from her fhoulders hung a Quiver of Arrows; in one hand a burning Lamp, the other leaning upon the heads of two ferpents, and before her feet a hound.

VII. The *Egyptians* worfhipped her under the name of *Ifis*; and depictured her covered with a black and fable veftment, in token that fhe her felf giveth no light; holding in one hand a Cymbal, in the other an earthen veffel of water, upon which as *Servius* faith, many thought her to be the Genius of *Egypt*.

By the Cymbal is fhewed the murmurings and roarings of Nilus, *when it overflows* Egypt ; *and by the other veffel the nature of the Country, which is moift and full of lakes, pools and rivers.*

VIII. She is alfo depicted with yellow hair, a glafs green mantle, trimmed with Silver; buskins Silver; bow Golden, Quiver of various colours.

IX. *Nymphæ Dianæ* in white linnen to denote their Virginity, and their garments girt about them, their arms and fhoulders naked, bows in their hands, and arrows by their fides.

C H A P. XI.

How the Antients depicted Janus.

I. **J**Anus is depicted with two faces; in the one of his hands is a long rod or wand; in the other a Key.

The two faces of Janus *fignifie time ; the one being withered and hoary, fhews time paft , the other youthful and beardlefs, time to come.*

II. *Pliny*

II. *Pliny* faith that *Numa* King of the *Romans*, caufed the ftatue of *Janus* to be hewed out in fuch fort, that the fingers of his hands appeared to be three hundred fixty five, to fhew that he was God of the year, whereupon they called the firft month of the year *Januarius*, from *Janus* their God.

Under the feet of Janus *is oftentimes placed twelve Altars, fhewing thereby the months of the year, or figns of the Zodiack, through which* Sol *makes his revolution.*

III. The *Phœnicians*, as *Cicero* and *Macrobius* report, framed his Image in the form of a ferpent, holding her tail in her mouth, and continually turning round.

IV. Some depicted *Janus* with four faces, (as were thofe ftatues which were found in divers places of *Tufcany.*

By the four faces was fignified the four feafons of the year, Spring, Summer, Autumn, *and* Winter : *which fome think to be* Venus, Ceres, Bacchus *and* Vulcan ; *and fometimes the winds with* Æolus *their Commander.*

CHAP. XII.

How the Antients depicted Aurora.

I. **H**Omer defcribes her like a young Virgin, having her hair difhevelled, and hanging loofe about her fhoulders being of the colour of the pureft gold, fitting in a golden chair, with all her veftments of that hue and colour.

II. *Virgil* faith, that upon the inftant time of the fable nights departure, fhe cometh with one of her
hands

hands full of Rofes, Gilliflowers and Lillies, taken out of a basket which fhe carries in the other hand, which fhe befprinkles on the marble pavement of the lower Heavens, adorning the Sun with unfpeakable beauty.

III. Others defcribe her, holding in one hand a flaming torch, and drawn in a gorgeous and ftar-befpotted Chariot, by winged *Pegafus*; which favour fhe obtained of *Jupiter* by many importunate requefts, prefently after the downfal of *Bellerophon*.

IV. She is as it were the Herald and Meffenger of *Phœbus*, who receives her being from the vertue of his beams; and is no other but that rubicund and Vermillion blufh in Heaven, which *Sol*'s firft appearance worketh in the *Orient*, and from thence defcending beautifies our *Hemifphere* with fuch a refplendency.

V. She is alfo depicted in a purple robe, in a blew mantle fring'd with Silver.

CHAP. XIII.

How the Antients depicted Juno.

I. SHE was fet forth by the Antients like a middle aged woman, holding in one hand a Silver veffel, in the other a fharp Spear: and *Homer* faith fhe was drawn in a Chariot glistering with precious ftones; whofe wheels were Ebony, and their nails fine filver, mounted upon a Silver Seat; and drawn with horfes, which were faftned with chains of Gold.

II. She is oftentimes depicted with a Scepter in her hand,

hand, to shew that she hath the bestowing of Govern-ments, Authorities and Kingdoms.

III. *Martianus* depicts her (sitting in a chair un-der *Jupiter*) with a thin veil over her head, with a Coronet upon it, inchased and adorned with many pre-cious Jewels; her inward vestment fine and glittering, over which depended a mantle of a sad and darkish colour, yet with a secret shining beauty; her shooes of an obscure and sable colour; in her right hand a thunberbolt; and in her other a loud noised Cym-bal.

IV. *Pausanias* saith that in a temple in *Corinth*, her sta-tue(made of Gold and Ivory)was adorned with a glori-ous Crown, on which was insculped the pictures of the *Graces*; with a *Pomegranate* in the one hand, and a Scep-ter(on the top of which a Cuckow) in the other:for that *Jupiter*, when he was first enamoured of *Juno*, transform-ed himself into that bird.

Touching this story (and others of like kind) Pau-sanias saith, that although he did not believe such things to be true, nor any others, which are so written of the Gods; yet saith he, they are not altogether to be rejected, in that there were no such things reported but that they were impleat-ed and filled with mysteries, and carried in themselves an inward meaning, and secret understanding, the which no doubt some might by their writings have unshadowed, if the tyranny of fore-passed times had not destroyed and obliterated the same.

V. *Tertullian* writeth that in *Argos* a City in *Greece*, the statue of *Juno* was covered all over with the boughs of a Vine, and underneath her feet lay the skin of a Li-on, which discovered the hatred and disdain she bare to-wards *Bacchus* and *Hercules*, to whom(as the Poets say) she was step-mother.

VI. Some have painted her a middle aged woman,
holding

holding in one hand a poppey-flower or head ; with a yoke or pair of fetters lying at her feet.

By the yoke was meant the hand of marriage, which tyeth man and wife together ; and by the Poppey, fruitfulness or the innumerable issue of children, which are brought forth into the world (signified by the roundness of the Poppey head, and its numberless seeds therein contained.) From hence many suppose her to be the goddess of marriage.

VII. She is also painted with black Hair and Eyes, adorned with a sky-coloured mantle, or pied ; wrought with Gold and Peacocks eyes ; like the orient circles in the Peacocks trains.

CHAP. XIV.

How the Antients depicted Ops *or* Tellus.

I. MArtianus saith, that Ops (the wife of *Saturn*) is an old woman, of great bigness, continually bringing forth children, with whom she is encompassed and set round, going in a green vestment, with a veil over her body, spotted with divers colours, wrought with infinite curious knots, and set with all sorts of Gems and Metals.

II. *Varro* (out of *Boccace*) thus describes her : she is crowned (saith he) with a Crown insculpt with Castles and Towers ; her apparel green, overshaded with boughs ; in the one hand a Scepter, in the other a Ball or Globe ; and near to her a Chariot of four wheels, drawn by four Lions.

By the Crown is signified the habitations of the earth ; by the greenness and boughs, the increase thereof ;

T   *by by the Scepter, the Kingdoms and Governments of the world ; by the Ball, the roundness thereof ; by the Chariot, the continual motion, change and alteration of things ; by the Lions, the wisdom and strength of mankind, by which things are carried on and managed.*

III. *Isidorus* saith, that this Goddess was painted holding a key in one of her hands : which shews, that in the winter the bowels of the earth are locked up by reason of cold ; which at the approach of Spring and Summer is unlocked again.

IV. She was sometimes depicted in the form of an antient woman, having her head circumcinct with ears of corn, holding in her hand a poppey-head : drawn in a Chariot (as *Orpheus* saith) with two fierce and untamed *Dragons.*

V. The earth is also called *Ceres,* which many have depicted with torches, lights and fire-brands in her hands ; as *Praxiteles* in a temple, seated upon a promontory of *Attica.*

VI. She is also pictured in a long green mantle.

CHAP. XV.

How the Antients depicted Neptune *and the Sea Gods.*

I. NEptune among the Antients is depainted with several countenances, sometimes with mild and pleasant looks, sometimes with lowring and sad, and at other times with a mad, furious and angry aspect ; naked, holding in his hand a silver trident or forked mace, standing upright in the concavity of a great Sea shell, forcibly drawn by two monstrous

horses,

horses, which from the middle downwards have the proportion and shape of fishes, as *Statius* saith.

That variety of Aspects (according to Virgil *and* Homer) *is given him from the Sea, in that it at sundry times sheweth it self so : and the trident, the three Gulfs of the Mediterranean Sea.*

II. Sometimes he is depainted with a thin veil hanging over one of his shoulders, of a *Cerulean* or blewish colour.

III. *Lucianus* setteth him down with marvellous long hair hanging down over his shoulders, of a very sad and darkish colour.

Yet Servius *and others affirm, that all the Gods of the Sea were for the most part in the shape of old men with white and hoary hairs, proceeding from the froth or spume of the Sea.*

IV. *Plato* describes him in a sumptuous Chariot, holding in one hand the reins of a bridle : in the other a whip, drawn by Sea-horses galloping.

V. *Martianus* describes him of a greenish complexion, wearing a white Crown : signifying thereby the spume and froth of the Sea.

VI. *Glaucus* (another Sea God) saith *Philostratus*, hath a long white beard and hair, soft and dropping about his shoulders, his eyes green and glistering ; his brows full of wrinkles, and green spots ; his breast all over-grown with greenish Sea-weed or moss, his belly, and from thence downwards fish-like, full of fins and scales.

VII. *Galatea* (a Sea Goddess) is described (by the said *Philostratus*) to be drawn in a strange framed Chariot, by two mighty Dolphins, which were guided by two silver reins held in the hands of old *Triton's* daughters ; over her head, a Canopy made of Purple silk and silver, with her hair hanging carelesly over her

T 2   shoulders.

ſhoulders. *See her deſcribed as a Nymph, Chap.32. Seſt.7.*

VIII. *Oceanus* (the father of all the Sea **Gods**) ſaith *Thales Mileſius,* is depainted, drawn on a glorious Chariot, accompanied and attended with a mighty company of *Nymphs*; with the face of an old man, and a long white beard.

IX. *Æolus* is depainted with ſwoln blub cheeks, like one that with main force ſtrives to blow a blaſt; two ſmall wings upon his ſhoulders, and a fiery high countenance.

He is called the God and Ruler of the winds , whoſe deſcriptions are in the thirty fourth Chapter of this Book.

X. *Thetis* (another Sea Goddeſs) is depicted by the ſixth Section of the two and thirtieth Chapter of this Book.

XI. *Neptune* is alſo depicted with long hoary hair, in a blew or Sea-green mantle trimmed with Silver, riding in a blew Chariot, or on a Dolphin of a brown black colour, with a Silver trident in his hand.

CHAP. XVI.

How the Antients depicted Nemeſis.

I. SHE was by *Macrobius* deſcribed with wings on her ſhoulders ; hard by her ſide the rudder of a ſhip, ſhe her ſelf ſtanding upright upon a round wheel; holding in her right hand a Golden ball, in the other a whip.

II. She is often depicted, holding the bridle of an horſe in one hand, and in the other a ſtaff.

III. *Chryſippus* (as *Aulus Gellius* ſaith) deſcribed her

her like a young Virgin, beautiful and modeſt, with an eye prying round about her, for which cauſe the ancients called her the all-diſcerning Lady.

This Nemeſis, *as* Pauſanias *and* Amianus Marcellinus ſay, *was held to be the Goddeſs of Puniſhments, who caſtigates the offences of Malefactors, with pains and torments according to their ſins and demerits; and rewarding the vertuous with honour and dignities : ſhe was the daughter of* Juſtitia *(who dwells and inhabits very ſecretly, within the houſe of Eternity, recording the offences of the wicked) and a moſt ſevere and cruel puniſher of arrogancy and vain glory.* Macrobius *ſaith, that this* Nemeſis *was adored among the* Egyptians *(by them called alſo* Rhammuſia*) as the revenger and chief enemy of* Pride, Inſolency *and* Haughtineſs; *and that ſhe had erect and dedicated unto her, a moſt ſtately and magnifique ſtatue of Marble.*

CHAP. XVII.

How the Antients depicted Pan.

I. **P**An (the God of Flocks and Sheep) is from the middle upwards in proportion like a man, with his face ruddy and ſanguine, being very hairy; his skin and breaſt covered with the skin of a ſpotted *Doe* or *Leopard*; in the one hand a ſhepherds hook, in the other a whiſtle : from the middle downwards the perfect ſhape of a Goat, in thighs, legs and feet.

II. *Juſtine* ſaith, that *Pan's* Statue was made in a Temple in *Rome*, near the hill *Palatine*, appearing to the view all naked, ſaving that it was lightly enſhadowed and covered with a Goats skin.

Thereby

Thereby is signified that (as it was reputed in those dayes) Pan kept his habitation among Hills, Woods and Groves, who was indeed most of any adored and worshipped by Shepherds, as he that had the peculiar care and Government of their flocks.

III. *Goat-ear'd Pan, his small tipt new grown horns*
Advance themselves, about whose either side
A flow'ry Garland twines, and there adorns
His curled Temples with a wond'rous Pride.
  His face is of a high and reddish blush,
  From which hangs down a stiff rough beard or bush.
And for his bodies vesture he doth wear
The finest skin of the most spotted Doe,
That ever any in those woods did bear,
Which from his shoulder loose hangs to his toe.
  And when he walks, he carries in his hand
  A Shepherds hook, made of a knotless wand.

Servius faith, by the horns is signified either the Beams of the Sun, or New of the Moon, at what time she is horned : his red face signifies the element of fire : his long beard, the Air : his spotted garment, the starry firmament : his Shepherds hook, the rule and Government of nature.

IV. After the form of *Pan* were the *Fauns, Sylvans, Satyres* and *Fairies* set forth, having little short horns growing on their heads, with small ears, and short tails.

These are held among some people in very great regard and observance, being of a wonderful speed in running. Plutarch *writeth, that there was one of these brought and presented for a rare gift unto* Sylla, *as he returned from the wars against* Mithridates.

V. *Plato* understandeth by *Pan*, Reason and Knowledge ;

ledge; which is twofold; the one of a man, the other
of a beast : by the upper part of *Pan*, he signifies truth,
accompanied with *Reason*, which being Divine, lifteth
man up towards *Heaven:* by the lower parts of him is
signified the falseness, beastliness and rudeness of those,
which living here in the World, are only delighted
with the pleasures and foolish vanities thereof.

CHAP. XVIII.

How the Antients depicted Pluto.

I. **M**Artianus faith, that *Pluto* sitteth (in the lower
region) majestically in a chair, holding in
one of his hands a black imperial Scepter, and on his
head a stately Crown ; at whose left hand sitteth his
wife *Proserpina*, attended with many Furies, and evil
Spirits, and at whose feet lyeth chained the Dog
Cerberus.

II. The Antients also have painted him drawn in a
Chariot, drawn with four furious black horses, from
out whose fiery nostrils proceedeth thick and ill-favoured smoak, as *Claudianus* faith.

III. Some say, that his head is encircled with a garland of *Cyprefs* leaves; others with *Narciffus* leaves.

*The first shew sadness and horror, used in burials, and
about the dead: the other are more grateful, and are used in
memory of the untimely death of that youth.*

IV. *Charon* (*Pluto*'s Ferriman, which carries souls
over the three rivers of Hell, *Acheron, Cocytus* and *Styx*)
is described old, yet exceeding strong, with a black
mantle hanging loosely over his shoulders, as *Boccace*
and *Servius* say.

By Charon *is underſtood time* ; *and whereas he is ſuppoſed to have the tranſportation of ſouls from the one ſide of thoſe rivers to the other*; *thereby is ſignifed, that time, ſo ſoon as we are born and brought forth into the world, doth carry us along by little and little unto our deaths*; *and ſo ſetteth us over thoſe rivers, whoſe names by interpretation ſignifie ſor-rowfulneſs, for that we paſs this life with miſery and ad-verſity.*

V. He is alſo depicted with long, curled black hair ; in a robe of cloth of Gold.

CHAP. XIX.

How the Antients depicted the Parcæ, *or Siſters.*

I. THE Siſters which are called *Parcæ,* are ſaid to attend upon *Pluto,* which are three, and are called *Clotho, Lacheſis* and *Atropos.*

II. *Clotho* takes the charge of the Births and nati-vities of mortals : *Lacheſis* of all the reſt of their life ; and *Atropos* of their death, or departure out of this world.

III. They are all three depicted ſitting on a row, very buſily employed in their ſeveral offices ; the youngeſt Siſter drawing out of a Diſtaff a reaſonable big thread : the ſecond winding it about a wheel, and turning the ſame, till it becomes little and ſlender : the eldeſt (which is aged and decrepit) ſtood ready with her knife, when it ſhould be ſpun to cut it off.

IV. And they are deſcribed to be inveſted with white veils, and little Coronets on their heads, wreathed about with garlands, made of flowers of *Narciſſus.*

CHAP.

CHAP. XX.

How the Antients depicted Minerva, *or* Pallas.

I. **M***Inerva* (as taken for *Bellona*) as *Licophrones* faith, was depicted with a flaming fire-brand in her hand by the Antients.

II. Moſt Writers have defcribed *Minerva* in the ſhape of a young woman, of a lively and freſh countenance, yet of an angry look, fix'd ſtedfaſt eye of a blewiſh green colour, compleatly armed at all weapons, with a long Spear in the one hand, and in the other a Cryſtal ſhield, or target : upon her helmet a garland of Olive branches, and two children, Fear and Horror, by her ſide with naked knives in their hands, feeming to threaten one another.

III. *Paufanias* faith, that in *Greece*, the ſtatue of *Minerva* was made with an helmet, on the top of which was the ſhape of a *Sphynx* ; and on the ſides thereof, two carved *Griffins*.

IV. *Phidias* making her ſtatue in *Greece*, placed on the top of her Helmet the form of a Cock.

V. She was alfo painted in *Greece*, ſitting on a ſtool, and drawing forth little ſmall threads from a diſtaff ; for that the Antients ſuppoſed her to be the Inventrefs of Spinning and the like.

VI. Laſtly ſhe is depicted with a blew mantle embroider'd with Silver : and is called the Goddefs of Wiſdom.

CHAP.

CHAP. XXI.

How the Antients depicted Vulcan.

I. **V**Ulcan is depicted, standing, working and hammering in a Smiths forge, on the hill *Ætna,* framing Thunderbolts for *Jupiter,* and fashioning Arrows for the God of love. *The opinions which the Antients had of* Vulcan *were various, in which respect he is shaped sometimes in one form, sometimes in another.*

II. Some make him lame of one leg, of a very black and swarthy complexion, as it were all smoaky ; of a general ill shaped proportion in all his Lineaments ; and because that he is the husband of *Venus,* often depicture her with him.

III. *Alexander Neapolitanus* relateth , that in one place of *Egypt* was erected the statue of *Vulcan,* which held in one of its hands, the true and lively proportion of a mole ; and in his other hand a Thunderbolt.

The mole was so placed , because they thought he sent unspeakable numbers of moles among them, as a plague to them, which did eat, gnaw and destroy every thing which was good.

IV. He is also painted lame in a scarlet robe.

CHAP. XXII.

How the Antients depicted Bacchus.

I. **P**Hilostratus saith, that his statue was framed in the likeness of a young man without a beard, of a corpulent and gross body, his face of an high colour
lour

lour and big; about his head a garland of Ivy leaves; upon his temples two small horns; and close by his side a certain beast, called a *Leopard* or *Panther*.

This description is drawn from the nature of wine, (of which as the Poets feign, Bacchus *is the God) whose inventer and finder out was certainly* Noah, *which not only* Moses, *but also* Josephus *and* Lactantius *specially affirm ; wherefore some suppose him to be this God* Bacchus.

II. *Claudianus* saith, that his Image or Statue is made all naked ; thereby shewing the nakedness of those which abuse themselves with wine , by which they reveal and open those things which ought to be concealed and kept hid.

III. *Diodorus Siculus* saith, that *Bacchus* among the *Grecians* was depicted in two several forms, the one of a very aged man, with a long beard, stiff and thick ; the other of youthful years, of a pleasant and amorous aspect.

By the first is shewed the effects of the intemperate use of wine, which overcomes nature and brings with it old age : by the other, how it cherishes and revives the heart, used moderately.

IV. *Macrobius* saith, that *Bacchus* was framed sometimes in the likeness of a young child, sometimes of a youth, sometimes of a man ; and sometimes in the likeness of decrepit old age.

By these was signified the four seasons of the year, the vine being dedicated to Sol, *in whom they all exist.*

V. This Picture was made in the likeness of a Bull (among the *Cyrenians*, a people inhabiting the farther part of *Persia.*)

The reason hereof was because Proserpina *(the daughter of* Jove *) brought him forth in that form.*

VI. *Philostratus* saith , that *Bacchus* was oftertimes
drawn

drawn clothed in womens garments, and in a long purple robe ; wearing upon his head a Coronet of Rofes, with companions and followers, all in like loofe and wanton garments, fafhioning themfelves fome like rural *Nymphs*, as the *Dryades*, *Oreadess*, &c. fome like Sea *Nymphs*, as *Nereides*, *Syrens*, &c. fome like *Satyres*, *Fauns*, and *Sylvans*, &c.

The womens garments fhews that wine makes a man faint, feeble, and unconftant like to a woman.

VI. *Paufanias* faith, that among the *Eleans*, the picture of *Bacchus* was made with a long beard, and clothed with a long gown hanging to the feet ; in one hand a fharp hook, and in the other a bowl of wine, and round about him many Vine-trees and other fruitful plants.

VII. The Statue of *Bacchus* alfo, was fometimes fet forth and adorned with Coronets made of fig-tree leaves, in memory of a *Nymph* (as fome fay) called *Pfyche*, which was by the Gods metamorphofed into that plant.

In like manner, the Nymph Staphilis (*on whom* Bacchus *was in like manner enamoured*) *was transformed into the Vine, from whence it is that thofe plants are fo exceeding grateful and pleafant unto this God.*

VIII. He is painted alfo with fhort brown curled hair, with a Leopards skin, or in a green mantle, a tawny face, with a wreath of Vine branches.

CHAP.

CHAP. XXIII.

How the Antients depicted Fortune.

I. **F**Ortune was depicted by some with two faces, one white and well-favoured ; the other black, and ugly.

And this was because it was held, that there were two Fortunes, the one good, from whom came riches, happiness, quiet, content and pleasure : the other bad, from whom came wars, afflictions, crosses, disasters, calamities, and all other miseries whatsoever.

II. The *Thebeans* made her in the shape of a woman ; in one of her hands a young child, to wit, *Pluto* or Riches.

So that in the hands of Fortune, they put the disposing of Wealth, Honour, Glory and all Happinesses.

III. *Martianus* describes her a young woman, alwayes moving ; covered with a garment of the thinnest silk ; her steps uncertain, never resting long in a place ; carrying in her spacious lap the universal fulness of the treasures, riches, honour and glory of this world ; which in hasty manner (with her hand) she offers ; which offer, if not instantly received, was utterly lost ; in her right hand a white wand, with which she smites such as offend her, slight her kindness, or are not nimble enough to receive them.

Oh cruel Fortune, stepdame to all joyes,
That disinheritst us from sweet content,
Plunging our hopes in troubled Sea's annoyes ;
Depriving us of that which nature lent!

When

When will thy proud insulting humour cease,
T'assuage the sorrows of an only one ?
That free from care, its soul may live in peace,
And not be metamorphos'd into stone.
But why entreat I thy unstable heart,
Knowing thy greatest pleasure, thy delight
Consists in aggravating mortals smart
Poyson'd with woes, by venom of thy spight ?
'Tis what thou wilt, must stand, the rest must fall,
All humane Kings pay tribute to thy might :
And this must rise, when pleaseth thee to call,
The other perish in a woeful plight.
And this is it, that chokes true vertues breath,
Making it dye, though she immortal be :
Fruitless it makes it ; subject unto death,
To fatal darkness, where no eye can see.
Oh come you wounded Souls, conjoin with me ;
In some adumbrate thicket let us dwell,
Some place which yet the Heavens ne'r did see,
There let us build some despicable Cell.

    Strength, Beauty, perish: Honours fly away :
    And with Estates, Friends vanish and decay.

IV. In a Temple in *Greece,* *Fortune* was made in the form of a grave Matron, clothed in a garment agreeable to such years, whose countenance seemed very sad ; before her was placed the Image of a young Virgin of a beauteous and pleasant aspect, holding out her hand to another ; behind these, the Image of a young child, leaning with one of its arms upon the Matron.

    The *Matron* is that Fortune, which is already past ; the young *Virgin,* that which now is : and the young child beyond them both, is that which is to come.

    V. *Quintus Curtius* saith, that among the people of
Scythia,

Scythia, Fortune was depicted in the form of a woman without feet, having round about her at her right hand a number of little wings.

Being without feet, shews that she never stands firm; and the many wings shew, that her gifts and favours are no sooner given, but are presently lost, and do as it were fly away again, before they be fully possessed.

VI. *Alexander Neapolitanus* relateth, that in *Greece,* her Image was made wholly of Glass; to shew that her favours are brittle, and subject to sudden decayes.

VII. *Cebes* the Philosopher resembled *Fortune* unto a Comedy, in which many Actors appear often as Kings and great Monarchs; and presently after become poor fishermen, slaves, bond-men, and the like.

VIII. *Socrates* compared her to a Theatre, or common meeting place, where without all order or observance men take their places and seats, without respect to the dignity of any.

Hereby is shewed, that she (without respect of birth, worth, merit or state,) blindly, unadvisedly, and without any order or reason, bestows felicities, riches and favours.

IX. In *Egira,* a City of *Achaia,* Fortune was drawn in the shape of a beautiful woman, who held in one of her hands a *Cornucopia;* in the other, the boy *Cupid.*

By which is signified (as Pausanias *saith) that beauty without riches avails nothing : and indeed I may say he is doubly fortunate, who in his love enjoys the fruition of both beauty and riches : but he is happy in the superlative degree, who with the other two meets with vertue and love also.*

X. *Giraldus* saith, that *Fortune* was with some depicted

picted riding on a horse galloping; with which swiftness she seems to pass invisible, after whom followeth
Destiny with great wrath and fury, holding in her hand
an Iron bow , and aiming to strike Fortune at the
heart.

By her swift galloping, is signified her mutability. See
Sect. 4. Chap. 28. *where she is taken as one of the powers.*

CHAP. XXIV.

How Vertue, Truth, Peace, Honour, Fame *and* Opinion *were depicted.*

I. VErtue in *Greece* was made in the form of a *Pilgrim,* like a grave and austere woman ; sitting
alone upon a four squared stone, melancholy, and leaning her head upon her knees.

*Being a Pilgrim, shews she hath no resting place, secure
abode, or certain habitation upon the earth: the form of her
sitting, shews her life to be full of troubles, dangers, crosses,
and miseries. See the 1. Section of Chap. 30. of this Book.*

Hæc angusta via horrendis scatet undique monstris,
Et vita innumeris est interclusa periclis.
Sed tamen incolumes hac virtus ducit alumnos
Extrema ut vitent, ne pes hinc inde vacillet.
Proclamat longe spes, hic sunt digna laboris
Præmia, & excipient mordaces gaudia curas.
Pax, sincera quies nullo temeranda dolore,
Lætitia hic habitant longum, sine fine, per ævum.

*Fierce Monsters do this narrow passage bound,
And deadly dangers it encompass round.
Yet vertue doth her Followers safely guide,
Lest they should go astray on either side.*

And

And Hope proclaims afar ; lo here you shall
Have Joy for Sorrow ; honey for your gall.
Here Peace and joyful rest for ever dwell,
Which neither cross nor time shall ever quell.

II. *Truth,* saith *Hippocrates,* was framed in the similitude and likeness of a beautiful woman, attired with gravity and modesty: *Philostratus* saith that she remaineth in the cave of *Amphiarus,* cloathed all in white garments of a beautiful hue : *Lucianus* saith that her statue was made in the form of a young woman, habited in rags, and base attire, with a superscription over her head, how she was *wronged and abused by Fortune.*

III. *Peace,* saith *Aristophanes,* was framed in the shape of a young woman, holding between her arms the Infant *Pluto,* the God of Riches, and Ruler of the lower Regions.
She is also called Concordia, *and is a special friend to the Goddess* Ceres, *from whom comes the encrease of Fruits, Corn, and other nutriments.* See Chap. 28.

IV. *Honour* is depicted with two wings on its shoulders; which as *Alciatus* saith, was made in the form of a little child, cloathed in a purple garment, having a Coronet or wreath of Laurel about his head ; holding hand in hand the God *Cupid,* who leads the child to the Goddess *Vertue,* which is depainted right over against it.

V. *Fame* is painted like a Lady, with great wings, and seeming to proffer a flight, and to mount from the *Earth,* and rove abroad : having her face full of eyes ; and all over her garments an infinite number of ears and tongues. *See the tenth Section of the twenty ninth Chapter of this Book.*

U   VI. *Opi-*

VI. *Opinion,* faith *Hippocrates,* refembles a young woman, not altogether fo fair and lovely as *Truth,* yet not deformed, or ill proportioned; being rather impudent than modeftly bold in her demeanour, with her hand ftretched forth to take whatfoever is offered and prefented to her.

CHAP. XXV.

How Night, Sleep, Silence, Pleafure and Fear were depicted.

I. Night (the mother of *Sleep* and *Death*) was depicted by the Antients in form of an old woman, having two great wings growing on her fhoulders, all coal black, and fpread abroad, as if fhe feemed to offer a flight; and that fhe is drawn in a Chariot, whofe wheels are made of Ebony: having a fad countenance, and an upper garment of a deep black, fpotted all over with filver fpots like ftars, as *Boccace* faith.

She is alfo depicted like an old woman in a black mantle fpotted with ftars of Gold.

II. *Sleep* (the brother of *Death*) faith *Hefiod,* was painted of a moft fowr, lowring, and fad afpect; aged, and holding in her left hand a young child very beautiful, and in her right, another child, of a moft fwarthy, black and dull complexion, with legs and arms very crooked. *Philoftratus* in a Tablet (which he made for *Amphiarus*) makes her like an aged woman, flothful and fluggifh, cloathed with feveral garments, the under black, the upper white; holding in one of her hands, a horn pouring forth feed.

By

By the garment is fignified night and day ; by the feed, reft, eafe and quiet.

III. *Harpocrates* (the God of *Silence*) called in Greek *Sigaleon*, was made, as *Mnrtianus* and *Apuleius* fay, in likenefs of a young child, who clofe to his lips held one of his fingers as a fign of fecrefie. Some portraict him without any face at all; all covered with the skin of a wolf, painted full of eyes and ears:

Shewing it to be good to fee and hear much, but to fpeak little.

IV. *Voluptia* or Pleafure, was depainted a Lady, having a pale and lean countenance, fitting in a pontifical and majeftick chair, embroidered and emboffed with ftars of gold, treading and trampling upon *Vertue.*

V. *Fear*, faith *Paufanias*, was fhaped in feveral forms by the Antients; fometimes with the head of a Lion among the Grecians (as on the fhield of *Agamemnon* :) and fometimes with the deformed face and body of a woman.

The Corinthians dedicated this Picture fo made unto the fons of Medea; *which were flain for bringing fuch fatal gifts to the daughter of old* Creon, *whereby fhe, and all that regal family perifhed, and were for ever extinct.*

CHAP. XXVI.

How the Antients depicted several wisemen and Philosophers, Lawgivers, Emperours, Kings and Queens.

I. S*Idonius Apollinarius* in the ninth Epiſtle of his ninth Book, ſaith that the Philoſopher *Zeuſippus* was painted with a crooked neck : *Aratus* with a neck bowed downwards : *Zeno* with a wrinkled forehead.

II. *Epicurus*, was painted with a ſmooth skin : *Diogenes*, with a hairy rough beard : *Socrates*, with whitiſh bright hair.

III. *Ariſtotle*, was painted with a ſtretched out arm : *Zenocrates*, with a leg ſomewhat gathered up : *Heraclitus*, with his eyes ſhut for crying.

IV. *Democritus* with his lips open, as laughing : *Chryſippus* with his fingers cloſe preſſed together, for numbering : *Euclid* with his fingers put aſunder, for the ſpace of meaſures.

V. In ſome ancient Bibles and many Pictures, *Moſes* is deſcribed with horns.

   " The ground of this abſurdity was a miſtake of the
" Hebrew Text, in that of *Moſes* deſcending from the
" Mount, upon the nearneſs of the words, קֶרֶן *Ke-*
" *ren*, *Cornu*, an horn, and קָרַן *Karan*, *Luceo*, to ſhine.
" The vulgar tranſlation (of *Exodus* 34. 29. 35.) a-
" grees with the former, to wit ; *Ignorabat quòd cor-*
" *nuta eſſet facies ejus.   Qui videbant faciem* Moſis *eſſe*
" *cornutam.* The tranſlation of *Paulus Fagius* is other-
" wiſe, viz. Moſes *neſciebat quòd multus eſſet ſplendor*
" *gloriæ vultûs ejus.   Et viderunt filii* Iſrael *quòd multa*
                             " *eſſet*

" *effet claritas gloriæ faciei* Mofis.   Tremelius *and* Ju-
" nius *have it thus, ut ignoraret* Mofche *fplendidam effe*
" *factam cutem faciei fuæ.   Quod fplendida facta effet*
" *cutis faciei Mofchis :* agreeing with the Septuagint,
" Δεδόξασαι ἦ ὅτις τῦ γρώματ⊙ τῦ προσώπε, *glorificatus*
" *eft afpectus cutis feu coloris faciei.*

VI. But *Mofes* is generally depicted with bright hair,
a very beautiful Vifage, with radiant fcintillations about
his head, in form of hoarinefs, which in Painting is called Glory.

VII. *Alexander* the great, with brown hair, and a
ruddy complexion, riding upon his horfe ; but by fome
riding upon an Elephant.

*The reafon of this is hard to be difcerned ; for as much
as I find not in hiftory, that ever he ufed that beaft in his
Armies, much lefs in his own perfon : except it were for
that remarkable battel which he fought with* Porus *King of*
India, *wherein were many Elephants : In which himfelf (as*
Curtius, Arianus *and* Plutarch *relate) was on horfeback,
the name of which beaft yet lives, and is famous in hiftory to
this day.*

VIII. *Numa Pompilius* with white hair Crowned with
a Silver bend or Diadem ; his robe crimfon trimmed
with Gold ; his mantle yellow trimmed with Silver ; his
buskins watchet and filver.

IX. *Æneas* the *Trojan* Prince in a purple mantle
trimmed with Gold.

X. *David* (the King of *Ifrael*) with brown hair, a ruddy complexion and a long beard.

XI. *Elizabeth* Queen of *England*, pale-faced, light
brown hair, and gray-eyed.

XII. *Dido* Queen of *Carthage* in a purple or fcarlet
mantle, her under-garments purple ; a Golden Quiver ; her hair yellow, tyed up with fpangles and knots
of Gold.

XIII.

XII. *Guſtavus Adolphus* King of *Sweden* with yellow hair.

XIV. *Mahomet* the *Turks* great Prophet, in garments all of green.

XV. *German Emperours* in a Violet-coloured robe, watchet, or light-coloured.

XVI. *Roman Emperours*, with yellow Carruſters embroidered with Silver ; the labels of their ſleeves, and ſhort baſes of watchet ; the under ſleeves, and long ſtockings white ; a Lawrel wreath, with a Silver jewel before ; and rays of Gold, iſſuing from the wreath.

XVII. *Pythagoras* in white garments with a Crown of Gold.

XVIII. *Empedocles*, in Violet, murry, or purple, and ſo generally the reſt of the *Grecian Philoſophers.*

XIX. *Eraſmus Roterdamus*, yellow haired, gray-eyed, and ſomewhat pale.

CHAP. XXVII.

The Painting of the Sibyls.

I. *Sibylla Agrippa*, a women in years, in a roſeal garment.

II. *Sibylla Libyca* an elderly woman, crowned with a garland of flowers, in purple garments.

III. *Sibylla Delphica*, with a black garment, a young woman with a horn in her hand.

IV. *Sibylla Phrygia*, in red garments, having an old Saturnian hard favoured face.

V. *Sibylla Herophila*, a young woman very fair in

a pura purple garment, and head covered with a vail of Lawn.

VI. *Sibylla Europea,* a comely young woman, having a high, red-coloured face, a fine vail on her head, and clad in a garment of Gold work.

VII. *Sibylla Perfica,* with a white vail, and a golden garment.

VIII. *Sibylla Samia,* a middle aged woman, clothed in Willow weeds, having a palm in her hand.

IX. *Sibylla Hellefpontica,* a young woman in green garments, with a round, lovely, fresh coloured face; holding in her left hand a Book; and in her right hand a Pen.

X. *Sibylla Tiburtina,* an old woman in purple garments, of a hard visage, holding in her Apron the books of the Sibylls.

These Sibylls *for their Prophecies of Christ are in high esteem: they are ten in number as* Varro *faith; yet others make twelve, of which we are not satisfied;* Boyfardus *in his Treatise of divination, besides these ten addeth two others,* Epirotica *and* Ægyptia. *Some, as* Martianus, *will have but two;* Pliny *and* Solinus, *but three;* Ælian *four; and* Salmafius *but the first seven. They are generally described as young women, yet some were old, as she that fold the books unto* Tarquin, *from whence we conclude the* Licentia pictoria *is very large.*

U 4

CHAP. XXVIII.

The Painting of Arts, Vertues, Paſſions and minor Gods.

I. **A**Rithmetick is painted in cloth of Gold : *Geometry* ſallow faced, a green mantle fringed with Silver, and a Silver wand in her right hand : *Aſtronomy* with a Silver Creſſant on her fore-head, an azure mantle, a watchet Scarf, with golden Stars.

II. *Faith* is painted in white garments, with a cup of Gold : *Hope* in blew, with a Silver Anchor : *Charity* in yellow robes ; on her head a tyre of Gold with precious ſtones ; her chair Ivory.

III. *Religion* in a Silver vail, with a garment, or mantle of white : *Juſtice* in a white robe, and a white mantle ; with a Coronet of Silver and white buskins : *Innocency* in white.

IV. *Concord* in a sky-coloured robe, and a yellow mantle ; *Peace* in white, ſcattered with ſtars, or a carnation mantle fringed with Gold, a vail of Silver, green buskins, and a palm in her hand in black : *Unanimity* in a blew robe, mantle and buskins ; with a chaplet of blew Lillies.

V. *Wiſdom* in a white robe, blew mantle, ſeeded with ſtars : *Law* in purple robes, ſeeded with Golden ſtars ; a mantle of Carnation fringed with Gold ; purple and yellow buskins : *Government* in Armour.

VI. *Watchfulneſs*, in a yellow robe : a ſable mantle fringed with Silver, and ſeeded with waking eyes ; a chaplet of turnſole, in her right hand a Lamp ; in her left, a Bell : *Confidence* in a particoloured garment : *Modeſty* in blew.

VII. *Eternity*

VII. *Eternity* in blew, feeded with Golden ftars; the *Soul* in white garments, branched with Gold and Pearl; and crowned with a Garland of Rofes: *Felicity*, in purple trimmed with Silver.

VIII. *Love*, in Crimfon fringed with Gold, a flame-coloured mantle, a Chaplet of red and white Rofes: *Natural-affection*, in Citron colour: *Envy*, in a difcoloured garment full of eyes.

IX. *Joy*, in a green robe, and a mantle of divers colours, embroidered with flowers; a garland of Myrtle; in her right hand a Cryftal Cruife, in her left a Golden Cup: *Pleafure* in light garments, trimmed with Silver and Gold: *Laughter* in feveral colours.

X. *Wit*, in a difcoloured mantle: *Jollity*, in flame colour: *Paftime* in purple trimmed with Gold.

XI. *Opinion* in black Velvet, black cap, with a white fall: *Impudence*, in a party-coloured garment: *Audacity*, in blufh colour.

XII. *Honour*, in a purple robe, wrought with Gold: *Liberty*, in white: *Safety*, in Carnation.

XIII. *Cupid* was painted (by *Zeuxis*) in a green robe: *Hymen*, in long yellow hair, in a purple or Saffron coloured mantle: *Triton* (*Neptunes* Trumpeter) with a blew skin, in a purple mantle.

XIV. *Urania*, in a mantle of azure, filled with lamps: *Aftrea* the Goddefs of Juftice, in a Crimfon mantle, trimmed with Silver: the *Graces* all alike, as Sifters, in Silver robes.

XV. *Tellus*, the Goddefs of the Earth in a green mantle: *Ceres*, with yellow hair, and a ftraw-coloured mantle trimmed with Silver: *Vefta*, daughter of *Saturn*, in white garments filled with flames.

XVI. *Flora*,

XVI. *Flora* in a mantle of divers colours: *Proser-pine* in a black mantle, trimmed with Gold flames: *Echo* , (the Goddess of the Air and daughter of speech, the intirely beloved of *Pan*) is an invisible Goddess.

Aufonus Gallus, reporteth that she hath oftentimes dissuaded, and reprehended such, who would undertake to depaint her, and repeats the same in an Epigram, whose sence in English is this.

Surceaſe thou medling Artiſt thy endeavour,
  Who for thy skill haſt reap't ſuch long liv'd fame :
Strive not to paint my body, ſhape, for never
  Did any humane Eyes behold the ſame.
In concave caverns of the Earth I dwell,
  Daughter o'th' Air, and of each tatling voice,
In Woods and hollow dales I build my Cell,
  Joying to re-report the leaſt heard noiſe,
To grief oppreſt, and men diſconſolate,
  That tell each grove their ſouls vexation,
Their dying agonies I aggravate,
  By their dole accents iteration.
    And he that will deſcribe my form aright,
    Muſt ſhape a formleſs ſound or airy ſprite.

C H A P. XIX.

To expreſs the Powers.

I. **E**Ternity, It is expreſſed in the form of a fair Lady, having three heads, ſignifying Time paſt, preſent, and to come ; in her left hand a Circle, pointing with the fore finger of her right hand up to Heaven:

Heaven : the Circle fignifies fhe hath neither beginning nor end.

In the Medals of Trajan, *fhe was figured red, fitting upon a Sphear, with the Sun in one hand, and the Moon in the other* : (by her fitting is fignified perpetual conftancy.)

In the Medals of Fauftina, *fhe is drawn with a Vail, and in her right hand the Globe of the World.*

Boccace, *writing of the Progenie of the Gods, faith that the Antients derived it from* Demogorgon, *as the principal and firft of them all, who inhabited in the middle or Center of the Earth,* encircled round about, and circumvefted with a dark and obfufcate cloud, breathing from his mouth, a certain liquid humidity.

But however what Eternity *is, the name doth clearly difcover, containing in* it *felf all Worlds and Ages, and not limited, or meafured by any fpace of time.*

Claudius *defcribes it by a Serpent that encompaffeth round with her body, the Cave or Den wherein it lyeth, fo as making a Circle, fhe holds in her mouth the end of her tail,* which with the Ægyptians *was the emblem of a year.*

All in a Circle thus fhe fits involv'd,
Whofe firm tenacity is ne'er diffolv'd :
She fends forth times, and them recalls again,
Ages to come, and paft fhe doth retain.

But according to Boccace, *as Eternity hath an abfolute command over all times, fo fhe lives far hence in fome remote and unknown vale, where humane fteps never approached, but is even unfound out of the cœleftial inhabitants, thofe happy fouls, who ftand before the prefence of the greateft, that only knows all things.*

II. *Time,* It is drawn ftanding upon an old ruine, winged,

winged, and with Iron teeth. *Or thus,* An old man in a garment of ſtars ; upon his head a garland of roſes, ears of corn, and dry ſticks, ſtanding upon the Zodiack, with a looking-glaſs in his hand; two children at his feet, the one fat, the other lean, writing both in one book ; upon the head of one the Sun, upon the other the Moon. *Or thus,* An old man, bald behind, winged, with a ſithe and an hour-glaſs, having a lock of hair on his forehead.

III. *Fate,* A man in a fair, long, flaxen robe, looking upwards to two bright ſtars encompaſſed with thick clouds, from whence hangs a golden chain.

IV. *Fortune,* A naked Lady having an Inſign or Sail overſhadowing her, ſtanding upon a Globe or ball.

Lactantius *ſaith that Fortune is a vain, idle and ſenſeleſs name , ſhewing forth mans weakneſs in attributing any thing thereto:* which Marcus Tullius *confirmeth, where he ſaith that this name of Fortune, was firſt brought in to cover the ignorance of man.* Alexander Neopolitanus *ſaith that in* Præneſte *in a temple ſhe was depicted in the ſhape and form of two ſiſters, both conjoined in one and the ſame ſtatue.* Pauſanias *ſaith that her moſt ancient ſtatue was that which* Bupalus *made in* Greece *in ſhape of a woman, upon whoſe head was a round ball, and in one of her hands a* Cornucopia. *She is called the blind Goddeſs, and partial Lady, by reaſon of the beſtowing of her unconſtant and mutable favours.*

> Imperious Ruler of the worlds deſigns,
> Lady of ſolace, pleaſure and of pains :
> Like Tennis balls thou beat'ſt us to and fro,
> From favours to diſgrace, from joy to woe ;
> From wars to peace, from rule to be commanded :
> But with unconſtancy thou now art branded.

Macrobius

Macrobius *saith she was set forth with wings on her shoulders,* (*to shew that she was always at hand among men*) *had by her side the rudder of a Ship* (*to shew that she doth rule and command*) *her self placed upon a wheel, holding in her right hand a golden ball, and in the other a whip ; shewing where she smiled, wealth and honour, and where she frowned, crosses and misery should follow.*

In Egypt *Fortune was depicted like a Lady turning a great glass wheel, on whose top were many men playing, others a climbing up; and others having attained it, precipitating themselves and falling down back again.*

V. *Equality,* A Lady lighting two Torches at once.

VI. *Victory,* Is expressed by a Lady clad all in Gold, in one hand a helmet, in the other a Pomegranate : *By the Helmet is meant force ; by the Pomegranate unity of wit and counsel.*

Augustus *drew her with wings ready to flye, standing upon a Globe, with a Garland of Bays in one hand, in the other a Coronet of the Emperor, with these words* Imperator Cæsar. *In the Medals of* Octavius, *she is drawn with wings, standing on a base, in one hand a palm, in the other a Crown of Gold.*

VII. *Peace,* Is drawn like a Lady, holding in her right hand a wand or rod downwards towards the earth, over a hideous Serpent of sundry colours; and with her other hand covering her face with a veil, as loth to behold strife or war.

Trajan *gave a Lady in her right hand an Olive branch, in her left a* Cornucopia. *In the Medals of* Titus, *a Lady having in one hand an Olive branch, the other leading a Lamb and Wolf coupled by the necks in one yoke. The Olive as always the emblem of peace.*

VIII. *Providence,* A Lady lifting up both her hands to Heaven with these words *Providentia Deorum.* Or

this,

thus, A Lady in a robe, in her right hand a Scepter, in her left a *Cornucopia,* with a Globe at her feet.

IX.*Concord,* A Lady fitting, in her right hand a charger for facrifice, in her left a*Cornucopia,* with the word *Concordia. Or thus,* A fair Virgin, holding in one hand a Pomegranate; in the other a Mirtle bunch.

The nature of thefe trees are fuch, that if planted though a good fpace one from another, they will meet and with twining embrace one another.

X.*Fame,* A Lady clad in a thin and light garment, open to the middle thigh, that fhe might run the fafter; two exceeding large wings, garments embroider'd with eyes and ears, and blowing of a Trumpet.

XI. *Deftiny,* a Lady, who with great fury, and exceeding celerity holds in her hand an Iron bow ready bent, aiming to ftrike fortune even at the very heart.

Deftiny and fortune can never agree; and therefore as fortune flies from deftiny, fo deftiny purfues fortune; for where deftiny fets her foot, there fortune is as it were inchanted and conjured, as having no power, efficacy or vertue.

CHAP. XXX.

Of Vertues and Vices.

I. **V**Ertue is reprefented by *Hercules,* naked, with his Lyons skin, and knotted club, performing fome one of his Labours; as offering to ftrike a dragon keeping an Apple-tree: or holding in his hand three golden Apples.

Hercules *is nothing elfe but Vertue, his name in the Greek*

Greek tongue is Ηεγχλῆς *, quaſi* ἥεςς κλεὸς *,* Junonis gloria : vel quia κλησεῖ τὸς ἥεωας, celebrat aut commemorat Heroas, *which is the property of Vertue : he is drawn naked to demonſtrate her ſimplicity: by the dragon is ſet forth all manner of vices : by the Lions skin, magnanimity and greatneſs : by his Oaken Club, Reaſon and Policy: by its knottineſs, the difficulty, pains and labour in ſeeking after vertue : by the three golden Apples, the three Heroical Vertues, Moderation, Content and Labour.*

II. *Piety* is drawn like a Lady, with a ſober countenance; in her right hand ſhe holdeth a ſword ſtretched over an Altar; in her left hand a Stork; and by her ſide is placed an Elephant and a Child.

The Stork is ſo called of ςὸςγη, *the reciprocal or mutual love of Parent and Child, of which this bird was ever an Emblem, for the love and care ſhe hath of her parents being old. The Elephant worſhips towards the riſing of the Sun.*

III. *Hope* is drawn like a beautiful child in a long robe hanging looſe, ſtanding upon tiptoes, and a trefoyl or three-leaved graſs in its right hand, in its left an Anchor.

The looſe veſtment ſhews, ſhe never pincheth or binds truth, ſtanding on tiptoes ſhews ſhe always ſtandeth dangerouſly ; the branch of trefoyl ſhews knowledge (the ground of faith) faith (the ground of hope) and hope it ſelf.

IV. *Mercy,* a Lady ſitting upon a Lion, holding in one hand a Spear, in the other an Arrow ; which ſhe ſeemeth to caſt away.

In the Medals of Vitellius *ſhe ſits with a branch of Bays in her hand, and a ſtaff lying by her.*

V. *Juſtice,* a fair young Virgin, drawing after her, with her left hand a black, hard, ill-favoured Woman,

man, haling her by main force, and ftriking her over the face in a fevere manner.

The young Virgin was Juftice, the other Injuria *: fhe is drawn young and a Virgin, to fhew, that Judges and adminiftrators of Law ought to be incorrupt and free from bribes, partiality or flattery, but juft; conftant and fincere.*

VI. *Felicity,* a Lady fitting in an imperial throne, in the one hand fhe holdeth a *Caduceus* or Rod, in the other hand a *Cornucopia.*

VII. *Fruitfulnefs,* a Lady fitting upon a bed, and two little infants hanging about her neck.

VIII. *Diffimulation,* a Lady wearing a vizard of two faces, in a long robe of changeable colour ; and in her right hand a Magpye.

IX. *Security,* a Lady leaning againft a pillar, before an Altar, with a Scepter in her hand.

X. *Calumnia,* a beautiful, rich and young woman, approaching towards a Judge, gorgeous in her habit, with an angry, fcornful and difcontented look, and red and fiery eyes; fhe holds in her left hand a flaming torch : and with her right fhe by force draws a young man by the hair of the head.

XI. *Envie,* a wonderful lean old man, with a pale and meagre face, in whofe withered cheeks Age hath wrought deep furrows and wrinkles.

XII. *Penitence,* a Woman in vile, ragged and bafe attire, infinitely deploring her being : and bemoaning her felf in paffionate fits above all meafure, continually weeping.

CHAP.

CHAP. XXXI.

Of Rivers.

I. **H**Erein you ought to obferve the Adjuncts and Properties of the fame ; which confifts in fome notable Accident done near them ; fome famous City, trees, fruits, or reeds fituate upon their banks ; fome fifh only proper to their ftreams ; or recourfe of fhipping from all parts of the world.

II. Therefore you had beft place the City upon their heads ; the fruits in a *Cornucopia* ; reeds, flowers and branches of trees in their Garlands, and the like.

III. **The River** *Tyber*. It is expreffed (in the *Vatican* in *Rome*) in a goodly Statue of Marble lying along (for fo you muft draw them) holding under his right arm a fhe wolf, with two little infants fucking at her teats, leaning upon an Urn or Pitcher, out of which iffueth its ftream : in his left a *Cornucopia* of delicate fruits, with a grave Countenance and long beard ; a garland of flowers upon his head ; and refting his right leg upon an Oar.

IV. **The River** *Nilus*. It is feen (in the *Vatican*) cut out in white Marble, with a garland of fundry fruits and flowers, leaning with his left arm upon a Sphynx ; from under his body iffueth its ftream ; in his left arm a *Cornucopia* full of fruits and flowers on one fide, with fixteen little children, fmiling and pointing to the flood.

The Sphynx was fometimes a monfter which remained by Nilus : *the Crocodile* ἀπὸ τῦ κϱόκον δειλιῷν, *from his hatred of Saffron, the moft famous monfter of* Egypt : *the fixteen children, the fixteen cubits of height, the uttermoft*

X   *of*

of the flowing of Nilus : *their smiling looks, the profit of it, which glads the hearts of the Sun-burnt inhabitants.*

V. The River *Tigris*. It was drawn like an old man (as the rest) and by his side a Tiger.

This beast was given it as well for its fierce streams, as for the store of Tigers which are there.

VI. The River *Ganges*. It bears the shape of a rude and barbarous savage, with bended brows, of a fierce and cruel Countenance, crowned with a palm, having, as other floods, his pitcher, and by his sides a *Rhinoceros*.

This River runneth through India, *and hath its head from a fountain in Paradise.*

VII. The River *Indus*. It is drawn with a grave and jovial aspect, with a garland of its countrey flowers, by its side a Camel (from χάμαι ·) it is represented pleasantly, grave, as an Emblem of the *Indian* policy.

This is the greatest River in the world, receiving into its channel threescore other great and famous Rivers, and above an hundred lesser.

VIII. The River *Thamesis*. In the house of an honourable friend, I saw the *Thames* thus drawn : A Captain or Soldier lying along, holding in his right hand a Sword, and under his arm the August tower : in the other a *Cornucopia* of all fragrancies, with a Golden chain which held four Crowns ; and with this he encompassed the streams, from under which bending of his left arm they seemed to flow : his temples were adorned with Bays , the River was empaled on one side with Anchors, and on the other stood *Cæsar*'s *Augusta*.

IX. The River *Arnus*. It is a famous River in *Italy*, drawn like an old man leaning upon his pitcher, pouring

ing out water: upon his head a garland of Beech, by his right side a Lyon, holding forth in his dexter paw a red Lilly or Flower-de-luce, the antient Arms of the chief City of *Tuscany.*

By the garland of Beech is set forth the great abundance of Beech-trees growing about Fasterona *in the* Appennines *where* Arnus *hath his head.*

X. The River *Po* or *Padus.* It is depicted with an Ox's face, having a garland of Reeds or Poplar on his head.

It is so called from the Sister of Phaeton, *whom the Poets feign destroyed with lightning, and drowned here : the head of the Ox, is from its horrid noise and roaring, whose crooked banks resemble the horns thereof ; by the sides whereof grows much Reed and many Poplars.*

XI. The River *Danubius.* In the antient Medals of the Emperour *Trajan,* it is depicted with its head covered with a veil.

It is so drawn, because its head or first spring is unknown. Ausonius *saith,*

Danubius periit caput occultatus in ore.

XII. The River *Achelous.* Ovid describes it with a garland of Reeds, Willow, and the like : having two Urns or Earthen Pitchers, the one empty , the other casting out water ; and upon its head two horns, the one whole, the other broken.

This River as it is the most famous of all Greece, *so it divides* Ætolia *from* Arcadia, *and then falls into the Sea. This is fetch'd from the fable of* Hercules *who combated him in the likeness of a Bull, and broke one of his horns for* Deianiras *sake, there turning both its streams into one, whereupon one of the Urns is empty.*

XIII. The River *Niger*. It is drawn like a Black-Moor, with Glory, or a Coronet of Sun-beams falling upon his Urn, having by its fide a Lyon.

By the Sun-beams and black, is fhewed the clime, lying under the torrid Zone, whofe inhabitants are Blacks or Moors; the Lyon is that which the Countrey Mauritania *and* Barbary *breed, being the fierceft in the World.*

CHAP. XXII.

Of Nymphs.

I. NΥ´ΜΦΗ, *Nympha*, a Bride (*from* νεὸν & φαί-νεϑαι *as it were a frefh or new creature: or as fome will have it from* Nympha quafi Lympha, *by changing* L. *into* N. *after the Dorick dialeft:*) it is nothing elfe but an Allegory, from the Vegetative humidity, which gives life to trees, herbs, plants, and flowers, by which they grow and increafe.

II. They are feigned to be the daughters of the Ocean, the mother of floods, the nurfes of *Bacchus*, and goddeffes of fields, who have the protection and charge of mountains, herbs, woods, meadows, rivers, trees, and generally of the whole life of man.

III. *Firft*, Napææ, *Nymphs of the Mountains.*

Let them be drawn of a fweet and gracious afpeft, in green mantles, girded about in the middle; and upon their heads garlands of honey-fuckles, wild-rofes, tyme and the like; their actions, dancing in a ring, making garlands, or gathering flowers.

They

They are so called from Ναπὸς, *the top of an hill,or woody valley.*

IV. *Secondly,* Dryades, *Nymphs of the woods.*

Draw these less fair than the former, of a brown or tawny complexion, hair thick like moss, and their attire of a dark green.

They are so called from Δρὺς *an Oak, having their beginning with trees, and dying again with them.*

V. *Thirdly,* Naiades *Nymphs of the floods.*

Draw them beautiful, with arms and legs naked, their hair clear as Cryſtal ; upon their heads garlands of water-creſſes, with red leaves : their actions, pouring out water.

They are so called from Νάω *to flow, or bubble as water doth.*

VI. *Thetis,* a Lady of a brown complexion, her hair ſcattered about her ſhoulders, crowned with a Coronet of Periwincle and Eſcallop ſhells, in a mantle of Sea-green , with chains and bracelets of Amber about her Neck and Arms, and a branch of red Coral in her hand.

VII. *Galatea,* a moſt beautiful young Virgin, her hair careleſly falling about her ſhoulders like ſilver threads, and at each ear a fair pearl with a double ſtring of them (ſometimes) about her Neck and left Arm a mantle of pure thin and fine white, waving as it were by the gentle breathing of the air, viewing in her hand a ſpunge made of Sea-froth, *ſhe is ſo called from* γάλα, lac, milk.

VIII. *Iris,* a Nymph with large wings, extended like to a ſemicircle, the plumes ſet in rows of divers colours, as yellow, green, red, blew or purple ; her hair hanging before her eyes, her breaſts like clouds, drops of water falling from her body, and in her hand *Iris,* or the Flower-de-luce.

X 3   *Virgil*

Virgil makes her the meſſenger of *Juno* (where ſhe is ta..en for the air *)* when he ſaith, *Irin de Cœlo miſit Saturnia Juno.*

IX. *Nymphæ Dianæ*; Let them be cloathed in white linnen to denote their Virginity, and their garments girt about them; their Arms and Shoulders naked; bows in their hands, and arrows by their ſides.

X. *Aurora,* the Morning. A young Virgin with carnation wings and a yellow mantle; in her forehead a ſtar, and Golden Sun-beams from the Crown of her head, riding upon *Pegaſus,* with a viol of dew in one hand, and various flowers in the other, which ſhe ſcattereth upon the earth.

CHAP. XXXIII.

Of the Nine Muſes.

I. **C**Lio, She is drawn with a Coronet of Bays; in her right hand a Trumpet; in her left a Book, upon which may be written *Hiſtoria*; her name is from praiſe or glory.

II. *Euterpe,* Is crowned with a garland of flowers, holding in each hand ſundry wind inſtruments; her name is from giving delight.

III. *Thalia.* Draw her with a ſmiling look, and upon her Temples a Coronet of Ivy, a Mantle of Carnation embroidered with ſilver twiſt and gold ſpangles, and in her left hand a vizard; her Ivy ſhews ſhe is miſtriſs of Comical Poeſie.

IV. *Melpomene.* Draw her like a Virago, with a majeſtick and grave countenance, adorn her head with Pearls, Diamonds and Rubies; holding in her left hand

Scepters

Scepters with Crowns upon them, other Crowns and Scepters lying at her feet: and in her right hand a naked Poniard, in a Mantle of changeable Crimson. Her gravity befits Tragick Poesie.

V. *Polyhymnia.* Draw her acting a Speech with her fore-finger, all in white, her hair hanging loose about her shoulders of an orient yellow, upon her head a garland of the choicest jewels intermixt with flowers, and in her left hand a book, upon which let be written *Suadere* ; her name imports memory, to whom the Rhetorician is beholden.

VI. *Erato.* She hath her name from Ἔρως , *Amor, Love :* draw her with a sweet and comely visage, her temples girt with Myrtles and Roses, bearing an heart with an Ivory Key ; by her side *Cupid,* winged, with a lighted torch ; at his back, his bow and quivers.

VII. *Terpsichore* ; a cheerful visage playing upon some Instrument ; upon her head a Coronet of Feathers of sundry Colours, but chiefly green ; in token of the victory which the Muses got of the Syrenes, *&c.* by singing.

VIII. *Urania.* A beautiful Lady in an azure robe ; upon her head a Coronet of bright stars ; in her right hand the Cœlestial globe, and in her left the Terrestrial. Her name imports as much as heavenly ; *Urania cœli motus scrutatur & Astra.*

IX. *Calliope.* Upon her head draw a Coronet of Gold ; upon her left arm Garlands of Bays in store, for the reward of Poets ; and in her right hand three books, upon which write *Homerus, Virgilius, Ovidius.*

The Muses had their names, as Eusebius *saith,* περὶ τὸ μυεῖν, *which is to instruct, because they teach the most honest and laudable disciplines.*

CHAP. XXXIV.

Of the four winds.

I. **E***Urus*, the Eaſt-wind. Draw a youth with puffed and blown cheeks (as all the other winds muſt be) wings upon his ſhoulders, his body like a Tawny-Moor, upon his head a Red Sun.

II. *Zephyrus*, the Weſt-wind. Draw a youth with a merry look, holding in his hand a Swan, with wings diſplay'd as about to ſing, on his head a garland of all ſorts of flowers.

'*Tis called* Zephyrus *quaſi* ζωὴν φέρων, *bringing life, becauſe it cheriſheth and quickneth.*

III. *Boreas*, the North-wind. Draw it like an old man, with a horrid, terrible look; his hair and beard covered with ſnow, or the hoar-froſt ; with the feet and tail of a Serpent.

IV. *Auſter*, the South-wind, is drawn with head and wings wet, a pot or urn pouring forth water, with which deſcends frogs, graſhoppers, and the like creatures which are bred by moiſture.

CHAP. XXXV.

Of the Months of the Year:

I. **J***Anuary* muſt be drawn all in white, like ſnow or hoar froſt, blowing his fingers ; in his left arm a billet, and *Aquarius* ſtanding by his ſide.

II. *February* is drawn in a dark skie colour, carrying in his right hand *Piſces*, or Fiſhes.

III. *March*

III. *March* is drawn tawny with a fierce look, a helmet upon his head, leaning upon a Spade: in his right hand *Aries*; in his left Almond Bloſſoms and Scions; and upon his arm a basket of Garden-ſeeds.

IV. *April* is drawn like a young man in green, with a garland of Myrtle and Hawthorn-buds, winged; in the one hand Primroſes and Violets; in the other *Taurus*.

V. *May* is drawn with a ſweet and lovely aſpect, in a robe of white and green, embroidered with Daffadils, Haw-thorn and Blew-bottles; on his head a garland of white, red, Damask-roſes; in the one hand a Lute; upon the fore-finger of the other a Nightingal.

VI. *June* is drawn in a mantle of dark graſs-green; upon his head a Coronet of Bents, King-cobs, and Maiden-hair; in his left hand an Angle; in his right *Cancer*; and upon his Arm a basket of Summer fruits.

VII. *July* is drawn in a Jacket of a light yellow, eating Cherries, with his face and boſome Sun-burnt, on his head a garland of Centaury and Tyme, on his ſhoulder a Sithe; with a bottle at his girdle, carrying a Lion.

VIII. *Auguſt* is like a young man of a fierce look, in a flame-coloured robe; upon his head a garland of wheat; upon his arm a basket of Summer fruits; at his belt a Sickle, bearing a Virgin.

IX. *September* is drawn in a purple robe, with a cheerful look, and on his head a Coronet of white and purple Grapes; in his left hand a handful of Oats, with a *Cornucopia* of Pomegranates and other Summer fruits; and in his right hand a ballance.

X. *October* is drawn in a garment of the colour of decaying flowers and leaves; upon his head a garland of Oak-leaves with the Acorns; in his right hand a Scorpion; in his left, a basket of Services, Medlars and Cheſtnuts.

XI. *November*

XI. *November* in a robe of changeable green and black : upon his head, a garland of Olives with the fruit, in his right hand *Sagittarius :* and in his left bunches of Pafnips and Turneps.

XII. *December* is drawn with a horrid afpect, clad in an *Irifh* rug, or courfe Freeze girt about him : upon his head three or four night-caps, and over them a *Turkifh* turbant ; his nofe red, beard hung with Iceikles ; at his back a bundle of Holly and Ivy, holding in furred mittens a Goat.

Where note, it will be good to give every month its proper and natural Landskip ; not making bloffoms and fruits upon trees in December *; nor a barren face of the Earth and trees in* June.

CHAP. XXXVI.

Of Painting of the Face and Skin.

I. *T* W O *wayes there be of adorning of the Face and Skin ; the firft is by Painting : the fecond is, by application of Excellent cofmeticks, which give a very natural, abfolute and lafting beauty.*

The firft way, which is that of Painting, is the fubject matter of this Chapter. Some may wonder that we fhould meddle with fuch a fubject as this, in this place ; but let fuch know ; the Painting of a deformed Face, and the licking over of an old, withered, wrinkled and weather-beaten skin, are as proper appendices to a Painter, as the rectification of his Errors in a piece of Canvafe : Nor is there any reafon, but that the Artift fhould fhew his care in the one, as well as to expofe his skill in the other, fince a *fingle deformity*

in

in the body , begets a complication of miseries in the mind, and a unity of defects a multiplication of Evils.

And though some think the Poets did not much amiss, to fancy the creature to be hatcht in Hell, by reason it brings with it such a torrent of dejections, yet let those darkned souls, (who are so much affrighted at its cloudy adumbrations) understand, that when time shall have made its full revolution, themselves may be the product of such a conception: But we confess, it seeks darkness, and only solaces it self in obscurity and dusky solitudes.   For such whose bodies have passed the stamp with some faults, and have missed the impressions or reflexions of beauty, which might make them delectable in humane society, *ever make choice of darkness as their chief companion. Deformity* is a disease esteemed the most pernicious, and its issue is a matter of dangerous consequence, chiefly *obstructions to Ladies Preferment.*   Now to prevent this danger, to take away these obstructions, and to deliver you from the embraces of so hideous a monster (which some esteem as a Fury of *Hell*) these *Cosmeticks* we have offered upon the *Altar* of your defects ; protesting that the use of these beautifiers, will make you as fit for the entertainment of Courtiers , as ever you were before for the courtship of *Grooms* or *Hostlers,* and make your *rusty skins* and *ill-look'd faces* , to outshine with a radiant lustre, the most splendid of all the *Nymphs* of *Diana.*   Though you may look so much like the Image of death, as that your skins might be taken for your winding-sheets, yet by our directions you may attain such a rosid colour, and such a lively cheerfulness, as shall not only make you look like natures workmanship, but also put admiration into the beholders, and fix them in a belief, that you are the first-fruits of the resurrection.   Thus we teach you

lippid

lippid mortals to retrace the steps of youthfulness, and
to transform the wrinkled hide of *Hecuba,* into the tender skin of the Greatest of beauties; which then you
will dull by the advance of your features, and make
all conceited shadows of glory, to vanish in your pre-
sence. When once your artificial heat shall appear,
others shall seem pale with envy for your perfections;
and their *natural ruddiness* shall only serve them to
blush, to see their features clouded by your splendor,
who will seem like brown bread compared with Man-
chet, or rather like wooden dishes upon a shelf of China ware, or as another once said, like blubber'd jugs in
a cupboard of Venice glasses, or as earthern piss-pots
in a Goldsmiths shop. By this means your spark-
ling Glories shall fire *Platonick* Lovers, so that none
though as cold as *Saturn,* shall be able to resist your
actuating flames, but shall force the stoutest heart, to
be a *Sacrifice to love.* If any remain unscorched, it
must be only those leaden hearted *Cowards,* who dare
not *approach* your flames, for fear of *melting*; or those
undeserving soldiers of *Venus* (of a frigid constitution)
who dare not so much as *look* upon your youthful fire,
for fear of being burnt to ashes. But it may chance
that some *Saint* or another, may condemn your *hearts*
for *evil,* because you strive to make your *faces good,*and
may like your *in-side* the *worse,* because your *out-side* may
look *so well*; yet with *Benjamin,* refuse not the many
messes of Pottage, nor yet the many changes of Rai-
ment (although one might well enough serve your
turn) but receive them from the hands of *Joseph,*
though all the rest of the Brethren be angry. Avoid
not company for want of beauty, when Art affords an
innocent supply, but with *confidence* crucifie that evil
conscience, which forbids the use of a little oyl to make
a cheerful countenance, and the drinking of a little
wine

wine to make a merry heart. Borrow our Artificial beautifiers, and become *splendid*, that you may be fit to be gathered by the hand of some metamorphosed *Hero*; left in the garden of *Deformities*, growing *green* with *sickness*, you should be taken for *thistles*, and so cropp'd by *Asses*.

II. *To cleanse the face and skin.*

Before any thing be used to paint, or make the skin beautiful, it must be made very clean thus: first wash with warm water, and sweet scented wash-balls very well; then rub the face with a cloth, and wash well with water in which Wheat-bran is boiled; so is the skin prepared.

Or thus, Take *Sublimate* one ounce, glair of six eggs, boil them in a glass vessel, till they grow thick, then press out the water, with which wash the skin.

III. *To make a white Fucus or Paint.*

Take Talk and powder it, by beating of it in a hot mortar, to the powdred Talk add distilled Vinegar, boil it at a gentle fire in a wide glass, let the fat froth that swims at top, be taken off with a spoon; then evaporate the Vinegar, and mix the remaining cream with flegm of common Salt, or a little *Pomatum*, with which wash or anoint the face, and it will beautifie it much.

IV. *Another very excellent.*

Take Crude Talk in powder one ounce, oil of Camphire two ounces, digest till the oil is white; it is a noble *Fucus* for Ladies faces.

V. *To make the aforesaid oil of Camphire.*

Take Camphire four ounces, Bole twelve ounces, make them into balls and dry them in the Sun, then distill them in sand in a glass retort, into a receiver that hath distilled rain water therein: first there will come forth a white matter, which melts in the Alembick, and

and falls into the receiver, then a clearer water ; and at last with a stronger fire, the oil we speak of, sweet scented, which rectified with spirit of wine will be yellow as Gold.

VI. *Another excellent Fucus made of Pearl.*

Dissolve Pearl in distilled Vinegar ; precipitate with oil of *Sulphur per Campanam* ; then sweeten and digest with spirit of wine ; abstract the spirit, and you have a magisterial *Fucus* will melt like Butter.

VII. *To make the best Fucus or Paint as yet known.*

Take Venetian Talk, cleave it into slices, digest it in the heat of the Sun, or of a horse-dunghil for a month, with distilled vinegar, made of Spanish wine, adding every day new distilled vinegar to the former, till the vinegar be mucilaginous ; which them distill by a luted retort and a large receiver with a naked fire. First there comes forth the vinegar ; then a white oil, which separate. After you have cleansed the skin by the second Section, then first wash with the vinegar, after anoint with the oil : if the face be first well wash'd from all impurity, this one anointing may hold for a month without fading. *This Cosmetick if rightly prepared , is worth about five pound an ounce.*

VIII. *An excellent Fucus made of Bulls gall.*

Take Bulls galls dryed in the Sun, whose tincture extract with spirit of wine, with which besmear the face, (being cleansed by the second Section) leaving it on for three or four dayes, without going abroad, or exposing the skin to the air : at the end of the time cleanse the face by the second Section : so almost to a miracle, the skin of the face and neck is rendred most gratefully white, soft, delicate and amiable. This is the *Spanish Fucus* which several Ladies now use.

IX. *To make an excellent red Fucus.*

Make a decoction of red Sanders in double distilled
vinegar,

vinegar, adding a little Alom, with a few grains of Musk, Amber-griese, or of some sweet Spices, and you will have a perfect red *Fucus* for the face.

X. *Another very excellent.*

Take juice of Clove-gilliflowers, with which mix a little juice of Limons: with this paint your face, and you shall have a pleasing red colour.

XI. *To do the same another way.*

Make a strong infusion of Clove-gilliflowers in rectified spirit of wine, adding a few drops of oil of Vitriol, or instead thereof a little Alom, and the juice of a Citron or Limon; so shall you have an excellent colour to beautifie the face with.

XII. *A Fucus or Paint not easie to be discovered.*

Take seeds of Cardamoms or grains of Paradise, Cubebs, Cloves, and raspings of Brazil, which infuse in rectified spirit of wine for ten dayes, over a gentle heat; then separate the spirit: this is so perfect a Fucus, that it may deceive any man, for this clear water gives a fresh, red and lovely colour which will last long.

XIII. *A Fucus or Cosmetick of river Crabs.*

Take of the flesh which remains in the extremities of the great claws of river Crabs (being boiled) a sufficient quantity, which dry gently, and then extract a deep tincture with rectified spirit of wine; evaporate part of the *menstruum*, till the tincture have a good thickness or body; with which (the skin being cleansed) anoint the checks first, applying over it some other albifying Cosmetick.

XIV. *Spanish wooll, wherewith women paint their faces red.*

Boil shearings of Scarlet in water of quick-lime half an hour, of which take two pound, to which put Brazil two ounces (rasped) Roch Alom, Verdegriese,

of

of each one ounce, Gum-Arabick two drachms, boil all for half an hour, which keep for use.

XV. *To do the same another way.*

Take Spirit of wine one pound, Cochenele half an ounce, rasped Brazil one ounce, Gum-Armoniack three drachms, mix and digest till the Gum is dissolved ; then boil it gently, and strain it for use, into which you may put old linnen rags, or Spanish wooll at pleasure.

CHAP. XXXVII.

Of Cosmeticks which beautifie without any thing of Paint.

I. *AN excellent Cosmetick or Liquor of Talk.*

Take powder of Talk (made by rubbing it with pumice stones ; or beating it in a very hot mortar ; or filing it with a Goldsmiths smoothing file) eight ounces, *Salis Tartari* sixteen ounces, calcine it twelve hours in a wind furnace, and set it in a Cellar, separating that which melts, from that which doth not : then calcine this dry Calx added to four times its weight of Sal-nitre, with a strong fire, so the Talk will be melted into a clear white mass, which being set in a Cellar will turn to a clammy liquor.

This wonderfully whitens and beautifies the skin, and takes away spots and freckles from the face : but you must not leave the liquor long on, but wash it off with decoction of wheat bran, that it corrode not the skin.

II. *To make the skin soft and smooth.*

The face being very clean, by the second Section of the six and thirtieth Chapter, wash it very well with a *Lixivium* of Salt of Tartar , and after that anoint

it

it with *Pomatum*; or which is better, oil of fweet Almonds, doing this every night going to bed. The *Pomatum* we have taught the way to make in our *Synopfis Medicinæ, lib. 3. cap. 58. Sect. 2.*

III. *A water to cleanfe the face from Scurfe and Morphew.*

Take diftilled rain water fix ounces, juice of Limons twelve ounces, mix them, and wafh with it morning and evening, anointing after it at night going to bed with the oil or *Pomatum* aforefaid.

IV. *An Unguent which brings the skin to an exquifite beauty.*

Take of our *Pomatum* one ounce, Salt of Tartar one drachm, Musk twenty grains, mix them well, and (the face or skin being very clean) anoint morning and evening.

V. *A wonderful Cofmetick of great worth.*

Take white Tartar twenty ounces, Talk, Salt, of each ten ounces, calcine them in a potters furnace very well; then grinding the matter upon a marble, put it into *Hippocrates* his fleeve, and fet it in a Cellar or other moift place for twenty or thirty days, and there will drop from it a precious oil; which being rubbed upon the skin foftly with a linnen cloth (the skin being duly cleanfed firft) takes away all kind of fpots, and makes the skin foft and delicate.

VI. *A cheap, yet excellent Cofmetick.*

Take Alom in fine powder, and fhake it with whites of new laid eggs, being a little heated, till fuch time as they grow thick to an ointment, with which anoint the face morning and evening three or four days; and it will take away fpots and wrinkles, and make the skin grow clear and fair.

VII. *An excellent Mercurial Cofmetick prevalent againft moft deformities of the skin.*

Y   Take

Take Mercury purified from all blackness half a pound, Mercury *Sublimate* in powder as much, mix them in a stone or marble mortar ; put them into an Alembick of a strait Orifice, put on distilled Vinegar, till all be covered three or four fingers, letting it stand four days, daily stirring the same at certain times, then it extracts a whitish powder ; the whitish Vinegar by inclination separate, rejecting it, and put on other Vinegar : the powder at bottom keep so for some days : which labour you must so often reiterate, till you have abundance of that white powder, which dry, and keep for use : anoint with it, by mixing with it a little distilled rain water, and it will take away all blemishes of the skin, as also Tetters. Use it not too often, and beware you touch neither eyes nor teeth with it.

VIII. *Another of great estimation.*

Take Mercury *Sublimate,* *Saccharum Saturni* of each two drachms, Rose water, juice of Limons of each two ounces, mix them like to an ointment, with which anoint gently at night, and the next morning with the Pomatum aforesaid.

IX. *To make a kind of* Lac Virginis, *an excellent Cosmetick.*

Take distilled rain water a quart, *Saccharum Saturni* crystallized one ounce, mix them, and then wash with the water, being settled : the fine white powder at bottom, is also an excellent fucus or paint, which may be laid upon the skin if very clear : note, some use Vinegar instead of the rain water.

X. *To make* Oleum Tartari *per deliquium.*

Take Salt of Tartar, which put into a bag with a corner in a moist Cellar, and the oil will distil therefrom in drops : with this oil you may mix a little fair water, and wash your face at night going to bed ; and
the

the next morning, the face being very clean, you may wash with the aforesaid *Lac Virginis*; thus continuing for some days, you may create an exquisite and lasting beauty.

XI. *A compound Cosmetick esteemed by some of great force.*

Take of the aforesaid *Lac Virginis* one ounce, oil of Tartar aforesaid half an ounce, mix them, with which wash morning and night for about a weak or more, as you shall see occasion; then anoint with the following ointment.

XII. *To make the Cosmetick Ointment aforesaid.*

Take musk three drachms, ambergriese two drachms, civet one drachm, grind them upon a porphyre or marble stone, with oil of Ben and Rhodium of each three ounces, with which anoint as aforesaid : note, some instead of the oil of Ben, use oil of sweet Almonds.

XIII. *A vetegable Cosmetick.*

Besmear your face or skin at night going to bed, with the juice of Wake Robin; it is excellent.

XIV. *An incomparable Cosmetick of Pearl.*

Dissolve Pearls in juice of Limons or distilled Vinegar, which digest in Horse-dung, till they send forth a clear oil, which will swim on the top : this is one of the most excellent Cosmeticks or Beautifiers in the world : *this oil if well prepared is richly worth seven pound an ounce.*

XV. *A Cosmetick ointment of great worth.*

Take of our *Pomatum* aforesaid six ounces, *Saccharum Saturni* two ounces, mix them, and anoint morning and evening.

XVI. *Another very good for the skin.*

Mix *Saccharum Saturni* one drachm, in Vinegar half an ounce, which mingle with the glair of eggs, and anoint with it.

Y 2   XVII.

XVII. *A Cosmetick wonderful to make a pleasing ruddy complexion.*

Take oil of Tartar four ounces, Alom, Sal Gem, of each one ounce, Borax, Camphire of each half an ounce, beat them well together, to which add of Briony water a pint, distil them in *Balneo*, and you will have your desire.

XVIII. *Another for the same.*

Take Madder, Myrrh, Saffron, Frankincense, of each alike, bruise and steep all in White-wine, with which anoint the face going to bed, and in the morning wash it off, and the skin will have a gallant pleasing blush.

XIX. *To make the Cosmetick of Myrrh, very excellent.*

Boil eggs till they are hard, slit them and take out the yolks, fill them up with powdred myrrh, close them together, and lay them in a moist Cellar, and the myrrh will dissolve into oil.

XX. *To make a very good Wash to whiten the skin, and give a good complexion.*

Take Limons, hens eggs boiled, of each twelve, Turpentine eight ounces, distil all in *Balneo Maria*, with which wash: when you wash, you may drop into it a drop, two or three of oil of Oranges or Cinamon, for fragrancy sake.

XXI. *A Cosmetick to make a rough skin smooth.*

Take sweet Almonds blanched four pound, moister them with spirit of wine and rose water mixt together, of each two ounces, beat them together and fry them; and when they begin to smoak, put them into a bag, and press them (in a press made for that purpose) and there will come forth a very clear oil which put into rain water, and beat it till it is exceeding white.

C H A P. XXXVIII.

Of Cofmeticks, which remedy the various Vices of the skin.

I. **T**O *take away Sun-burnings.*

To glair of ten eggs put Sugar-candy one ounce, and anoint with it going to bed : or anoint with the juice of Sow-bread at night going to bed ; and in the morning with oil *Omphacine.* The like effects hath our *Lac Virginis* at the ninth Section of the feven and thirtieth Chapter, as alfo *Oleum Tartari,* and other things of like nature.

II. *To take away rednefs and Pimples.*

Firft prepare the skin by bathing it often with the decoction of wheat-bran, and applying pultifles of bread, milk and oil thereto : when the skin is thus fuppled and rarified, you may cure them either by our liquor of Talk, at the firft Section of the feven and thirtieth Chapter, or mercurial Cofmetick at the feventh Section of the feven and thirtieth Chapter, or our *Lac Virginis* and oil of Tartar at the ninth and tenth Section of the feven and thirtieth Chapter, or by often wafhing with juice of Limons.

III. *To take away Freckles.*

Take juice of Limons, put it into a glafs bottle, to which put fine Sugar, and *Borax* in powder, digeft it eight days in Sand, then ufe it ; or mix *Sal Tartari* with whites of eggs, and apply it ; or often ufe our compound Cofmetick at the eleventh Section of the feven and thirtieth Chapter, or oil of Tartar alone, for fome weeks ; but if all fail, you muft have recourfe to our Liquor of Talk at the firft Section of the feven

and

and thirtieth Chapter, or Mercurial Cofmetick at the feventh Section of the feven and thirtieth Chapter.

IV. *To take away fpots from the face or skin.*

This is done by anointing with oyl of Tartar for ten days ; and after all that to wafh it with a *Lixivium* of *Quick-lime* in which *Sal-armoniack* hath been diffol-ved for a long time : or you may ufe the Cofmetick at the third Section of the feven and thirtieth Chapter camphorated.

V. *To cleanfe a fcurffy skin.*

If the creature be fat, foment firft with a *Lixivium* of Salt of Tartar ; but if lean, make a fomentation of Borrage, Buglofs and Mallow leaves, which ufe for fome days : this being done, bath the place where the fcurf is, with *Spiritu Nicotianæ* made by fermentation, which being dryed in, anoint firft with oil of Tartar, then with oil of Almonds ; repeating the three laft works, fo often till the fcurf goes away.

If all thefe fail, you muft have recourfe to our liquor of Talk, or Mercurial Cofmetick; or thofe at the fifth and eighth Section of the feven and thirtieth Chapter, which without doubt will perform your defire.

VI. *To free the Skin from Tetters and Ring-worms.*

Diffolve *Sublimate* one ounce in a glafs of Red-wine by boiling, with which wafh the place morning and evening, letting it dry of it felf, for three or four days together, and it will certainly cure : if they be not in-veterate, our liquor of Talk at the firft Section of the feven and thirtieth Chapter, or Mercurial Cofmetick may fufficiently do; or you may anoint with this oint-ment. Take *Sal Tartari* two drachms, burnt Alom three drachms, powder and incorporate with whites of eggs : Or this, take *Sulphur vive* three drachms, Camphire one drachm, Hogs-griefe two ounces, mix and make an ointment.

VII.

VII. *To take away wrinkles from the skin.*

Take oil of Almonds, lees of oil Olive, and make them into an ointment with wax, powder of Camphire and Maſtich, with which anoint. Oil of Myrrh to anoint with, is eminent in this caſe : or waſh with a decoction of Briony roots and figs of each alike : or diſſolve Gum Tragacanth in *Lac Virginis,* and waſh with that. Excellent good is a ſtrong decoction of Pomegranate pills in White-wine , to waſh often with.

VIII. *To take away Warts.*

The juice of the greater Spurge with Salt anointed, takes them away, ſo alſo a continual waſhing with a Lixivium of Quicklime and Salt of Tartar. The juice of *Verrucaria* performs the ſame. A plaiſter of *Cantharides* with a defenſative is very good in this caſe : ſo alſo this following waſh : take *Saccharum Saturni* three ounces, *Sal-Armoniack* one ounce, Vitriol common ſix drachms, Quicklime eight ounces, boil all in water four pound to the conſumption of the half, with which often bath the warts, and then waſh with our Mercurial water. Black Soap hath often been found very good ; but eſpecially a plaiſter of Turpentine.

IX. *To heal Chaps in the skin.*

Our *Pomatum* in this caſe is moſt excellent : yet this following is commendable. Take Capons grieſe mixed well with Camphire, and anoint with. Oil of Turpentine two drachms, mixed with *Vnguentum Populeon* two ounces, is very good. So alſo oil of Roſes mixed with Sheep Suet and wax to an ointment.

X. *To heal Burnings and Scaldings.*

Excellent good is the *Vnguentum Rubrum* in our *Synopſis Medicinæ lib.* 3. *cap.* 58. *Sect.* 1. both to draw out the fire, and to heal. To draw out the fire alſo, glair of eggs mixed with Roſe-water, is very prevalent :

ſo

fo alfo is Salt, raw Onions, Soap, Yeft, Oil of Tartar and the like. To hinder the rifing of the blifters, Hens dung three ounces, mixed with hogs griefe four ounces, and Salt of Tartar one ounce is very good; fo alfo a cataplafme of Honey and crums of bread; but beft of all a plaifter of ftrained *Opium*, which performs all the intentions to admiration. If the blifter break, it may be prefently skinned by anointing with oil of eggs, and wafhing often with *Lac Virginis*, ftrewing upon the fore, powder of Bole, Tutty, Cerufe or the like.

XI. *To take away fcars and marks of the fmall Pox.*

Take of oil of Tartar one ounce and half, Cerufe diffolved in oil of Rofes one ounce, *Borax* and *Sal Gem* of each one drachm, mix and make an ointment, with which anoint. Oil of Tartar alone performs this work well: fo Salt of Tartar, mixed with powder of Myrrh and oil of Rofes.

XII. *To beautifie the hands.*

To make them foft, often anoint with the oil of Almonds or our *Pomatum* at night going to bed, wafhing them the next morning with decoction of wheat-bran: after a while wafh them with Salt of Tartar, diffolved in fair water, perfumed with oil of Cloves, Oranges, Rhodium or Cinnamon. Or this, take Venice Soap diffolved in juice of Limons one pound, Virgin-honey four ounces, Sublimate, Orice root, Sugar, Salt of Tartar, Alom, Borax of each one ounce, Balfom of *Peru* two drachms, oil of Cloves one drachm, oil of Rhodium and Cinnamon of each half a drachm, make a mixture to wafh the hands withal: Or this, take powder of Venice Soap one pound, Orice root eight ounces, *Amylum* fix ounces, mix them and make an ointment with *liquid Storax* and oil of *Benjamin* a fufficient quantity; it wonderfully whitens, fmooths and

fweetens

sweetens the hands.   To anoint also with a Bulls gall is very good.

XIII. *To help hands which are swoln, and look red or blew with cold.*

What we even now said (in the last Section) may be said again here : to which we add, that a long bathing of them in a lather of Castle Soap, is very good if it be done : or if a repercussive plaister be applied made of barley meal, *Saccharum Saturni*, and oil of Myrtles ; washing (after the coming off of the Cataplasme) with juice of Limons or white-wine Vinegar : a plaister of Turpentine mixed with Salt is good. Often to anoint the hands with oyl of Roses, Almonds, or *Pomatum* at night, and the next morning with the *Lac Virginis* prevails much.   Oil of Annifeeds, Caraways and Fennel prepared chymically, as also Cloves and Oranges, mixed with oil of Almonds and often used, are eminent above all other things.

C H A P. XXXIX.

Of making a sweet Breath.

I. A *Stinking Breath comes from one of these four causes,* viz. *Putrified Lungs, defective Teeth, a distemper of the Head, or obstruction of the Stomach.*

II. *To remedy a Stinking Breath coming from putrified Lungs.*

Take *Unguentum Nicotianæ* one ounce, *Oleum Succini* two drachms, mix them and anoint the breast outwardly ; inwardly give cleansers, (as oil of Sulphur allayed with Rose water) morning and evening ; as also *Antimonium Diaphoreticum* ten grains five times a
day

day for several days together ; then heal by giving oil
of Almonds mixed with a few drops of oil of Cinnamon, or Pills of Turpentine : Lastly, morning, noon
and night let this bolus be abhibited, take Nutmegs,
Mace, Ginger, of each fifteen grains, honey two
drachms, oil of Cinnamon ten drops, mix them, and
continue it for some weeks.

III. *To help the defects of the Teeth.*

1. *If the teeth be furred over,* rub them every morning
with *cremor Tartari* in powder, and wash them with
White-wine. 2. *If the teeth be black* ; allay oil of Sulphur or Vitriol in Rose-water, and scowr them well
therewith, with the end of a stick and a rag, till all the
blackness be gone ; then rub them with oil of Almonds
perfum'd with oil of Cinnamon. 3. *If the teeth be
loose,* first rub them with this powder, take Galls, Pomegranate flowers, Sumach, Cyperus, of each one ounce,
Roch Alom half a pound, powder them all for use :
then use this Gargarisme. Take Galls one ounce ,
Myrrh, Pomegranate peels of each half an ounce, boil
them in White-wine vinegar for a Gargarisme. Lastly,
morning, noon and night wash the gums with good
red Wine ; by this means the teeth will be fastned and
the gums restored. 4. *If they be in danger of rotting* ;
take ashes of Harts-horn, magistery of Coral of each
one ounce, musk, or instead thereof oil of Cinnamon,
ten grains, mix for a dentifrice to rub the teeth withal,
it will keep them white and sound. 5. *If they be rot-
ten and hollow* ; make little pellets of strained Opium,
Myrrh and oil of Cinnamon, and put them into the
hollow tooth. 6. *If they ach* ; use the aforesaid pellets,
or make little ones of *Laudanum Paracelsi,* and put
them into the hollowness : or if they be not hollow,
tye a little pill of the same up in a fine thin rag, and
hold it between the aking teeth. 7. *If they stink* ; often
wash

wash them with wine or spirit of wine, in which a few drops of oil of Cinnamon and *adeps Rosarum* is dissolved.

IV. *To rectifie a Stinking Breath arising from distemper of the head.*

Consider the cause of the distemper, whether it arises from the Pox, Imposthumes, or the like, and follow the method instituted in the cure of those diseases, and then the cause being taken away, the effects you will find will soon cease; yet neverthelefs these following pills are excellent : take *Calx* of refined Silver made by spirit of Nitre, and well dulcified by washing in warm rain water, one ounce, *Resina Scammonii* one ounce and half, mix them for a mass of pills, of which take eight or ten grains at night going to bed every third, fourth or fifth day.

V. *To rectifie a Stinking Breath arising from the obstruction of the Stomach.*

This is done by opening and cleansing the Stomach thus. Take every evening going to bed half a drachm of *Pil. Ruffi* for ten or twelve days together : Or thus, first vomit with *Vinum Benedictum* one ounce or more, according as Strength requires, twice or thrice; then take *Pilula Rudii* half a drachm at a time, in the morning fasting, drinking after it some warm broth or posset drink, which repeat every third or fourth day four or five times.

VI. *To rectifie the Breath, when it smells of any thing that is eaten.*

Chew Coriander seed or Zedoary in the mouth, drinking a good draught of wine after; the scent of the wine is taken away by eating sowr apples or Quinces, or by chewing troches of Gum-Tragacanth perfumed with oil of Cinnamon.

CHAP.

C H A P. XL.

Of beautifying the Hair.

I. **T**O *dye the Hair black.*

This is done with the *Calx* of *Luna* (made by Spirit of Nitre) mixed with fair water, and the hair waſhed therewith, with a Spunge : it is the moſt excellent thing of that kind thatis yet known.

II. *To keep the hair from falling off.*

Take Myrtle berries, Galls, Emblick Myrobalans of each alike, boil them in oil Omphacine, with which anoint : it is an excellent Medicine, yet as old as *Galen.*

III. *To remedy Baldneſs.*

This is a hard thing to cure, yet the following things are very good. Rub the head or bald places every morning very hard with a coarſe cloth, till it be red, anointing immediately after with Bears griefe : when ten or fifteen days are paſt, rub every morning and evening with a bruiſed Onion, till the bald places be red , then anoint with honey well mixed with Muſtard-ſeed, applying over all a plaiſter of *Labdanum* mixed with mice dung, and powder of Bees: do this for thirty days. If all the former fail, bath with a decoction of Bur-dock roots, made with a Lixivium (of Salt of Tartar) two parts, and muskadel one part ; immediately applying this Unguent: take *Thapſi* or *Turbeth* one drachm(in powder)Bears griefe one ounce, mix them, which uſe for ſixty days ; if this make not the hair come, the defect is incurable.

IV. *To take away hair from places where it ſhould not grow.*

Take Quicklime four ounces, *Auripigmentum* one
ounce

ounce and a half, *Sulphur vive,* Nitre, of each half an
ounce, *Lixivium* of Salt of Tartar a quart, mix and
boil all ſo long in a glazed earthen pot, till putting a
quill therein, all the feathers peel off, and it is done.
Firſt foment the place with warm water a little before
you uſe the aforeſaid medicine ; a quarter of an hour
after waſh with very hot water ; then anoint with the
aforeſaid Unguent, and in a quarter of an hour it will
do the work : when the hairs are faln away, remember to anoint with oil of Roſes; now to keep them
from ever growing again, anoint for ſome days with an
ointment made of the juices of Henbane and Night-
ſhade, *Opium* and Hogs griefe.

V. *To make the hair curl.*

Waſh the hair very well with a *Lixivium* of Quick-
lime, then dry it very well, that done anoint it with
oil of Myrtles, or oil *Omphacine,* and powder it well
with ſweet powder, putting it up every night under a
cap : if the party be naturally of a cold and moiſt con-
ſtitution, the waſhing, anointing and powdring muſt
be perpetually uſed once or twice a week during life,
the hair being put up every night.

VI. *To make hair lank and flag that curls too much.*

Anoint the hair throughly twice or thrice a week
with oil of Lillies, Roſes, or marſh-mallows, combing
it after it very well.

VII. *To make the hair grow long and ſoft.*

Diſtil Hogs griefe or oil Olive in an Alembick with
the oil that comes there-from anoint the hair, and it will
make it grow long and ſoft : uſe it often.

VIII. *To preſerve the hair from ſplitting at the ends.*

Anoint the ends thereof, with oil Omphacine, or oil
of Myrtles, they are eminent in this caſe to preſerve the
hair from ſplitting, ſo alſo an ointment made of Honey,
Bees wax and oil Omphacine or Bears griefe.

CHAP.

CHAP. XLI.

Of the Art of Perfuming in general.

I. IN this Art two things are to be confidered, *viz.*
    1. The way and manner of making of Perfumes.
    2. The way and manner of Perfuming.

II. The Perfume it felf is confidered, 1. In refpect of its Form. 2. In refpect of its Compofition.

III. The Form of the Perfume is either Water, Oil, Effence, Unguent, Powder, or Tablets.

IV. The Making and Compofition is taken from the Form and matter.

V. The Matter is either Vegetable, Animal or Mineral.

VI. The way of Perfuming is according to the matter to be perfumed.

VII. The matter to be perfumed is either natural, as Hairs, Skins, Cloaths, Air, *&c.* or Artificial, as Pomanders, Powders, Wafh-balls, Soaps, Candles, and other things of like nature.

CHAP. XLII.

Of the matter of which Perfumes are made.

I. THE ground of *Vegetable* Perfumes, is taken from *Flowers, Seeds, Herbs, Roots, Woods, Barks* and *Gums.*

II. The chief *Flowers* for this ufe, are of Clove-Gilliflowers, Rofes, *Jafemin,* Lavender, Oranges and Saffron.

III. The

III. The chief *Seeds* or fruits are Nutmegs, Cloves, Carraways, Grains, Seeds of *Geranium Mofchatum*, and the Nut Ben.

IV. The chief *Herbs* are *Geranium Mofchatum*, Bafil, fweet Marjoram, Tyme, Angelica, Rofemary, Lavender, Hyfop, fweet Trefoyl, Mint and Bay-tree leaves.

V. The chief *Roots* are of *Calamus Aromaticus*, Ginger, China, *Caryophyllata*, Indian Spicknard and fweet Orrice or Iris.

VI. The chief *Woods* are of yellow Sanders, *Xylobalfamum*, *Lignum Aloes*, and *Rhodium*.

VII. The *Barks* and *Peels* are of Cinnamon, Mace, Oranges, Limons and Citrons. ·

VIII. The chief *Gums* are Frankincenfe, *Olibarum*, Labdanum, Styrax, liquid Styrax, *Balfamum Verum*, Ambergriefe, *Styrax Calamita*, Benjamin, Amber, Camphire.

IX. The chief matters of Perfumes taken from *Animals*, are Musk, Zibet, Cow-dung and other turds.

X. Of *Minerals* there are two only, which yield a Perfume, and they are *Antimony* and *Sulphur*.

C H A P. XLIII.

Of the Oil of Ben.

I. THE little Nut which the Arabians call *Ben*, is the fame which the Latins call *Nux Unguentaria*; and the Greeks *Balanus Myrepfica*; out of which is taken an Oil, of great ufe in the Art of Perfuming.

II. *To make the Oil of* Ben. Blanch the Nuts, and beat them very carefully in a mortar, and fprinkle them with wine, put them into an earthen or Iron Pan,

and

and heat them hot, then put them into a linnen cloth, and press them in an Almond press; this work repeat, till all the Oil is extracted, so have you Oil of *Ben* by expression.

III. In like manner you may express the Oil out of Citron seeds, incomparable for this purpose, to extract the scent out of Musk, Civet, Amber and the like, because it will not quickly grow rank, yet Oil of the *Nut Ben* is much better.

IV. This oil of *Ben* hath two properties; the one is, that having no scent or odour of it self, it alters, changes or diminishes not the scent of any Perfume put into it : the other is that it is of a long continuance, so that it scarcely ever changeth, corrupts or putrifies, as other oils do.

V. To make a Perfume thereof, put the Musk, Amber, *&c.* in fine powder thereinto, which keep in a glass bottle very close stopped, for a month or more, then use it.

VI. Or thus, Blanch your Nuts, and bruise them, (Almonds may do though not so good) and lay them between two rows of Flowers, suppose Roses, *Jasemin, &c.* or other Perfumes; when the Flowers have lost their scent and fade, remove them, adding fresh ones; which repeat so long as Flowers are in season; then squeez out the oil, and it will be most odoriferous.

VII. Lastly, by this last you may draw a sweet scent out of those Flowers, out of which you cannot distil any sweet water.

CHAP.

CHAP. XLIV.

Of sweet Waters.

I. *The first sweet water.*

Take Cloves in powder two drachms, yellow Sanders, *Calamus Aromaticus* of each one scruple, *Aqua Rosarum Damascenarum* fifteen pound , digest four days, then distill in an Alembick; to this new distilled water put in powder Cloves, Cinnamon , Benjamin, *Storax Calamita* of each one drachm , distil again in *Balneo* ; lastly put the water into a glass-bottle with Musk and Ambergriese of each ten grains, keep it close stopt for use.

II. *The second sweet Water.*

Take Damask Roses exungulated three pound , Flowers of Lavender and Spike of each four ounces, Clove-gilliflowers, and Flowers of *Jasemin*, of each two pound, Orange-flowers one pound, Citron peels four drachms, Cloves two drachms, Cinnamon, *Storax Calamita*, Benjamin, Nutmegs, of each two scruples all in powder, *Aqua Rosarum* six pound, digest ten dayes, then distil in *Balneo:* to the distilled water add of Musk and Ambergriese of each thirty grains.

III. *The third sweet Water.*

Take Roses, Clove-gilliflowers of each one pound, Flowers of Rosemary, Lavender, *Jasemin*, Marjoram, Savory, Time, of each three ounces, dry Citron peels one ounce, Cinnamon, Benjamin, *Storax Calamita*, of each two drachms, Nutmegs, Mace, of each one drachm, bruise the Herbs and Spices well, digest in the Sun two days, then distil in *Balneo:* to the distilled water add Musk in powder one scruple.

Z　　　　　IV. *The*

IV. *The fourth sweet Water.*

Take Cloves, Cinnamon of each one drachm, Mace, Grains, Musk, Ambergriefe, Citron peels of each half a scruple, Benjamin, *Storax Calamita* of each one scruple, *Aqua Rosarum* twelve pound, digeft fifteen days, then diftil in *Balneo.*

V. *The fifth sweet Water.*

Take Rofemary-flower water, Orange-flower water of each five pound, Ambergriefe one fcruple, digeft ten days, then diftil in *Balneo.*

VI. *The fixth sweet Water.*

Take Rofes two pound, Macaleb half a drachm, Ambergriefe ten grains, bruife what is to be bruifed, digeft in fand three days, then diftil in *Balneo.*

VII. *The seventh sweet Water.*

Take green peels of Oranges and Citrons of each four drachms, Cloves half a drachm, flowers of Spike fix ounces, *Aqua Rosarum Damascenarum* fix pound, digeft ten days, then diftil in *Balneo.*

VIII. *The eighth sweet Water.*

Take of the water at the fifth Section fix pound, Musk ten grains, mix and digeft them for ufe.

IX. *The ninth sweet Water.*

Take *Aqua Rosarum*, *Aqua Florum de Jasemin* of each four pound, Musk one fcruple, digeft ten days, then diftil in fand.

X. *The tenth sweet Water.*

Take Damask-rofes, Musk-rofes, Orange-flowers of each four pound, Cloves two ounces, Nutmegs one ounce, diftil in an Alembick, in the nofe of which hang Musk three fcruples, Amber two fcruples, Civet one fcruple, tyed up in a rag dipt in bran, and the white of an egg mixed.

XI. *The eleventh sweet Water, called* Aqua Nanfa *or* Naphe.

Take

Take *Aqua Rosarum* four pound, Orange-flower-water two pound, waters of sweet Trefoyl, Lavender, Sweet Marjoram of each eight ounces, Benjamin two ounces, Storax one ounce, Labdanum half an ounce, Mace, Cloves, Cinnamon, Sanders, *Lignum* Aloes of each one ounce, Spicknard one ounce; all being grosly beaten, digest a month, then in a glass retort distil in *Balneo.*

XII. *The twelfth sweet water, called* Aqua Moschata.

Take spirit of wine two pound, Musk three scruples, Amber two scruples, Civet one scruple, digest in the Sun twenty days close stopped in a glass vessel; a drop of this water put into any other liquor, will very well perfume it.

So may you extract the scent out of sweet Flowers, with this difference, that they lie but a little while, because their earthy substance will make the spirit ill-favoured.

CHAP. XLV.

Of Perfuming Oils.

I. **T**O *make Perfuming Oils by infusion.*

This is taught fully at the fifth Section of the three and fortieth Chapter aforegoing.

II. *To make* Oleum Imperiale.

Take Ambergriese four drachms, *Storax Calamita,* eight ounces, Rose-water, *Oleum Rosarum* of each two pound, oil of Cinnamon and Cloves of each half a drachm, put all into a glass, and digest in horse dung twenty days: this done, gently boil all for a quarter of an hour, which then let cool; with a spoon take off the oil which swims a top, to which put of Musk and

Zibet of each two drachms, digeſt all in a gentle heat for twenty days, and keep it for uſe. Where note the Amber and Storax at bottom will ſerve to make ſweet balls of, to lay among cloaths, or beads to carry in ones hands; or for a perfume to burn.

III. *To make Oil of Cinnamon.*

Digeſt Cinnamon groſly bruiſed in ſpirit of Wine, ſharpned with oil of Salt, in a glaſs veſſel, with a blind head cloſely luted, in a gentle heat for ten days, then diſtil in an Alembick, as we have more at large taught in our *Synopſis Medicinæ, lib.* 3. *cap.* 47. *ſect.* 1. it is a wonderful Perfume, the moſt fragrant and pleaſant of all Oils, as well in taſte as ſmell: the uſe of it will certainly take away a ſtinking Breath.

IV. *To make Oil of Roſes, called* adeps Roſarum.

Take Damask Roſes, pickle them with Bay ſalt, and after three months, with a large quantity of water diſtil in aſhes with a gentle fire, ſo have you Oil, and Spirit or water, which keep for other diſtillations. *Weckerus* hath it thus,

Roſarum folia in umbra aliquandiu aſſervata in matula vitrea magna ponuntur, cujus ſit fundus latus, & ad dimidium vas impletur: inde affunditur ipſis Roſarum foliis tantum aqua roſacea ſtillatitiæ, quantum ſatis fuerit, ut optimè madeant: appoſitóque pileo vitreo cæco, ſtipatiſque optimè rimis cera gummata, quindecim diebus equino fimo macerantur: ſic tamen, ut mutato, cùm frigeſcere cœperit, fimo, calor æqualis ſervetur. Appoſito mox matula roſtrato pileo, igne moderato cinerum, aqua omnis elicitur: quæ rurſus in eadem matula, optime priùs à fæcibus mundata, ablutáque ponitur, & calentis aqua balneo lentiſſimo igne elicitur, dum tota in vas recipiens abeat. Nam in fundo matula remanebit oleum roſarum, colore rubrum, perſpicuum, & Moſchi odore ſuaviter fragrans.

This

This is the greatest of all vegetable perfumes, and of an inestimable value.

V. *To make Oil of Calamus Aromaticus.*

It is made as oil of Cinnamon: it is a very great perfume, helps a stinking breath, vomiting, weak memory, &c.

VI. *To make Oil of Rhodium.*

It is made as oil of Cinnamon : is a very excellent perfume, good for the head, breath and the senses.

VII. *To make Oil of Indian Spicknard.*

By infusion it is made by the first Section ; by distillation, as oil of Cinnamon. It is an eminent Perfume.

VIII. *To make Oil of Benjamin.*

Take Benjamin six ounces in powder , which dissolve in oil of Tartar and *Aqua Rosarum* of each one pound, which distil with a close pipe in an Alembick. So is made oil of *Storax* and *Labdanum.*

IX. *To make Oil of Storax compound.*

Take oil of Ben, or sweet Almonds one pound, Storax grosly beaten four ounces, Benjamin, Cloves, of each two ounces, digest (till the Gums are melted) over hot coals; then press out the oil diligently.

CHAP. XLVI.

Of Perfuming Essences.

I. **T**He way to extract Essences is somewhat difficult, viz. by *Distillation, Calcination, Digestion* or *Menstruum.*

II. If by *Menstruum* , use not a watry one for a watry essence; nor an oily one for an oily essence ; because being of like natures, they are not easily separated;

rated; but on the contrary, chuſe an oily *Menſtruum* for a watry eſſence, and a watry *Menſtruum* for an oily eſſence.

III. If the eſſence of any metal be to be extracted by a *corroſive menſtruum*, after the work is done, ſeparate the ſalts from the waters, and uſe only thoſe ſalts which will be eaſily taken out again; *Vitriol* and *Alom* are very difficult to be ſeparated by reaſon of their earthy ſubſtance.

IV. *To extract the eſſence out of Musk, Ambergrieſe, Civet, and other Spices or Aromaticks.*

Mix the perfume with oil of Ben, which in a glaſs-bottle ſet in the Sun or Sand for ten days, then ſtrain it from the dregs, and the eſſence will be imbibed in the oil. Then take ſpirit of Wine, and diſtilled fountain water, which mix with the ſaid oil, and digeſt for ſix days: then diſtil in ſand; ſo will the eſſence and water aſcend, (the oil remaining at bottom without any ſcent) that eſſence and water diſtil in *Balneo* in a glaſs veſſel, till the water be come off, and leave the eſſence in the bottom in the form of oil.

V. *Another way to do the ſame.*

Infuſe the matter in ſpirit of Wine a ſufficient quantity, digeſt and ferment for ten days, then diſtil in ſand, as long as any water will come over (but have a care of burning) which diſtilled Liquor draw off in *Balneo*, with a very gentle heat and the quinteſſence will be left in the bottom, of a liquid form.

VI. *To extract the eſſence out of Herbs and Flowers, as of Sweet Marjoram, Baſil, Orange-flowers, Jaſemin, &c.*

Bruiſe the matter, and put it into a glaſs veſſel to ferment in Horſe-dung for a month; then diſtil in *Balneo*: ſet it in dung for a week again, and diſtil in *Balneo* again; which reiterate ſo long as it will yield any liquor; put the diſtilled matter upon the *Caput mortuum,*

tuum, diftilling thus for fix days : draw off the water in *Balneo*; and the effence remaining exprefs in a prefs : which being a week fermented in dung, will yield the perfect fcent, colour and vertues of the matter defired.

VII. *To extract the effence out of Salts.*

Calcine the Salt, and grind it very fmall, then lay it upon a marble in a moift Cellar, fetting under it a pan to receive the diffolution ; therein let it ferment for a month, then with a gentle fire diftil in *Balneo*: caft away the infipid water, which comes from it; and fet that which remains in the bottom, to ferment another month, then diftil out the infipid water as before; repeating this work fo long as any infipid water may be drawn : then evaporate away all the moifture, and what remains is the quinteffence of Salt.

Where note, 1. *That thefe Saline quinteffences as they may be ufed, will draw forth the perfect and compleat effence of any vegetable whatfoever.* 2. *That the effence of Salts thus drawn, will fcarcely come to two ounces in a pound.*

CHAP. XLVII.

Of Perfuming Unguents.

I. **T**O *make* Unguentum Pomatum, *or Ointment of Apples.*

Take Hogs Lard three pound, Sheeps Suit nine ounces, bruifed Cloves one drachm, *Aqua Rofarum* two ounces, Pomwaters pared and fliced one pound, boil all to the Confumption of the Rofe-water; then ftrain without preffing, to every pound of which add oil of *Rhodium* and Cinnamon of each thirty drops.

Z 4

II. *To*

II. *To make a compound Pomatum.*

Take of the Pomatum aforesaid, (without the oils) four pound, Spicknard, Cloves of each two ounces, Cinnamon, Storax, Benjamin of each one ounce (the Spices and Gums bruised and tyed up in a thin rag) Rose-water eight ounces; boil to the Consumption of the Rose-water, then add white wax eight ounces, which mix well by melting, strain it again being hot ; and when it is almost cold, mix therewith oil of Musk(made by the first Section of the five and fortieth Chapter) then put it out, and keep it for use.

III. *Another excellent Ointment.*

Take hogs griese one pound , *Saccharum Saturni* two ounces, mix them well by gently melting them ; to which add oils of Musk and Ambergriese of each half an ounce, let them all cool, and beat the Unguent well in a mortar, and keep it for use.

IV. *To make Unguentum Moschatum.*

Take hogs griese one pound, Ambergriese, Mosch of each one drachm and a half , (ground with oil of Jasemin upon a marble) *adeps Rosarum* half an ounce (ground with Civet one drachm) mix all together into an ointment which keep for use.

CHAP. XLVIII.

Of Perfuming Powders.

I. TO *made Powder of Ox dung.*

Take red Ox dung in the month of *May* and dry it well, make it into an impalpable Powder by grinding : it is an excellent Perfume without any other addition; yet if you add to one pound of the former,

Musk,

Musk, and Ambergriese of each one drachm, it will be beyond comparison.

II. *To make Cyprian Powder.*

Gather Musk mofs of the Oak in *December, January* or *February,* wafh it very clean in Rofe-water, then dry it, fteep it in Rofe-water for two days, then dry it again, which do oftentimes; then bring it into fine Powder and fierce it; of which take one pound, Musk one ounce, Ambergriefe half an ounce, Civet two drachms, yellow Sanders in powder two ounces, mix all well together in a marble mortar.

III. *Another way to make the fame.*

Take of the aforefaid powder of Oak-mofs one pound, Benjamin, Storax of each two ounces in fine Powder; Musk, Ambergriefe and Civet of each three drachms, mix them well in a mortar.

IV. *A Sweet Powder to lay among cloaths.*

Take Damask-rofe leaves dryed one pound, Musk half a drachm, Violet leaves three ounces, mix them and put them in a bag.

V. *Another for the fame or to wear about one.*

Take Rofe leaves dryed one pound, Cloves in powder half an ounce, Spicknard two drachms, Storax, Cinnamon of each three drachms, Musk half a drachm, mix them and put them into bags for ufe.

VI. *Powder of fweet Orrice, the firft way.*

Take Florentine Orrice root in powder one pound, Benjamin, Cloves of each four ounces in powder, mix them.

VII. *Powder of Florentine Orrice, the Second Way.*

Take of Orrice root fix ounces, Rofe leaves in powder four ounces, Marjoram, Cloves, Storax in powder of each one ounce, Benjamin, yellow Sanders of each half an ounce, Violets four ounces, Musk one drachm,

Cyperus

Cyperus half a drachm, mix them : being grosly powdered, put them into bags to lay amongst linnen : but being fine, they will serve for other uses, as we shall shew.

VIII. *Powder of Orrice roots, the third way, excellent for linnen in bags.*

Take roots of Iris one pound, sweet Marjoram twelve ounces, flowers of Rosemary and Roman Camomil, leaves of Time, *Geranium Moschatum*, Savory of each four ounces, Cyperus roots, Benjamin, yellow Sanders, *Lignum Rhodium*, Citron peel, *Storax*, *Labdanum*, Cloves, Cinnamon of each one ounce, Musk two drachms, Civet one drachm and a half, Ambergriese one drachm, powder and mix them for bags. This composition will retain its strength near twenty years.

IX. *Powder of Orrice, the fourth Way.*

Take Orrice roots in powder one pound, *Calamus Aromaticus*, Cloves, dryed Rose leaves, Coriander seed, *Geranium Moschatum* of each three ounces, *Lignum Aloes*, Marjoram, Orange peels of each one ounce, Storax one ounce and a half, *Labdanum* half an ounce, Lavender, Spicknard of each four ounces, powder all and mix them, to which add Musk, Ambergriese of each two scruples.

X. *Pulvis Calami Aromatici compositus.*

Take *Calamus Aromaticus*, yellow Sanders of each one ounce, Marjoram, *Geranium Moschatum* of each one ounce, Rose leaves, Violets, of each two drachms, Nutmegs, Cloves of each one drachm, Musk half a drachm, make all into powder, which put in bags for Linnen.

XI. *Another of the same.*

Take *Calamus Aromaticus*, Florentine Iris roots of each two ounces, Violet flowers dryed one ounce, round Cyperus roots two drachms, *adeps Rosarum* one drachm

drachm and a half, reduce all into a very fine powder : it is excellent to lay among Linnen, or to ftrew in the hair.

XII. *An excellent perfuming Powder for the hair.*

Take Iris roots in fine powder one ounce and a half, *Benjamin, Storax,* Cloves, Musk of each two drachms : being all in fine powder, mix them for a Perfume for hair Powder.   Take of this Perfume one drachm, Rice-flower impalpable one pound, mix them for a powder for the hair.   Note, fome ufe white ftarch, flower of French Beans and the like.

CHAP. XLIX.

Of Perfuming Balsams.

I. **N**Atural Balfam perfumed.
     Take *Balfamum verum* one ounce, Musk, Ambergriefe, Civet of each two fcruples, mix them, for a Perfume : it is the moft fragrant and durable of all Perfumes.

II. *An odoriferous compound Balfam.*

Take of the aforefaid Balfam perfumed one ounce, oils of *Rhodium* and Cinnamon of each two drachms, mix them : this is an incomparable Perfume, and better than the other for fuch as are not affected fo much with musk.

III. *Balfamum Mofchatum.*

Take oil of Musk one drachm, oil of Cinnamon half a fcruple, Virgin wax one drachm and a half, melt the wax, and mix them according to Art.

IV. *Another very good.*

Take Cloves, Cinnamon, Lavender, Nutmegs of
each

each two drachms, oils of Cloves and *Fhodium* of each half a drachm , Wax three drachms, Musk and Amber-griefe of each ten grains, mix them into a Balſam.

V. *Another very excellent for thoſe that love not the ſcent of Musk and the like.*

Take oil of *Geranium Moſchatum* (made as *adeps Roſarum* by the fourth Section of the five and fortieth Chapter) *adeps Roſarum*, oil of Cinnamon of each one drachm, Virgin wax ſix drachms, melt the wax, and mix the oils for a Perfume.

CHAP. L.

Of Perfuming Tablets.

I. **T**O make red *Muskardines or Tablets.*

Diſſolve Gum *Tragacanth* in Roſe-water, ſo that it may be as thick as Gelly: which make into paſte with the following compoſition. Take *Amylum* one pound, fine Sugar half a pound, *Cochenele* two ounces, Musk three drachms, all being in fine powder, mix them, and make Tablets with the aforeſaid Mucilage of Tragacanth, ſquare, long, round, or of what form you pleaſe, which dry in an Oven, out of which bread hath been lately drawn : but be ſure you dry them till they be as hard as horns.

II. *Another ſort of red Tablets.*

Take of the aforeſaid compoſition one pound, Cloves, Cinnamon, Nutmegs, Ginger of each two ounces, Cochenele one ounce, all being in fine powder, make into Tablets, with the aforeſaid Mucilage, and dry as aforeſaid.

III. *To*

III. *To make yellow Tablets.*

Take *Amylum* one pound, fine Sugar half a pound, yellow Sanders four ounces, Saffron two ounces, (or you may dip the *Amylum* in ſtrong tinᵭure of Saffron, and then dry it again) Musk four drachms, all being in fine powder, make the maſs into Tablets with the aforeſaid Mucilage, adding oil of Cinnamon in drops two drachms, dry them carefully in the ſhade.

IV. *Another ſort of yellow Tablets.*

Take *Amylum* dyed with tinᵭure of Saffron one pound, Sugar half a pound, Saffron two ounces, Nutmegs, Cinnamon, Ginger of each one ounce, Carroways half an ounce, Musk three drachms, Ambergrieſe one drachm, all in fine powder make into Tablets, as aforeſaid, adding oil of Cinnamon two drachms; which dry in the ſhade, till they be as hard as Horn.

V. *To make Muſcardines or Tablets of any other colour.*

You muſt make them after the ſame manner, only adding the colour you do intend; and in this caſe we think that it is better that the *Amylum* be dipt in the tinᵭure, and dryed firſt before you uſe it. Where note, that theſe Tablets when uſed are to be held in the mouth, in which they will diſſolve, thereby cheering the heart, reviving the ſenſes, comforting the ſpirits, ſtrengthning nature, reſtoring the body, and indeed nobly perfuming the breath. For them that do not love Musk, you may make them without, uſing inſtead thereof ſo much the more oil of Roſes or Cinnamon.

CHAP.

CHAP. LI.

Of making Pomanders for Bracelets.

I. THe *first sort.* Take Orrice powder, Cloves, Mace, Cinnamon, of each half an ounce, yellow Sanders, Styrax, sweet *Assa* of each two drachms, Ambergriese, Musk of each one drachm, Balsam of *Peru*, oil of *Rhodium* of each one scruple, Civet two drachms, all being in fine powder (except the Balsam and Oil) mix together, and make into paste with mucilage aforesaid, of which form Beads, drying them in the shade for use.

II. *The second sort.* Take *Storax Labdanum* one drachm and a half, Benjamin one drachm, Cloves, Mace, Spicknard, *Geranium Moschatum* of each ten grains, Musk, Ambergriese of each six grains; with mucilage make a *Pomander* for Bracelets.

III. *The third sort.* Take Damask-Rose leaves exungulated two ounces, beat them impalpable: Musk, Ambergriese of each two scruples, Civet one scruple, *Labdanum* one drachm with mucilage of gum Tragacanth, in Rose-water aforesaid, make a *Pomander* for Bracelets.

IV. *The fourth sort.* Take Storax, Benjamin of each an ounce and half, Musk two drachms, oil of Cinnamon one drachm, with Mucilage aforesaid make a paste of *Pomander*, very excellent.

CHAP.

CHAP. LII.

Of Perfuming Wash-balls.

I. *To make Barbers Wash-balls.*

Take purified Venetian Soap six ounces, Macaleb four ounces, *Ireos, Amylum* of each seven ounces, Cloves two ounces, *Labdanum,* Anniseeds of each one ounce, Nutmegs, Marjoram, Cypress-powder, *Geranium Moschatum,* Camphire of each half an ounce, *Storax liquida* half a drachm, Musk ten grains, all being in fine powder, with a little fine Sugar, beat all in a mortar, and make them up into Wash-balls.

II. *To do the same another way.*

Take of the said Soap two pound, juice of *Macaleb* two ounces, Cloves, Orrice of each three ounces, *Labdanum* two ounces, Storax one ounce, all being in fine powder, mix with the Soap, of which make balls, drying them in the shadow.

III. *To make Balls of white Soap.*

Take of white Soap five pound, *Iris* four ounces, *Amylum,* white Sanders of each three ounces, Storax one ounce, all in powder, steep in Musk-water, of which make paste for Wash-balls.

IV. *Another sort very good.*

Take of white Soap four pound, Orrice six ounces, *Macaleb* three ounces, Cloves two ounces, all in powder mix with the Soap, with a little oil of Spike, Rhodium or the like, of which make Balls.

V. *Another way to make them of Goats fat.*

Make a strong *Lixivium* of Pot-ashes, as that a new laid egg will swim thereupon, which boil with Citron peels: take of this Lye twenty pound, Goats fat two pound,

pound, boil it for an hour, then ſtrain it through a linnen cloth into broad platters of fair water, expoſing it
to the Sun, mix it often every day till it begins to grow
hard, of which you may form balls, which you may perfume with Musk half a drachm, Civet one ſcruple, oil
of Cinnamon ten grains.

CHAP. LIII.

Of perfuming Soaps.

I. **T**O *purifie Venetian Soap.*
Cut it ſmall, to which put ſome Roſe-water,
or other perfuming water, boil them a while, then
ſtrain it and it will be ſweet and good, then take off
the Soap which ſwims a top with a ſpoon, and lay it
upon a tyle, and it will preſently be dry, being white,
free from filth and unctuoſity.

II. *Another way to do the ſame.*
Grate the Soap, and dry it in the Sun, or an Oven,
powder and ſierce it, then moiſten it with ſome ſweet
water or oil of Spike, which dry again (in the ſhadow)
and keep it for uſe.

III. *To make white musked Soap.*
Take white Soap purified as aforeſaid three pound,
Milk of *Macaleb* one ounce, Musk, Civet of each ten
grains, mix them and make all into thick cakes or
rouls.

IV. *Another kind of ſweet Soap.*
Take of the oldeſt Venice Soap, which ſcrape and
dry three days in the Sun (purifying it as aforeſaid)
two pound, *Ireos, Amylum* of each ſix ounces, *Storax
liquida* two ounces, mix them well whilſt hot; which
put into pans to form Cakes.

V. *To*

T. *To make soft Soap of Naples.*

Take of *Lixivium* of Pot-aſhes (ſo ſtrong as to bear an egg) ſixteen pound, Deers Suet two pound, ſet them upon the fire to ſimper ; put all into a glaſed veſſel with a large bottom, ſet it in the Sun for a while, ſtirring it five or ſix times a day with a ſtick, till it wax hard like paſte.   Then take of this paſte, to which put Musked Roſe-water ; keep it eight days in the Sun, ſtirring it as aforeſaid, ſo long as it may be neither too hard nor too ſoft ; then put it up in boxes or pots.

VI. *To make the ſame Soap, musked.*

Put to the ſaid Soap, Roſe-water two pound, fine musk in powder half a drachm, then mix the ſaid water as before.

VII. *Another exquiſite Soap.*

Take of the aforeſaid *Lixivium* or oil of Tartar *per deliquium* twelve pound, oil Olive three pound, mix them, *Amylum* two pound, Roman Vitriol one ounce in powder, Glair of eggs two ounces, put all together, and ſtir continually for four hours time, then let it ſtand the ſpace of a day and it is done. You may perfume it as before ; this makes the hair fair.

VIII. *Another exceeding the former.*

Take Crown-ſoap, Vine-aſhes of each one pound, make it into Cakes with powder of Roch Alom and Tartar of each alike, which you may perfume at pleaſure.

IX. *To get the juice or milk of Macaleb.*

Take the ſweet and odoriferous grains of *Macaleb,* which beat in a mortar (with Roſe-water, or ſome perfuming-water) till it becomes like pap, then preſs out the juice or milk ; which uſe within two or three days left it ſpoil.

CHAP. XIV.

Of Burning Perfumes.

I. *To make perfumed lights.*

Take *Olibanum* two ounces, Camphire one ounce, beat them into powder, of which make, with wax, balls or rowls, which put into a glafs lamp with Rofe-water and lighted with a candle, will give a fair light, and a very good fcent.

II. *Another for a Lamp.*

Take fweet oil Olive one pound, Benjamin, Storax in powder one ounce, Musk, Ambergriefe of each one fcruple, mix all with the oil, which put into a lamp to burn : and the oil will yield a fragrant odour.

III. *To make perfumed Candles.*

Take *Labdanum*, Myrrh, *Xylo-aloes*, *Styrax calamita* of each one ounce and a half, Willow Charcoal one ounce, Ambergriefe, Musk of each ten grains, make them into pafte with mucilage of Gum *Tragacanth* in Rofe-water, which make into rouls like Candles, and dry for ufe.

IV. *A perfume to fmoak and burn.*

Take *Labdanum* two ounces, Storax one ounce, Benjamin, Cloves, Mace of each half an ounce, Musk, Civet of each ten-grains, all in fine powder, make up into cakes with mucilage of gum Tragacanth in Rofe-water, which dry; and keep among your cloaths, which when occafion requires, you may burn in a chafing-difh of coals.

V. *Another fmoaking perfume to burn.*

Take *Labdanum* two drachms, Storax one drachm, Benjamin, Frankincenfe, white Amber, Xylo-aloes of each

each two fcruples, Ambergriefe, Musk of each five grains, make all into Cakes as aforefaid.

VI. *Another very excellent.*

Take Storax, Benjamin of each one ounce, wood of Aloes half an ounce, Ambergriefe, Musk, Civet, Balfam of *Peru*, oil of Rhodium, of each two fcruples, Ivory burnt black a fufficient quantity, powder what is to be powdered, and mix all together; which make into a pafte, with the Ivory black and the mucilage aforefaid; make little cakes and dry them, which keep in glaffes clofe ftopt for ufe.

VII. *Another very good, but of lefs coft.*

Take Olibanum one pound, *Styrax Calamita* and *Liquida* of each eight ounces, *Labdanum* fix ounces, Willow charcoal a fufficient quantity, with mucilage of Tragacanth, make a pafte as aforefaid.

CHAP. LV.

Of Animal and Mineral Perfumes.

I. *THe Animal Perfume of* Paracelfus.

Take Cow-dung in the month of *May* or *June*, and diftil it in *Balneo*; and the water thereof will be an excellent perfume, and have the fcent of Ambergriefe. See our *Synopfis Medicinæ lib.*3. *cap.*75. *fect.*5.

II. *Lard muskified, a great perfume.*

Tak hogs lard very pure one drachm, Musk, Civet, of each half a drachm, mix them well for boxes.

III. *The Mineral Perfume of Antimony.*

Diffolve Antimony in oil of Flints, Cryftal or Sand, coagulate the folution into a red mafs, put thereon Spirit of Urine, and digeft till the Spirit is tinged;

pour

pour it off, and put on more, till all the tincture is extracted; put all the tinctures together, and evaporate the Spirit of Urine in *Balneo*; and there will remain a blood-red liquor at bottom; upon which put Spirit of Wine, and you shall extract a very pure tincture smelling like Garlick: digest it a month, and it will smell like Balm; digest it a while longer, and it will smell like Musk or Ambergriese.

Besides being a perfume, it is an excellent sudorifick, and cures the Plague, Fevers, *Lues Venerea*, &c.

IV. *After the same manner you may make as substantial a perfume of Sulphur or Brimstone. The making of the oil of Flints, we have taught at the seven and fiftieth Section of the nine and twentieth Chapter of the third Book.*

CHAP. LVI.

Of the Adulteration of Musk, Civet and Ambergriese.

BY reason that these choice Perfumes are often adulterated or counterfeited, we shall do our endeavour to discover the cheat, lest any being deceived thereby should suffer loss.

I. *Musk is often adulterated* by mixing Nutmegs, Mace, Cinnamon, Cloves, Spicknard of each alike in a fine or impalpable powder with warm blood of Pigeons, and then dryed in the Sun, then beaten again, and moistned with Musk-water, drying and repeating the same work eight or ten times; adding at last a quarter part of pure Musk by moistning and mixing with Musk-water; then dividing the mass into
several

several parts, and rouling them in the hair of a Goat, which grows under his tail.

II. *Others adulterate it thus :* By filling the Musk-cods with Goats blood, and a little toasted bread, mixed with a quarter part of Musk, well beaten together. The cheat is discerned by the brightness of the Goats blood.

III. *Or thus,* Take Storax, *Labdanum,* powder of Xylo-aloes, of each four ounces, Musk and Civet of each half an ounce, mix all together with Rose-water. The cheat is discerned, by its easie dissolving in water, and its different colour and scent.

IV. *Or thus,* Take Goats blood, powder of Angelica roots, Musk, of each alike, make a mixture.

V. *To adulterate Civet :* Mix with it the Gall of an Ox, and Storax liquefied and washed : or you may adulterate it by the addition of Honey of *Crete.*

VI. *To restore the lost scent to Musk, or Ambergriese.*

This is done, by hanging it some time in a Jakes or house of Office ; for by these ill scents its innate vertue and odour is excited and revived.

CHAP. LVII.

Of the way of Perfuming Cloth, Skins, Gloves and the like.

I. *To Perfume Skins or Gloves.*

Put a little Civet thereon here and there, (if Gloves, along the seams) then wash in Rose or musked water four or five times, or so long as that they savour no more of the leather, pressing them hard every time ; then lay them in a platter, covered with the said water,

mixed

mixed with powder of Cyprefs, a day or two; take
them out, prefs them, and dry them in the fhadow: be-
in half dry, befmear them a little with Civet mix'd
with oil of Jafemin or Ben, on the inward fide chafing
them with your hands before a fire, till you think that
the Civet hath pierced or gone through the leather;
leaving them fo a day or more; then rub with a Cloth
that the Gloves or Leather may grow foft; leaving
them fo till they are almoft dry, being drawn and
ftretched out; then hold them over fome burning Perfume to dry, and wetting them again with Musk-water,
do thus twenty times; laftly, take Musk and Ambergriefe a fufficient quantity, which mix with oil of Jafemin, Benjamin or Ben, diflolve at the fire with a little
perfumed water, with which (with a pencil) ftrike the
Gloves or Leather over on the outfide, befmearing the
feams with Civet; laftly lay them for fix or eight days
between two mattrefles, fo will the Skins or Gloves be
excellently perfumed.

II. *Another way very excellent.*

Take three pints of Wine, Sheeps fuet or fat one
pound, boil them together in a veffel clofe covered, this
done, wafh the Griefe fix or feven times well with fair
water, then boil it again in White-wine and Rofe-water
of each one pound and a half, with a fmall fire, till the
half be confumed: then take the faid griefe, to which
put pulp of fweet Navews roafted half a pound, boil all
in Rofe-water half an hour, then ftrain it, and beat it
in a mortar, with a little oil of Jafemin and Musk, with
which befmear your Gloves (after due wafhing as aforefaid) rubbing it well in by the fire.

III. *Another way for Gloves.*

Wafh new Corduban Gloves, wafh them well three
or four days (once a day) in good White-wine, preffing and fmoothing them well; laftly, wafh them in
musked

musked water, letting them lye therein for a day, then dry them with care.   This done, steep *Musk*, *Amber*, *Bazil* of each one drachm in a quart of sweet water, in which dissolve gum *Tragacanth* three drachms, boil all gently together, and in the boiling add *Zibet* one scruple, with which besmear the Gloves, rubbing and chafing it in, then drying them according to Art.

IV. *Or thus*, First wash the Gloves or Skins in white-wine, then dry them in the shade ; then wash them in sweet water, mixed with oil of Cloves, and *Labdanum* of each alike : lastly, take Musk, Civet, Ambergriese of each the quantity of six grains, oil of Musk half a drachm, mucilage of gum Tragacanth fifteen grains, mix them well together in a mortar, which chafe into the wash'd Gloves before the fire.

V. *Cloths, Linnen or Woollen, Coffers, Trunks* and the like, are best perfumed(with little cost) with the smoak of burning Perfumes.

CHAP. LVIII.

Of making various sorts of Ink.

I *TO make good black writing Ink.*
    Take ponderous galls three ounces in pow-der, White-wine, or in place thereof rain-water, which is better, three pound, infuse them in the Sun or in a gentle heat two days : then take Roman Vitriol well coloured and powdered, which put therein, and set all in the Sun for two days more ; shake all together, to which add of good gum Arabick in little bits one ounce with a little white Sugar, which dissolve over a gentle fire.

II. *To make red writing Ink.*

Take Raſpings of Brazil one ounce, white lead, Alom, of each two drachms, grind and mingle them, infuſe them in Urine one pound, with gum Arabick eight ſcruples.

III. *Another way to make red Ink.*

Take Wine-vinegar two pound, Raſpings of Brazil two ounces, Alom half an ounce, infuſe all ten days; then gently boil, to which add gum Arabick five drachms, diſſolve the Gum, ſtrain, and keep it for uſe.

IV. *To make green Ink to write with.*

Make fine Verdigrieſe into paſte with ſtrong Vinegar, and infuſion of green galls, in which a little gum Arabick hath been diſſolved, let it dry, and when you would write with it, temper it with infuſion of green Galls aforeſaid.

V. *Another way to make green Ink to write with.*

Diſſolve Verdigrieſe in Vinegar, then ſtrain it, and grind it with a little honey and mucilage of gum Tragacanth, upon a porphyry ſtone.

VI. *To make blew Ink to write with.*

Grind Indico with honey mixed with glair of eggs of glew-water, made of Iſinglaſs diſſolved in water, and ſtrained.

VII. *To make red writing Ink of Vermilion.*

Grind *Vermilion* well upon a porphyry ſtone, with common water; dry it and put it into a glaſs veſſel, to which put Urine, ſhake all together, let it ſettle, then pour off the Urine; and putting on more Urine, repeat this work eight or ten times, ſo will the *Vermilion* be well cleanſed; to which put glair of Eggs to ſwim on it above a fingers breadth, ſtir them together, and ſetling abſtract the glair: then put on more glair of eggs, repeating the ſame work eight or ten times alſo,

to

to take away the scent of the Urine : lastly, mix it with fresh glair, and keep it in a glass-vessel close stop'd for use. When you use it, mix it with water or vinegar.

VIII. *To make Printers black.*

This is made by mingling Lamp-black with liquid varnish, and boiling it a little, which you may make thick at pleasure. You must make it moister in winter, than in Summer ; and note that the thicker Ink makes the fairer letter.

If it be too thick, you must put in more Linseed oil, or oil of Walnuts, so may you make it thicker or thinner at pleasure.

IX. *To make red Printing Ink.*

Grind Vermilion very well with the aforesaid liquid Varnish or Linseed oil.

X. *To make green Printing Ink.*

Grind Spanish green with the said Varnish or Linseed oil as aforesaid : And after the same manner, may you make Printers blew, by grinding Azure with the said Linseed oil.

CHAP. LIX.

Of making Sealing Wax.

I. **TO** *make red Sealing Wax.*

Take white Bees-wax one pound, Turpentine three ounces, Vermilion in powder well ground, oil Olive, of each one ounce, melt the wax and Turpentine ; let it cool a little, then add the rest, beating them well together.

II. *To do the same otherwise.*

This is done by taking away the Vermilion, and adding
ding

ding inſtead thereof red Lead three ounces, to the former things,

III. *To make green Wax.*

Take Wax one pound , Turpentine three ounces,
Verdigrieſe ground, Oil Olive of each one ounce, compleat the work by the firſt Section.

IV. *To make black Wax.*

Take Bees-Wax one pound , Turpentine three
ounces, black earth, Oil Olive of each one ounce, mix
and make Wax as aforeſaid.

V. *To make Wax perfumed.*

This is done by mixing with the Oil Olive aforeſaid,
Musk, Ambergrieſe, or any other eminent Perfume, as
oil of Cinnamon, *adeps Roſarum,* or the like one drachm,
more or leſs, according as you intend to have its ſcent
extended.

VI. After the ſame manner you may make Sealing
wax of all colours, having what ſcent you pleaſe ; by
mixing the ſcent intended, with the Oil Olive, and putting the colour in, in place of the Vermilion.

CHAP. LX.

Of the various wayes of making Artificial Pearls.

I. **T**He *firſt Way.* Diſſolve mother of Pearl in ſpirit
of Vinegar, then precipitate it with oil of
Sulphur *per Campanam* (not with *Oleum Tartari,* for
that takes away the ſplendor) which adds a luſtre to
it ; dry the precipitate, and mix it with whites of eggs ;
of which maſs you may make Pearls, of what largeneſs
you pleaſe , which before they be dry, bore through
with a ſilver Wire , ſo will you have pearls ſcarcely

to

to be difcerned from thofe which are truly natural.

II. *The fecond way.* Take Chalk, put it into the fire, letting it lye till it breaks ; grind it impalpable, and mix it with whites of eggs, of which form pearls, boring them as aforefaid ; dry them, then wet and cover them with leaf filver.

III. *The third way.* Take prepared Crabs-eyes, ground into impalpable powder, and with glair make Pearls ; which bore, as aforefaid ; dry them, and boil them in Cows milk ; then in the fhade (free from duft) dry them well ; they will pleafe.

IV. *The fourth way.* Take Potters earth, and make them of what form you pleafe ; dry them in the Sun, or in the gentle heat of a furnace ; then wet them with glair of eggs, lightly coloured with Bole-armoniack, and cover them with leaves of filver, being firft wet with water : when they are dry, polifh them with a tooth, and they will be Oriental. Then take bits of Parchment, and wafh them in warm water, till the water grows fomewhat thick, boil and ftrain it, and ufe it warm : then faften each pearl through its hole upon a fine piece of wire, and plunge them into the water of Parchment, taking them out again ; then turn them round, that the glewy liquor may equally cover them ; thus the filver whitenefs will the better fhine through, fo that the pearls will feem to be truly natural, and being compared, will rather exceed.

V. *The fifth way.* Calcine Mufcle and fnail fhells in a Crucible, till they are very white, even as fnow ; with glair make Pearls, which bore by the firft Section, dry them in the Sun ; dip them in red wine, dry them again, and they will be fair.

VI. *The fixth way.* Take *Sublimate* two ounces, *Tinglafs* one ounce, mix them, and fublime them together, and you will have a fublimate not inferiour to
the

the beſt orient Pearls in the world, of which with glair, you may form what you pleaſe.

VII. *The ſeventh way.* Take any of the aforeſaid particulars, and mix them (inſtead of glair) with ground Varniſh, (made of gum *Anima*, and the *Alcool* of wine) of which make pearls; theſe will in all reſpects be like the natural; for theſe will no more diſſolve in water, than the truly natural; which all thoſe that are made of glair of eggs are unavoidably ſubject to.

VIII. *The eighth way.* After diſſolution, precipitation, edulcoration, ſiccation and formation, put the pearls into a loaf of bread, and bake it in the Oven with other bread, ſo long till the loaf is much burnt, then take them out, and waſh them, firſt in good juice of Limons, then in clear Spring-water; and they will be as fair as the truly natural. Or after baking, give them to Pigeons to eat, keeping them cloſe up, and in the dung you will find the pearl exceeding fair: where note, you muſt give the Pigeons nothing to eat in three days time.

IX. *The ninth way.* After diſſolution of ſmall oriental pearls in juice of Limons, make the form thereof with clarified honey, moiſtning your hand with *Aqua Mellis*; this done, perfect them as before.

X. *The tenth way.* Take filtrated juice of Limons, powder of pearl, of each ſix ounces, *Talk* one ounce, put them into a glaſs, and ſtop it cloſe, ſet it fifteen days in horſe-dung, and it will be a white paſte; of which form pearl, bore them, and dry them in the Sun; at laſt in paſte of barley meal (*viz.* a barley loaf) four fingers thick, ſtick the pearl, ſo that they may not touch, ſtop the holes, and cover them with paſte; ſet it into an Oven, and bake it with bread, and you will find them hard and clear.

XI. The

XI. *The eleventh way.* Having formed them of the matter intended, bored and dryed them, put them into Quickſilver, ſet over a glowing heat, ſtirring them well about, that the Quickſilver may ſtick to them ; then dip them into glair of eggs, upon a glowing heat, and they are done ; or being dry, boil them in Linſeed oil, and waſh them in warm water.

XII. *The twelfth way.* Take pearl three ounces, prepared Salt one ounce, filtrated juice of Limons, ſo much as will cover them four fingers breadth : let it ſtand ſo long till it be a paſte; the glaſs being very cloſe ſtopped, ſhake all together five or ſix times a day ; and when it comes to paſte, put it into a glaſs with ſtrong ſpirit of Vinegar, lute another glaſs over it ; digeſt it three weeks in a cool place under the earth, ſo long till all be diſſolved, then mix it with a little oil of eggs, or ſnail-water, till it be like pearl in colour ; then put this paſte into ſilver moulds and cloſe them up for eight days ; after which take them out, and bore them by the firſt Section, and put them again into the mould for eight days ; this done, boil them in a ſilver porringer with milk ; laſtly, dry them upon a plate, in a warm place, where neither wind nor duſt may come, and they will be much fairer than any oriental pearl.

XIII. *The thirteenth way.* After the preparation of the matter in juice of Limons, or *Aqua fortis*, with clean hands make them into paſte, and waſh them in diſtilled water, which put into edulcorate calx of ſilver, and digeſt in Horſe-dung for a month, ſo will they be fair and very oriental.

XIV. *The fourteenth way.* Diſſolve the matter in *Aqua fortis* (which let over-top it a fingers breadth) in a glaſs gourd, till all be incorporated into one body, which put into ſilver moulds, which have holes through them, and having ſtood one day, bore them

through

through the holes, as they lye in the mould with a filver needle: being quite dry, take them out, put them
into a glafs clofe covered in the Sun, till they be quite
dry; then put them upon a filver wire; and let them
lye covered in their own fat, (that is, that fatty fubftance, which fwims on the top of the menftruum in
their diflolution) fo long till they are very fair, then
being ftrung, put them into a glafs egg, and let them
ftand nine days in digeftion, and they will be as fair as
the natural.

XV. *The fifteenth way.* Take Tobaccopipe clay,
of which form little beads (by *Sect.* 14.) dry them
in the Sun, and burn them in a Potters furnace, then
cover them with Bole-Armoniack, tempered with
whites of eggs; being dry, dip them in water, lay
on leaf filver, which dry again, and polifh them with
a tooth: then take clean fhavings of parchment, cut
fmall, and wafhed well with warm water; boil them
in a new pot, with a flow fire, till they become fomewhat thick, ftrain it, and being warm, put in the pearl
upon a needle or fine wire, that the hole may not be
ftopped, take them out, turn them round, that the
water or glew may not fettle in one place, dipping
them fo often (drying them every time) till they be
thick enough, and they will appear full as fair as the
truly natural.

XVI. *The fixteenth way.* Take the impalpable and
fnow-white calx of Talk, and with our beft Varnifh
make a pafte; of which form peals, and bore them
with a filver wire, on which let them dry: this done,
make a mixture of the Alchool of the incomparably
pure red diaphoretick Mercury, calx of talk aforefaid,
fhell gold and filver (in *Lib.* 2. *Chap.* 21. *Sect.* 1.)
in a juft and due proportion (as by many tryals you
may find out) in which roul your pearls till they be
all

all over perfectly covered , then vernifh them with our
aforefaid vernifh, which let dry according to Art, and
if need be,polifh with the impalpable powder of Putty
and water.

CHAP. LXI.

*A brief difcourfe of Alchimy , and firft of
Metals in General.*

I. THe Mineral Kingdom is divided into *Metals,*
Semi-metals, Salts and Stones.

II. Metals are in number feven, *viz. Saturn, Jupiter, Mars, Sol, Venus, Mercury* and *Luna,* called by the
Vulgar, Lead, Tin, Iron, Gold, Copper, Quickfilver
and Silver.

III. The Semi-metals are *Antimony, Tin-glafs, Cinnaber* and *Zink.*

IV. The Salts are chiefly Vitriol, Sulphur, Arfnick,
Allom, Nitre, Borax and Salt.

V. The chief Stones are *Lapis Calaminaris, Tutia,
Lazuli,* and Lime ftone.

VI. Now out of thefe the *Alchymift* defigns three
things, to wit, 1. Either the *Counterfeiting* of the fine
Metals. 2. Or the *feparation* of fine Metals out of the
bafe : or, 3. The *Generation* of the fine Metals out of
the bafe, by *tranfmutation.*

VII. The *counterfeiting* of the fine Metals, is done by
giving the colour, and body, of a fine Metal to that
which is bafe : as the tinging of Lead into a Gold Colour ; the whiting of Copper ; the reduction of Mercury or Quickfilver.

VIII. The *Separation* of fine Metals out of bafe, is
done

done by attracting of the particles or Atoms of the fine (contained in that bafer) into one heap or mafs, that they might not be carried away by the wings of the Volatile or bafer Metal.

Thus it appears, there is a large quantity of Gold, in Lead, Tin, Copper and Silver: and much Silver in Tin, Copper, and Iron: the proof of this is manifeſt by the parting ſay (as they call it) to wit the teſt by ſtrong waters ; by which you may find that one pound of Lead will yield near three or four penny weight of ſilver, and one of Gold: One pound of Tin will yield ſomething above an ounce of Silver ; and about two penny weight of Gold or more ; One pound of Silver will yield about one ounce of Gold ; and Copper about a quarter of the ſame quantity or more, &c. but this is according to the goodneſs of the Metals, and the skill of the undertaker ; for by this way of Separation, what is gotten will never pay the coſt, it remains therefore, that we ſearch out ſome way more profitable, the which in the following lines, to the true ſons of Art, we ſhall faithfully preſent according to the beſt of our knowledge: But we are bound to be a little the more obſcure, for the ſakes of ſome ingrateful men by whom we know our juſt meaning will be. traduced ; our skill in Art abuſed ; and our perſon ſought to be rent and deſtroyed, ſhould we but adventure to be ſo open, as to give them the clear knowledge thereof. Let others ſearch as we have done, it is ſome ſatisfaction, that the matter here ſought, is really in rerum natura ; *the which joined to the certainty of anothers attaining thereof, may give life to future hopes, which as the precurſor of better things may point at the great work it ſelf.*

IX. The matter of tranſmutation is done by that great **powder, *tincture, Elixir*, or *ſtone*** of the Philoſophers, which according to the opinion of *Paracelſus,*and others **the moſt** learned, we ſhall ſignifie in few words.

By

By this *tincture* or *Elixir* according to the judgement of Philosophers the whole body of any Metal (being separated from its impurity) is changed into fine Gold.

CHAP. LXII.

Of Saturn, *or Lead.*

I. S*Aturn* is a cold, grofs, dull and heavy body, replete with much impurity, yet full of a golden feed.

II. It is tinged into a pure golden colour by calcination thereof with Antimony, and imbibing the calx thereof with the fpirit of *Venus, lapis calaminaris, tutia,* and *Zink,* feverally prepared, and mixt *ana.* and then reduced, adjoining to every ounce of Lead in *calx* a penny weight of the golden fulphur of *Venus.*

III. Its *Lunar property* is extracted, by a fimple calcination with *Arfnick* and *Nitre ana.* and imbibition of the faid *calx* for about feven days in the *Oil of Salt.*

IV. *Or thus,* Take of our Seed or Salt of *Luna* one ounce, of the Salt of *Venus* one ounce and a half; of the crude body of *Saturn* one ounce, mix, and melt them; then feparate, and you fhall have the *Saturnian Luna,* with confiderable advantage.

CHAP. LXIII.

Of Jupiter *or* Tin.

I. J*Upiter* is much a more noble body than *Saturn*, and (as we said before) abounds much more with a *Solar* and *Lunar* seed.

II. It is reduced into the *Imitation* of silver by often melting of it, and quenching of it in the spirit of *Arsnick*; or by calcination of it with *Lime* (three ounces to a pound of *Jupiter* granulated) and then by often extinguishing of the same in the spirit of *Arsnick* aforesaid.

III. The *Luna* is extracted out of it thus: Let *Jupiter* be married to our *Luna* of the same stature by the Priest *Mercury*, after which let them drink their fill of the *Mineral spirit* of the Grape; then put them to bed in *Taurus* the exaltation of *Luna* and house of *Venus*, and the next morning let them drink very well of the fruitful Wine of the daughter of *Luna*; this being done, you will find *Luna* like a bride coming forth out of the marriage chamber; but with the wings of an *Eagle*, which wings you must clip by the means of *Mars*, else you will lose her: Thus, take of the Seeds of *Mars*, and the eldest Son of old *Saturn ana.* make them contend with mother *Tellus*, for three whole days and nights, till they conjoyn and beget a Son, white as *Luna*, and fixt as *Sol*. This Sun will by force take *Jupiters* wife from him, and being fruitful cause her to bring forth a plentiful and profitable issue.

IV. *Or thus,* Kill *Jupiter* (in conjunction with
Luna)

Luna) by the fire of *Tellus*, then revive the dead body (after it is impregnated with the *Mineral spirit* of the Grape) by the help of *Saturn*, and you have a numerous off-spring of *Luna*.

V. *Or thus*, Marry *Jupiter* to *Luna* ; then marry him to her daughter, and join these issues together , and they will sympathetically attract and join all the seed of *Luna* into one family or lump.

VI. *Or thus*, Which is both the best and easiest way. Take *Jupiter* and melt him, then quench him ten times in the *spirit* of mother *Tellus* , till he is reduced very small and low : this done, join him with the *Daughter of Luna* calcined with mother *Tellus*, and the work is over.   *This is very profitable, and the most useful of all, but by reason of the unworthiness of this generation, it cannot admit of any explication.*

VII. The Gold is thus extracted : marry *Jupiter* to *Venus*, and their off-spring to *Sol* by the means of Priest *Mercury* ; put them to bed (in the life of *Phœbus*) for three whole days and nights, afterwards make them drunk with the spirit of the daughter of *Venus*, then make a perfect conjunction with the eldest Son of *Saturn*, and you shall have what you sought.

VIII. *Or thus*, Calcine *Jupiter* granulated one pound, with *Quick-lime* four ounces, mix all with the *Calx* of *Venus* and *Luna ana.* calcine again for three days, imbibe in the spirit of *Venus* (that is, the fixed oil) for seven days, then reduce to a *regulus* with *Saturn*, and afterwards separate with *Antimony.*

CHAP. LXIV.

Of Mars, *or Iron.*

I. **M***Ars* is yet a more noble body, but harder and more replete with *scoria* or filth, yet very full of a Solar and Lunar sulphur.

II. It is converted into Copper by the *Oil or spirit of Venus:* into brafs by the means of *Lapis Calaminaris,* and made to imitate silver by impregnating its *calx* in the burning spirit of *Arsnick.*

III. It has much Silver and Gold in it, but they are extracted with great difficulty ; thus, firſt melt the body with an equal quantity of *Tin, Lead and Copper ;* this done, *granulate* it and imbibe the body with *Oil of Venus* very ſtrong, then calcine it with the butter of *Arsnick* (if you extract its Silver,) or *Antimony* (if its Gold) imbibe this *calx* over a gentle heat in the ſtrongeſt oil of Flints or Sand for ten days : then reduce it.

CHAP. LXV.

Of Sol, *or Gold.*

I. **S***Ol* is the pureſt of all Metals, and the very per- fection of the Mineral kingdom, at the which, all our pains, labours and endeavours aim.

II. This *Gold* of it felf is dead and without force or power, but being quickned, and enlivened, it has

an

an inward *feminating germinating* property, which being raifed and brought forth by its *innate life* (till now
lockt up) can dilate it felf (*having a fitting womb to
receive it*)into an hundred times its own quantity ; and
thereby *tranfmute* and *change* the Mercurial property
(which is indeed immature Gold) of all Metals into
its own nature and kind.

III. This *immaturate Gold* in the bodies of all Metals
would have come to perfection of its own accord, had
it been ennobled with a fufficient life and heat, to have
caufed fuch a natural *fermentation and excretion* of the
abounding filth and drofs, in which the fo fmall particles and Atoms of the Seminal golden property was
latent, or buryed.

IV. The quickning of the inward life of this Metal is
folely done by the help of the Seed of Metals, to wit
Mercury, but how or after what manner we fhall more
plainly fhew in *Chap.* 77.

CHAP. LXVI.

Of Venus, *or* Copper.

I. **V***Enus* is the fineft of the bafe Metals, and contains more of a *Golden fulphur* than them all.

II. She is *Whitened*, and made like unto *Silver*, by
calcining it with butter of the daughter of *Luna*, and
Salt of Tartar, and then reduced by *Saturn*, and being
often melted and extinguifhed in the faid butter.

III. Or thus, To the afore reduced *Venus*, being

melted add (for an ounce of *Venus*) two penny weight of our white fixed *Mercury.*

IV.She is made of a Golden colour by often changing the *calx* (calcined with the Son of *Saturn*) in the spirit of *Antimony, Zink, Lapis Calaminaris,* and *lapis tutia :* then reduced by being melted with a sufficient quantity of *Lapis Tutia,* and ten or twelve times melted, and quenched in the aforesaid spirit.

V. Her *Silver* is extracted as that of Tin by the third *Sect.* of *Chap.* 63. *Or thus,* Calcine her, with *butter of the daughter of Luna,* to which *calx* adjoin the *calx of Luna ana.* and reduce with *Saturn.*

VI. Her *Gold* is extracted thus : Calcine her with the Son of *Saturn :* then calcine *Luna* with the same also : put both these calces together and calcine for three days with the *Son of Saturn* mixt with *Mother Tellus ;* to which add the *Calx* of *Sol* calcined with the same *Son of Saturn, ana.* put all together and calcine them for twenty four hours, reduce them with *Antimony,* keep them all in a melted heat for three days, then take it forth, and quench it being melted ten or twelve times in the tinging and fixing spirit of *Lapis Calaminaris, Antimony* and *Zink, ana.*

This is very profitable, and not difficult to perform ; it may be done also (as before) without calcination.

CHAP.

CHAP. LXVII.

Of Mercury, *or Quickfilver.*

I. **M**Ercury is the Seed of Metals, and pure immaturate Gold.

II. By this the body of *Sol* is opened thus : make an Amalgama of *Sol* and *Mercury* fo long till the *Mercury* will fwallow up no more : Separate and you fhall find your Gold like Earth newly broken up : this Gold being put into the fweet oil of Salt becomes more perfectly diffolved , which being diftilled till it comes over the helm will anfwer your intention : but there is a more noble and excellent way of opening of the body of Gold which here we may not declare, yet in its due and convenient place fhall be manifeft, and that is only by the help of a perfect fweet, or rather *infipid menftruum.*

III. *To make our white Mercury* ; this is only done by a fimple diffolution in the aforefaid *infipid menftruum.*

By this white *Mercury,* is Copper made of a durable white, after a thoufand meltings.

IV. *To make our red Mercury* ; this is done by a diffolution in the fpirit of Mother *Tellus,* and then tinged by the mineral fpirit of the Grape : and laftly *perfectly fixed by the green fpirit of* Venus. *This will perfectly unite with Gold,* never more to be feparated by all the Art of man.

CHAP. LXVIII.

Of Luna, *or* Silver.

I, **L**Una, is the meaneſt of the fine Metals, and (as it were) *white Gold.*

II. She is tinged of a *Golden Colour* by our red *Mercury* (calcine *per ſe* for twenty eight days in a *Pelican* or other convenient veſſel; till ſuch time as the ſaid *Mercury* will endure the ſtrongeſt fire) the yellow colour this *Mercury* gives is fixed.

III. Her *Gold* is exactly extracted by the method delivered in *Chap.* 66. *Sect.* 6.

IV. *Or thus,* Calcine her with the *Son of Saturn,* to which add of our red *Mercury,* *ana.* put all into *Oil of Salt* for ten or twelve days; heat it *red hot,* and extinguiſh in oil of *Flints or Sand* ten times; to this *calx* add of fine *Lapis Tutia ana.* reduce all and ſeparate with *Antimony.*

CHAP. LXIX.

Of the ſecret Hermetick *Myſterie, or great Philoſophick Work.*

WE *cannot be ſo vain as to pretend to the world that we have attained the knowledge of this great Secret, much leſs to be the Maſter thereof, or the inſtructor of other men : but this we can ſay, we have converſt with moſt Authors that ever have wrote thereof, we have with a great deal of diligence and ſtudy com-*
pared

*pared their sayings one with another ; and we have by a
long and continued exercise and practice in the Mineral work, found out not only the natures of Metals, and in
what degrees of purity they stand in one to another ; but
we have also found out many excellent Secrets, of real
Worth and Value, by which, although we cannot pro-
fess a knowledge of the great work it self, yet we thereby
see not only a possibility, but also a probability thereof in
nature (to that man whom it shall so far please God to
enlighten) and therefore judge we may in some measure
the better undertake to discourse the sayings of those Wor-
thies, who having attained the Mysterie thereof, thought
good in Cloudy and Mysterious terms to publish the same to
the world, that none but the truly worthy Sons of Art might
be partakers thereof.*

*In the following lines then, we shall tell you what has
been told us, and what we do conceive thereof by the comparing of the sayings of the most excellent men together, such
as were* Paracelsus, Lullius, Ripley, Bacon, *and others ;
and this in so concise a manner, that the opinions and judgements of all those men (though far asunder in words) may
center not only in truth it self, but also in the narrow com-
pass of the following Sections ; the which that we might so
perform, we express our conceptions of their sense in a language consonant thereto.*

I. *The seed of Gold is lodged in all Metals.*

This is apparent from their generation, whose origi-
nation is *Mercury,* which is indeed immaturate Gold ;
and so remains immaturate in the baser Metals till a
ripening and meliorating spirit quickens that seminal
property lodged in the womb of impurity.

II. *This seed of Gold may be quickned or made to
live.*

This is done through the death of the first matter,

ter, and difpofition of the fecond to a refufcitation
or refurrection of that innate, energetical, and feminal life , and that only by the fpirit of Mother
Tellus.

III. *This femen being quickned, dilates it felf into
other bodies , and tranfmutes them into its own property.*

That is juft as the feminal life of Vegetables
tranfmutes or changes that fuccus or humidity of the
Earth proper to themfelves into their own forms
and natures ; and fo of a little feed there becomes
a great tree: fo that as the Earth is the womb out
of which fo fmall a feed becomes a great tree, by the
tranfmuting property of the innate feminal life in the
feed : fo all the bafe Metals are the womb unto that
feminal purity : in which womb if the feed be difpofed rightly, there will be as certain a generation and
encreafe ; and the purity of the bafe Metals will be
tranfmuted into that feminal property to a vaft augmentation.

IV. *That this may be rightly done, the bodies of the bafe
Metals muft be opened and prepared.*

That is, they muft be brought into a mortification,
that that ftrong band which has hitherto chained
the *feminal life* may be broken, and fo the *energetick
vertue* may be fet at liberty : this is performed by
the *flying dragon* who devours all that he comes near :
this being done, the *femen* muft be caft into this
mortified body (impregnated with the fpirit of Mother *Tellus*) that it may there generate, tranfmute
and fix.

V. *This may be done in any of the bafe Metals ; but they
(like the Earth) yield an encreafe according to their degree in purity; fo that more of the body of a pure Metal is
tranfmuted, than of an impure.*

As

As barren Earth cannot yield fo great an encreafe as a fertil foil; fo neither can a bafe Metal yield fo great an augmentation as a more fine.

VI. *The body of the bafer Metals being fitted , the femen muft be caft into the fame to generate.*

That is, there is to be a conjunction of the *femen* or true *Golden effence* with the prepared body to be tranfmuted : now you muft be careful you ufe not the fimple body of any Metal for this *femen* , for then you will be deceived; the matter in which the generative fpirit is lodged is another thing : if you bury a whole tree or plant in the Earth, that will not generate, and bring forth another tree, but perifh and rot, the feminal or generative vertue and life is clog'd and loaded, and fo is ineffective; but if you bury the feed of the fame tree, you may have another or more according to the quantity of feed fown; the fame you muft underftand in the generation of Metals, and of the Golden work ; it is not Gold which will generate Gold, but the feed of Gold.

VII. *This femen muft be Volatile.*

Otherwife it cannot *tranfmute,* for nothing but a *Volatile* fpirit or effence can dilate and fpread it felf: a *fixed* matter cannot operate at all, for all *fixed* things are dead, and their life remains in a central ftate, not fit for *coaction.*   This is evident in the *Volatile* Salts of *Vinegar* and *Quick-lime,* which furpafs the Art of man to attain fimple; but if you mix a *Lixivium* of *Quick-lime* with *Vinegar,* you may have a large quantity of Salt, and that *fixed,* which was before unattainable. Thus you fee out of two *Volatile* things, a third abfolutely fixed is produced; and this is the condition of this great work.

VIII. *It muft be of an unchangeable blood-red colour.*

Otherwife it could not ting; for were it only yellow,

low, it would create only a faintiſh kind of green : but this our Philoſophick tincture, generates Gold of the higheſt and pureſt nature , and having the deepeſt yellow.

IX. *This* Semen *is made Volatile by the deſtruction of its external form.*

That is, nature muſt be brought to action, that the inactive body may let fall its *Semen*, out of which the Golden tree of the Philoſophers is produced.

X. *This* Semen *is made blood-red by impregnating of it with the ſpirit of Mother* Tellus.

It is neceſſary that there be a common band to conjoin the bodies, which are to be united : as the bodies of the baſe Metals which are the womb for this ſeed are to be mortified : ſo muſt that body be,out of which you extract the *Semen*: and as that mortified and prepared body is to be impregnated with the ſpirit of *Mother Tellus,* ſo muſt this *Semen,* that there may be as well a ſympathy and likeneſs in nature, as a unity in body.

XI. *The matter out of which this* Semen *is to be extracted is* Mercury *or Gold.*

We mean ſimply, and without Metaphor, Quickſilver and Gold; for if there be an innate life, power and vertue, in the baſe Metals, why not in theſe ? if Lead, Tin, Iron,Copper and Silver,contain the Seminal life of Gold, why ſhould *Mercury* or Gold be excluded, which are the thing it ſelf?

XII. *The* Semen *being caſt into the body prepared for it, is there to be digeſted, till both be perfectly united , whoſe ſimple conjunction is the product of the Golden kingdom.*

This digeſtion is perfected only by the force of an external fire, conjoined with the inward Seminal life.

CHAP.

CHAP. LXX.

A brief difcourfe of Chiromancy, and firft of the Line of Life.

I. **K**Aρδιαχὴ [*Linea Vitalis*] The Line of Life is that which includeth the Mount of the Thumb.

II. This Line broad and of a lively colour well or largely drawn without interfections and points, fhews long life and one fubject to few difeafes : but flender, fhort and broken or cut with little crofs lines, of a pale or black colour, fhews fhort Life with many infirmities.

III. If it makes a good Angle with the *Hepatica,* and the Angle be adorned with parallels or little Croffes, fhews a good wit and a pleafant difpofition.

I. This *Linea Vitalis* abounding with branches towards the upper end, and thofe branches extending themfelves towards *Linea Hepatica* forefhew riches and honour , but if thofe branches defcend towards the *Reftricta,* they threaten poverty, contempt and deceitful fervants.

V. If this line be cut with little lines like hairs, it fignifies difeafes, which if they fall towards the *Hepatica,* fhews in the younger years, in the middle of the line in the middle of the Age, if toward the *Reftricta,* in the latter years.

VI. If this line be any where broken, it threatens great danger of life in that Age which the place of the faid breach betokeneth, which you may find out with a great deal of exactnefs if you divide the line

into

into feventy equal parts, beginning to number them from A towards B.

VII. If the Character of *Sol*, (*viz.* ☉) be found in this line, it fhews the lofs of an Eye, if two fuch figures, the lofs of both Eyes.

VIII. A line paffing through this *Vital* to the *Triangle* of *Mars* fhews wounds and fevors, and many misfortunes in journeying.

IX. A line proceeding from the Vital beneath the Angle it makes with the *Hepatica* to the Mount of *Saturn*, fhews an envious man, as alfo fome dangerous *Saturnian* difeafe, as a Confumption, *&c.* which fhall fall in thofe years fignified by that part of the Vital Line which the faid Line toucheth.

X. But fuch a line paffing from the Vital to the ring-finger, fhews honour and wealth, and that by means of fome noble woman.

CHAP. LXXI.

Of the Epatick, or Natural Line.

I. THe *Natural or Liver Line* is that which runs from the Life iine or Mount of *Jupiter* through the middle of the Palm, terminating generally upon the Mount of *Luna*.

II. This line ftraight continued and not cut by other oblique lines, fhews a healthy conftitution and long life, but fhort or broken, not reaching beyond the middle of the Palm, fignifies a fhort life replete with many difeafes.

III. The longer this line is, fo much the longer life

it

it fignifies, if it be cut at the end thereof, it threatens the end of Life with fome dangerous difeafe.

IV. If any breach appears, (yet fuch an one as feems almoft continued) it fhews a change of life, if under the middle finger, in ftrength of years, if under the ring-finger, in declining Age.

V. If the upper part of it be far diftant from the *Vital*, it fhews manifold difeafes of the heart, and alfo a Prodigal perfon.

VI. If it be crooked, unequal, of various colours, and cut by other lines, it fhews an evil habit of the Liver and difeafes thence proceeding, one ill natured and foolifh.

VII. If ftraight drawn and well coloured, fhews wit, honour and health.

VIII. If it has a *parallel or fifter*, it gives inheritances.

IX. If continued with *little hard knots*, it fhews Murder according to the number of thofe knots.

X. If it terminates with a Fork or Angle towards the *Mount of Luna*, it fhews a foolifh, hypocritical, ill-natured perfon, if it tends to the *Menfal*, it fhews a flanderous and envious perfon.

XI. When it cuts the Vital eminently to the *Mount of Venus* or *foror Martis*, efpecially if the fame be of a ruddy colour, fhews danger of thieves and many ill difeafes, threatning life.

CHAP.

CHAP. LXXII.

Of the Cephalica or head-line.

I. THe *Cephalica* ariseth below from the *Cardiaca*, and is drawn thence to the *Epatica*, thereby making a *Triangular* Figure.

II. Making such a perfect figure, and it having a lively colour, without intersection, declares one of great *prudence*, and a person of no *Vulgar Wit* or Fortune.

III. So much the more perfect the *Triangle*, so much the more *Fortunate*, and it shews a man very wise, temperate and couragious.

IV. If the *Triangle* be obtuse, it shews an evil nature, *clownish and rude*, if there be no *Triangle*, it is still worse, and shews the person to be *foolish*, *a liar and prodigal*, and generally one of a short life.

V. The *higher Angle* being *Right*, or not very *Acute*, shews a generous man ; but if it be *very acute*, or if it touch the *Line of Life* under the mount of the *middle finger*, it declares a miserable , hard and covetous wretch, it also foreshews a *consumption*.

VI. The *left Angle* made upon the *Epatica* in the *ferient* (being a right Angle) shews a profound understanding.

VII. The *Cephalica* casting *unequal* and irregular clefts to *Mons Lunæ*, thereby constituting strange Characters, shews a *dull head, and danger by the Sea*, in Men : but in Women *discontents, miscarriages* and the like.

VIII. But casting *equal lines*, it presages the contrary in both Sexes : to wit, in men *wisdom, and suc-*

cefs at Sea, and in Women, *contentment, and happy child-bearing.*

IX. If the *Cephalica* make a cleft or apparent Star, *upward* to the *Cavea Martis,* it shews boldnefs, and magnanimity of mind : but if it let the fame fall *downward,* it manifefts *deceit and cowardife.*

X. The *Cephalica* joyned to the *Reftrilla,* by a remarkable concourfe, fhews a happy and joyful old Age.

XI. But if it be drawn *upwards,* (*in form Lke a Fork*) towards the place of *Fortune,* it fhews much fubtilty and craft in the management of affairs.

XII. If in this *Fork* the Character of ⊕ *Sors* be found, it fhews *Riches and Honour,* by the mans own induftry.

CHAP. LXXIII.

Of the Menfal Line, or Line of Fortune.

I. THe *Menfal* or Line of *Fortune* (called alfo *Linea thoralis*) takes its original from under the *Mount of Mercury,* and extends it felf towards the *Mount of Jupiter.*

II. This line if it be *long enough* and without *incifures,* fhews ftrength of body, and conftancy of mind ; the contrary if it be *fhort, crooked or cut.*

III. If it terminates under the *Mount of Saturn,* it fhews a *foolifh, idle and deceitful perfon.*

IV. If in this line be found certain pricks or points, it fhews a *lecherous perfon.*

V. If the *Epatica* be wanting; and the *menfal* be

C c *annexed*

annexed to the *Vital*, it foreshews either *beheading*, *hanging* or other *untimely death*.

VI. If from the *Menfal*, a line ascends to the space between the Mounts of *Jupiter* and *Saturn*, another to the space between the Mounts of *Saturn* and *Sol*; and a third to the space between the Mounts of *Sol* and *Mercury*, it signifies an envious, turbulent and contentious person.

VII. A little line only thus drawn to the space between the *Mons Saturni & Solis*, shews labour and forrow.

VIII. If annexed to the *Epatica*, making therewith an acute Angle, *the fame.*

IX. The *Menfal* projecting small branches to the *Mons Jovis*, shews honour and glory.

X. But if it be *naked* or *single*, it shews *poverty* and *distress.*

XI. If it cuts the Mount of *Jupiter*, it shews a covetous mind, and great pride.

XII. If it fend a branch between the *Mons Jovis & Saturni*, it shews *in a Man*, a wound in his head; but *in a Woman*, miscarriage or danger in child-bearing.

XIII. Confufed little lines in the *Menfal*, shew sickness and diseases: if under the *Mons Saturni*, in youth: under the *Mons Solis*, in the middle Age: under the *Mons Mercurii*, in old Age.

XIV. Lastly, If there be no *menfai* at all, it shews one faithless, base, inconstant and malicious.

CHAP.

CHAP. LXXIV.

Of the Reſtricta , *or* Cauda Draconis.

I. THe *Reſtricta* is that Line which divides the Hand from the Arm, either by a ſingle, duple, or triple *tranſcurſion* ; thereby determining the τὸ ὑποκεί-μενον or *ſubject of Art* ; which by ſome is called the *Diſcriminal line.*

II. If the *Reſtricta* be double or treble, and extended in a right and continued tract, it ſhews a *healthful con-ſtitution of body, and long life.*

III. That line which is neareſt the hand continued without *inciſure,* and *of a good colour,* ſhews riches.

IV. But if it be *pale* or *crooked,* or *cut in the middle,* it ſhews weakneſs of body and poverty.

V. A line drawn from the *Reſtricta* to *Mons Lunæ* , ſhews poverty , impriſonment and private enemies.

VI. If that line be *crooked,* it doubles all the evil, and ſhews a perpetual ſlavery or miſery.

VII. But ſuch a line being clear and ſtraight, and extended to the *Mons Lunæ,* ſhews many journeys and *peregrinations* both by Sea and Land.

VIII. If it extend to the *Mons Jovis,* it foreſhews *eſtimation* and *Eccleſiaſtick dignity,* but that the man ſhall live in a ſtrange countrey.

IX. If to the *Epatica,* it ſhews honeſty, truth and ſin-cerity, and one of a healthful and long life.

X. If to the *Mons Solis,* a great and certain good, and gives honour and command in the Common-wealth.

XI. And

XI. And so from the *same reason*, passing to the *Mons Mercurii*, it shews a learned and ingenious soul : but if it reach not that *Mount*, but is *broken about the middle*, it shews a lying, prating, idle person.

XII. If it *ascends directly to the Mons Saturni*, it shews an *inheritance in land* : but if it be *crooked*, it shews a covetous person, and one of a very ill nature.

XIII. A line running from the *Restricta* through the *Mons Veneris*, shews poverty, adversity and want, and that by means of some women or womankind.

XIV. A *cross or star* upon the *Restricta*, shews a happy and long life.

XV. One or more Stars upon the *Restricta* by the *Mons Veneris* in *Women*, shews lewdness, dishonour and infamy.

CHAP. LXXV.

Of the Saturnia, or Line of Saturn.

I. **T**His *Line* is that which ascends from the *Re stricta* through the middle of the *Vola*, to th *Mons Saturni*, which line if it be cut or parted, i called *Via combusta*.

II. This being full, and extended to the *Mon Saturni*, shews a man of *profound cogitations*, of grea wisdom ; and an admirable counsellor in all *grea actions*.

III. If it be *combust*, it is an evil sign, foreshewin

many misfortunes, and poverty in one part of life.

IV. A *line* drawn from the *Vital* through the *Epatica* to the *Mons Saturni*, making an angle with the *Linea Saturnia*, forefhews imprifonment, and captivity, and many misfortunes.

V. The *Saturnia* bending backwards in *Cavea Martis* towards the *ferient*, the fame.

VI. This *line* filled with *unufual* and *inaufpicious characters*, fhews unhappinefs and difafters.

VII. A *grofs line* running from the *interval* of the *Mons Jovis* to the *menfal*, and *breaking or cutting* of it, fhews difeafes or wounds in the belly or parts adjacent.

CHAP. LXXVI.

Of the Mount of Jupiter.

I. THE *Mount of Jupiter* is the *tuberculum* under the fore-finger.

II. If upon the *Mount of Jupiter* there be a *Star or a double* crofs it forefhews, riches, profperity, and happinefs, one born to noble and glorious actions, one honeft, affable, courteous, and renowned, a generous foul indeed, and faithful in all their undertakings.

III. *The fame*, if this *Mount* is adorned with a *parallel line*, or a line fweetly drawn, between it and the *Vital*; it fhews great dignities, and eftimation with great men.

IV. But if this *Mount* be vitiated, with a *Character* like a half *Gridiron*, it fhews unhappinefs, cala-

mities,

mities, poverty, difgrace and depofition from honours and dignities; loffes by women-kind, and difeafes in the heart and lungs.

V. *The fame,* If a line cutting this Mount, tends to the *Mount or line of Saturn* ; this alfo threatens an Apoplexy.

VI. *Laftly,* A *Crofs,* but efpecially a *clear red Star* on this *Mount,* is a fignal and fure demonftration of a *fplendid life, repleat with honour and glory, riches and an Eternal name.*

CHAP. LXXVII.

Of the Cavea *of* Mars, *and the* Via Martis.

I. THe *Cavea Martis* is the hollow in the middle of the *Palm,* commonly called the *Triangle* of *Mars,* made of the three principal lines, to wit, the *Cardiaca, Cephalica, & Epatica.*

II. The *Via* or *linea Martis* (called alfo the *Vital fifter* and *foror Martis*) is a parallel to the line of Life on the *Mons Veneris.*

III. *Mars* is Fortunate fo often as the *foror Martis* appears red, clear and fwectly drawn, and when either *Stars* or *Croffes* are found in his *Cavea* or *Triangle :* and thereby is fignified courage, boldnefs, magnanimity, fortitude and ftrength: the man is imperious, ftrong, and a great eater.

IV. But if the *Triangle* be infortunated by evil lines from the *Mons Veneris* or *Luna,* the perfon is litigious, fcornful, proud, difdainful, deceitful and wicked; a thief, lecher, robber, murtherer, and fhall have a life wholly filled with unhappinefs.

V. The

V. The Character ♄ *Saturn* in the *Triangle*, shews a danger of falling from some high place.

VI. A *crooked line* ascending from the *Triangle* to the *Mons Saturni*, shews imprisonment.

VII. A line from the said *Triangle* towards the *Restricta*, terminating under the *Mons Luna*, shews many peregrinations, journeys and travels.

VIII. The *soror Martis* augments all the good signified by the *Cardiaca* or line of life, but particularly it promises success in war, and the love of Women.

CHAP. LXXVIII.

Of the Mount of the Sun, *and* Via Solis.

I. THe *Mount of the Sun* is the *tuberculum* under the ring-finger.

II. The *Via Solis*, is a right line running down from the *Mount of Sol*, to the *Triangle of Mars*.

III. A *Star* or *Stars* upon the *Mons Solis*, shews one faithful and ingenious, and that he shall attain to great honour, glory and dignity, be honoured of Kings, Princes and great men; one of a *great and magnanimous spirit*, wise, just and religious.

IV. But a *perpendicular* thereon cut or crost with a line from the *Mons Saturni*, shews pride, and arrogancy, a boaster, a poor base spirit, and one that shall fall into *irrecoverable miseries*.

V. The *Via Solis* clear, and not broken, or cut by any ill line, shews honour in the Common-wealth, and the favours of *Kings and great Princes*.

VI. But it being cut or confused, or hurt by any

line

line from either the Mount or line of *Saturn*, it shews the contrary, poverty and the hatred of great men.

CHAP. LXXIX.

Of the *Mount of* Venus, *and the* Cingulum Veneris.

I. THe *Mount of Venus* is the *tuberculum* of the Thumb.

II. The *Cingulum Veneris* or girdle of *Venus*, is a piece or segment of a Circle drawn from the interval or space between the *Mons Jovis & Saturni*, to the interval or space between the *Mons Solis* and *Mercurii*.

III. A clear Star, or furrows that be red and *transversly parallel* upon the *Mons Veneris*, and it much elevated, shews one merry, cheerful and amorous; it shews also one faithful, just and intire, *one with whom an incorrupted tye of friendship (being once made) is durable for ever* : it also signifies great fortune or estate and substance by a sweet-heart or lover.

IV. But this *mount* infortunated by evil lines, or lines from evil places, and irregular figures shews a *lecherous person, an adulterer*, a poor, base, sordid wretch, who shall spend his substance on whores.

V. The Character of the △ *Trine Aspect* on this *mount*, shews a great fortune by marriage.

VI. The *Mount of Venus* void of lines and incisures, shews a rude, effeminate and foolish person, and one ridiculous, and unfortunate in wedlock.

VII. The *Cingulum Veneris*, or girdle of *Venus*, shews

shews intemperance and lust in both Sexes, a base and bestial life; a filthy *Sodomite*, who abuses himself with beasts.

VIII. If it be *broken or dissected*, it shews infamy and disgrace by *lust and lechery*.

CHAP. LXXX.

Of the Mount of Mercury.

I. THe *Mount of Mercury* is the *tuberculum* under the little finger.

II. This *Mount* happy and fortunate with a Star, or *parallel crosses*, or the Character of the △ *Trine Aspect*, shews wit and ingenuity, and makes the person a great Orator, gives him substance by Arts and Sciences, and the underſtanding of secret mysteries in *Alchymy, Mu-sick, Painting, Astrology, and Philology*, and raises the person to dignity by means of his own wit, prudence and industry.

III. But this *Mount afflicted*, or without lines, or hurt by a line from the *Mount of Saturn*, (cutting the *Mount of Sol*) or from the *Triangle of Mars*, shews a poor, low and dull wit, a person of no audacity or courage, a meer coward, a lyer, pratler, thief, cheat, traitor, and one faithless, and sometimes melancholy; mad or frantick.

IV. These judgements are the more firm where the lives and signatures are fair, firm and clear: but if they be dull or obscure, these judgements are more dubious and intricate.

V. A line from the *Mons Luna* to the *Mons Mercurii* not cut or broken, shews a man eminent and famous

in

in his trade or profeſſion (among the common people)
let it be what it will.

CHAP. LXXXI.

Of the Mons Lunæ, *and the* Via Lactea.

I. THe *Mons Lunæ* (called alſo *feriens à feriendo*, the
ſmiting part) is the mount comprehended un-
der the *tuberculum* of *Mercury*, between the *menſal* and
Reſtricta.

II. The *Via lactea*, or Milky way, is the line running upwards from the *Reſtricta* through the *feriens*
or *Mons Lunæ*.

III. The *Mons Lunæ* filled with happy Characters
(as we have before hinted) ſhews one honeſt, juſt
and honourable, and makes a man famous through a
Kingdom, gives him the praiſe of the common people, and the acquaintance of great and noble Ladies ;
and makes him happy in Navigation.

IV. But being unfortunated by evil Characters, or
a *trapezia*, or evil lines from the Triangle of *Mars*,
or lines broken, or cut with oblique Angles, it ſhews
one of a various, poor and inconſtant life, a beggar,
a perſon envied by almoſt all people, one wicked,
treacherous and deceitful, a perſon ſubject to travel,
captivity or baniſhment.

V. If the good lines on the *ferient* be fair and comely, they premonſtrate ſo much the more happineſs,
and *in women fruitfulneſs :* but the evil lines pale, ſo
much the more evil.

VI. The *Via lactea* or milky way , well proportioned

tioned and continued, ſhews fortunate journeys, both by Sea and Land, great wit, and the love and favour of Women-kind, chiefly of Ladies and great Women.

VII. But if this line be cut or crooked, it ſhews unhappineſs, and a poor and low eſtate.

VIII. If it be whole and extended to the little finger, it ſhews a great good beyond expectation.

CHAP. LXXXII.

Of the Menſa, *or* Table.

I. THe *Menſa* is the interval or ſpace betwixt the *menſal* and *Epatica,* the which is given or attributed to *Fortune* ; from whence the Table is called the place of *Fortune.*

II. The *Menſa being large and broad,* and repleat with good figures, ſhews riches and treaſure, one of a liberal *magnanimous ſpirit,* and of long life.

III. But *ſmall and narrow,* ſhews poverty or a ſlender and mean fortune, a niggard, a coward, a *pitiful poor, fearful and mean ſoul.*

IV. A little circle in the *Menſa* ſhews a great wit, and a profound perſon in *Arts and Sciences.*

V. The *Menſa* terminating in an *Angle* under *Mons Jovis* by the concourſe of the *Menſal* and *Cardiac* or *Vital line,* ſhews falſhood and treachery, and one of ſhort life.

VI. A *Croſs or Star,* within it, clear and of good proportion, eſpecially under the *Mount of Sol,* ſhews honour and dignity, by means of great and Noble men, and

encreaſe

encreafe of Noble men : if it be the Character of ♃ *Jupiter*, it fhews *Ecclefiaftical preferment.*

VII. The fame *Crofs* or *Star*, being doubled or tripled wonderfully encreafeth the aforefaid good fortune ; but cut or confufed by other little lines, the faid good is much diverted, and *Anxieties* and troubles threatned.

.VIII. Good and equal lines in the *Menfa*, fhew good fortune ; evil and diftorted or crooked, the contrary.

IX. A *Crofs* or *Star* in the *Menfa* over *Mons Luna*, fhews fortunacy in travelling.

X. If there be no *menfa*, it fhews a cloudy and obfcure life and fortune.

CHAP. LXXXIII.

Of the Thumb and Fingers.

I. A Line furrounding the *Pollex* or Thumb in the *middle joint*, fhews the perfon fhall be hanged.

II. A line paffing from the *upper joint* of the *Pollex* to the *Cardiaca*, fhews a violent death, or danger by means of fome married woman.

III. *Overthwart lines*, clear and long underneath the nail and joint of the Thumb, fhew Riches and Honour.

IV. *Equal furrows* drawn under the lower joint thereof, fhew Riches and Inheritances.

V. The *firft and fecond joint* free from incifures, fhew a flothful and idle perfon.

VI. *Overthwart lines* in the uppermoft joint of the *Index*

Index or fore-finger, shew inheritances; but such in the middle joint, shew a subtil person.

VII. *Right lines* running between those joints in the *Index,* shew (*in Women*) a plentiful issue; (*in Men*) a nimble tongue.

VIII. If they be in the *first joint* near *Mons Jovis,* they shew a pleasant and courteous disposition; and a man of a *generous soul.*

IX. But a Woman who hath a *Star* in the same place, is *lascivious and whorish.*

X. Little *gridirons* in the joints of the *Medius* or middle-finger, an unfortunate and melancholy person: but Equal and parallel lines shew fortune by dealing in Metals.

XI. A *Star* there, shews a violent death by drowning or Witchcraft, or the like.

XII. A *Cross line* rising from the *Mons Saturni,* through the whole finger to the end thereof, shews a meer fool or mad person.

XIII. In the *Annular* or Ring-finger, a line rising from the *Mons Solis,* straight through the joints thereof, shews honour and glory.

XIV. In the *first joint* of the *Annular,* equal lines shew treasure and honour: *overthwart* lines, the hatred of Kings and great men; but if interfected, their envy shall be abated.

XV. In the *Auricularis* or little-finger, a Star in its *first joint* near the mount thereof, shews one of ingenuity, and a good Orator.

XVI. *Evil Characters* and *obtuse Angles* the contrary: those unfortunate signs in the *first and second joints,* shew a thief: in the *last joint,* one perpetually inconstant.

XVII. Some Authors predict the *number of Wives or Husbands,* by the number of little lines in the outmost

moſt part of the *Mons Mercurii* ; but in my opinion
thoſe things ought rather to be ſought out in the *Mount
of Venus.*

XVIII. And as in the *Mounts* good or evil Characters, are *Omens* of good or evil fortunes ; ſo alſo on
the fingers they ſignifie the ſame.

XXIX. The *firſt joint* near the mount ſhews the
firſt Age : the *ſecond joint, middle Age :* and the *laſt
joint, old Age :* but it is *our opinion*, that the directions
of the principal ſignificators in every Geniture, more
properly demonſtrate the times in which the good or
evil ſignified by thoſe marks or lines, ſhall more certainly happen.

A note concerning the Good and Evil Lines, Marks or Characters.

XX. *The good lines, marks or Characters* are parallels,
as = or ‖ double or treble, and the like , Croſſes
as + or × : double Croſſes and the like : Stars as
the Sextile Aſpect ✳ or the like : Ladders-ſteps and
Quadrangles as □ or ▭ : the trine aſpect as △ : Angles as the right or acute, or a mult-angle, &c. the
Characters of *Jupiter* and *Venus*, as ♃ ♀, and other the
like a kin to theſe.

XXI. The *Unfortunate and evil Characters* are deformed, irregular and uncouth figures, broken lines,
crooked lines, gridirons, the Characters of ♄ *Saturn*
and ♂ *Mars :* the oppoſition ☍ : irregular Circles, ob-
tuſe angles and the like.

XXII. Laſtly, as *the quantity of lines* conſidered in
their length and depth ; *their quality*, in their ſhape
and complexion ; *their Action*, in touching or cutting
other lines ; *their paſſion*, in being touched or cut of
others ; and *their place* in which they are poſited or
located ;

located, *ought to be observed*; so also *their time of appearing or disappearing*, ought to pass our cognizance.

For it is most certain, that some lines are prolonged to certain years of our Age, othersome shortned; sometimes they wax pale, sometimes grow red; some of one shape quite vanish, while others of another shape rise : Now the cause without doubt is the various progressions of the Aphetical places in the geniture, to their various and contingent promissors, to the influence of which, the whole man it self is subjugated; and therefore it behoves the industrious and studious Artist, not to determine all things at first sight, for no man can attain the knowledge of all particulars at one inspection; But yearly to make new observations, as the person encreases in Age.

Experience framed Art by various use,
Example guiding where it was abstruse.

Qui in manu omnium hominum signa posuit, ut cognoscerent opera ejus singuli. Job 37. 7.

Moreover it is to be observed, that these judgements be not delivered simply alone, but by being compared with the rules delivered in Chap. 25. Lib. 1. from whence many other Prognosticks more than what we have here mentioned will arise, to the infinite pleasure of the Artist, and satisfaction of the curious inquisitor.

FINIS.

The CONTENTS.

The TABLE.

The Table.

The Table.

The Table.

The Table.

The Table.

The Table.

Original

The Table.

Pro-

The Table.

The Table.

The Table.

The Table.

FINIS.

A Catalogue of some Books sold
by *John Crumpe* at the *Three Bibles* in St. *Paul's* Church-yard.

Folio.

HEylin's Cosmography.
Causin's Holy Court.
Clark's Lives of the Fathers.
————Martyrologie.
Cassandra, a Romance.
Stapletons Juvenal.
Parthaniffa, A Romance compleat.

Quarto.

Sport upon Sport.
Don *Belianis* of G ecce.
Phyrophane's Secrets.

Octavo.

Mary Magdalen's Tears.
Evago as, A Romance.
Parson's Law.

How's Delighting in God.
Sport upon Sport.
Fowler's Free Discourse.
Busby's Latin Grammer.
Nomenclatura.
Powel's Concordance.
Grew of Vegetables.
Lucius Florus in English.
William's Poems.
New Academy.
Canting Academy.
Bayfeild's Exercitationes Anatomicæ.
Tokens for children, Compleat.
Directions for Study of the Law.
Sparrow's Rationale upon the Common prayer.
The Life and Death of *Oliver Cromwel*, the Late Usurper.
Beraldus, A Novel in two parts.
Don *Carloss*, an Historical Novel.
Salmon's Synopsis Medicinæ.